sustaining civil society

PHILIP OXHORN

sustaining civil society

Economic Change, Democracy,
and the Social Construction
of Citizenship in Latin America

The Pennsylvania State University Press
University Park, Pennsylvania

Library of Congress Cataloging-in-Publication Data
Oxhorn, Philip.
Sustaining civil society : economic change, democracy,
and the social construction of citizenship in Latin
America / Philip Oxhorn.
    p.   cm.
Includes bibliographical references and index.
Summary: "Devoting particular emphasis to Bolivia, Chile,
and Mexico, proposes a theory of civil society to explain
the economic and political challenges for continuing
democratization in Latin America"—Provided by publisher.
ISBN 978-0-271-04894-9 (cloth : alk. paper)
ISBN 978-0-271-04895-6 (pbk. : alk. paper)
1. Citizenship—Latin America.
2. Civil society—Latin America.
3. Democratization—Economic aspects—Latin America.
4. Latin America—Politics and government—1980- .
5. Bolivia—Politics and government—2006- .
6. Chile—Politics and government—1988- .
7. Mexico—Politics and government—2000- .
I. Title.

JL967.A2O94 2011
300.98—dc22
2011009776

The Pennsylvania State University Press is a member of the
Association of American University Presses.

It is the policy of The Pennsylvania State University Press to
use acid-free paper. Publications on uncoated stock satisfy
the minimum requirements of American National Standard
for Information Sciences—Permanence of Paper for Printed
Library Material, ANSI Z39.48–1992.

contents

List of Figures and Tables   vii

Acknowledgments   ix

List of Abbreviations   xi

1   Civil Society and the Social Construction of Citizenship   1

2   Controlled Inclusion and the Elusive Goal of Citizenship as Agency   29

3   Dictatorship or Democracy: The Rise of Neopluralism and Citizenship as Consumption   51

4   Testing the Limits of Citizenship: Chile's Democratic Transition   91

5   The Failure of Citizenship: Bolivia's Popular Participation Law   138

6   The Promise of Citizenship: Civil Society and Mexico's Transition to Democracy   186

7   Latin America's Democratic Crossroads: The Challenge of Making Civil Society Relevant   230

Notes   239

References   251

Index   273

figures and tables

figures

1.1   Civil society, the public sphere, and the social construction of citizenship rights   22

6.1   Total crimes: preliminary findings, 1997–2009   220

6.2   Kidnappings: preliminary findings, 1997–2009   221

tables

3.1   Average crime victimization rates   69

3.2   Select characteristics of case study countries   89

4.1   Income inequality   113

4.2   Levels of education by income   117

4.3   Public perceptions of Chilean democracy   120–121

4.4   Trust in institutions   122

5.1   Impact of the Popular Participation Law   151

6.1   Economic growth rates   200

6.2   Gini coefficients   200

6.3   Public opinion and the evaluation of Mexican democracy   218

acknowledgments

It would have been impossible to complete a project as ambitious as this book without the support of a long list of people and institutions, even if the ultimate responsibility remains my own. At an institutional level, generous research support from the Fonds pour la Formation de Chercheurs et l'Aide à la Recherche and, in particular, the Social Sciences and Humanities Research Council allowed me to undertake extensive fieldwork. A grant from the Inter-American Development Bank funded my first trip to Bolivia, while support from the Ford Foundation helped me complete fieldwork in Chile.

Chapters 1–3 draw on revised versions, used with permission from the publisher, of the following: "Neopluralism and the Challenges for Citizenship in Latin America," in *Citizenship in Latin America*, edited by Joseph S. Tulchin and Meg Ruthenburg, © 2007 by Lynne Rienner; "Social Inequality, Civil Society, and the Limits of Citizenship in Latin America," in *What Justice? Whose Justice? Fighting for Fairness in Latin America*, edited by Susan Eckstein and Timothy Wickham-Crowley, © 2003 by the Regents of the University of California, published by the University of California Press; "Conceptualizing Civil Society from the Bottom Up: A Political Economy Perspective," in *Civil Society and Democracy in Latin America*, edited by Richard Feinberg, Carlos H. Waisman, and Leon Zamosc, © 2006 by Palgrave Macmillan; "Is the Century of Corporatism Over? Neoliberalism and the Rise of Neopluralism," in *What Kind of Democracy? What Kind of Market? Latin America in the Age of Neoliberalism*, edited by Philip Oxhorn and Graciela Ducatenzeiler, © 1998 by Pennsylvania State University Press; "The Social Foundations of Latin America's Recurrent Populism: Problems of Class Formation and Collective Action," *Journal of Historical Sociology* 11 (June 1998): 212–46, permission granted by Wiley and Sons; and "When Democracy Isn't All That Democratic: Social Exclusion and the Limits of the Public Sphere in Latin America," North South Agenda Paper 44, North South Center at the University of Miami, Coral Gables, Florida, April 2001. Chapter 4 also draws on "Neopluralism and the Challenges for Citizenship in Latin America."

Over the years, I have benefited intellectually from a variety of people, including the dozens of graduate students who took my various seminars, both at McGill and in the Programa de Posgrado en Ciencias Políticas y Sociales at the Universidad Nacional Autónoma de México. Among them, I would like to thank Catherine Slakmon and especially Monica Treviño. I would also like to thank Luiz Carlos Bresser Pereira, Richard Feinberg, John Hall, Terry Karl, Joel Migdal, Eugenio Ortega, Philippe Schmitter, Bill Smith, Joe Tulchin, Federico Vázquez Calero, Carlos Waisman, and Leon Zamosc, all of whom have commented on various aspects of the arguments I develop here. Bryan Roberts and John Peeler read the first draft of the manuscript, and their comments have helped improve it in important ways.

The Bolivian case study would not have been possible without the assistance and helpful feedback of Sonia Fleury, Manuel Contreras, Roberto Laserna, and Fernando Calderón. I would also like to thank Maria Eugenia Brockmann for her invaluable research assistance in Bolivia. The Chilean case study benefited considerably from the input of Sergio Bitar, Augusto Varas, and Alfredo Navarrete. In Mexico, I was fortunate enough to be able to count on the research support of Carlos Chávez Becker.

While my appointment first as director of the Centre for Developing-Area Studies and then as director of the Institute for the Study of International Development at McGill in some ways slowed down the completion of this book, it also brought with it important institutional support. I would like to thank Jennifer Nicols and, in particular, Iain Blair, who helped prepare various versions of the manuscript. I would also like to thank Sandy Thatcher, who has encouraged my efforts to bring this project to fruition for more years than I care to remember, and Susan Silver for her meticulous copyediting, as well as others at the Pennsylvania State University Press who have made the publication of this book possible.

Finally, a number of people helped complete this project in various more intangible ways. The support and encouragement, as well as intellectual input, of Susan Eckstein, Judit Bokser, and Michael Brecher probably meant more to me than they realize. To my wife, Rosa, and son, Gabriel, the only people who are probably happier than I am to finally finish this book, I owe more than I can put into words.

abbreviations

AC	Civic Alliance (Alianza Cívica)
AD	Democratic Alliance (Alianza Democrática)
ADN	Nationalist Democratic Action (Acción Democrática y Nacionalista)
APPO	Popular Assembly of the Peoples of Oaxaca (Asamblea Popular de los Pueblos de Oaxaca)
ASP	Assembly for the Sovereignty of Indigenous Peoples (Asamblea para la Soberanía de los Pueblos)
CEPAL	Economic Commission for Latin America and the Caribbean (Comisión Económica para América Latina y el Caribe)
CESCO	Community Economic and Social Councils (Consejos Económico-Sociales Comunales)
CNC	National Peasant Confederation (Confederación Nacional Campesina)
COB	Bolivian Workers Central (Central Obrera Boliviana)
CTM	Confederation of Mexican Workers (Confederación de Trabajadores Mexicanos)
CUD	Unitary Committee of Earthquake Victims (Coordinadora Única de Damnificados)
CV	Vigilance Committee (Comité de Vigilancia)
DC	Democratic Current (Corriente Democrática)
ECLAC	Economic Commission for Latin America and the Caribbean
ENUSC	National Urban Survey of Citizen Security (Encuesta Nacional Urbana de Seguridad Ciudadana)
EZLN	Zapatista Army of National Liberation (Ejército Zapatista de Liberación Nacional)
FDN	Democratic National Front (Frente Democrático Nacional)
FMLN	Farabundo Martí National Liberation Front (Farabundo Martí para la Liberación Nacional)
HIPC	Heavily Indebted Poor Countries

IDB	Inter-American Development Bank
ISI	Import Substitution Industrialization
LOCE	Organic Constitutional Law for Education (Ley Orgánica Constitucional de Enseñanza)
LPP	Popular Participation Law (Ley de Participación Popular)
MDP	Popular Democratic Movement (Movimiento Democrático Popular)
MIR	Revolutionary Left Movement (Movimiento Izquierda Revolucionaria)
MNR	Nationalist Revolutionary Movement (Movimiento Nacionalista Revolucionario)
NAFTA	North American Free Trade Agreement
OECD	Organisation for Economic Co-operation and Development
OTBs	Base-Level Territorial Organizations (Organizaciones Territoriales de Base)
PAN	National Action Party (Partido Acción Nacional)
PC	Communist Party (Partido Comunista)
PDC	Christian Democratic Party (Partido Democrática Cristiana)
PDT	Democratic Labor Party (Partido Democrático Trabalhista)
PNR	National Revolutionary Party (Partido Nacional Revolucionario)
PPD	Party for Democracy (Partido por la Democracia)
PRD	Party of the Democratic Revolution (Partido de la Revolución Democrática)
PRI	Institutional Revolutionary Party (Partido Revolucionario Institucional)
PRM	Party of the Mexican Revolution (Partido Revolucionario Mexicano)
PRONASOL	National Solidarity Program (Programa Nacional de Solidaridad)
PS	Socialist Party (Partido Socialista)
PT	Workers' Party (Partido dos Trabalhadores)
SNTE	National Educational Workers Union (Sindicato Nacional de Trabajadores de la Educación)
UNDP	United Nations Development Programme (Programa de las Naciones Unidas para el Desarrollo)

1 CIVIL SOCIETY AND THE SOCIAL CONSTRUCTION OF CITIZENSHIP

At first glance, the events of September–October 2003 in Bolivia seemed reminiscent of a bygone era of military regimes. Mass mobilizations demanding the ouster of a government accused of insensitivity toward the nation's poor majority and its replacement by a more "democratic" one were met by fierce repression that left dozens dead. Unlike past mobilizations against dictators, particularly in Bolivia, the protesters got what they wanted relatively quickly: President Gonzalo Sánchez de Lozada resigned on October 17, just fifteen months after he had assumed office for the second time. Vice President Carlos Mesa took over the presidency, maintaining at least the facade of respect for democratic institutions.

The immediate cause of the wave of protests that led to Sánchez de Lozada's ouster was a proposed natural gas pipeline through Chile that would allow landlocked Bolivia to export untapped natural gas reserves to the United States. More fundamentally, the project's imminent approval by the president served as a catalyst for opposition leaders to ignite popular frustrations that, in some cases, literally went back centuries.

Bolivia was one of the first countries in the region to implement a series of far-reaching market-oriented economic reforms in Latin America, beginning in the mid-1980s and continuing during Sánchez de Lozada's first term as president (1993–97). Yet after almost twenty years of sometimes painful economic reforms, 58 percent of Bolivia's population still lived in poverty in 2003; indigenous peoples made up the majority of this group. The promised prosperity obviously did not arrive, recalling bitter memories of centuries of exploitation—first by the Spanish during the colonial period, and then later by a small criollo elite also closely tied to international economic interests. In the popular imagination, the international mining consortium behind the natural gas project seemed to be no different from the foreign interests that historically had benefited so handsomely from Bolivia's rich natural resources. Moreover, the consortium insisted on routing the pipeline through Chile, so the country that had deprived Bolivia of its access to the sea in the aftermath of the 1879 War of the Pacific would also reap the benefits of Bolivia's natural riches. Compounding matters even more, the most active groups in the protests were indigenous coca growers suffering the consequences of a U.S.-sponsored coca eradication program that, despite years of promises, still had not provided them with alternative sources of livelihood. Once again, the protestors apparently got what they wanted: the project was indefinitely put on hold, and its ultimate fate remains uncertain.

The events of September–October 2003 are full of tragic ironies. The poorest country in South America abandoned a potentially lucrative development project in defense of an ambiguous set of national interests related more to national pride and the settling of old scores than a reasoned assessment of the alternatives. This nationalist fervor was expressed most forcefully by impoverished indigenous communities, even though racism and extreme poverty have historically excluded them from any meaningful integration into Bolivian society. Although democratic institutions survived, the process through which Sánchez de Lozada was removed from power marked the resurgence of a conservative populism that lacked a clear set of policy alternatives for future socioeconomic development and posed a real threat to democracy (Alfredo Navarrete, personal interview, Iquique, July 22, 2001; see also Laserna 2003). Bolivian society, particularly its indigenous majority, had flexed its muscles by removing an unpopular government, and the military had remained subordinated to civilian rule. But is this a victory for Bolivian civil society? How did Bolivia end up in such a dramatic situation and what does it bode for the country, particularly the future of its democracy?

Sánchez de Lozada's resignation, forced not by the military but by popular repudiation despite the absence of a clear alternative, is not an isolated event.[1] In Argentina, in the space of just over a week in early 2001, more than two dozen people died, and Fernando de la Rúa and three interim presidents were forced to resign as a result of widespread protests against economic policies. Intended to resolve Argentina's growing economic crisis, the market reforms implemented by de la Rúa's predecessor, Carlos Menem, failed miserably. Two years after the 1999–2002 economic recession ended, more than 50 percent of the population still remained below the poverty line. Argentina—known as the "richest" country in Latin America—eventually did experience some economic growth. But its road back to prosperity will be a long one. Unfortunately, neither the protests nor Argentina's politicians were able to produce even a semblance of a coherent long-term plan for traveling that road.

Although markedly less violent than the Bolivian and Argentine experiences, a mass protest by the country's large indigenous population in Ecuador was joined by a faction of the military led by Colonel Lucio Gutiérrez in January 2000, resulting in a short-lived coup and the assumption of power by the incumbent vice president, Gustavo Noboa. Prolonged economic recession and a rejection of market-oriented economic reforms provided the context for the protests, and the immediate catalyst was the plan to dollarize the economy. The protesters succeeded in removing the unpopular president associated with those policies, but Noboa passed most of them (including dollarization), providing little relief for Ecuador's poor. Gutiérrez went on to win the presidency in January 2003, largely because of his role in the coup.

Popular mobilizations do not necessarily lead to a change in presidents, as in the case of Paraguayan president Gonzalez Macchi. In July 2002 he declared a state of emergency in response to massive protests demanding his resignation and the end of market reforms; he then won a congressional vote to delay his removal from office until December.

Such a "failure" was most dramatic in Venezuela, where Hugo Chávez achieved political prominence after leading a failed coup attempt in 1992. He was elected president in 1998 on the promise of ending political corruption and reversing the same market-oriented reforms that he had targeted in 1992. Continued economic decline and a conservative backlash against his vague promises of Cuban-style social and economic policies increasingly polarized the country, culminating in a national protest on April 11, 2002. In sharp contrast to the other examples, where the poorest segments of society, with allies from the middle and working classes, led protests against the elected government, Venezuela's poor supported Chávez while the other classes demanded his resignation. Three days of near-chaos ensued, pitting hundreds of thousands of people from both sides against one another in the streets, leaving at least forty-five people dead and risking serious divisions within the military. The protest was marked by a failed coup attempt that saw Chávez leave the presidential palace in disgrace, only to return triumphantly two days later. Temporarily cowed but not subdued, the opposition regrouped. In a region where national strikes are considered successful if they slow down the economy for even a day, it brought the economy to a virtual standstill for the nine weeks from December 2002 to February 2003. Yet Chávez survived, in part because the opposition was united only in its resistance to him and lacked any clear or coherent vision for the future.

These examples and the violence they frequently entailed recall the struggles between the state and civil society associated with "popular upsurges" (O'Donnell and Schmitter 1986) under authoritarian regimes, yet in each case the mobilizations were against governments elected in free and fair elections. Whereas the mobilizations against dictatorships offered hope and a positive democratic vision for their respective countries after years of authoritarian rule, those against popularly elected presidents reflected the frustration and despair of large groups of people who had lost confidence in their democratic leaders and who increasingly saw themselves as marginalized socially, economically, and politically. While such mobilizations certainly offered a vague promise of a better future for their participants, they are better characterized by their power to paralyze government and exercise a de facto veto over specific policies; presidents were forced to resign because they could no longer govern, not because there was an obvious candidate who could govern better. In striking contrast to democratic transitions, whose success depended on the emergence of a preferable, viable alternative (Przeworski 1986), these mobilizations were marked by a surprising amount of trust in generally unproven, often unknown leaders with few concrete policy alternatives. For this reason, one also cannot escape the conclusion that such mobilizations contain an important cathartic element, especially in a country such as Bolivia, where centuries of accumulated injustices seemed to converge.

In general, these mobilizations represent extreme examples of a principal characteristic of democratic politics in the region today: a plebiscitary quality defining the relationship between citizens and their leaders (Oxhorn 1998a; O'Donnell 1994). Presidential elections are the most important aspect of this, but so too is the "thumbs-up or thumbs-down" (and it is usually thumbs-down) quality of mobilizations. Meaningful elections are more prevalent in the region than ever before, and a majority of Latin Americans prefer democracy over other forms of government, yet their dissatisfaction with their actual elected governments and political parties implies a hollowness to democratic rule.

A number of trends contribute to this situation. Lackluster economic performance has generated growing insecurity, at the same time that poverty and crime continue at unacceptably high levels. Latin America remains the most unequal region in the world, and citizens perceive traditional politicians and political parties as corrupt and self-interested. During most of the 1990s, outsiders such as Chávez in Venezuela, Gutiérrez in Ecuador, and Alberto Fujimori in Peru enjoyed considerable popularity (at least initially) and were able to mobilize support by appealing to these frustrations, even if their solutions were ephemeral at best.

Many of these problems, of course, are not new, although they are assuming new forms and rising in intensity. Poverty, inequality, and self-interested politicians are not unique to the current period. That populist leaders such as Chávez or Gutiérrez emerge because of their ability to take advantage of pent-up frustrations and feelings of marginalization is also not a new phenomenon. What is surprising is that these "durable inequalities" (Tilly 1998) are greater and more enduring in Latin America than anywhere else, despite considerable social progress since the 1930s. As Chilean president Ricardo Lagos noted in his speech inaugurating the Special Summit of the Americas in Monterrey, Mexico, in January 2004, "South America is not the poorest continent in the world, but it may very well be the most unjust" (*Santiago Times,* January 14, 2004).

What is unique to the current period is that all these problems, including the periodic outbursts that enduring inequality is likely to bring, are unfolding in a context in which political democracy is more firmly entrenched than ever before—despite its often poor quality and frequently weak institutions. This is at the heart of the Latin American conundrum: the paradoxical convergence of unprecedented political rights while other rights are precarious at best, and declining at worst.

Today's paradox of rights did not emerge in a vacuum but is, in many ways, the culmination of historical processes dating back at least to the 1920s, with the Great Depression and the emergence of the developmentalist state. Violent authoritarianism resurged in the 1960s and 1970s, while the exhaustion of the import substitution industrialization (ISI) model in the 1970s dramatically punctuated the course of development. The debt crisis followed in the 1980s, along with the concomitant emergence of a new market-oriented development model, commonly referred to as neoliberalism.

Taking inspiration from the rich political sociology of the 1960s—particularly the classic works by Barrington Moore (1966), Reinhard Bendix (1964), and Fernando Enrique Cardoso and Enzo Faletto (1970)—the focus here is on how different groups are (or are not) incorporated into national socioeconomic and political processes. To do so, the book takes as its starting point the nature of civil society and its relationship with the state.

In particular, I reinterpret T. H. Marshall's (1950) classic work to better understand this decades-long process as a series of distinct struggles over the definition of citizenship: who is or is not included and the rights that citizenship entails. I call this approach the *social construction of citizenship*, basing it on the simple premise that it matters greatly which organized groups do or do not participate in struggles over the definition of citizenship rights. Today's paradox of rights represents the most recent turn in a long path in the social construction of citizenship that is markedly distinct from the paths taken in the now developed democracies of the West. The book is an effort to understand how Latin America arrived at this point and to examine the nature of the challenges this paradox poses not only to democratic stability but, more important, to the quality of Latin America's democratic regimes.

As part of this effort, I develop a theory of civil society that stands in contrast to the current aversion of researchers working on Latin America to building "grand theories" after the polemical 1970s and confusing 1980s. Tentative influential efforts at building grand theories have been offered by non–Latin Americanists. They tend, however, to herald a new liberal triumphalism that explains why "all good things come together" in development (Fukuyama 1989), promotes a new global cultural bipolarity dividing "us" from "them" (Huntington 1996), or describes a universal rationality that ignores difference completely, effectively blinding itself to context, history, culture, and more structural approaches in general (Bates 1981). Such efforts are less grand theories than ideological projects that proclaim, if not the "end of history" itself, the growing irrelevance of economic and other structures in determining the course of human events. In part a counterreaction to these more conservative tendencies and their frequent ethnocentricity, the postmodern perspective rejects the very possibility of generalizable theories (Escobar 1995; Hann and Dunn 1996).

A useful theory of civil society must accomplish several tasks. First, there is the need to define the concept in a way that avoids equating it with a narrow set of historical phenomena found principally in Western Europe, Canada, and the United States. This does not mean that civil society is necessarily found in all societies, only that its possibility is not defined away *ex ante* by reducing it to a set of values that are culturally determined and not universal. Second, the theory must establish a framework for understanding how civil society emerges that allows for meaningful comparisons between different forms in particular contexts. Finally, such a theory must explain the role that civil society plays within political systems independent of its definition.

In the remainder of this chapter, I develop the basic outlines of a theory of civil society. I use this framework in chapters 2 and 3 to analyze general patterns in the changing modes of interest intermediation in Latin America from the postwar period to the present. I then apply the framework to detailed case studies of three countries: Chile, Bolivia, and Mexico.

Civil Society as a Concept for Comparative Analysis

A surprisingly large amount of theorizing about civil society focuses on the intellectual evolution of the concept and the normative content associated with it.[2] At one extreme, civil society is considered present to greater or lesser degrees in almost all social contexts, both past and present (Chambers and Kymlicka 2002; Ehrenberg 1999). On the other extreme, the concept itself is so normatively and historically determined by the experience of Western Europe and the United States that it is almost impossible to find in other contexts (Hann 1996) and may even be increasingly difficult to maintain in the changing socioeconomic contexts of the countries in which it originates (Seligman 1992). For others somewhere in between, the "bewildering plurality of normative justifications of 'civil society'" found in the literature deprives the concept of any analytical usefulness (Keane 1998, 53).

This excessive, if not exclusive, focus on the intellectual and normative basis of civil society is, if not ironic, all the more puzzling, given that the authors who are associated with the concept's modern usage (Ferguson 1966; Tocqueville 1969) explicitly sought to develop a theory for understanding what they felt were the principal socioeconomic developments of their day—the spread of the market economy and the struggle against authoritarian rule. Today the normative biases of authors tend to determine how (or if) empirical studies are incorporated into their understandings of civil society as a concept.[3] This only tends to reinforce the polemical nature of debates about civil society as a concept, raising fundamental questions about its universal applicability.

Despite the obviously contested nature of the concept, debates about civil society are further complicated by the increasing predominance of a particular liberal perspective in the North American social science literature. This has taken place even though conceptions of civil society within Western political thought reflect at least two distinct, if not mutually exclusive, intellectual traditions: a liberal or Lockean perspective and a collectivist perspective associated with the work of Montesquieu and, more recently, communitarians (C. Taylor 1990). While the specific elements of civil society that one perspective focuses on co-exist to a greater or lesser degree with the elements emphasized in the other, each highlights different aspects of modern societies in ways that influence both the substance and conclusions of the comparative research they inspire.[4] For a variety of reasons—including the end of the cold war, the diminished role of the state in influencing economic and social processes, and the concomitant rise of market dynamics throughout the world—the liberal/Lockean perspective has become the focal point in civil society debates (Oxhorn 2006).

The increasingly dominant liberal perspective defines civil society in terms of individual rights and obligations and is characterized as being coterminous with the spread of the market economy. Rational individuals who decide to live together to further private, individual interests create civil society. Individual freedom is valued above all, requiring the rule of law and respect for private property. Membership in any group becomes a function of interest maximization. Groups and group identities lose any sense of intrinsic value. Voluntarism and the absence of coercion, in turn, have historically justified unequal status by restricting citizenship rights for those who are defined as incompetent or dependent (such as women, youths, illiterates, the poor, and the working class). "Liberal" societies, principally the United Kingdom and the United States, have come to represent the ideal of civil society (Seligman 1992).

The increasing tendency in recent years to equate civil society with a very liberal normative framework centered around an exclusive focus on the individual has meant the concomitant marginalization of perspectives focusing more on collectivities and group identities.[5] This tradition is heavily influenced by Alexis de Tocqueville (1969), who saw the rich array of voluntary organizations in the United States as an important bulwark of democracy and a counterbalance to the centralizing and authoritarian tendencies of European states. An important turning point came with the publication of Robert Putnam's (1993) influential book on democracy in Italy, which put the concept of social capital at the forefront of studies of civil society. But even earlier, important theorists of civil society were emphasizing its normative foundations in terms of norms of "civility" (Shils 1991), "civil spiritness" (Gellner 1991), and the broad set of liberal values of trust, associability, and so on, associated with a liberal "civic culture" (Almond and Verba 1963).

Although it is never very clear how such values become predominant—at the very least, the trust that is generally seen as pivotal for people to organize and form vibrant civil societies—their presence within a society is seen as a prerequisite for civil society's emergence. Because of the lack, stemming from an exclusive focus on individuals, of any intrinsic value attributed to group and organizational identities, an appropriate political culture in effect becomes synonymous with civil society itself. Its absence is seen as precluding civil society's emergence while an appropriate political culture presumes its inevitable existence.

From the liberal civil society perspective, the requisites for a highly organized, vibrant civil society are quite high. This is consistent with the historical fact that such civil societies have been relatively rare and have been most closely associated with the development of Western (and now democratic) countries. The problem is not that the "bar" for entering what is a rather exclusive club is so high, but the way in which that bar is set. This perspective deliberately posits a *thick* notion of the consensual basis for civil society's emergence that tends to be equated with a narrow set of Western values and unique cultural experiences. For societies that do not share those values and history, such as most Latin American countries, where, for example, the level of societal trust is notoriously low (Lagos 1997), this conception of civil society is extremely alienating. As Chris Hann (1996, 1) notes, "There is something inherently unsatisfactory about the international propagation by western scholars of an ideal of social organization that seems to bear little relation to the current realities of their own countries; an ideal which, furthermore, developed in historical conditions that cannot be replicated in any other part of the world today."

The individualism inherent in this perspective seriously limits the relevance of such a model to different historical contexts and regions of the world. Many societies do not recognize the centrality of the individual in the public or political realm and instead emphasize communities and larger social networks. In Latin America, this is particularly true of indigenous communities. This view also ignores the important collective dimension of rights in established Western democracies (Oxhorn 2003). On the one hand, rights—regardless of their legal and normative justification as individual rights of citizenship—are in effect granted to groups of people such as women, the elderly, illiterates, and so on.[6] On the other hand, such rights for disadvantaged groups are frequently the result of collective struggles, as people often must organize to ensure that their rights are respected by the state and other individuals. Moreover, a principal threat to civil society may actually be individuals' unrestrained pursuit of their own self-interest.

With some notable exceptions (Migdal, Kholi, and Shue 1994; Waltzer 1999; Skocpol 1996), protecting the necessary autonomy of civil society is generally seen to require a virtually impermeable barrier between the state and civil society. This view has been reinforced (if not reified) by the prominent role civil society played in opposing the state during recent transitions to democracy. Cooperation was obviously ruled out for most of civil society. This sharp separation between civil society and the state was further accentuated by the shift to a new market-oriented development paradigm beginning in the late 1970s, which has dramatically changed the role of the state in society and the economy. Civil society has concomitantly been called on to play a much more important role, particularly in the provision of social services and, in Latin America at least, in helping people cope with the economic dislocations and instability the shift in development models has entailed.

The banner of "civil society" is increasingly being adopted by a variety of actors around the world, including international organizations (e.g., the Organization of American States, the World Bank, and Inter-American Development Bank) and donor governments (including the United States). One would hope for more practical insights from academia, yet basic questions often go begged in the literature: Does civil society as a concept represent a contingent phenomenon that can be expected to emerge only in the unique historical contexts generally limited to Western Europe and the United States? Or does civil society represent an ideal that can allow for the elucidation of fundamental sociopolitical dynamics in a wide array of societal contexts? If the latter, what does such a concept entail?

To begin to answer these questions, in what follows I develop a collectivist perspective that draws on the intellectual tradition associated with Montesquieu and the communitarians (C. Taylor 1990; Waltzer 1992), as well as a more traditional political economy perspective. I define civil society as the social fabric formed by a multiplicity of self-constituted territorially and functionally based units, excluding families and business firms, which peacefully coexist and collectively resist subordination to the state, at the same time that they demand inclusion into national political structures.

This definition shifts the study of civil society away from a focus on civil society's normative content to an emphasis on power relations within a given society. Power and power resources are understood principally in terms of economic resources and the organizational capacity to autonomously define and defend collective group interests. The latter can be based on a strong sense of collective identity, an ideology, and organizational skill. It can also derive from the availability of selective incentives for members. Coercive power is not relevant here because it is generally used for ends that are antithetical to the development of civil societies.

This emphasis on power relations and the way power is defined stands in stark contrast to more predominant (and liberal) views on civil society that downplay the existence of conflict within civil society and the inherent advantages that dominant groups enjoy, even in democratic regimes.[7] I define "inclusion" much more broadly than electoral inclusion and the existence of electoral or political rights, although this is an integral part (Oxhorn 2003). In this way, the approach draws attention to the limits of political democracy in much of Latin America. It also reflects historical problems of inequality that continue to condition the development of civil society throughout the region and the need to understand the obstacles that high levels of inequality create for achieving more equitable societies independently of the existence of the political right to vote (Karl 2003; Guidry and Sawyer 2003). But this ideal of inclusion is not limited to new democracies; the so-called new social movements that emerged throughout Western Europe, Canada, and the United States starting in the 1960s reflect the same dynamic, albeit in the less dramatic circumstances of consolidated political democracies and modern welfare states.

This dual dynamic of demanding inclusion and resisting subordination to the state may be latent or so routinized in established democracies that it is taken for granted. The voluntary organizations that are the hallmark of civil society in countries such as the United States would not generally be expected to either actively demand inclusion (since political inclusion is already firmly established more broadly) or actively resist subordination to the state (given that a variety of institutions exist for negotiating the limits on state action within civil society). On specific policy issues, however, organizations of civil society can be quite active at all levels of government as they attempt to influence policy making and determine the appropriate boundaries of state action within civil society.

Historically, this dynamic was central to the emergence of both civil society and consolidated democratic regimes—and their strength today is a measure of earlier "victories" (Bendix 1964; Keane 1988b). Critical turning points in national histories reflect the emergence of new groups within civil society trying to effect change through demands for inclusion and/or resistance to what are perceived as unacceptably intrusive state policies. In the United States, for example, this was the case with the civil rights and women's movements in the 1960s, as well as the antiwar movement during the Vietnam era. Moreover, resistance to state subordination has been a historical demand of civil society in the United States, stemming back at least to the War of Independence. One must not forget that the associational tendencies so admired by Tocqueville laid the foundation for successful armed struggle against the distant, closed state of the British Crown. Today, resistance is best reflected in the American Civil Liberties Union and the National Rifle Association, not to mention various right-wing militia groups and a variety of conservative political groups. In Western Europe—in addition to the rise of women's movements—environmental, antinuclear, and peace movements have had an important impact on both the state and society, to give just a few examples. And one must not forget that one of the principal impetuses for the emergence of new social movements in Europe was the rejection of the welfare state's increasing penetration of everyday life (Offe 1984; Melucci 1989). In Latin America, where social inequalities are far greater, the importance of this dual dynamic is more critical, first to the establishment of democratic political regimes and later to their subsequent "deepening" (K. Roberts 1998).

From this perspective, a strong civil society reflects a relative dispersion of political power throughout entire polities. This, in turn, "contributes to the advent of stable democratic regimes supported by already strong, vibrant civil societies whose component elements struggled for democracy in the first place" (Oxhorn 1995a, 253; Keane 1988b; Cohen and Arato 1992). In societies where political power is more concentrated, civil society is weaker and, correspondingly, the prospects for long-term democratic stability are lower.

Civil society has an ambiguous relationship to economic structure. Civil society is characterized more by "institutionalized societal pluralism" (Schmitter 1986, 6) than by the relative strength of class-based functional organizations such as employers' groups and trade unions. The class struggle that pitted workers against capitalists was perhaps the defining dynamic of civil society in much of Western Europe during the period in which democratic regimes were consolidated there, but even in this sense social class is a contingent concept (Katznelson 1986). "Labor" and "capital" are heuristic concepts whose concrete organizational manifestations are determined by a number of factors that vary from case to case. Moreover, civil society's roots predate capitalism (Keane 1988b; C. Taylor 1990) and arguably contributed to the demise of feudalism in Western Europe. The primary societal cleavages that initially established the foundations for democratic political systems in Western Europe also were not based on class, although this changed with the advent of the second industrial revolution (Lagos 1997; Lipset and Rokkan 1967). Today, with the emergence of the so-called new social movements in these same countries, class again is not as central to explaining the dynamic of civil society as it was as late as the immediate postwar period (Offe 1987; Melucci 1985; Cohen 1985). In other contexts, nonclass identities have been even more important for organizing subaltern groups demonstrating the potential to form part of a civil society (Bonner 2003; Calhoun 1991; Jaquette and Wolchik 1998; Avritzer 2002).

That said, economic structure does condition civil society in fundamental ways. First, dominant social classes have been key actors in civil society (and in society at large) due to the economic resources at their disposal. This is particularly true under capitalism, since markets by definition create economic resources outside the state's control.[8] For similar reasons, the working class has often been a key actor after a minimum level of industrialization has been reached, as Karl Marx recognized, albeit in an exaggerated way. Working together in factories, workers were relatively easy to organize compared with peasants in the countryside, and stable employment (when it existed) meant workers could pay dues to maintain organizations. Various ideologies, particularly Marxism and socialism, often served as important resources for identity creation and the mobilization of the rank and file.

These examples underscore how economic structure creates shared interests that can serve as a basis for the emergence of important collective actors (e.g., workers, professionals, businesspeople, and peasants). It also affects the availability of resources for sustaining different forms of organizational activity and may influence the ability of different groups to engage in collective action (for example, the difficulties of organizing workers in the informal sector of the economy compared to the formal sector). As economic structures evolve over time (due, for example, to periods of prolonged economic growth, processes of industrialization or deindustrialization, changes in state development policies, and changes in a particular country's insertion in the international economy), the potential for civil society to continue to develop is also affected.

In general, different patterns of development affect the distribution of resources in distinct ways (Huber 2002b). The nature of a country's insertion in the international economy also has important distributional consequences that are relevant to the potential development and contours of civil society (Cardoso and Faletto 1970). To the extent that a given set of economic development policies contributes to a greater dispersal of power resources and increases the capacity of subaltern groups to organize themselves, it should facilitate greater levels of social inclusion and democratization. Conversely, if economic development policies increase the level of economic concentration or are accompanied by the erection of new barriers to collective action on the part of subaltern groups, they tend to undermine civil society and allow for a greater contraction of social inclusion and democratization.[9]

Civil societies vary, not only in terms of the relative strength of their component units, but also in terms of the nature of the units themselves. As a result, the normative content of civil society is necessarily ambiguous. It is in large part a function of the historical specificities of a given society, which in turn reflect which groups are organized. Any societal consensus (or lack thereof) within society is a reflection of conflict, negotiation, and compromise. It is therefore of paramount importance to understand who is and who is not participating in this process of social construction. The autonomy of such groups is reflected in their ability to define and defend their own interests in interactions with other actors, including the state. Civil society itself becomes a realm of conflict and compromise, not consensus—at least initially and certainly not on many issues relevant to a given polity.

This focus on power relations and the importance of multiple, self-constituted collective actors raises important questions about social cohesion and the level of difference a society can tolerate before centrifugal forces tear it apart. This is equally important to a more individual or liberal view, but the thick normative census that this perspective presumes tends to obscure it. The reality in much of Latin America (and, historically at least, in many of the now established de-mocracies) is that such a thick consensus is either utopian or masks forms of exclusion that are inherently undemocratic by their nature and frequently quite coercive. Following the seminal work of Dankwart Rustow (1970), a *thin* notion of the consensual basis for civil society's emergence consists of a shared sense of national identity. This may be the basis for a thick notion of societal consensus, but it can also reflect societal stalemate or the practical infeasibility of secession-ist alternatives or both. In other words, just as democracy was seen by Rustow as a "second best alternative," so too might the acceptance of belonging to a given national community on the part of different actors in civil society.

A strong civil society can begin to emerge only on the foundation of such acceptance, however begrudgingly it might be given. Such a thin consensus necessarily requires that civil society actors be self-limiting in terms of their demands and expectations to coexist (even reluctantly) with other civil society actors (Cohen and Arato 1992). Recalling Thomas Jefferson's famous insight that "it does me no injury for my neighbor to say that there are twenty Gods or no God," such a thin consensus is similar to what John Keane refers to as a "higher 'amorality': an agreement to disagree about matters of conscience" (1998, 57–58). More specifically, demands for inclusion cannot have as their objective the permanent exclusion of other actors, ruling out both revolutionary movements on the left and reactionary movements on the right, as well as fundamentalist movements and other groups whose objectives are not readily classifiable on a left–right spectrum. The normative ideal is that different actors in civil soci-ety ultimately "bond together in difference" (C. Taylor 1998, 153) or, to take the specific example of religious difference, create "a space for continuous dialogue among religious traditions and between the religious and the secular" (Nandy 1997, 333). The precise content and extent of the moral consensus underpinning any strong civil society is a contingent outcome. And for this reason it matters which groups participate in the social construction of that consensus.

The achievement of this ideal is often a tremendous challenge. The violence of ethnic nationalism shows how difficult it can be to achieve if social mobili-zation escapes the bounds of civil society. The decades-long struggle for Irish independence in the United Kingdom—the other paragon of liberal civil so-ciety after the United States—is the most poignant example. In contrast, the recent experience of indigenous mobilization in Latin America is a significant example of the importance of such self-limiting goals. Similarly, the difficulties that revolutionary movements throughout Latin America have faced in trying to integrate themselves into democratic politics after years of exclusion can be understood in these terms. Conversely, it becomes even more apparent why movements such as Peru's Sendero Luminoso (Shining Path) would deliberately target organizations that fall within the realm of civil society: it represents alternative, mutually exclusive forms of organization compared to insurrectionary movements. Indeed, the strength of civil society organizations can help mitigate the centrifugal forces of diversity and inequality through the successful management of conflict, while successful revolutionary movements tend to reflect the weakness of civil society because they represent the only alternative available to subaltern groups after prolonged periods of often violent exclusion by the state.

Two other consequences of this collectivist perspective need to be highlighted. First, in focusing on self-constituted units as the component parts of civil society, the importance of organization in generating political power is emphasized. In particular, the capacity of subaltern groups within a society to organize themselves autonomously from other actors is a key defining characteristic of strong civil societies capable of supporting stable democratic regimes.[10] Whether it be peasant groups organizing to assert their rights vis-à-vis feudal lords in Europe at the end of the Middle Ages (Putnam 1993; Brenner 1976; C. Taylor 1990), the great working-class struggles of the nineteenth and early twentieth centuries for basic rights of citizenship (Bendix 1964), or the self-help organizations in the shantytowns of Latin America (Eckstein 1989; Escobar and Alvarez 1992), the capacity of disadvantaged groups to organize affords them the potential to define and defend their interests in larger political processes. Contributing to the dispersion of political power in their favor, this clout avoids or lessens the tendency in capitalist societies for the interests of dominant actors to completely subordinate the interests of other less powerful actors.

Conversely, the lack of organization in more or less spontaneous demonstrations of protest suggests that they do not yet constitute civil society, even if they are generally peaceful. Such mobilization could eventually lead to a strengthening of civil society if those involved subsequently begin to organize for the definition and defense of their interests. The lack of organization makes it difficult to maintain the requisite autonomy necessary to participate as collective actors in competition with other actors. Such mobilizations have been quite effective in forcing policy change and, in particular, the resignation of officials; they even caused the collapse of regimes in the former Soviet bloc. Yet to the extent that they are successful, massive demonstrations are double-edged swords that invite manipulation of the crowd by opportunistic leaders at the same time that they establish the undemocratic precedent of extraconstitutional popular vetoes.

The second consequence of adopting the collectivist perspective is somewhat paradoxical: civil society cannot be conceptualized independently of the state. In other words, if there is no state, there cannot be a civil society. Instead, civil society must be understood in terms of its specific relationship with the state.

While the autonomy of civil society from the state needs to be stressed, it does not imply isolation. Instead, it refers to the ability of societal units to define their collective interests and act in open pursuit of them, in competition with one another. As part of that competition, societal units seek to influence state policy. Their relationship with the state may be fluid and mutually reinforcing, as is the case in established liberal democratic regimes. But it can also be more selective, with preference given only to certain groups, as is the case in many newly formed democratic governments. It can even be openly antagonistic in countries where civil society is engaged in ongoing struggles against authoritarian regimes. The precise nature of this relationship, however, is best understood in terms of a related concept, the public sphere.

Civil Society, the Public Sphere, and the Social Construction of Citizenship

There are few systematic studies of the relationship between civil society and the public sphere (Keane 1998, 157). The most prominent have focused on deliberation and publicity as the defining characteristics (Cohen and Arato 1992; Avritzer 2002). While the approach taken here is not necessarily incompatible with this work, the focus on power relations and struggle in understanding civil society shifts the emphasis from the potential democratic contributions of publicity and deliberation toward a better understanding of the obstacles and limits to such a contribution.

The public sphere is best understood as the nexus between civil society and the state. As such, the public sphere is shaped by both civil society and the state in a variety of fundamental ways. To appreciate this, I adopt the following definition of the public sphere: "The public sphere denotes a contested participatory site in which actors with overlapping identities as legal subjects, citizens, economic actors and family and community members form a public body and engage in negotiations and contestations over political and social life" (Somers 1993, 589).

The public sphere is characterized according to its inclusiveness in terms of the multiplicity of actors who can actively participate and the capacity of those actors to "alter patterns of integration or the overall exercise of power" (Calhoun 1993, 278). In other words, the public sphere should be evaluated according to who is included and excluded, as well as the ability of those actors to pursue their self-defined interests.

The latter point about the effectiveness of the public sphere needs to be emphasized. As Jürgen Habermas (1992, 452) warns, "discourses do not govern." The public sphere becomes politically relevant "only to the extent to which it enables the participants in the economy, via their status as citizens, to mutually accommodate or generalize their interests and to assert them so effectively that state power is transformed into a fluid medium of society's self-organization" (431).[11] Similarly, Charles Taylor (1990, 4) suggests that this public dimension of civil society demonstrates its very existence "whenever the ensemble of associations can significantly determine or inflect the course of state policy." The proliferation of identity-based groups, defined by gender and ethnicity, for example, which undoubtedly have been very important to their members and the communities in which they have emerged, need to be seen in this light. The existence of such organizational activity is significant and unprecedented given the centuries of oppression that these groups have experienced (Alvarez, Dagnino, and Escobar 1998). Yet their existence is ultimately insufficient unless it is accompanied by meaningful changes in state policies, institutions, and social practices. This is especially true in developing countries like those of Latin America, where the lack of noticeable impact from such movements can feed frustration and, perhaps paradoxically, further shrink the public sphere as people withdraw from it. Moreover, social heterogeneity has historically created collective action problems among Latin America's lower classes that have served to reinforce social hierarchy rather than empower subaltern groups (Oxhorn 1998b).

Similarly, locally based actors need to be situated in larger national contexts to understand their ultimate impact on the societies in which they emerge (Oxhorn 1999). Unless such actors are able to project their influence onto national agendas and begin to influence larger socioeconomic and political processes that affect their ability to pursue their self-defined interests, their concrete achievements will at best be quite limited. Whether it be to influence the distribution of resources by the central state, seek protection from the negative consequences of globalization, reverse or compensate for discriminatory social practices, pursue environmentally sustainable development with some level of social equity, to name but a few examples, many of the principal objectives of social actors cannot be achieved in isolation from decision-making processes that determine the overall direction of the larger societies of which they form a part. This is particularly true in Latin America, where centuries of national centralizing tendencies still predominate (Véliz 1980), despite recent efforts at state decentralization in many countries.

In conflating the mere existence of civil society with the public sphere, much of the literature ignores important questions about the composition and effectiveness of the public sphere (Calhoun 1993). Social movements and civil society organizations become ends in themselves, regardless of their capacity to effect meaningful changes at the level of the state or society that go beyond the role (however important) such movements and organizations play in their members' lives. Frequently such activity, particularly activity that positively affirms the identities of disadvantaged or marginalized groups, is only a foundation for achieving social and political change. The challenge that these movements and organizations face is to successfully move beyond this beginning stage in their development. The concept of the public sphere as developed here best captures the complexity of that challenge.

Conversely, by ignoring the public sphere as a separate phenomenon, the literature on civil society sidesteps key issues about the nature of civil society's relation to the state. This further reinforces the tendency to draw a rigid line of separation between the two, often portraying civil society as confronting an antagonistic state. While this was certainly true during periods of authoritarian rule and may to a lesser degree also characterize relations between some segments of civil society and new democratic regimes, the most successful democratic regimes in terms of inclusion and respect for citizenship rights achieve this because the state works closely with civil society. The arena in which this takes place is the public sphere.

As Calhoun (1993, 273) notes, the public sphere is an "operationalization of civil society's capacity for self-organization." In this way, the public sphere is in reality the definitive demand of civil societies, and its creation is one of their principal victories. It is at the level of the public sphere that the dual dynamic of resistance to state subordination and the demand for inclusion plays itself out. The interaction of civil society and the state through the public sphere historically has been responsible for shaping the principal rights of citizenship actually enjoyed by citizens (Somers 1993; Oxhorn 2003). The public character of the various social actors who compose civil society and drive this dynamic embodies the thin social consensus on which civil society is based. It defines the limits of the competition among them for influence, effectively allowing a peaceful coexistence. Conversely, to the extent that civil society remains weak, the public sphere necessarily excludes large segments of the population.

Just as civil society cannot be understood in isolation from the state, the state also plays an important role in structuring the public sphere. In extreme cases, the public sphere is severely circumscribed as a result of the state's physical repression of civil society actors. States also play a role in directly creating or strengthening civil society actors, thereby conditioning the nature of the public sphere through the kinds of relations it establishes. This has been the case historically in the United States (Skocpol 1996), and is a hallmark of corporatist modes of interest intermediation in both developed and developing countries (Schmitter 1974). The public sphere reflects this, both through the kinds of actors who are present in it, as well as through the specific channels the state establishes with them.

The state directly structures the public sphere in several important ways that reflect a "state in society" perspective for understanding patterns of social domination (Migdal 1994). First, state institutions create both opportunities and incentives for different groups to organize and attempt to influence policies (Oxhorn 1998a; Skocpol 1985; Tilly 1981). The degree of openness of state institutions determines the kinds of groups that have access and how such access is achieved. The policies a state addresses, the scope of its influence in the economy and society, and the resources the state has at its disposal for distribution are all key variables that help determine the contours of the public sphere. Similarly, state institutions vary in terms of the degree to which they enable citizens to relate to one another in a variety of different ways that can help institutionalize the participation in the public sphere of the myriad social identities present in any society (S. Bickford 1999; L. Bickford 1999).

A second way in which states condition the public sphere is through the provision of legal rights of citizenship. Laws are essential for guaranteeing the gains of civil society (Cohen and Arato 1992), and in fact legislative initiatives are often at the forefront of civil demands. Important formal rights such as the freedom of expression and association, as well as universal suffrage, are obvious prerequisites for any public sphere to function democratically. The effective provision of other rights of citizenship, particularly basic civil rights, is also important for understanding the nature of the public sphere in Latin America. Such rights often are anything but universal and in practice lead to the exclusion of large segments of the population from active participation in the public sphere. Indeed, the effective rule of law is an important "complement to the efforts of less privileged groups to organize themselves" (Evans 1997a, 181).

More fundamentally, the state and civil society frequently must work together to achieve a variety of important outcomes that would otherwise be unattainable. This creates a more fluid relationship between the state and civil society that can be called *synergy,* or what Keane (1998, 11) labels a "power sharing perspective."[12] Under these circumstances, the state and civil society are not in competition with one another; a positive rather than zero-sum game is the result. Yet the rigid dichotomy of the state versus civil society found in much of the literature would rule this out, even though reality suggests that some of the most important achievements of the Western European welfare states, for example, would have been impossible without the close cooperation between organized business interests, labor movements, and the state (Goldthorpe 1984; C. Taylor 1990).

This synergistic relation has two principal dimensions. First, there is what could be called the negative or prescriptive dimension. At this level, civil society plays an essential role by insisting on respect for existing rights, including "the new politics of society" intended to ensure that politicians and state officials remain accountable for their actions (Smulovitz and Peruzotti 2000).[13] This is achieved through a variety of means, including resorting to the judiciary, media campaigns, and protests. It is often taken for granted in established Western democracies, but its importance was dramatically demonstrated by the activities of human rights movements throughout the developing world, in democracies and undemocratic regimes alike.

Equally important is a second dimension, which is positive, or proscriptive. States obviously do much more than enforce laws and ensure that basic rights are respected. Civil society can often play a crucial role in many of these activities. First, civil society actors frequently play important roles in setting public agendas, including demanding new laws and new rights. Agency is a crucial question when trying to understand the prospects for socially progressive reforms. Civil society can play a direct role, advocating change in the corridors of power within the state and developing alternative policies. It also plays an indirect role, prodding reformers within the state to act and campaign so that more of them attain positions of authority. As Bendix (1964, 50–51) notes, Tocqueville tended to exaggerated the influence of medieval politics on modern conceptions of the state and society: "The collective pursuit of private ends . . . is not necessarily incompatible with an increase of central government, because today voluntary associations frequently demand more rather than less government action in contrast to the medieval estates whose effort to extend their jurisdiction was often synonymous with resistance to administrative interference from outside."

Beyond that, civil society can play a critical role by working with the state in the design and implantation of important policies. For example, successful state development policies are dependent on the linkages between state institutions responsible for economic policy and key actors who can provide the state with information and then assist in policy implementation (Evans 1995; Stallings and Peres 2000). The achievement of policy priorities, including effective law enforcement and quality education, actually depend on a close cooperation between relevant state institutions and civil society actors (Oxhorn 2006). This is particularly true in developing countries where the lack of resources and institutional legitimacy are compounded by the effects of extremes in social inequality. In these contexts, cooperation with civil society can help compensate for the weakness of state institutions in terms of their resources and ability to reach out to all segments of society.

One consequence of these interactions is that the boundaries separating the public and private spheres is constantly contested and in flux (Maier 1987). Indeed, some of the most divisive political issues in many societies reflect competing visions of where that boundary should be drawn. Whether it be calls to keep the state out of individuals' lives regarding issues of sexuality and reproduction, insistence that formerly private issues of family violence cannot be ignored by the state, or demands that authoritarian regimes respect human rights by publicly insisting that "the personal is political" (Navarro 1989), the boundary separating the public from the private is frequently contested. Such debates only reinforce the inherently contingent nature of the public sphere, again underscoring the importance of which groups are active.[14] Of course, the state and civil society are not the only factors conditioning the nature of the public sphere. In particular, the media and political parties play an important intervening role.

The impact on the public sphere of the mass media is ambiguous. At a minimum, it is difficult to think of a public sphere without free mass media, and restrictions on the media are one way in which states attempt (sometimes violently) to constrain the public sphere. Conversely, a free medium is not the same as an unbiased one, particularly in countries where there is a predominance of conservative social agendas linked to business interests. Yet recent history is rich in examples of candidates winning elections despite mass media opposition, including the dramatic but otherwise disparate elections of Alberto Fujimori in Peru, Hugo Chávez in Venezuela, and Luís Inácio ("Lula") da Silva in Brazil. Perhaps even more dramatically, opposition to the Augusto Pinochet military regime was able to successfully use the mass media to defeat him in the 1988 national plebiscite and thus begin a transition to democracy. In general, the obviously commercial nature of much of the mass media, particularly television, has to a certain extent neutralized its ability to influence policy debates. Also for commercial reasons, perhaps the most notorious influence exercised by media on the public sphere is through their often powerful impact on popular fears, particularly concerning crime and official corruption. These fears can have the perverse effect of narrowing the public sphere as public opinion shifts in support of authoritarian, nondemocratic remedies.

While it is arguable whether political parties should be considered part of civil society given that they uniquely compete to win control over the state, their influence on the public sphere is determined in important ways by their roots in civil society. This, in turn, has important implications for the public sphere. The weakness and loss of legitimacy that traditional political parties experienced in Venezuela and Peru, for example, were important factors explaining the electoral victories of populists such as Fujimori and Chávez, who successfully campaigned against traditional parties and politicians. Conversely, the strength of political parties in Chile was a principal reason for the opposition's ultimate victory, at the same time that parties had to overcome years of repression and the direct assault on their legitimacy by the military regime.

The nature of the ties between voters and political parties crystallizes in the public sphere, as part of political parties' unique representational function in democracies. Parties affect the public sphere directly, through the agendas or platforms that they debate and through the state policies that they advocate or oppose. The weaker the links between political leaders and the grassroots, the more distant and inaccessible the public sphere will appear. Indeed, this is one reason behind the widespread support of populists, both today and in the past: they appear to listen to the common person when traditional elites do not.

From the perspective of understanding the depth and quality of democratic rule, one of the most important processes that take place within the public sphere is the social construction of citizenship. As Charles Tilly (1996, 9) notes, historically, it was the "struggle and bargaining between expanding states and their subjects [that] created citizenship where it had not previously existed." While today there is perhaps greater consensus than ever before on the normative content of democratic citizenship rights, these rights are still contested in practice as a consequence of their uneven coverage and their ambiguous impact on important aspects of a given society (gender relations, land-owning patterns, indigenous cultures, and the environment, for example). There also is still no consensus on how to implement specific rights of citizenship. In most Latin American democracies, conflicts over basic citizenship rights were central yet unresolved issues in the transition process. The failure of democratic institutions to address these shortcomings after the transition is often the principal source of their fragility. Agency is the key to understanding how citizenship rights actually evolve or stagnate. The pressures for expanding citizenship rights that emerge (or fail to emerge) from within civil society through the public sphere, and how those pressures are dealt with by the state, are central to any causal theory of citizenship. In other words, citizenship reflects which groups participate and how in their social construction through the public sphere.

Viewed from this perspective, the strength of civil society is mirrored in the scope and depth of citizenship rights. As civil society expands to include different collective actors, their ability to define and defend their interests in the public sphere ultimately is reflected in the breadth and depth of the rights enjoyed by citizens in any particular country. Conversely, when civil society is weak or repressed by the state, the result is a more or less severe constriction of the rights people enjoy as citizens. This is clearest in nondemocratic states, but it is also reflected in the evolution of citizenship rights as a result of the historical successful mobilization of different groups.

If an inclusive, socially constructed body of universal citizenship rights is the ideal, its antithesis is represented in populism. As a form of mass mobilization, populism represents the ability of relatively small, privileged groups to gain greater access to state power and resources by capitalizing on disadvantaged groups on the basis of the latter's perceived socioeconomic or political exclusion (Oxhorn 1998b; K. Roberts 1994). Such disadvantaged groups are characterized by the lack of autonomous, self-constituted organizations, and their interests continue to be defined by and subordinated to the interests of whichever elite groups are able to mobilize them. This is true even though populist mobilization is invariably associated with some short-term distributional benefits and limited citizenship rights in exchange for continued support. Rather than a more complete dispersion of power within a society and the universalization of citizenship rights, power remains concentrated and new forms of inequality are introduced. Civil society itself is tightly constrained, with important negative consequences for citizenship rights, the public sphere, and the prospects for democratic rule.

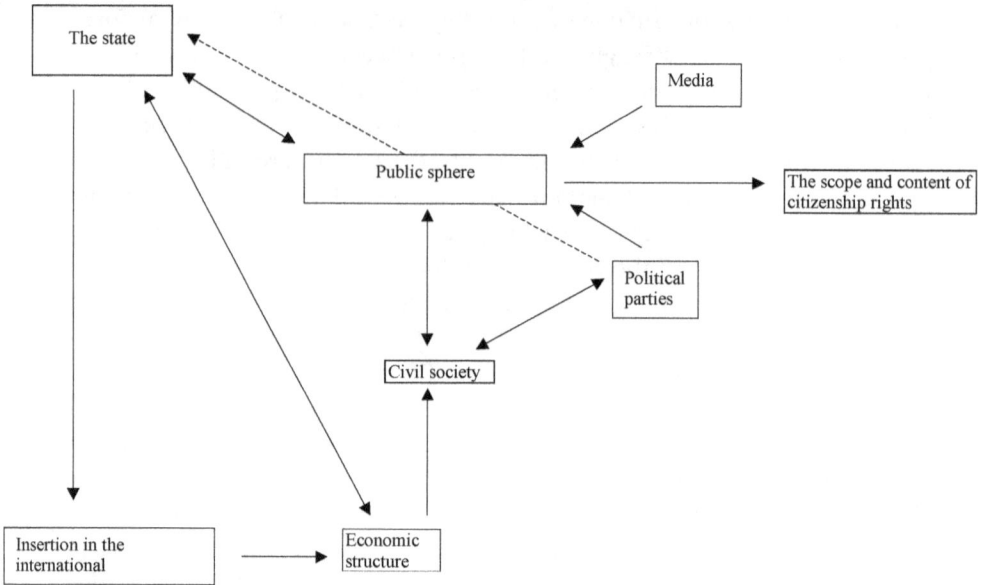

Fig. 1.1 Civil society, the public sphere, and the social construction of citizenship rights.

The state plays a central role in conditioning the nature of both civil society and the public sphere. Changes in state policy and a given country's insertion in the international economic system interact to create processes of economic change. The social and political consequences of these changes are mediated by the existing nature of the country's civil society and understood in terms of their ultimate effects on the distribution of power resources within that polity. At the same time, the resultant distribution of power resources affects the nature of civil society itself. To the extent that there is a greater dispersion of power resources, civil society should be strengthened, while social equity and democratization should improve. Conversely, civil society is undermined by increases in the concentration of power resources, with concomitant declines in social equity and a corresponding increase in the long-term threats to democratic stability.

This relationship is expressed through the public sphere, which mediates the interaction between the state and civil society (see figure 1.1). The strength of civil society, in particular, provides for a more inclusionary public sphere, while the state shapes the public sphere through the institutional spaces it creates for participation and the provision of citizenship rights. It is through the struggles (or lack thereof) of different organized groups within civil society vis-à-vis one another and the state that citizenship rights are socially constructed. In societies characterized by weak civil societies, or closed authoritarian regimes that deliberately seek to control (if not destroy) civil society, citizenship rights are severely constrained. Conversely, the strength of civil society is reflected in the breadth and multifaceted content of citizenship rights through civil society's capacity to expand rights and check authoritarian tendencies at the level of the state.

The mass media also have a clear, albeit ambiguous, effect on the public sphere. Political parties similarly play an important role in shaping the public sphere in a variety of ways. Whether political parties promote or restrict the public sphere is to a large extent determined by the kinds of linkages they have to civil society.

Figure 1.1 is expressed in ideal terms that focus on the dynamic relationships that are central to the social construction of citizenship. It is neither exhaustive of all public sphere activity nor necessarily incompatible with other approaches that emphasize the role of the individual in defining civil society or the deliberative qualities of the public sphere.[15] It is, however, useful for identifying the principal power relations within any polity that ultimately determine its democratic prospects.

A European Excursus

Given the emphasis on the Western European experience for understanding civil society in much of the literature, a brief discussion of that experience offers a particularly useful way to understand some of the implications of the perspective developed here. This excursus also provides a relevant historical backdrop for understanding the particular challenges facing Latin America.

As a starting point, the theory of civil society developed here can be used to reinterpret and contextualize the classic work by T. H. Marshall (1950) on citizenship and social inequality by focusing on the implications of his work for civil society's role in the social construction of citizenship (Oxhorn 2003). In what would prove to be a truly virtuous circle over the course of some three hundred years of British and, by extension, European history, Marshall suggests that the evolution of citizenship rights began with the establishment of civil rights.[16] Once civil rights were recognized in eighteenth-century Britain, citizenship then continued to expand to include, first, political rights in the form of universal male suffrage and, later, the social rights of citizenship associated with the modern welfare state. In the process, according to Marshall, the social inequality associated with capitalism was legitimated, at the same time that the social and political foundations on which modern capitalism could thrive were successfully put into place.

Central to Marshall's argument is the functional necessity of citizenship for modern capitalist development. The emergence of modern, universal rights of citizenship parallels the growth of the market economy. The process began in the eighteenth century, both because the emerging capitalist economy required the institutionalization of property rights through the enforcement of basic civil rights and because the new capitalist society had to legitimate the resultant social inequality with the new principle of citizenship. Civil rights thus became the cornerstone of modern conceptions of citizenship. Over the course of the next century, universal political rights were established and the process, as understood by Marshall, culminated after World War II with the establishment of the universal social rights of citizenship associated with the modern welfare state. For Marshall, decreased economic inequality due to economic development, combined with social integration achieved through universal civil, political, and social rights of citizenship, generated a new societal consensus for the minimization of social inequality.

The criticisms of Marshall's work from a number of perspectives (Mann 1996; Turner 1992; Walby 1994) reflect the inadequacies of his essay from the perspective of the social construction of citizenship rights. Despite some isolated references, the role of class conflict and social struggle in defining and expanding citizenship rights is largely ignored. Marshall adopts a deterministic, almost functionalist, view of the evolution of citizenship rights from the perspective of capitalist economic development and political stability.[17] There is an implicit assumption that the interests of the working class and capitalists are complementary rather than contradictory and that all actors will act (albeit slowly in the case of Britain) to institutionalize their mutual interest in universal citizenship rights. In the first instance, capitalists required civil rights to protect their interests. This, in turn, was portrayed by Marshall as unleashing a seemingly inevitable teleological process by which economic development created a new societal consensus surrounding universal rights of citizenship. The institutionalization of citizenship rights in Britain was able to keep pace with changing public attitudes in large part because continued economic prosperity raised levels of economic equality independently of state redistributive policies. Ultimately, British economic prosperity and the new social consensus that it created allowed for an increasingly direct attack by the state on any remaining sources of social inequity.

Yet Marshall's account of the evolution of citizenship rights is not inconsistent with approaches stressing the role of conflict and contingency in the social construction of citizenship. British capitalists may have enjoyed economic prosperity and relative political stability for centuries, but this is better understood as the consequence of concessions brought about as a result of social struggles initiated by workers and other social classes, rather than the outcome of any teleology of capitalist development.[18] In other words, once civil rights for subaltern groups, particularly the working class, were conceded by Britain's elite, these groups used their new rights to organize and eventually force reluctant elites to grant political rights in the form of universal suffrage, with their ultimate conquest being the creation of modern welfare states. Capitalists elsewhere have done extraordinarily well by following distinct paths of political and economic development in which limited social rights of citizenship were in effect given to workers as a way of co-opting or controlling worker mobilization in the absence of effective political and civil rights (Mann 1996; Oxhorn 1995a, 1998b). This is particularly true for Latin America, and a useful theory must be able to account for these different results.

Rather than the outcome of the functional requirements of capitalism or a consequence of a new social consensus associated with modernity, a causal theory of citizenship rights needs to focus on the development of civil society within particular countries and its interaction with the state. In other words, the expansion of citizenship to include civil, political, and, ultimately, social rights as described by Marshall should be reinterpreted to recognize the conflictual nature of the process and the central role played by civil society. This demonstrates how the contingent outcomes of such struggles are also compatible with a diverse range of rights that Marshall's more economic perspective would seem to preclude, including gender, ethnicity, ecology, and community. Such rights reflect the diversity of the actors participating in their construction through the public sphere.

Citizenship struggles are also constitutive of the growing strength of civil society. Through struggle, collective identities are created and redefined as new sources of political power. When rights are granted as a result of social struggle, a certain prior distribution of power resources is recognized and institutionalized by the state, contributing to a further relative dispersion of power resources and concomitantly strengthening civil society. From this perspective, the path followed by Britain as described by Marshall may be "ideal," but it is also unique. In sharp contrast to most recent (and many historical) transitions to democracy, working-class mobilization was deliberately intended to change an existing (according to the standards of the day) democratic regime rather than overthrow a violent authoritarian one. This continuity allows for a progressive accumulation in the strength of different actors in civil society that is much more problematic in cases of a more radical regime change.

However "ideal" the British experience may have been, it also was not unproblematic or lacking in violence, as stressed by Moore (1966). In Moore's groundbreaking study of the paths to the modern world, the early commercialization of agriculture ensured that "modernity," which Moore equated with high levels of industrialization and urbanization, would be democratic in Britain. The commercialization of agriculture eliminated the peasantry as a class that could be mobilized either by the forces of reaction or revolution. It also created a bourgeoisie capable of providing a more or less equal ally for the aristocracy in creating an effective counterbalance to the state and curbing the latter's authoritarian tendencies.

In terms of civil society and the social construction of citizenship, the early introduction of the market with the commercialization of agriculture created new, more widely distributed power resources. As Moore notes, it clearly increased the power of the bourgeoisie. Equally important, these new resources were largely independent of the state (although the state played a critical role in regulating new markets and facilitating Britain's growing trade relations). This balancing and effective (albeit reluctant) cooperation between the state, the oligarchy, and Britain's rising capitalist class served as the foundation for democratic governance and represents an early variant of the state-society synergy.[19]

Along with early industrialization, there was also a significant increase in the potential power of the working class in Britain, helping to ensure further democratization in the future. This increased power was reflected in the steadily increasing wage incomes of workers. It also was the result (as Marx appreciated early on) of the relative ease of organizing workers who were concentrated in factories and shared clearly identifiable common interests and whose cooperation was becoming increasingly indispensable for continued capital accumulation.[20]

In sharp contrast to the example in Britain, Moore identifies two alternative paths to modernity: revolution from above, or fascism; and communist revolution from below. Both alternatives, in turn, reflect very distinct patterns in the emergence of civil society and its subsequent relationship to the state. In both paths, the relative weakness of the bourgeoisie and the oligarchy's resort to "labor-repressive agriculture" were decisive, according to Moore. From the perspective of civil society and the social construction of citizenship, they reflect varying levels of concentration of power resources and a progressive narrowing of the ability of different actors to work with the state through the public sphere.

Labor-repressive agriculture, which Moore defines as the use of political coercion to tie peasants to the land, reflects nothing more than a disproportionate concentration of power in the hands of the oligarchy and its allies in the state. In the extreme case of communist revolution, power was so concentrated in the oligarchy and state that civil society was virtually nonexistent. Indeed, it is the weakness of the bourgeoisie as a potential ally that, according to Moore, left the oligarchy with few alternatives and contributed to a polarization of society that allowed for the emergence of revolutionary movements seeking complete control of the state.

Similarly, the intermediate path of fascism, as exemplified by both Germany and Japan prior to World War II, reflected the consequences of a greater dispersion of power resources than found in the cases of communist revolution, but significantly less than was the case in Britain.[21] In these cases, according to Moore, the relatively late commercialization of agriculture was not sufficient to provide the social base for a bourgeois democratic revolution. Instead, the bourgeoisie became the oligarchy's junior partner in fostering state-led industrialization. The consequence was that democracy could be installed only after the defeat of the Axis in World War II.[22]

The rich and varied historical experience of Europe further highlights the general implications of the social construction of citizenship perspective developed here.[23] As early as the Middle Ages, civil society's uneven emergence in Europe demonstrated a variety of different paths to modernity that, grosso modo, laid the foundations for divergent developments between Eastern and Western Europe.[24] It was in the Middle Ages that sharp distinctions were first drawn between the church, political organization, and society in Western Europe. At the same time, the emergence of new collective actors, beginning with the first cities and guilds, contributed to a greater dispersion of power as they competed with traditional feudal institutions, effectively putting important constraints on emerging absolutist states. This process was reinforced by early struggles between organized peasants and the oligarchy as feudalism slowly gave way to the Renaissance and the early emergence of capitalism. In sharp contrast, absolutist states in Eastern Europe generally faced fewer constraints in a socioeconomic context marked by fewer large cities, the slower emergence of market relations, and fewer autonomous actors who could challenge the increasing centralization of power—long before the emergence of the Soviet bloc's communist regimes.

At the same time, the European experience demonstrates the significance of alternative paths in the development of citizenship. In contrast to Marshall's idealized sequence of rights, there are important examples of social rights of citizenship preceding political rights, often for the purpose of co-opting middle- and lower-class actors to forestall demands for more effective political rights. For example, Michael Mann (1996) persuasively argues that social rights of citizenship were historically often a substitute for civic and political rights in Germany under Bismarck.

The importance of the sequencing of citizenship rights and the development of civil society is highlighted in a different way by examining the fate of women's rights in the former Soviet Union and in post-Soviet Eastern Europe. As is well known, the social rights enjoyed by women under Soviet-style communism were often quite significant in terms of their potential for empowering women. Indeed, the communist order claimed to champion many women's rights (regardless of how effective or genuine such claims actually were), and that is part of the problem. The granting of such rights by the communist state in the absence of any autonomous demands for them from within civil society stymied the development of civil society by preempting the potential for women's mobilization. When the communist regimes fell, a new stigma was attached to feminist movements because their demands were so closely associated with the now discredited communists. In the face of considerable setbacks in rights that would have been considered major gains for women had they been won in other contexts (access to social services and health care, reproductive rights, to name

but a few), one finds a "cultural narrative that reasserts an essentialized sexual-
ized woman, who seeks to reclaim her natural domesticity denied to her under
the former regime" (Hobson and Lindholm 1997, 501).

As even this simplified history of Europe attests, both regional and national
dynamics condition the emergence of civil society and its interaction with the
state through the public sphere in fundamental ways. The admittedly "thick"
societal consensus underpinning both democracy and civil society in Western
Europe is the culmination of this experience in a select number of states, but it
is one of a multiplicity of historically contingent outcomes when looking both
at the region as whole or individual countries over time. As we will see in the
next chapter, the unique regional and national dynamics in Latin America have
produced a different set of experiences that have been far less conducive to such
a thick consensus and democracy.

2

CONTROLLED INCLUSION AND THE ELUSIVE GOAL OF CITIZENSHIP AS AGENCY

Far from achieving a thick societal consensus, Latin American societies have historically been characterized by the lack of even a minimal level of consensus. This lack of consensus reflects extremes of inequality and high levels of poverty. The stakes in Latin American politics are thus unusually quite high: the loss of immense privilege for dominant groups and the hope for improved standards of living for the often impoverished majority. Among the principal consequences of this are varying levels of political instability and violence, weak democratic institutions, and the stymied development of civil society.

Despite a very high level of historical continuity in terms of inequality, poverty, and instability, Latin America has been anything but static economically, socially, and politically. This dynamic quality can be understood in terms of the social construction of citizenship. The extreme nature of social, political, and economic exclusion inherited from the colonial period and institutionalized after the wars of independence meant that national political processes until the early part of the twentieth century were completely dominated by elites, who often begrudgingly shared power among themselves. Toward the end of the nineteenth century in countries such as Argentina and Chile, new groups began to challenge the elite's monopoly over political power. During periods of oligarchic rule, the best evidence of this was the repression that the state would unleash against mobilized lower-class groups, or the popular sectors, as well as, albeit to a lesser extent, the middle sectors.[1] Although repression did not end with the advent of a new period in the region's economic and political development, the dominant classes could no longer sidestep the issue of incorporating other groups. Citizenship became the axis around which the issue was addressed, particularly with the rise of the first populist leaders in the 1930s. It defined the principal political struggles in the region, even if the exact nature and outcomes of those struggles varied considerably.

Struggles over citizenship had profound consequences. Most obviously, they would determine who would be included in the category of "citizen" and what this would entail in terms of rights for specific groups; most rights were anything but universal in practice. More important, they juxtaposed two quite different models of citizenship: *citizenship as co-optation* and *citizenship as agency,* which is why struggles over citizenship frequently led to extreme levels of violence and polarization in the 1960s and 1970s throughout Latin America.

As suggested in chapter 1, the concept of the social construction of citizenship highlights the importance of knowing who participates in defining citizenship rights. Citizenship as co-optation captures what has been the predominant historical tendency throughout the region: citizenship rights were granted selectively to co-opt particular actors and contain popular sectors' pressure for greater structural change and inclusion.[2] Rather than responding to the direct influence of subordinate groups in defining the content of citizenship, citizenship tended to be created in a top-down fashion. This minimized the potential contribution of citizenship to social change because citizenship rights were granted to subordinate groups on the terms set by those already in highly privileged positions they did not want to see undermined. Because the focus here is on agency (or lack thereof), citizenship as co-optation is very different from the apathetic citizen lauded in the early literature on democratic pluralism (Dahl 1961) or the feared active citizen in the literature on democratic governability (Crozier et al. 1975). In the former case, apathy is viewed as a consequence of successful democratic governance (people choose not to participate because there is little need), whereas citizenship as co-optation captures its coercive aspects. In the latter case, such fear presumes that citizen demands are fundamentally illegitimate, even when they respect democratic norms and institutions, whereas citizenship as co-optation underscores how existing citizenship rights are disconnected from actual demands of citizens or potential citizens.

In contrast to citizenship as co-optation, citizenship as agency ideally reflects the active role that multiple actors, particularly those representing disadvantaged groups, must play in the social construction of citizenship so that democratic governance can realize its full potential. Historically, it is synonymous with strong civil societies in Western Europe, where advanced social welfare states can be seen as one of its principal achievements. Given Latin America's historical extremes of inequality and exclusion, as well as the predominance of citizenship as co-optation, the ideal of citizenship as agency was typically championed by the radical Left. For this reason, citizenship as agency was quite different from the ideal represented by Western Europe and not compatible with civil society and the thin social consensus discussed in chapter 1. Citizenship as agency in this context was linked with the revolutionary capture of the state and the exclusion of actors not directly linked with the revolutionary party. Political democracy was, at best, generally viewed by the Left as something to be used instrumentally or, at worst, as a bourgeois trap that inherently blocked structural change. However, this instrumental view of democracy was not limited to the Left, and citizenship in Latin America had a very ambiguous relationship to political democracy during this period.

In this chapter, I first discuss the nature of Latin America's independence struggles and their aftermath during the period of oligarchic rule that began to break down in the early part of the twentieth century. I then analyze the political economy of the new order that consolidated itself in the aftermath of World War II, which I characterize as a period of controlled inclusion. This period came to an end with the debt crisis and the region's economic collapse in the early 1980s, although the social construction of the citizenship dynamic had already led to increasingly violent forms of authoritarian rule throughout the region, beginning with Brazil's 1964 military coup. The chapter then concludes with a discussion of some of the implications of this period for understanding the social construction of citizenship in Latin America.

Reactionary Independence, Oligarchic Rule, and the Pursuit of Order

While the precursors of West European civil societies had already been evolving for hundreds of years when Spain and Portugal began to colonize at the end of the fifteenth century, the conquest quickly destroyed anything that one day might develop into strong civil societies in Latin America. The decimation of indigenous populations, which in turn necessitated the massive importation of African slaves, the monopolization of political and economic power in the hands of the colonial elite, and the nature of the colonial economy based on natural resources and extreme forms of labor repressive extraction (Moore 1966), laid the structural foundations for future extremes of socioeconomic inequality that would be antithetical to the emergence of civil societies throughout the region (Karl 2003; De Ferranti et al. 2004).

In many crucial respects, the dynamics driving civil society's early emergence in Western Europe were the polar opposite in Latin America. Whereas numerous West European cities struggled for their autonomy vis-à-vis political authorities, the relatively few cities established in Latin America served as the seat of colonial administrations, reinforcing centralization and hierarchy rather than contributing to a dispersion of power resources. At the same time, vast expanses of territory lacked any colonial state presence. The power struggles between an emergent urban bourgeoisie and the rural aristocracy that provided a key dynamic in the emergence of West European civil societies were largely absent in Latin America during the colonial period. Instead, often absentee landlords and the emerging urban bourgeoisie generally sought to defend a common interest in maintaining their own privileges and reinforcing the concentration of power rather than opening opportunities for the incorporation of new actors.

The problems colonialism created for the future emergence of strong civil societies are clearest in the reactionary nature of the region's wars of independence in the early nineteenth century.[3] For the criollo elite (people of Spanish descent born in the colonies), the Spanish Crown had become both a hindrance to their personal advancement and a threat to their continued privileged position. The economic underdevelopment of Spain in relation to Britain and France led the Spanish Crown to exert increasing political control over the colonies, displacing criollo elites with more trustworthy Europeans in the colonial administration. At the same time, the Spanish monopoly over trade sought to extract ever more resources from the colonial economy to maintain Spain's own position in the evolving international system.

To make matters worse, criollos watched in horror as Bourbon reforms increased the social mobility of the lower classes. Policies designed to lessen social tensions by removing the most blatant forms of discrimination began "to blur the lines between whites and castes, and to enable many who were not clearly Indian or black to be regarded as socially and culturally Spanish" (Lynch 1984, 155). The successful rebellion against the French by former slaves in Haiti in 1803 only served to remind the criollo elite of its own vulnerability as a small minority sitting atop large indigenous and slave populations upon whose continued quiescence their position depended. France's inability to quash the rebellion graphically demonstrated the danger of depending on the much weaker Spanish Crown to defend their position in the face of any popular revolt.

When the Spanish Crown collapsed with Napoleon Bonaparte's invasion in 1808, the criollos sought to fill the political vacuum in the colonies by mobilizing to win their independence and firmly take destiny into their own hands to prevent the lower classes from doing so (Lynch 1984). To succeed, the criollo elite turned to locally based strongmen, or caudillos, whose private armies would wrest control from forces still loyal to Spain, keeping nationalist mobilization of the lower classes to a minimum and under tight control (Centeno 2002; Lynch 1992).

Under these circumstances, it is no surprise that the newly independent countries of the region were marked by important contradictions and paradoxes. Because of the extreme concentration of power resources, Latin American societies would not be economically integrated until well into the twentieth century (Thorp 1998). State authority over national territories was recognized externally (initially by Spain's rivals) decades before this was achieved internally. As a result, Latin American elites had to quickly confront their primordial challenge of maintaining domestic political stability. Scarce resources were allocated to augment the state's coercive apparatus as "the new states made their presence felt mainly as instruments for repression and social control" (Oszlak 1981, 21).

Once again, the criollo elite turned to the caudillos, whose role in the wars of independence "legitimized the bandit chief and guerrilla leader and made him into a military hero," not to mention leaving the elites with large private armies, to erect "the necessary barriers to limit social change and preserve political privilege" (Lynch 1992, 82, 205). The criollo elite recognized that the struggle for independence had represented a social protest against all forms of social and political inequality for lower-class groups. Now in power, they were determined to ensure that such expectations were blocked as they set about creating new political institutions intended to contain any mass-based threats to their continued hegemony.

Reliance on the caudillos, however, was a double-edged sword. With few exceptions (principally Chile and Costa Rica), the region was wracked for decades by political instability and civil war as the various caudillos fought for control over the central state and its resources. The caudillos' internecine wars inevitably undermined the rule of law (Lynch 1992). Their personalism and reliance on patron-client relations to guarantee the support of their followers made it impossible to build strong state institutions to provide basic governability and long-term development, let alone ensure any accountability of the ruling elite. State institutions did grow, but as a source of patronage. This was the beginning a process of politicizing state institutions that continues to plague much of the region to this day, even though states remained largely incapable of extracting sufficient economic resources from the elite to finance such expansion (Karl 2003). States instead turned to debt and dependence on external rents from trade—another problem that continues to haunt much of the region.

The criollo elite's racist views toward the majority of Latin Americans, combined with the effects of chronic political instability and the concomitant insecurity of the elite's property rights during times of civil war, generated a growing fear of anarchy. The pursuit of domestic political order became the primary preoccupation of most of Latin America's elite (Safford 1987, 51). In this way, order was seen as a prerequisite for progress (Oszlak 1981, 21), establishing a perceived trade-off between citizenship rights and development that elites would continually resort to in their justification of the suspension of democratic institutions well into the twentieth century.

Order was eventually established, largely so that the criollo elite could take advantage of increasing opportunities for economic progress that were opening up with the rapid expansion of international trade in the second half of the nineteenth century (Oszlak 1981; O'Donnell 1988). This marked the beginning of Latin America's first sustained export-led expansion, under the normative guidance of economic liberalism, with striking similarities to the predominance of neoliberal economic policies introduced more than a century later. Facing little or no pressure to change structural sources of inequality, the region's elites not only left them intact but actually exacerbated them in fundamental ways through reforms obeying the exigencies of the new laissez-faire development model (Karl 2003; Thorp 1998). Inequality was still functional to the continued maintenance of economic prosperity, and a variety of institutions were created to further the economic interests of the elite by securing property rights and keeping labor costs to a minimum (Thorp 1998). For example, under the guise of liberal modernization, many of the collective property rights enjoyed by indigenous communities during the colonial period were revoked. This further increased land concentration "as landowning become more solidly entrenched as a source of wealth, political power and access to other inputs such as credit and water" (Thorp 1998, 95).

For both Latin America and the now developed West, this growth phase ended with the Great Depression. In the West, the societal reaction against the vagaries of unregulated markets led to a "Great Transformation" (Polanyi 1944), culminating in the creation of inclusionary welfare states based on universal citizenship rights. Latin America also experienced a great transformation, ushering in a new period in the region's economic and political development that lasted roughly from the end of World War II to the early 1980s. But Latin America's transformation bore only the most superficial resemblance to anything envisioned by Karl Polanyi or T. H. Marshall. The distribution of power within Latin American societies and the consequences this had for the emergence of strong civil societies ensured a very different outcome. Major structural change took place throughout the region after World War II, including massive urbanization and a growing socioeconomic role for the state that led to rapid industrialization in a number of countries. The political and economic domination by the traditional oligarchy was increasingly losing its viability as Latin American societies became more complex. New collective actors, particularly an incipient industrial bourgeoisie, middle sectors, and a growing working class, were entering the national stage for the first time and demanding unprecedented levels of inclusion. Even the peasantry began to assert itself politically. To contain these growing pressures, a new mode of political inclusion and social integration emerged throughout the much of the region.

Controlled Inclusion:
Attempting to Contain the Swelling Tide of Civil Society

The defining characteristic of Latin America's political economy in the postwar period was a unique process of controlled inclusion. Controlled inclusion consisted of top-down processes of political and social inclusion in which citizenship rights were segmented, partial, and, ultimately, precarious. It epitomizes the idea of citizenship as co-optation, which explains why political alternatives based on citizenship as agency would prove so destabilizing in the 1960s and 1970s. Rather than substantially alter structures of inequality, controlled inclusion reflected and reinforced them. Some countries attempted controlled inclusion relatively late (e.g., Peru, Bolivia) and others (those in Central America, apart from Costa Rica, and Paraguay) never really made any attempt at inclusion. However, processes of controlled inclusion formed the principal axis around which the social construction of citizenship in Latin America played itself out until the introduction of an alternative axis—dictatorship or political democracy—in the late 1970s and 1980s.

The catalyst for this change was the region's new insertion in the international economy and the accompanying socioeconomic and political changes. After the shock of the Great Depression and the continued contraction of the international economic system during World War II, various countries began to redefine their development model based on ISI. In sharp contrast to the liberal free trade model preceding it, ISI revolved around extensive state intervention in the economy and society, with internal markets protected from international competition. The ensuing economic growth and ability of manufacturers to absorb labor costs due to the lack of competition allowed for relatively higher wages and minimal social rights for growing segments of the population, particularly among the middle sectors and workers in the formal sector. Yet, central to understanding the political significance of controlled inclusion, such gains were restricted to specific segments of the population and generally excluded the majority.

Virtually all Latin American countries underwent a process of social modernization between 1960 and 1980, as national societies became less agrarian and more urban and industrial (CEPAL 1991, 1989). Although countries modernized at different rates and with various levels of success, almost every country experienced important social transformations based on the internal expansion of market relations, substantial rural migration to cities, and real or expected upward social mobility for large portions of the population. This process of social modernization was driven by a twenty-year period of strong and relatively sustained economic growth of 5 to 6 percent annually, which resulted in a doubling of per capita GDP in the region. Despite the disequilibrium and inequalities associated with it, "this growth represented a true process of development" that affected the majority of people in practically every country of the region (CEPAL 1991, 22).

Throughout Latin America, there was a transfer of people from low productivity activities, especially in agriculture, to areas of greater productivity in manufacturing and the service sector. In 1950 more than 50 percent of the economically active population (EAP) in three-quarters of the twenty countries included in the CEPAL study was engaged in agricultural activities, primarily in subsistence farming or traditional agriculture on low-productivity latifundia. This still was true for the majority of Latin American and Caribbean countries in 1960. By 1980, however, only three countries had populations that were primarily engaged in agricultural activities—El Salvador, Guatemala, and Haiti. In a number of countries, the EAP in agriculture had fallen to approximately 30 percent (CEPAL 1989, 51–54).

Increased investment in capital and improved skills in the workforce allowed for the absorption of a growing proportion of the EAP in activities that were characterized by not only higher levels of productivity but also higher incomes and social status. The manufacturing sector was the engine of growth for the first time in Latin America (Thorp 1998). In particular, employment in the formal sector grew at a rate of 4 percent per year from 1950 to 1980 (Altimir 1998, 5) and real wages rose as well (Thorp 1998). One important consequence of these rapid socioeconomic changes was that 26 percent of the EAP experienced upward mobility in terms of social status and income between 1960 and 1980, according to a CEPAL study of general "structural mobility" in ten countries at various levels of social modernization.[4]

Younger generations were the primary beneficiaries of this social mobility, a fact that was central to the viability of controlled inclusion. Even if the social position of the older generations was more or less static and the structural causes of inequality largely unaffected by social modernization, continued economic dynamism served as a source of optimism about the future. Moreover, this reflected the importance of educational expansion, particularly at the primary level, and a rapid reduction of illiteracy (Altimir 1998; Thorp 1998).

The constraining impact of ISI and controlled inclusion on civil society was accentuated by the fact that this period also coincided with a generalized and very rapid process of urbanization.[5] The region's particular pattern of urbanization served as a pillar of controlled inclusion. Between 1940 and 1975, regional urbanization had doubled, from 19.6 percent of the population to 40.5 percent, with a number of countries experiencing much higher rates (B. Roberts 1981, 7). Yet, in sharp contrast to Western Europe, much of this urbanization was concentrated in a few large cities, further constraining the growth of civil society. Geographic centralization with its concomitant growth of political power resources was reinforced as those cities became the loci for industrialization and economic investment, as well as home to a disproportionate share of national populations.

This massive influx of migrants had important implications for popular-sector inclusion (B. Roberts 1981, 2005; Roberts and Portes 2006; Roberts and Wood 2005a). The sheer volume of urban migration, combined with the state's unwillingness or inability to invest sufficiently in urban services to satisfy popular-sector needs, meant that the popular sectors ultimately assumed the responsibility for creating their own cities through various forms of self-help in the provision of housing and basic urban services. This required the creation of important networks within and across urban communities, but such networks belied the existence of a strong civil society for several reasons. Collective action remained locally focused, but ultimately with little autonomy in the political realm. Although networks were essential for the poor to be able to survive in the new urban environment and allowed them to address a range of needs, from the provision of sewage disposal and fresh water to finding a job and a place to live, the focus inevitably was on immediate needs. A pragmatic concern with "the capacity of the poor to fend for themselves and to cope with urban life" was more important than ideals of citizenship or rights (B. Roberts 2005, 141). The poor were much less concerned with demanding inclusion than with finding a solution to pressing needs, at the same time that they were in no position to be able to effectively resist subordination to the state.

This pragmatic focus of collective action also made the poor susceptible to various forms of clientelism and co-optation (Castells 1983; B. Roberts 1981). Housing and urban infrastructure were very expensive, even if the required labor was essentially free. This gave political parties or other actors with access to state resources considerable leverage by being able to offer even minimal assistance. At the same time, the popular sectors were extremely vulnerable to eviction, particularly if they had no clear property rights or if they fell behind in their rent. The state took advantage of these circumstances by alternating repression with selective benefits, reinforcing popular-sector dependence despite the necessity of self-help mobilization. Combined with the pervasive negative impact of informality and its intrinsic insecurity, the poor were essentially "active but unincorporated members of urban populations" (B. Roberts 1981, 3). Not surprisingly, this pattern of urbanization was essential for the success of populism. The urban poor often felt that their situation had improved, albeit marginally, as a result of the policies enacted by populist leaders (B. Roberts 1981; Castells 1983), even though they still remained highly disadvantaged in political, social, and economic terms as a result of pervasive inequality.

Fundamentally, this period represented an increased dispersion of power within most Latin American societies compared to the period of oligarchic rule, reflected in a relative strengthening of civil society and a more inclusive public sphere. Yet despite often remarkable and rapid socioeconomic change, controlled inclusion meant that the region remained among the most unequal in the world. If anything, inequality increased in most countries (Thorp 1998; Altimir 1998; De Ferranti et al. 2004).

Persistent and worsening inequality reflected the lack of effective redistributive policies; social mobility and modernization resulted largely from economic growth and any efforts at redistribution were either rebuked or quickly reversed (De Ferranti et al. 2004; Karl 2003; Morley 2003; Thorp 1998; Altimir 1998). As Rosemary Thorp (1998, 6) explains, "governments and private sectors were in large measure responding to the existing socioeconomic structure, so the significant gains in building institutions did little to ameliorate the inequality embedded in the status quo."

Several factors account for this. First, although the oligarchy's hegemony was no longer viable politically, landowners still exercised sufficient political power to block meaningful land reform—the principal cause of rural urban migration with its concomitant augmentation of the already large unskilled urban labor force. Business groups were often closely linked economically to the oligarchy and also saw land reform as a threat to their own property rights. Where large-scale land reform was instituted (for example, Mexico and Bolivia after their respective revolutions, Peru under a reformist military regime in the late 1960s, and Chile under both the reformist Christian Democratic government of Eduardo Frei and Salvador Allende's socialist government), it had no significant long-term impact on distribution (except, of course, in Cuba). The continued political dominance of these two upper classes, increasingly supported by the middle sectors, also meant that taxation levels remained extremely low and regressive, while state expenditures remained skewed in favor of these same social classes. This is particularly clear in the educational sector, where popular-sector participation in secondary and postsecondary education remained low even as overall rates of literacy improved. Perhaps the most poignant indication of this lack of redistribution was the way in which the urban poor essentially constructed their own cities because the state would not provide even minimal public goods, in sharp contrast to what the state provided economically better-off neighborhoods.

Ultimately, the persistence of extremes of inequality both reflects and reinforces the weakness of civil society and the impact of controlled inclusion on civil society's continued evolution, particularly the ability of civil society actors to work through the public sphere to change social structures. The nexus of high inequality, weak civil society, and controlled inclusion is found in the region's highly asymmetrical, segmented class structure.

In his comprehensive study of Latin American class structures, Alejandro Portes (1985) defines classes in terms of three criteria: control over the means of production, control over the labor power of others, and the mode of remuneration. On this basis, he identifies five distinct social classes in Latin America: the dominant class, the bureaucratic-technical class (middle sectors), the formal proletariat, the informal petty bourgeoisie, and the informal proletariat.

What is most striking about Portes's findings is the extreme asymmetry of Latin America's class structure. The dominant and middle sectors together accounted for less than 10 percent of the EAP for all of Latin America in the 1970s. In no country did they exceed 15 percent, and only Venezuela and Panama came close to even that low percentage. Moreover, Portes's data on income distribution show that these two classes on average received more than 45 percent of the national income.

Portes found a similar pattern among the three subordinate social classes. While the size of the formal proletariat (which Portes classifies as those workers who receive wages on a contractual basis and an indirect wage through social welfare programs prescribed by law) varied more widely throughout the 1970s, it represented more than half of the EAP in Argentina, Uruguay, and Chile. The weighted regional average in 1972 was just 22.4 percent, and in most countries it hovered at around 12 percent.

This, of course, means that the informal sector of the economy was quite large at the beginning of the 1980s. The informal petty bourgeoisie accounted for approximately 10 percent of the regional EAP. As a social class, it linked the informal proletariat to the modern sector of the economy by subcontracting out for firms in the formal sector to lower costs and by supplying low-cost goods and services to the formal proletariat. The informal proletariat receives neither regular money wages nor the indirect wage of social security coverage. Their economic activity includes a wide range of activities, from doing piecework at home to street vending to collecting anything recyclable on the streets or in garbage dumps—performing any tasks that at best provide for a subsistence living. In all countries except Uruguay, workers in the informal sector (the informal proletariat and the informal petty bourgeoisie combined) represented at least 20 percent of the EAP in 1980. For the region as a whole, the informal sector represented roughly 60 percent of the EAP, or 80 percent of all workers.

This extreme class asymmetry prevented the emergence of even the minimal social consensus necessary for a strong civil society. In particular, the classic class compromise underlying social democracy between dominant business interests and the working class proved all but impossible to achieve (Przeworski 1985; Huber 2002b; Bresser Pereira and Nakano 1998). For the dominant classes, the state was both a source of wealth and privilege, as well as an institutional buffer to protect its interests from encroachment by other classes, particularly the popular sectors. Just as the state was the guarantor of order during the previous period of export-led growth, the dominant classes continued to resort to it in the face of the growing threat posed by the greater dispersion of power resources associated with ISI and its potential for strengthening civil society. Controlled inclusion became a state project intended to mediate this threat by selective and partial incorporation for subordinate groups. But the dominant classes were also the first to abandon it when such perceived threats appeared to overwhelm its institutional bulkheads. With the growth of a new business elite in control of production for domestic consumption, an important segment of the dominant classes was also dependent on the state for continued protection and subsidies. This new business elite was particularly concerned with ceding control of the state apparatus to interests that could undermine this relationship, particularly representatives of the lower class.[6]

The middle sectors were the principal beneficiaries of controlled inclusion. While their incorporation was rarely unproblematic and generally resulted after varying levels of political instability and political violence, controlled inclusion effectively became institutionalized through their insertion into a new ruling coalition with the dominant classes. Where growth of the middle sectors was stunted by the continued dominance of a traditional oligarchy (usually allied with the military), as was the case in Central America (apart from Costa Rica) and Paraguay, controlled inclusion was absent.

Political inclusion was possible in cases of controlled inclusion because the middle sectors had already achieved an important level of socioeconomic inclusion as a byproduct of development and social modernization. They essentially mobilized to demand commensurate political power. Because the middle sectors benefited from the existing social structure, they were much less of a threat than the popular sectors. At the same time, they would continue to benefit disproportionately from the expansion of the state and public sector of the economy under ISI. The middle sectors were particularly vulnerable to lower-class advancement and control of the state given their dependence on the public sector for employment. Yet the middle sectors had been key actors in the struggles of the region's first democratic regimes and were hesitant to give up their political rights. This explains why controlled inclusion often lasted longer than the dominant classes would have preferred. The middle sectors became the indispensable lynchpin for creating successful "coup coalitions" when controlled inclusion was violently reversed in the 1960s and 1970s throughout the region (O'Donnell 1979a). Ultimately, when confronted by their fear of increasing political power of the popular sectors, the middle sectors sided with the dominant classes to preserve the status quo and their privileged position within it.

For the dominant classes, middle-sector incorporation was the lesser of two evils, given that the political representatives of the middle sectors frequently mobilized workers to pressure reluctant regimes (Rueschemeyer, Stephens, and Stephens 1992; Collier 1999; Collier and Collier 2002). By more or less fully incorporating the middle sectors, controlled inclusion sought to undermine the emergence of strong, multiclass coalitions. This was a typical "divide-and-conquer" strategy that was controlled inclusion's hallmark. The middle sectors were more than willing to comply, given their own political vulnerability.

Yet workers were mobilizing and, as industrialization proceeded, their economic strength grew. Demobilizing them would involve high levels of state violence, which became feasible during the last breaths of the oligarchic state as the region was swept by violent waves of worker repression in the aftermath of World War I (Spalding 1977). Middle-sector incorporation limited (but by no means eliminated) this option (Collier and Collier 2002). Middle-sector support for authoritarian alternatives would require extremes of political polarization in the context of economic crisis, and the goal of controlled inclusion was to avoid this. At the same time, the growing importance of ISI as a development strategy meant that labor unrest had to be subdued, in particular to attract foreign investment (Thorp 1998).

To deal with this challenge and maintain the order needed for future economic progress, processes of controlled inclusion reinforced the segmented, highly unequal nature of civil society. Key societal actors were deprived of any autonomy through policies of state corporatism, clientelism, and populist appeals, which were made possible by the resources at the disposal of political elites as a byproduct of rapid economic growth. Economic success, in turn, helped institutionalize rigid hierarchical patterns of political participation, excluding large segments of the population from economic and political power.

Starting with the working class, the autonomy of organized labor was severely circumscribed through state intervention in union affairs (Cook 1998). As Collier and Collier (2002, 7) conclude, "in most cases the result was ultimately the creation of an organized labor movement and system of industrial relations in important measure controlled and regulated by the state."[7] In its most extreme form of state corporatism (Schmitter 1974), the state literally (re) created the labor movement relatively early in the industrialization process, preempting the emergence of strong autonomous labor movements with independent social bases. In Brazil and Mexico, for example, corporatist labor structures were virtual appendages of the state.[8]

In countries such as Argentina and Chile, where the strength of organized labor's roots in civil society created conditions approximating what Philippe Schmitter (1974) characterized as societal corporatism in Western Europe, the autonomy of labor was constrained by other factors in addition to high levels of state intervention. Hierarchical structures subordinated these movements to elite actors responsible for the mobilization, whether it was the Peronist movement in Argentina or the Left in Chile. It is not a coincidence that controlled inclusion generally coincided with the growth of mass-based political parties that began to assume central roles in most countries of the region, conditioning the strength of civil society and the expansion of the public sphere in important ways. It is also not a coincidence that none of these party systems was able to produce the kind of social democracies found in Western Europe. The control exercised by parties over their constituencies and the limits this imposed on the autonomous mobilization of collective civil society actors precluded a social democratic construction of citizenship in Latin America.

From the perspective of the social construction of citizenship, this reflected an important dispersion of power within civil society, with the result that workers in these countries generally achieved higher levels of socioeconomic and political inclusion. Yet such gains were uneven and ultimately came at the high cost of violent political repression when working-class inclusion threatened to overflow the limits imposed by controlled inclusion and elite domination of the state.

In all these cases, the institutions of controlled inclusion, whether they were state corporatist institutions or party structures, were eventually consolidated by granting important social rights of citizenship to workers. These rights included higher wages, social security protection, and contract claims, including collective bargaining (however circumscribed). It was the granting of these rights that distinguished the formal and informal economies, highlighting their segmented rather than universal qualities. Workers in the formal sector became the new elite within the popular sectors, as labor legislation that would be considered progressive in the Western European context had the pernicious effect in many Latin American countries of segmenting labor markets and leaving the majority of workers unprotected (Portes 1994; Thorp 1998).

Compared to advanced market economies, it was relatively easy to impose institutions of controlled inclusion in Latin America. The relative size and strength of the industrial proletariat in Latin American countries never approached that achieved in the first countries to industrialize (Rueschemeyer, Stephens, and Stephens 1992; CEPAL 1989; Fajnzylber 1990). Industrialization in the "late-late industrializers" (cf. Kurth 1979) was conditioned by the capital-intensive nature of modern technology, which reduced the capacity of manufacturing industries to absorb labor, and a parallel expansion of the service sector in the world economy, which would outpace industry. Manual and low-paid nonmanual workers in the service sector typically represented a third or more of the EAP in all but the least modernized countries of the region (CEPAL 1989, 49–50).

The limited capacity for labor absorption in industry is particularly significant. The size of the urban workforce tended to rise markedly faster in Latin America than in Western Europe during its industrial revolution because of the coincidence of rapid population growth rates, high levels of rural migration, and increasing female participation. This created significant downward pressure on urban wage rates, forcing a growing "marginal mass" to try to survive "by inventing employment around the fringes of the urban economy" (Portes 1985, 8; CEPAL 1989). Given that formal-sector workers were important consumers of the low-cost goods and services produced in the informal sector, a perverse relationship was created that meant rising standards of living in the informal sector would reflect higher costs for goods and services consumed by formal-sector workers. High levels of income concentration, capital flight, and investment in speculative rather than productive activities further constrained the growth of productive employment so that upward social mobility was barely sufficient to allow for a gradual decrease in the relative level of poverty in the region, which declined from 50 percent of the population in 1960 to 35 percent in 1980. Despite this relative reduction, the number of people living in poverty actually increased by 16 percent in the 1970s alone, due to the growing size of the population (CEPAL 1989, 55).

These findings raise serious doubts as to the capacity of the proletariat, as a class, to act as the principal agent for social change and for the integration of all subordinate classes in Latin America. Organized labor has further accentuated, even institutionalized, new forms of inequality. Considerable conflicts of interest exist, particularly as the large informal sector represents not only downward pressure on wages in the formal sector but also a major threat to stable employment.

This social heterogeneity, combined with high levels of inequality, offers a fertile terrain for populist mobilization, particularly in periods of intense economic dislocation. For this reason, populist movements were often pivotal in ushering controlled inclusion, as the experience of countries as diverse as Argentina, Brazil, and Mexico would suggest.[9]

As a form of interest intermediation, populism allows relatively small, privileged groups to gain greater access to state power and resources by mobilizing mass followings among the lower classes on the basis of the latter's socioeconomic and political exclusion. In the absence of collective identities capable of unifying the lower classes, populism can provide an overarching identity by claiming to address at least some of the lower classes' concerns. During the first half of the twentieth century, these concerns focused on popular-sector political incorporation for the first time. This popular-sector ascendant variant of populism was the primary form assumed in the region until relatively recently.[10] Social hierarchy and heterogeneity were reinforced, if not accentuated, by populism. The potential for autonomous lower-class collective action was further limited, as was the viability of competing alternatives to populist modes of interest intermediation.

At its core, populism represents an asymmetrical multiclass coalition. This asymmetry reflects the dominance of the relatively privileged middle-sector groups leading the coalition and the lack of autonomous organizations representing lower-class interests (Di Tella 1965), causing an unequal distribution of power (and benefits!) within the coalition. Ultimately, the interests of the lower classes are subordinated to those of the more privileged groups in Latin America's social hierarchy.

The lower classes have been offered a variety of enticements in exchange for their support. In addition to particularistic benefits through clientelism, populism historically has been associated with the important collective rights and benefits for workers in the formal sector of the economy, forming part of the foundation for controlled inclusion.

A second characteristic of populism is that it mobilizes broad popular support. This mobilizational aspect of populism distinguishes it from more explicitly authoritarian regimes and explains populism's affinity with electoral politics. Indeed, the success of populism often reflects the fact that electoral support is a form of power and political legitimation that populist leaders wielded more effectively than established elites. Populism is ambiguously related with political democracy, and aspiring populist leaders saw elections as the best means, given their power in numbers, for attaining political power. Populism represents a struggle among groups of elites (or emerging elites) demanding greater access to the political system and the removal of restrictions on their freedom to act. They attack the existing power holders and offer the limited incorporation of subaltern groups as part of their strategy for obtaining and retaining power. In paving the way for the introduction of controlled inclusion, mobilization was deliberately directed against the "enemies of the people," the oligarchy and imperialism.

Co-optation and repression were central for keeping pressures for change (if not revolution) in check, associating populism with a paternalist and elitist leadership style. Populism is organized hierarchically, from the top down. In the popular-sector ascendant version that ushered in controlled inclusion, a char-ismatic leader was able to mobilize followers through bypassing intermediate organizations completely, establishing a direct relationship with followers. This particular form of mass mobilization required that adherents to the populist movement remain passive recipients of paternalist social policies formulated by the elite in exchange for their support, encapsulating the concept of citizenship as co-optation. Ultimately, hierarchy within the populist movement and lower-class dependence served as a break on excessive demands from the mobilized masses, at the same time that any organizational autonomy from the populist elite was eliminated.[11]

Despite the importance of at least some emphasis on distributional issues, populist movements tend to downplay, or even oppose, class conflict. Instead, integration and the non-zero-sum nature of development are emphasized along with the ideal of expanding the economic pie. No real social change is being proposed, which is why populism was the hallmark of controlled inclusion in a number of countries. This is also why the economic power of traditional elites was left intact to help finance industrialization. Populist leaders sought conces-sions from upper classes rather than their overthrow.

Aside from its obvious authoritarian and elitist aspects, populism blocks so-cial change that could successfully reverse historical problems of inequality and political instability in the region. Populism (like controlled inclusion) not only depends on social heterogeneity to succeed but actively encourages and even ex-acerbates it. Although a relatively small segment of the lower classes might real-ize important gains in terms of rights and improved standards of living (at least in the short term), populism simultaneously imposes rigid patterns of participa-tion with sharp limits to how far reform is allowed to go. Civil society remained fundamentally weak under controlled inclusion, including its populist variant, as large segments of the population remained unorganized, and organized seg-ments of the lower classes enjoyed only limited autonomy from the state and the elite interests to which they were subordinated.

The Demise of Controlled Inclusion and the Backlash of Coerced Marginalization

Although controlled inclusion imposed constraints on civil society's development and the social construction of citizenship, the mobilization of civil society continued to impact politics in significant ways. Important rights were won
through social struggle, even if they often tended to be segmented rather than
universal and were generally subordinated to narrow elite interests. Given the
historical depth of problems of inequality and the stunted development of civil
society, the challenges civil society faced were immense, but not necessarily insurmountable. This process through which civil society evolved and citizenship
was socially constructed was by no means predetermined. Alternatives were
possible (Cardoso and Faletto 1970), although more democratic ones were increasingly less likely as political polarization intensified in the 1960s and 1970s.[12]
So while the potential for citizenship as agency was generally quite limited, it
was not totally absent; it played an important, albeit limited, role in the social
construction of citizenship under controlled inclusion.

In particular, organized labor was an important actor, particularly on a symbolic level that went beyond its structural strength (Garretón 1996). Workers
often played decisive roles in the establishment of the region's first democratic
regimes (Collier 1999; Rueschemeyer, Stephens, and Stephens 1992), even if the
outcome was marred by the institutions of controlled inclusion that accompanied it. Social mobilization was directly associated with the depth and breadth
of social policies, which varied widely throughout the region during this period.
Where social mobilization was highest, in Argentina, Chile, and Uruguay, the
result was a social welfare system characterized as "stratified universalism" that
"cushioned rather than reinforced the prevailing pattern of social stratification"
(Filgueira and Filgueira 2002, 137). Where there was little or no effective social
mobilization (e.g., most of Central America), the result was "exclusionary" welfare regimes and not even the semblance of controlled inclusion. In between
these extremes, welfare systems in Brazil and Mexico were characterized by
their dual nature, where large segments of the population were excluded from
corporatist institutions and access to state services was dependent on patron-
client relations (Filgueira and Filgueira 2002).

The extent and nature of popular-sector mobilization also determined the
ultimate fate of controlled inclusion. Because even limited incorporation of
lower-class groups was empowering when it raised expectations for continued
social mobility, controlled inclusion was a potentially risky strategy for dominant groups. Such risks were multiplied by the radicalization of the Left after
the Cuban Revolution. The inability of reform programs to solve basic problems
of inequality and high levels of poverty led to calls for more dramatic structural

change by the same people who had designed the original reform projects, further contributing to political polarization by delegitimating the basic tenants of controlled inclusion (Hirschman 1979). Where processes of controlled inclusion could not contain social mobilization, the result was the violent imposition of authoritarian rule in Argentina (twice, in 1966 and 1976), Brazil (1964), Chile (1973), and Uruguay (1973). With the exception of Brazil, these are the same countries that had achieved the most inclusionary welfare regimes as a result of civil society's active role in the social construction of citizenship. From the perspective of the dominant classes and the middle sectors, controlled inclusion could no longer constrain civil society actors from entering the public sphere to demand social change, even in Brazil, except through resorting to increasing repression.

These regimes, the most violent in the region's history in terms of the state's systematic abuse of basic human rights, represent processes that can be characterized as *coerced marginalization,* in contrast to the processes of controlled inclusion that they replaced. Coerced marginalization reflects the extreme political and economic exclusion of the popular sectors. It is marginalization in the most fundamental sense: subordinate classes are violently denied basic citizenship rights that they had previously enjoyed or aspired to and the public sphere is sharply constrained, if not entirely eliminated, through deliberate state policies.[13]

The fate of controlled inclusion in the cases that avoided the harsh authoritarian backlash associated with coerced marginalization is also telling from the perspective of the social construction of citizenship. Costa Rica in many ways epitomizes the potential and limits of controlled inclusion. Its democratic regime, which dates to 1948, is the oldest in the region and its stability is directly tied to a welfare state. While often characterized as a "transition by imposition," in which elite actors reached political pacts that laid the foundation for democratic rule (Karl 1990), the nascent agro-industrial bourgeoisie that dominated this process only reluctantly accepted a democratic regime based on important social rights as a consequence of earlier popular mobilization (Paige 1997).[14] Paradoxically, after a brief civil war that preceded the installation of the democratic regime, the victors implemented the reform agenda of the defeated president, who was allied with the Communist Party (Partido Comunista, PC) and enjoyed the support of working-class organizations and the Catholic Church. As Jeffrey Paige argues, the viability of reform reflected the inability of the coffee agrarian elite to displace farmers with small and medium-sized lots during the nineteenth century. In fact, as James Mahoney (2001) argues, reformers at that time actively promoted small farms, leading to a coffee export economy based on them. The result was cooperative relations among coffee growers on small and medium-sized farms, which served as a foundation for the national myths of equality and class cooperation that Costa Rica's social democracy reinforced. This is linked to the fact that the state was able to secure its monopoly over the legitimate use of force relatively soon after independence because there had been no serious threat from a divided elite since the 1830s (Mahoney 2001).

From the perspective of civil society, landowning patterns meant that power was relatively more dispersed in Costa Rica than the rest of the isthmus. Among the elite and middle-sector groups, this necessitated compromises that were foreclosed in countries where the hegemony of agrarian coffee elites was more firmly established. A working-class / leftist coalition could then emerge and, although defeated militarily, effectively set the political agenda for a reformist government bent on stopping the spread of communism in the 1950s. As Paige (1997, 249) concludes, "It was pressure from below, not simply enlightenment from above, that established the Costa Rican welfare state." Costa Rica thus avoided the more violent, protracted civil wars that wracked the region in the 1980s. This country (along with Uruguay) comes closest to approximating West European social democracy in Latin America (Sheahan 2002) and has one of the lowest levels of income inequality, even though, as Paige demonstrates, its underlying social structure of socioeconomic exclusion for large segments of the population was remarkably similar to the rest of Central America.

In Mexico (see chapter 6), Colombia, and Venezuela, relatively weaker civil societies allowed processes of controlled inclusion to continue much longer, but with results far less satisfactory than in Costa Rica. Even if they were able to avoid the violence associated with coerced marginalization, they were no more able than the other countries in the region to enact the kinds of long-term structural reforms needed to overcome extremes of inequality and weak civil societies. Colombia and Venezuela boast the region's two longest-lasting democracies after Costa Rica's, founded in the late 1950s. Yet the quality of their democratic regimes was severely limited by elite pacts that circumscribed democratic participation and political competition well into the 1970s (Karl 1990; O'Donnell and Schmitter 1986). Since then, Colombia has been wracked by civil war and drug-related violence, threatening to tear the social fabric apart rather than serve as a foundation for inclusionary democracy. Venezuela, on the other hand, is experiencing a new populist threat to democracy led by President Hugo Chávez, a man who first entered the political stage by leading an unsuccessful military coup in 1992. Since then, Chávez has successfully campaigned against the corruption of the country's political parties and trade unions, replacing the country's flawed democratic institutions with institutions intended to concentrate political power in the presidency at the expense of a strong autonomous civil society.[15] In both countries, historical problems of inequality and weak civil societies went largely unresolved and were often exacerbated as a result of controlled inclusion, despite prolonged democratic stability.

Controlled Inclusion and the Social Construction of Citizenship: Latin America's Unique Path

Although controlled inclusion seriously constrained the development of strong civil societies in Latin America, it could not prevent their continued evolution. Conditioned by the nature of economic development under state-led ISI policies, exacerbating historical problems of extreme social inequality and heterogeneity, with powerful dominant classes bent on preserving their privileged position, the scope of civil society was quite limited. Yet its interaction with the state through the public sphere is central to understanding the political dynamics of the period. For the first time, citizenship became a central axis for political struggles, juxtaposing ideals of citizenship as co-optation and citizenship as agency.

Ironically, given that these two ideals of citizenship are otherwise diametrically opposed, both prioritized social rights over political rights. For proponents of controlled inclusion, social rights—limited and anything but universal—were a mechanism for co-opting key segments of the popular sectors, dividing them from the majority to prevent the emergence of political coalitions with the strength to institute social change. There was no inevitable trade-off between political rights and social rights under controlled inclusion, as the examples of Chile and Uruguay demonstrate. But even in these cases, political democracy was viewed instrumentally and tolerated only insofar as it allowed key actors to achieve other ends. When political democracy no longer was seen as allowing this to happen or, even worse, was seen as an obstacle to achieving those ends, it was abandoned. For the extreme Left, democratic institutions at best offered potential stepping-stones for achieving revolution. But even for more moderate elements of the Left and much of the population in general, decades of abuse by dictators and traditional elites had robbed existing democratic institutions of any intrinsic legitimacy (Garretón 2003).

This stands in sharp contrast to the ideal citizenship path sketched by T. H. Marshall. In Latin America, not only were rights explicitly not universal, but the relationship between types of rights was very different: social rights were prioritized, with a secondary, instrumental, emphasis on political rights. There was little emphasis on civil rights, which (turning Marshall's teleology on its head) could hardly be universal given the very nature of exclusion for those outside the institutions of controlled inclusion and the hierarchical, often arbitrary, relations between different groups and the state within the institutions of controlled inclusion. Unlike nineteenth-century British capitalism, which may have required civil rights to function, Latin America's twentieth-century associated dependent development welcomed both the protection and rents that large public sectors provided (Cardoso and Faletto 1970; F. Cardoso 1973). This

3

DICTATORSHIP OR DEMOCRACY:
THE RISE OF NEOPLURALISM AND
CITIZENSHIP AS CONSUMPTION

Although coerced marginalization signaled the end of controlled inclusion throughout much of the region, its ultimate death knell came with the economic crisis of the 1980s and the search for an alternative to ISI—the infamous "lost decade." Per capita GDP for the region as a whole was 8.1 percent lower in 1989 than it had been in 1980 (Iglesias 1990, 347), although one estimate suggested that per capita income may have declined by as much as 15 percent through 1990 (Altimir 1998, 10). The number of households living below the poverty line increased from 35 percent in 1980 to 39 percent in 1990 (CEPAL 1996, 35). In absolute terms, this meant that there were 71 million more people living in poverty at the end of the 1980s compared to 1970, for a total of 183 million people, of whom 88 million lived in absolute poverty—28 million more than in 1970 (CEPAL 1991, 78). Not surprisingly, inequality became significantly worse throughout the region (Korzeniewsicz and Smith 2000; Psacharopoulos et al. 1997).

Like the economic crisis of the 1930s, the economic dislocations of the 1980s led to a second "great transformation" (Smith and Korzeniewsicz 1997). While individual countries varied considerably in terms of the timing and extent of their reforms, there has been an increasing convergence of economic policy making around a set of market-oriented economic reforms. Designed to minimize the role of the state in the market and dramatically change its relationship to society, these reforms include the privatization of public firms and, in a growing number of countries, public welfare provision, as well as deregulation, free trade, state decentralization, and new social welfare policies specifically for the poor. "By 1995, the main elements of the reform package had been adopted across almost all the countries of the region" (Stallings and Peres 2000, 47). Often referred to as neoliberalism, it has led to the dismantling of many institutional pillars of ISI and controlled inclusion. These policies have radically transformed both the state and the region's insertion in the international economy.

At the same time, the region has experienced an unprecedented resurgence of democracy. Although the relationship between transitions to democracy and the adoption of market-oriented economic reforms is indirect at best (Oxhorn

One reason for this success was that the shared demand for democracy allowed previously antagonistic actors to set aside their differences, which would be addressed once the overriding objective of ending authoritarian rule had been achieved. The litmus test for belonging to the opposition was unqualified support for democratic rule, placing the onus on the Left and, when relevant, the Right to demonstrate that they had abandoned their past ideological animosity toward electoral politics. Indeed, minimizing differences among opposition groups was often a principal challenge as unity in purpose was often perceived as an essential prerequisite for forcing authoritarian elements among the elite and within civil society to relinquish political control.[2] For the first time, democracy came to be valued as an end in itself, if not a panacea for resolving future political conflicts. The importance of this achievement cannot be underestimated. But it also inevitably meant that conflicts over basic citizenship rights were central yet unresolved issues in the transition process.

This so-called resurrection of civil society proved short-lived as elite actors and political parties ultimately determined the final course of the transitions (O'Donnell and Schmitter 1986; Oxhorn 1995b). The clearest expression of this can be found in the political pacts that in many cases not only determined the rules of the game for the future democratic regime and the actors who could participate but set limits on the substantive issues that elected governments could address (Karl 1986, 1990). Among those limits were concessions to outgoing authoritarian regimes regarding future prosecutions for human rights abuses and the preservation of various "authoritarian enclaves" within the institutions of the new democracy (Garretón 1989). These enclaves often included new institutionalized channels of political influence for nonelected officials, particularly the military and intelligence community, and well-entrenched civilian bureaucracies that were held over from the authoritarian regime.

The process by which elite actors and political parties came to dominate politics during the transition necessarily entailed a demobilization of mass actors and their subordination to the interests of ensuring a successful transition. This demobilization appeared necessary to avoid an authoritarian backlash by depriving extremists within the authoritarian regime of any pretense for halting the transition process (O'Donnell and Schmitter 1986). Even though there was widespread agreement within civil society on the overriding importance of achieving this goal, demobilization was not without tensions.

Fundamentally, demobilization cut short the process of building civil society that had started as a prelude to the transition. This problem was exacerbated by the continued dominance of elite actors, particularly political party elites, after the transition and a widespread perception of a growing distance between party leaders and the population at large. The available space for popular participation often seemed circumscribed to the electoral arena by the kind of democratic institutions that were erected during the transition process. Even the women's destabilizing effects of their activities or had them as their explicit goal. Now the fear (often amplified by political elites) was that any autonomous mobilization would be counterproductive.[4]

This general experience contrasts sharply with the working-class mobilization in Britain referred to by T. H. Marshall (1950). There, mobilization was deliberately intended to change an existing democratic regime (according to the standards of the day) rather than overthrow a violent authoritarian one. The alternative was more, rather than less, democracy, not authoritarian rule. Success did not entail a complete rethinking of previous organizational experiences. The new spaces created by winning new rights could more readily be filled by the newly empowered actors who had opened them up in the first place. Because regime change was the dominant, if not only, demand of the actors involved in recent transitions in Latin America, there was a tendency to view political rights almost as a panacea for resolving a variety of social ills rather than as an indispensable starting point. Whereas the Latin American transitions cut short a process of building civil society, in Britain the process was continuous and cumulative—hence the apparent teleology of Marshall's analysis. Political rights were a clear victory of civil society in both Marshall's England and Latin America, but only in England did this victory lead to an accumulation of power resources on the part of subaltern groups, creating a cumulative process that would culminate in the creation of welfare states guaranteeing a wide range of universal social rights.

The contrast is even sharper when looking specifically at organized labor in Latin America. The British labor movement was significantly strengthened through its struggles to win civil rights and went on to help create the British Labour Party and secure its political integration. In most Latin American countries, organized labor played an important role in the mobilizations that helped bring about transitions to democracy (Drake 1996; Collier 1999), yet to this day its situation remains considerably weakened in virtually every country in the region. Rather than experience growing political influence and power, labor movements throughout the region were hard-hit by the rolling back of the social rights they had been granted in the earlier period of controlled inclusion.

The goal of this discussion is not to draw attention to the limits of Latin America's democratic transitions. Rather, it is to discuss how these transitions inevitably limited civil society's continued development. While with hindsight it is possible to imagine how the outcome might have been different, the reality is that the stakes were quite high as the transitions unfolded. Latin America's problematic history of democratic stability and civil society increased the risks of failed transitions to democracy, at the same time that it underscored the importance of what had been achieved: more or less universal political rights exercised through participation in relatively free and fair elections. The challenge of unelected (and unaccountable) power holders, particularly the military and de facto powers, including dominant economic interests, exercise control over key state decisions (McSherry 1998; Garretón 2003).

The logic of neopluralism, undergirded by market-based economic reforms, permeates entire political systems in a variety of ways. In particular, market principles and market-based incentives come to play a defining role in collective action. Individuals' personal economic resources largely determine the extent and nature of their political and social inclusion. Economic resources also directly determine the quality of education, health care, and even legal protection. Just as the state is assigned a minimal role in ensuring the smooth functioning of the market in the economic realm, it largely abdicates its role in providing incentives (both positive and negative) for collective action. The public and private goods formally available at the state level to those mobilized in earlier periods, as well as the coercive incentives for the hierarchical organization of economic interests under state corporatism (Schmitter 1974), no longer exist or have been significantly reduced. Group identities and collective interests lose any intrinsic value, yet these are a primary potential source of power for subaltern groups. Instead, organizational activity within civil society is the outcome of individual, self-interested decisions to join. This, in turn, is both a cause and consequence of a marked "individualization of rights and responsibilities" (Roberts and Wood 2005a, 14).

Countries vary according to the degree to which they conform to the ideal-typical model of neopluralism, although there is a remarkable level of convergence, particularly in comparison with the preceding period of controlled inclusion. This convergence reflects the spread of liberal economic reforms and the unprecedented strength of political rights, juxtaposed with Latin America's shared structural problems of highly unequal, segmented social structures. The changing international geopolitical and economic environment, particularly the end of the cold war and the move toward greater levels of economic integration at the global level, reinforce this convergence. In contrast to state-centered processes of controlled inclusion, the requisites for neopluralism are also lower. Aside from the existence of democratic political rights, neopluralism as a mode of political incorporation and social integration is not a direct response to actual or potential societal pressures the way controlled inclusion was. The existence of neopluralism therefore is not directly related to a country's level of economic development or the strength of its civil society, which was not the case with controlled inclusion. Similarly, neopluralism's emphasis on a minimal state means that states are increasingly adopting similar institutional structures as the often bloated, highly developed state institutions associated with ISI and controlled inclusion are progressively reformed, if not dismantled. Conversely, because of the role of social struggle for transitions to democracy and a new

Neopluralism and the Limits of Democratic Citizenship

Neopluralism erodes the quality of democratic governance through its negative impact on civil society and the ability of citizens to access the public sphere as part of the social construction of citizenship. More specifically, neopluralism imposes serious limits on the exercise of citizenship rights through its pernicious consequences in four areas of central importance to most Latin Americans: (1) growing economic inequality and insecurity, (2) segmented educational systems and diminished long-term social mobility, (3) heightened citizen insecurity and what I describe as the marketization of the rule of law, and (4) a general crisis of representation and the weakening of the public sphere.

Growing Economic Inequality and Insecurity

Economic insecurity is one of the region's most pressing challenges, the significance of which is only exacerbated by neopluralism's reliance on market mechanisms for resolving social problems. Since 1996 employment-related problems have been at the top of citizen concerns, according to public opinion surveys conducted by Latinobarómetro (2009b, 73). For example, in 1996, a total of 85 percent of Latin Americans reported that they were either unemployed or concerned about losing their jobs, and that percentage increased in eleven of the seventeen countries surveyed in 2001 (IDB 2004, 57). Such economic insecurity threatens democracy by directly decreasing the ability of workers to engage in it, individually and collectively, severely circumscribing the social construction of citizenship. Indirectly, it threatens to undermine democracy, as people's often desperate search for survival mechanisms leads them to support nondemocratic alternatives. The remarkably high levels of support enjoyed by an increasingly authoritarian Fujimori in Peru during the first half of the 1990s (with approval ratings approaching 90 percent) is the most dramatic example of this danger (Conaghan 2005).

This increased insecurity is a direct result of neopluralism's reliance on the market for determining the best allocation of resources and opportunities for members of society. Part of the problem emerges from lackluster growth rates in the 1990s. While the average annual growth rate for 1990–98 of 3.9 percent was a vast improvement compared to the 1980s average of 0.2 percent, it was significantly lower than the annual average growth rate of 5.2 percent achieved over the period 1950–80, and a far cry from the 6 percent per year average needed to tackle growing social problems (Stallings and Peres 2000, 77, 89–91). Moreover, it was insufficient to raise per capita income in the region, which remained stagnant through the early part of this century (PNUD 2004, 39).

The significance of slow growth rates for poverty alleviation is particularly alarming, since economic growth, rather than social policies, was the principal structures of inequality in labor markets and its relation to high levels of poverty (CEPAL 2009a, 26).

Compounding these labor market problems, labor codes throughout the region have been modified to generally make it easier for firms to hire temporary workers (who generally do not enjoy any social security protection) and fire current employees (IDB 2004; Tokman 2002; CEPAL 2003). This new labor market flexibility allows for the maintenance of international competitiveness on the basis of low wages by eliminating key social rights associated with controlled inclusion. Moreover, governments increasingly "informalize themselves vis-à-vis their own laws in their quest for even more foreign investment" by creating special production zones that exempt foreign firms from labor legislation and taxation policies applicable in the rest of the nation (Portes 1994, 168). A full 40 percent of new jobs in the formal sector in the 1990s had no social security safeguards (PNUD 2004, 122). Where existing rights are not taken away outright, their systematic violation is often ignored by the state. Clear examples of this are the high percentages of workers in some countries who do not receive a full minimum wage and the more than half of all workers in Latin America who did not receive legally mandated social welfare safeguards (IDB 2004). These lapses in enforcement, combined with greater resort to temporary contracts, threaten to undermine the impact of any positive advances, such as increased indemnities for laid-off workers, in labor legislation enacted in the 1990s (CEPAL 2003). They also threaten to create a vicious cycle of a low-paid, unskilled labor force as the precariousness of employment diminishes employers' incentives to invest in worker training and workers lose their motivation to improve their own productivity (Tokman 2002; Levy 2008).

One dimension of the magnitude of these problems is the International Labour Organization's measure of Latin America's primary deficit of decent jobs. This measure captures the combined levels of current unemployment in comparison to the historical average level of unemployment (1950–80), underemployment in the informal sector and those workers in both the formal and informal sectors who enjoy no social security coverage. In 1990 the primary job deficit was 49.5 percent of the urban workforce. By 2002 it reached 50.5 percent of the urban workforce—93 million more workers than in 1990 (PNUD 2004, 122).

Another dimension of these problems is reflected in persistently high levels of income inequality. Even though eleven of the eighteen countries included in its study experienced a decline in poverty levels and fifteen experienced increased per capita incomes between 1991 and 2002, the level of inequality in each country was still above the world average in 2002 (PNUD 2004, 26). While differences in data sets and periods studied have resulted in some disagreement over which countries might have experienced modest improvements in income decline in the real minimum wage, which on average was 25–26 percent less in 1999 compared to 1980 (Tokman 2002, 161; Gurrieri and Sáinz 2003, 161–62). This is the result of the concentration of employment creation during the 1990s in the low-productivity informal sector, which implies that the poor's income will continue to grow more slowly than the average when there is growth (Tokman 2002). More troubling, the poor's pressing need for an income means that they tend to accept lower-paying jobs as they are continually forced to find new ones given the high volatility of informal-sector employment (IDB 2004, 70), reinforcing the tendency toward a vicious cycle of rising poverty and inequality. The ultimate consequence of this is that the number of working poor is skyrocketing, with estimates of those whose incomes are insufficient to surpass the poverty level ranging from 50 percent of all workers to as high as 75 percent (IDB 2004; Kliksberg 2000). As Alejandro Portes and Kelly Hoffman (2003, 59) note, "75 percent of the employed population . . . does not generate enough income from their jobs to surpass the poverty level. This implies that with few national exceptions, to be a worker in Latin America means to be poor."

Unfortunately, changes in state social welfare policies that are closely linked to neopluralism have limited the state's ability to compensate for, much less reverse, these trends toward greater inequality and economic insecurity. Social spending has generally increased since the 1990s in Latin America, and a greater commitment to addressing growing social problems throughout the region has meant that it did not decline in per capita terms as growth slowed in the late 1990s (Stallings and Peres 2000, 23–25). While this is unquestionably good, social expenditures remain procyclical—increasing during periods of economic growth and remaining stagnant (if not decreasing) during periods of economic downturn (CEPAL 2009a). Focusing on government spending directed specifically to the poor based on need—the so-called targeted assistance—each 1 percent decline in GDP led to a decline of 2 percent or more in targeted spending per poor person. While the share of the budget devoted to targeted assistance remained the same, overall spending declined along with the GDP at the same time that more people were eligible for such assistance (De Ferranti et al. 2004).

Moreover, overall levels of expenditure may hide the true distributional impact of social policies. Rossana Mostajo's (2000) study found that social expenditures increased the total income share of the poorest 20 percent of the population from 3.5 percent to 6 percent at the apparent expense of the richest 20 percent of the population, whose income share decreased from 53.9 percent to 50.4 percent when government expenditures are factored in. Yet the actual redistributive impact is much less given that people with sufficient resources "opt out of public services and purchase their own because of poor quality, especially in education and health—what appears to be progressive in quantitative terms actually is regressive" (34–35). Gross figures also hide considerable leakage through corruption and the misdirection of funds for the administratively cumbersome process, easily abused when state institutions are characterized by high levels of corruption and clientelism.

One of the lasting impacts of market-oriented state reforms has been a significant reduction in the state's capacity to positively influence income distribution. This is best exemplified by conditional cash transfer programs that place important obligations on recipients, including ensuring children attend school and meet other requirements relating to nutrition and health care. Implementation of these programs began in the mid-1990s, and by 2008 they had been adopted by seventeen countries with a total coverage of 101 million people—17 percent of the region's population (CEPAL 2009a, 31). Extreme income inequality means that the income level required for the poor to rise above official poverty levels is so low relative to the incomes of other groups that even large declines in poverty will not lead to any appreciable narrowing of income gaps. For example, Brazil's Bolsa Família (Family Grant) program has become a model for development assistance, helping 11 million families (almost a quarter of Brazil's population) and is responsible for reducing poverty by 12–19 percent, but it represents only 0.5 percent of household income in Brazil (Power 2010; Veras Soares, Perez Ribas, and Guerreiro Osório 2010). In general, conditional cash transfer programs represent only 2.3 percent of regional public social expenditures and a paltry 0.25 percent of regional GDP. Even if funded completely by progressive income taxes (which they are not), the redistributive impact of these programs is essentially nil. At the same time, approximately 90 million people considered to live below the poverty line were not covered by these programs in 2009, exacerbating tensions between recipients and nonrecipients. Moreover, unless conditional cash transfer policies are accompanied by corresponding investments in the public services recipients are required to use (e.g., education and health care), there will be growing pressures on the existing quality of those services (CEPAL 2009a, 31–34).

Targeted assistance, including conditional cash transfer programs, also exacerbates the marginalization of the poor. Recipients become beneficiaries of state assistance rather than active participants in the design and implementation of social policies (Garretón 2003), which then lose their capacity for promoting greater social integration (Tokman 2002). As Manuel Antonio Garretón (2003, 66) concludes, the combination of the privatization of social services and targeted assistance "has generated stable, lasting conditions for the dualization of society: on one side, are those able to gain access to market mechanisms; on the other, those who necessarily will be forced to be 'assisted' forever by the state."

Under these circumstances, it is not surprising that poverty rates remained persistently high throughout the 1990s, even though the percentage of people living in poverty declined significantly from 48.3 percent in 1990. Poverty rates actually increased by half a percentage point, from 43.5 percent in 1997 to 44.0 percent in 2002. Population growth has also meant that the number of people levels of national economic productivity in an era marked by growing levels of free trade and the need to base international competitiveness on productive, qualified labor rather than low wages. Yet despite "a general context of sharply increasing international and domestic attention to the need to improve educational achievement throughout the region" (Nelson 2004, 252), trends in the region's educational system seem to epitomize how market influences permeate entire societies under neopluralism, with their pernicious long-term impact on the effective exercise of citizenship rights.

The inability of the region's educational systems to overcome structural inequality is not new. During the period of controlled inclusion, the contributions of increasing access to education were at best relatively limited, even though such expansion contributed to social mobility and rising standards of living for a significant segment of the population. Had educational expansion in Latin America followed the path of other countries at similar levels of economic development, inequality in the region would have peaked in the mid-1970s and declined thereafter. Southeast Asia, for example, reduced the number of people in the labor force without education by one-fifth and stabilized functional illiteracy between 1965 and 1995. In Latin America the number of people entering the labor market without education increased by one-sixth, while functional illiteracy doubled (Londoño 1996, 14–16).

These basic problems are only exacerbated by neopluralism. While most countries had achieved almost 100 percent enrollment rates at the primary level by the mid-1990s (Stallings and Peres 2000, 115–16), this is no longer sufficient to achieve improvements in the level of socioeconomic well-being similar to what expanding literacy during the 1960s and 1970s accomplished. Growth is increasingly knowledge intensive, which places a premium on access to secondary education and, in particular, quality education at all levels (Tokman 2002). Wage differentials between skilled and unskilled workers have generally increased in the 1990s and are the highest in the world (Baumann 2002; Korzeniewsicz and Smith 2000). Already in 1982 such wage differentials were twice as high in Latin America compared to advanced market economies and 50 percent higher than in Asia; since then they have fallen everywhere except Latin America (Morley 2003, 64–65). One reason for this is the alarmingly low rate of secondary education (Filgueira and Filgueira 2002). Only sub-Saharan Africa has a lower proportion of workers with at least some secondary education (IDB 1998, 45).

This problem is compounded by very low quality of public education throughout the region (IDB 2004, 1998; PNUD 1998). One study of forty countries, which included six from Latin America, found that almost half of the Latin American students were functionally illiterate (PNUD 1998, 121). This educational deficit disproportionately affects the poor: "all evidence for Latin America indicates that, in fact, the poor receive an inferior education" (IDB 1998, 53).

The mass media also have a deleterious impact on the public sphere. Crime and violence sell, causing the media to often exaggerate the extent of crime. People's natural fears are raised disproportionately, at the same time that they are encouraged (if only implicitly) to see violence as an appropriate way to resolve conflicts (Carrión 2003; Arriagada and Godoy 1999; Morrison, Buvinic, and Shifter 2003; Tulchin and Fagan 2003). The mass media also often contribute to the sense of frustration and deprivation felt by the popular sectors, who continuously are exposed to lifestyles beyond their reach (Morrison, Buvinic, and Shifter 2003). The sense of marginalization on the part of the popular sectors is further reinforced by the negative images of the poor generally found in the mass media. Typically portrayed either as the victims of crime in need of charity or as criminals to be feared, the lack of positive images makes it difficult for the poor to identify with the public sphere, much less actively participate in it.

Neopluralism's reliance on market mechanisms to address social problems affects how crime and violence are addressed in Latin America, reflecting the drastically unequal resources available to different segments of Latin American societies. Transitions to democracy throughout the region brought about a substantial reduction in the systematic violation of human rights by the state for political reasons. Yet the overall level of state violence in Latin America has generally not declined. Instead, it has undergone a qualitative change, as it is no longer directed against the political opposition, but against the poor (Méndez 1999b, 19–20; PNUD 1998; Carrión 2003). To deal with rising crime rates, the poor are often targeted by police efforts to control crime in what amounts to criminalizing poverty. As Paulo Sérgio Pinheiro (1999, 2) explains, "the poor continue to be the preferred victims of violence, criminality, and human rights violations." Moreover, the military is increasingly becoming involved in basic law enforcement, particularly in the growing area of drug-related crimes (McSherry 1998; Kincaid and Gamarra 1996). This not only increases the level of violence involved in crime control but also makes police reform more difficult because militaries are reluctant to cede power to civilian authorities once they become involved (Frühling 2003).

In some cases, the criminalization of poverty is even formalized into law. For example, after more than a decade of civil war ended in El Salvador, the growing desperation of the citizenry led its democratic government to pass the Emergency Law Against Crime and the Law for Social Defense on March 19, 1996. The laws were backed by all parties with the exception of the Farabundo Martí para la Liberación Nacional (Farabundo Martí National Liberation Front, FMLN). These laws, portions of which were eventually declared unconstitutional, amounted to nothing less than "the imposition of a state of siege without the army which would give rise to an authentic witch hunt" ("Ley de emergencia," 8). People would be considered potential criminals subject to imprisonment and the loss of rights because of their appearance. The unemployed, young own political intervention in the courts (Méndez 1999a). As a result, people are reluctant to cooperate with law enforcement agencies, even to the extent of reporting crimes. In Chile, for example, only 40 percent of all burglaries and thefts were reported in 1997, despite the fact that this is the only country in the region where most citizens approve of police performance. In Peru, where trust in the judicial system is much lower, only 25 percent of crimes are reported to the authorities (Arriagada and Godoy 1999, 11).

This lack of citizen cooperation leaves few alternatives because effective law enforcement and crime prevention are dependent on community involvement. Yet repressive police measures do little to improve the image of law enforcement agencies. They have invariably failed to control crime, at the same time that they have added to its violent consequences (Arriagada and Godoy 1999). There is a real danger that the situation will only grow worse as local communities withdraw further from the legal community (Neild 1999).

The criminalization of poverty and resort to repressive police methods also reflect the widespread marketization of the rule of law. Basic civil rights are in effect allocated according to people's purchasing power. Although equal protection under the law exists on paper, the poor cannot access it because of their limited economic resources. The state is incapable (because of corruption and its own lack of resources) of filling the void. For example, in eight of the fourteen countries for which there is information, there was fewer than one public defender per a hundred thousand citizens (PNUD 2004, 109). The seriousness of this is only exacerbated by the antiquated inquisitorial systems that are still prevalent in the region and strongly biased against the poor (Duce and Pérez Perdomo 2003). Perhaps the most graphic illustration of this bias against the poor is the fact that 54.8 percent of people in prison in Latin America had not been convicted or charged in accordance with due process (PNUD 2004, 109).[8]

Legal systems further reinforce structural problems of inequality and social exclusion. Middle-sector and upper-class white collar crimes and corruption are largely ignored, despite their huge monetary and institutional costs (Tulchin and Fagan 2003; Arriagada and Godoy 1999). As Pinheiro (1999, 4–5) points out, "police and other institutions of the criminal justice system tend to act as 'border guards,' protecting the elites from the poor. . . . Middle-class and elite crimes," including corruption, fraud, tax evasion, and the exploitation of child or slave labor, however, are ignored by judicial systems that focus on the crimes committed by the poor (see also Tulchin and Fagan 2003; Arriagada and Godoy 1999). While respondents did note substantial progress had been made in reducing corruption in recent years, 61 percent of respondents in the 2009 Latinobarómetro survey felt that either no progress had been made or corruption had worsened in the past two years (40).

Privileged segments of society are also able to use their economic and political resources to ensure that limited state resources are concentrated in those constant from 1996 through 2000, averaging 60–63 percent. In 1996 it was less than 50 percent only in Honduras. Due to the regional economic crisis that began in the late 1990s, support for democracy reached its lowest level in 2001 at 48 percent. By 2003 support for democracy had again risen to a regional average of 53 percent (down from 56 percent in 2002), although support declined since 1996 in every country except Honduras, where it had gone up 13 percent; Venezuela, where it increased by 5 percent to 67 percent; and Mexico, where it remained unchanged at 53 percent, despite the transition to democracy in 2000.

Since 2003 support for democracy continued to increase, even though it remained lower than the peak in support for democracy of 67 percent reached in 1997. In 2006 the a year in which economic growth in the region was the highest that it had been in forty years, support reached 58 percent and was actually 59 percent in 2009—the first full year of the region's latest economic recession (Latinobarómetro 2009b, 16–17).

In a region that has historically been characterized more for its lack of consensus on political models and frequent authoritarian lapses, this consistent and relatively high (at least by Latin American standards) support for democracy is very significant. As Marta Lagos (1997, 136), the director of the Latinobarómetro, concluded, "democracy . . . is the only thing that citizens agree upon so massively."[12]

Leaving aside the fact that this unprecedented level of consensus still leaves sizable minorities that explicitly accept the legitimacy of nondemocratic governments, such findings mask important contradictions within survey results that reflect neopluralism's mix of democratic and authoritarian characteristics. For example, when asked if democracy was preferable to economic development, only 44 percent of respondents in the 2009 Latinobarómetro agreed (29).[13] Similarly, 43 percent of respondents in 2009 felt democracy could exist without a Congress, and 40 percent felt democracy was possible without political parities—percentages that have varied only minimally since the late 1990s (27). While only 24 percent of respondents indicated they supported the 2009 Honduras military coup, 35 percent said that under certain circumstances they would support a military coup in their own country (7, 12). The authors of the 2009 Latinobarómetro survey conclude that a composite index of support for democracy based on the various dimensions of democracy—rejection of authoritarian governments, support of democracy over other forms of political regime, the necessity of political parties and legislatures—would show that only 40–45 percent of respondents had democratic attitudes on more than two of the dimensions, while "in Latin America, 'perfect democrats' who respond 'correctly' to all the questions relating to democracy would not surpass 8 percent of citizens" (17).

Educational levels are also important in accounting for democratic attitudes. People with the lowest level of education generally are less supportive of usefulness of public opinion polls for determining policy, polling epitomizes the limits of the public sphere in Latin America: the decision to participate is deliberately random and initially made by others, the participant has no choice but to remain anonymous, there can be no debate among participants, and the decision regarding the focus of the poll is not made by the participant.[17]

This distance between political leaders and the average person reflects various factors. In some countries, these include the still lingering impact of repression prior to the return of democratic rule, which had the effect of severing institutional links between the political elite and any mass base (Oxhorn 1995b). It also often reflects the weakness of political parties, which are little more than vehicles for the personal advancement of the individuals or the small group of people who founded them (Mainwaring and Skully 1995). Political parties increasingly have come to represent a political class rather than society or "a view of the common good" (Garretón 2003, 75). The popular sectors are the most disadvantaged by this, given the lack of alternatives for articulating their interests (Huber, Rueschemeyer, and Stephens 1997).

This distance is reinforced by the nature of the state, which leaves little space for effective citizen participation apart from elections (Huber, Rueschemeyer, and Stephens 1997). Citizens must deal with state organizations that are overly bureaucratic, difficult to understand, and, ultimately, biased in authoritarian ways that reflect the extreme inequalities in Latin American societies (PNUD 2004). Fully 96.7 percent of the respondents in the 2002 Latinobarómetro survey who had contact with state agencies reported that the experience was in some way negative; 27.6 percent felt they had been humiliated (83). In the 2003 survey, corruption was singled out as the second-most pressing problem, after those stemming from economic inequality, and the principal cause for lack of trust in state institutions. Yet only 28 percent of respondents felt progress had been made in combating it.[18] As the United Nations Development Program concluded in its report on the state of democracy in Latin America (189), this reflects a "perverse privatization of the state" whose institutions have been captured by special interests. Not surprisingly, for most Latin Americans "democracy is still seen as a privilege of the few" (Latinobarómetro 2003, 3), as nonelected de facto powers appear to exercise increasing influence over government policies and the issues that are of the most urgency to the vast majority of Latin American citizens (Garretón 2003).

Despite this privatization and the dismantling of many state institutions with the rise of neopluralism, the state continues to play a significant role vis-à-vis the poor. Targeted-assistance programs, particularly the now massive conditional cash transfer programs, mean that the state is more intrusive in its relationship with the poor than ever before.[19] Strict eligibility and compliance criteria are central to these programs' objectives, and they are measured by states that now have the capacity to reach out to the poor to a degree that is without precedent.

compared to workers' rights, which have generally declined (PNUD 2004). As a result, successful businesses have been able to adapt to unregulated markets (Huber 2002a), and their incomes have increased faster than those of other social classes (Portes and Hoffman 2003). A potentially self-perpetuating imbalance in the power exercised by employers and labor in their interactions is the inevitable consequence (Tokman 2002; Huber, Rueschemeyer, and Stephens 1997; Weeks 1999).

In sharp contrast to their situation in controlled inclusion, the middle sectors have been disadvantaged by the rise of neopluralism. The shrinking of the public sector throughout the region has meant they have lost jobs and seen their wages decline. At the same time they are forced to pay higher prices for public services due to their privatization or the elimination of subsidies, as a result of targeting state resources toward those most in need (Tokman 2002). Many have been forced to create their own sources of employment to cope, and microenterprises accounted for 30 percent of all jobs created from 1990 to 1998. Another 29 percent of new jobs were formed through self-employment (Portes and Hoffman 2003, 45). The middle sectors, often their most impoverished elements, have thus become principal employers of the informal proletariat. Along with the business elites, they also are key players in a new "veto coalition" that rejects policies for the poor because "after their own sufferings through economic crisis and adjustments, [they] feel that is they who deserve preferential treatment" (O'Donnell 1998, 51). The region's relatively privileged classes are even more resistant to paying increased taxes in a region notorious for having the lowest income taxes in the world (Karl 2003)

The problems created by increasingly powerful business interests and the insecure middle sectors are accentuated by the lack of any effective counterweight representing the popular sectors. One of the principal representatives of the lower classes historically has been organized labor. Yet labor movements throughout the region have been weakened under neopluralism. Union membership declined in almost every country during the 1990s, with an average union density of the nonagricultural labor force of just 14 percent (IDB 2004, 41). Workers in the informal sector and most free trade zones are only rarely organized (Barrera 1999; Organización Internacional 1996). Declining union membership and organizational fragmentation have combined to reduce the collective bargaining power of organized labor, independently of legal changes designed to have a similar effect (Huber 2002a; Organización Internacional 1993). Economic liberalization has seriously diminished the effectiveness of strikes in those sectors of the economy facing international competition (Murillo 2003), and even those relatively few unions with resources and bargaining power have generally been forced to accept the fact that "employers throughout the region have preferred the unilateral imposition of workplace changes" to labor negotiations (Cook 1998, 316). The diminished economic clout of organized labor and the growth and other economically disadvantaged groups to participate in the public sphere, another important consequence has been the erosion of their will to participate. As Carlos Vilas and Steve Ellner (1999, 20) note, the growing phenomenon of the working poor is radically altering what they call "the culture of work": "The idea of employment as the means which permits a living to be earned . . . is now diluted by the evidence that having a job does not necessarily permit one to live better. The vision of the union as the instrument of the defense of rights and access to benefits is likewise losing ground. The idea of belonging to a group of fellow workers—a class—is brought into question by fragmentation. The sentiment of solidarity with fellow workers is undermined by the competition for all against all for a decent job."

To the extent that people participate, it is to pursue short-term interests at the expense of long-term projects for society (Oscar Muñoz and Francisco Rojas, quoted in CEPAL 1999). As Raúl Urzúa explains, expecting people to participate in civil society is "like building a social fabric in a moment when there is an ideological effort to convince people that they will triumph due to their own efforts. We are struggling against the current" (29). "Individual action is overtaking collective action," as notions of solidarity from earlier periods are lost (Tokman 2002, 190). There is an inherent tension between the individualism associated with neopluralism and the need for societies to make collective decisions regarding their future, with the result that "politics becomes almost exclusively an activity with few ties to the identities, the interests and the aspirations of society" (PNUD 2004, 184).

Targeted social welfare reforms in many ways epitomize this tension between individual initiative and collective action. Normatively, they deliberately emphasize helping individuals participate in the market by targeting those most in need of assistance until they can resolve their own situation. In practical terms, targeted assistance focuses exclusively on individuals and their immediate families, without any mediation by communities or other collectivities. These dynamics only generate political apathy as people's efforts are devoted to participating in the market and they have less time to become politically active, at the same time that they have few illusions that political participation will improve their situation. State agencies frequently play popular organizations against one another in a competitive scramble for limited resources, particularly when social welfare budgets remain tight to curtail government spending (Piester 1997; Gay 1990; Eckstein 1988; R. Cardoso 1992).

Decentralization of social welfare services further fragments potential popular social movements, restricting popular-sector organizational activity to narrowly circumscribed communities (B. Roberts 2005; Roberts and Portes 2006). Like so many other aspects of neopluralism, decentralization reflects a contradictory set of dynamics that Evelina Dagnino (2005) eloquently characterizes as a "perverse confluence": one based on participatory practices that could help

achieve state-society synergy and another associated with neopluralism's economic criteria for social and political inclusion. As local and to a lesser extent
regional governments assume responsibilities for administering a variety of
public services, including education, health care, and aid to the poor, demands
become increasingly focused on local, if not individual, concerns. This severely
limits the potential for mass social mobilization that might contribute to more
inclusionary citizenship rights and often pits communities against one another
as they compete for scarce resources. While such reforms can potentially create
new spaces for state-society synergy and a more inclusive social construction
of citizenship, in most cases the responsiveness achieved by bringing the administration of public services closer to the people through decentralization is
measured in terms of market-based efficiency criteria, including competition.
There is little concern for nonmarket considerations, the absolute price levels
of services, or competing priorities. Consumer participation is seen as an important source of information to make de facto local markets function, but it
is generally limited to the implementation of policies designed by experts or
politicians. The ultimate political decision-making authority remains with the
central government, and the result is that "the diffusion of power promoted by
the new model of development has brought officials closer to the poor, but often
without the means to resolve their problems" (Roberts and Portes 2006, 76).

The deleterious effects of targeted assistance and state decentralization tend
to be exacerbated by what Bryan Roberts and Charles Wood (2005a, 10) label
the "maturing of urbanization" (also see B. Roberts 2005; Roberts and Portes
2006; Roberts and Wood 2005b). With Latin America now largely urbanized,
massive migration to cities is now complete. Whereas under controlled inclusion the poor essentially constructed their own cities, the formalization of ir-
regular settlements and their provision of urban infrastructure mean that the
challenge now is the urban renewal of slums. Self-help has similarly given way
to greater dependence on state services. At the same time, community and city-
wide collective action is undermined as individuals and their immediate families turn inward to focus on personal or at best specific local problems.

Ultimately, the atomization and fragmentation of civil society is reflected in
the abysmally low levels of interpersonal trust that have characterized the region
since the return to democratic rule. In 1996 the Latinobarómetro survey found
that only 20 percent of respondents felt they "can trust people"; by 2003 just 17
percent of respondents felt this way, although it was again at 21 percent in the
2009 survey, having reached a peak in of 23 percent in 1997. Such high levels of
distrust reflect widespread perceptions of inequality and their consequences,
leading to a spiral of distrust in which social cooperation, not to mention state-
society synergy, become all but impossible. As the authors of the Latinobarómetro surveys (2003, 25) conclude, "The poor do not trust business; business

and the rich do not trust the poor. Workers do not trust employers, business does not trust government, politicians do not trust business, etc."

Combined with problems of social organization created by increased economic insecurity, along with the impact of crime and efforts to control it, the public sphere is often closed to Latin America's lower classes. The necessity of day-to-day survival often makes public participation and collective action seem, at best, a luxury one can no longer afford and, at worst, a wasted effort. As Victor Mejia, president of the Association for Community Development in San Salvador, explained, there is an unavoidable decline in organizational activity when "the people in the communities are thinking about what they will eat today, despite all their other problems" (personal interview, San Salvador, May 6, 1997).

This fragmentation and atomization of civil society is propitious for the re-emergence of populism (K. Roberts 1995; Weyland 1999, 2001). Just as the 1930s and 1940s proved to be a fertile terrain for populism in its popular-sector ascendant variant, the socioeconomic dislocations of the 1980s and 1995s have given rise to a new popular-sector defensive variant (Oxhorn 1998b). In contrast with populism's earlier incarnation, in which middle-sector actors mobilized the popular sectors against the oligarchy and international system to achieve at least a minimum level of inclusion, populist movements now emerge as the popular sectors become concerned with halting their growing socioeconomic marginalization as the limits of their political incorporation become increasingly apparent. Distrust in state institutions and political parties, as well as the weakening of organized labor and its perceived self-interested nature, has created a representational void that populist movements seek to fill. They attempt to do so by mobilizing the popular sectors against the principal actors and institutions of political democracy, including those segments of society most privileged by controlled inclusion. The protagonist role that the popular sectors appeared to assume in earlier periods and that gave populism its progressive character has been replaced by a more reactive secondary role. This new role reflects changes in the nature of popular-sector expectations because their political incorporation has already been formally guaranteed through the (re)establishment of democratic political regimes. Rather than representing a new opportunity for the popular sectors' social advancement, the popular-sector defensive variant of populism may represent their last hope for avoiding further marginalization.

While there has been "a stunning resurgence [of populism] in the 1980s and 1990s" (Weyland 2001, 6–7), the two most important examples are Alberto Fujimori, who dominated Peruvian politics for most of the 1990s, and Hugo Chávez in Venezuela. Both effectively channeled the frustrations and fears of the informal proletariat against traditional actors to take power and dominate their respective country's politics, polarizing their societies between the haves and have-nots after years of economic mismanagement, growing economic inequality, and rising rates of poverty. Both men were political outsiders who successfully mobilized the informal sector, taking advantage of their growing marginalization in the context of universal political rights. These reasons are why they are both examples of popular-sector defensive populism, even though Fujimori and Chávez espoused diametrically opposed economic models.[22] Like all populist movements, they have failed to fundamentally transform the structural sources of inequality (which Fujimori actually made much worse), and any social advances realized by segments of the popular sectors were at best short-lived in the case of Peru and are dependent on the availability of oil revenues in Venezuela.

Latin America's Democratic Crossroads

The apparent inability of citizens to use their political right to vote to find democratic solutions for their most pressing needs is perhaps the greatest threat to democracy in the region. At best, it could suggest to Latin Americans that democracy is irrelevant to improving the quality of their lives; at worst, democracy could appear as an obstacle to finding solutions to the most serious everyday problems people confront. There are signs that both possibilities are beginning to emerge. As CEPAL researcher Héctor Assale wryly notes,

> Starting with the problem of employment, of employment security, following with education, continuing with health, citizen security, access to judicial systems, that is what is important to people. To those who have to get up at 6 in the morning every day and go to work, who hang from buses and return exhausted to their homes at 10 at night, institutional democracy is important, but it is not their real worry. They go and vote every so often, they believe that things are getting better or worse, but in terms of their effective personal situation, democracy really does not matter much. (CEPAL 1999, 27)

It seems incongruous that, so soon after successful transitions to democracy, the question of democracy's relevance is even being raised. As Garretón (2003, 24) states, "politics in and of itself works better than before, and people participate somewhat more, but its radius of action is becoming smaller and smaller, and to society on the whole it seems more irrelevant." Despite the often considerable efforts needed to achieve a successful transition, it is as if there is an increasing collective sigh of "so what," now that people have often fatalistically grown accustomed to the peculiarities of neopluralist democracy.

While lamentable, democratic relevance would not be such a pressing problem if it led to the kind of political apathy originally lauded by democratic pluralists in the 1960s. But the problems of growing economic and citizen insecurity, low-quality education, and a crisis of representation represent anything but the alleged contentment associated with pluralist apathy. Living in Latin America's actually existing democracies is not easy! It represents a daily challenge for the vast majority of citizens, who are confronting increasingly daunting challenges. According to pluralist theory, the assumption was that one's life chances and consumption possibilities would be improved by democratic politics so that one did not need to participate—since it made no difference to outcomes, there would be no incentive to become engaged in politics. In Latin America, it is not a question of whether or not democratic politics matters in practice, but that it should matter given the potential power that political rights are expected to grant majorities and the obviously pressing needs they must somehow resolve. In a new permutation of what is essentially a historical vicious cycle, neopluralism, with its unique combination of universal political rights with declining and segmented civil and social rights, limits the quality of democratic citizenship at the same time that it severely constricts the ability of civil society.

This problem is a direct consequence of the neopluralist zeitgeist of markets and economic liberalism. The quality of people's citizenship increasingly depends on their economic resources, as the arena for resolving pressing social and political problems shifts away from the institutions of democratic rule and outside of the public sphere into the private sphere of markets and the economy. Yet it is also in this sphere that, for historical reasons amplified by neopluralism, the popular sectors are at a tremendous disadvantage.

To cope with the problems associated with the perceived irrelevance of democratic politics, the growing danger is that people will look for nondemocratic political alternatives. Turning away from civil society and abdicating even the possibility of state-society synergy, support for populist leaders such as Fujimori and Chávez suggests that people might be convinced that democracy is replaceable by alternatives that promise to be more effective in dealing with their most pressing problems. These alternatives may be more relevant to people's daily lives.

There are disturbing signs that this may be taking place throughout the region. In addition to the extreme (but still isolated) examples of Fujimori and Chávez, as well as popular support for repressive policing to curb crime, the responses to the Latinobarómetro surveys continue to demonstrate a surprising level of tolerance for authoritarian alternatives (2009b). This general sentiment was most cogently expressed by Daniel Vargas, a twenty-four-year-old university student who was interviewed after his father was accused of orchestrating the lynching of an elected Peruvian highlands mayor: "I believe in an authoritarian government, if it works. They do this in other countries and it works. Look at Cuba, that works. Look at Pinochet in Chile, that worked" (*New York Times*, June 24, 2004).

Latin America's democratic crossroads reflects this uncertainty about its future. While neopluralism has proven to be more politically stable than controlled inclusion, the inherent tensions between the existence of universal political rights and precarious social and civic rights will not disappear. Whether the result is a reversion to old patterns of social (and perhaps greater civic) rights in exchange for political rights, or something generally unprecedented in the region in the form of greater social and civic rights with universal political rights, a change seems inevitable. The choice will signify a new stage in the social construction of citizenship and ultimately reflect the role that civil society plays.

To better understand the dynamics of neopluralism, the second part of this book analyzes three cases in greater depth: Chile, Bolivia, and Mexico. As shown in table 3.2, the three countries offer a considerable mix of relevant experiences. They exhibit different levels of development, as reflected in their Human Development Index rankings and per capita incomes (UNDP 2010). While all three experimented with controlled inclusion, their experiences varied considerably in terms of when the experiments started and their level of inclusion, with each country's social policy regime providing a rough proxy for the latter. The three also represent varying levels of state strength. While this could be defined in a variety of ways, Transparency International's (2010) Corruption Perceptions Index rankings are a useful rough gauge. From the perspective of state-society relations, the level of corruption is one indicator of the strength of institutions in resisting capture by special interests and offers a good insight into the capacity of states to effectively design and implement policies in a democratic fashion. The indexes also conform to a general sense in the literature that Bolivia's state is notoriously weak, while Chile's is one of the strongest institutionally and Mexico's is somewhere in the middle, but closer to Chile's. The countries also vary in terms of the strength of their party systems and civil society, although there is no shorthand indicator of civil society strength. All three countries experienced revolutionary moments, in which the popular sectors temporarily played a central role in national politics. As discussed in the case studies, these moments varied considerably in terms of civil society's role and their long-term impact on the evolution of citizenship. Finally, the three countries are now all democracies with considerable experience with economic liberalization.

In addition to overviews of each country's political economy beginning with the period leading up to the installation of the processes of controlled inclusion, the case studies focus on particular aspects of their current politics to highlight central dimensions of more general characteristics. Chile clearly represents the most successful neopluralist democracy in the region. The case study focuses on the lessons to be learned from this success, the sources of growing dissatisfaction with the country's democratic regime, and the surprisingly close 1999–2000 presidential elections. It also looks at a failed attempt to establish a free trade zone in the northern desert, highlighting the problems posed for

Table 3.2. Select characteristics of case study countries

	HDI rank[a]	PCI (2002)[b]	Start of controlled inclusion	Social policy regime (1970s)[c]	CPI rank (2003)[d]	Party system	Relative strength of civil society	Revolutionary moment	Transition to democracy	Start of economic liberalization[e]
Bolivia	114	2,460	1952 revolution	Exclusionary	106	Weak, fragmented multiparty	Weak	1952 revolution	1982	Mid-1980s
Chile	43	9,820	1925 Constitution	Stratified universal	20	Strong, institutionalized multiparty	Strong	Allende government, 1970–73	1990	Mid-1970s
Mexico	53	8,970	Consolidation of revolution, 1934–40	Dual	64	Intermediate, one-party dominant[f]	Intermediate	1917 revolution	2000	Mid-1980s

[a] Human Development Index. SOURCE: Data from UNDP (2004).

[b] Per capita income in purchasing power parity, U.S. dollars. SOURCE: Data from UNDP (2004).

[c] SOURCE: Data from Filgueira and Filgueira (2002).

[d] Corruption Perceptions Index. SOURCE: Data from Transparency International (2003).

[e] SOURCE: Data from Morley, Machado, and Pettinato (1999).

[f] This classification best captures the fact that the PRI's seventy-year hegemony was broken by PAN, which was founded in the late 1930s, and that various other smaller parties have always competed in elections. The PRI's impressive electoral comeback, especially given widespread predictions of its quick demise after its 2000 electoral debacle, would also seem to substantiate its dominance.

state-society synergy by weak collective actors, including representatives of business.

The focus of the Bolivian chapter is on one of the most radical state reforms in recent history, the Popular Participation Law (Ley de Participación Popular, LPP). The LPP introduced an unprecedented level of state decentralization, creating institutions of participatory democracy that were explicitly designed to address problems of institutional development, rent seeking, and national integration. The LPP seemed to offer the possibility of state-society synergy in one of the poorest countries in the region. Its inability to achieve that underscores the challenges that both civil society and the state must overcome to achieve higher levels of economic, political, and social inclusion.

Finally, the principal focus of the Mexican case is the role civil society played in its transition to democracy and in addressing the problems that the new regime's neopluralist quality soon created. As the most recent democratic transition in the region, this case study serves to highlight some of the central lessons that must be learned if neopluralist democracy is to give way to democratic regimes characterized by more complete, less exclusionary processes of the social construction of citizenship.

4

TESTING THE LIMITS OF CITIZENSHIP: CHILE'S DEMOCRATIC TRANSITION

For much of the twentieth century, Chile has proven to be a veritable laboratory for the emergence of alternative modes of political inclusion and models of citizenship. Several factors contributed to this, including Chile's unprecedented level of political stability, the early consolidation of a strong centralized state, and the emergence of an institutionalized political party system beginning in the mid-nineteenth century that quickly spanned the ideological spectrum from left to right.[1] This confluence of factors meant that Chile was in a unique position within the region to push the limits of dominant modes of political inclusion and models of citizenship, beginning with controlled inclusion and citizenship as co-optation prior to the 1973 military coup and, since the transition to democracy in 1991, neopluralism and citizenship as consumption.

At the same time, the combined dominance of a strong centralized state and equally strong centralized political parties had ambiguous consequences for civil society. While Chilean civil society was arguably among the strongest in Latin America for much of this period in terms of its organization and the participation of growing segments of the population, its autonomy from political parties and the state was also severely constrained. For this reason, even as the Left surged in terms of its ability to mobilize subordinate groups in civil society in the late 1960s and early 1970s, such mobilization represented only a qualified potential for exercising citizenship as agency because political parties, and not the popular sectors, would ultimately determine the political agenda and nature of any social transformation. These constraints on the autonomy of civil society were so great that, paradoxically, the strength of an autonomous civil society reached its peak in the 1980s, during the long interregnum of a brutal dictatorship under which it was difficult to envisage the presence of any meaningful model of citizenship.

In attempting to understand the constraints that neopluralism and citizenship as consumption place on democracy in Latin America, Chile without a doubt represents the so-called best case. Economically, Chile is the only country in the region to have experienced continuous economic growth (with the exception of the 1999 recession) since 1986, resulting in a dramatic decline in poverty rates. Politically, Chile's strong state and institutionalized party system have allowed for a level of democratic political stability since the democratic transition in 1990 that has few parallels in the region. Yet this success has also been conditioned by the legacy of an authoritarian regime that transformed the Chilean economy and state in profound ways, laying the institutional foundations for entrenched neopluralism and citizenship as consumption. As Chilean sociologist Manuel Antonio Garretón notes, since the transition "public freedoms are enforced and it has been the one of the best periods in our history with the best governments in our history," despite the fact that this "has happened under the framework of the worst constitution in the world, the most authoritarian, least democratic, the only one in the world that is the complete legacy of a criminal dictator" (2007, 103). The result is that Chile faces the same threats to citizenship as the rest of the region—growing economic inequality and insecurity, segmented educational systems and diminished long-term social mobility, heightened citizen insecurity, and a general crisis of representation and the weakening of the public sphere—even though economic and political success has mitigated the severity of their impact. In other words, Chile represents both the promise and shortcomings of neopluralism and citizenship as consumption better than any other country in the region.

The chapter is divided into five sections. In the first, I discuss the historical context ending with the 1973 coup and the imposition of military rule. The next section then focuses on some of the principal ways in which the military dictatorship transformed Chile and the transition to democracy. In the third section, I examine the nature of neopluralist democracy in Chile and the concomitant threats to the quality of citizenship there, despite its impressive economic and political success. The fourth section then focuses on a new style of politics that emerged in the 1999–2000 presidential election campaign as an important example of how neopluralism and citizenship as consumption constrain the quality of democratic rule in Chile. In the concluding section, I then briefly explore some of the implications of the Chilean experience for other countries in the region with less favorable contexts for the emergence of citizenship as agency.

Pushing the Limits of Controlled Inclusion: State-Society Relations and the Breakdown of Chilean Democracy

In sharp contrast to most of Latin America, Chile was able to consolidate strong central state institutions under civilian authority relatively early after it achieved formal independence from Spain (Garretón 1989; Gil 1966; Loveman 1979; Oxhorn 1995b; Pinto 1970). Between 1830 and 1860, the central state became the principal arena for resolving social conflict, with the result that power struggles were resolved through constitutional means rather than through military force. Elections were central to this, allowing Chile to trace its democratic roots to this period, even if citizenship was restricted to a very small minority.[2] This was the result of several factors, including the successful tutelage of Diego Portales, the founder of the modern Chilean state, and his ability to create institutions that reflected the economic power of the oligarchy. The task was made relatively easier by the fact that Chile's dominant class and principal geographic centers formed a more or less homogeneous whole, allowing the country to avoid the years of civil war among regional caudillos that plagued most of the region (Oszlak 1981). This, in turn, reflected Chile's relative poverty and the subsequent lack of extensive colonial involvement.

Once in place, the importance of the central state as an arena for resolving social conflict would quickly grow. The War of the Pacific (1879–83) was a major turning point. As a result of defeating Peru and Bolivia, Chile acquired the mineral-rich Atacama Desert. Because foreign capital soon came to dominate Chile's new export economy, *"the government and not national owners of the export sector* is the agent which administers, spends and distributes a considerable fraction of the rent generated by external trade" (Pinto 1970, 10; italics in original). This economic windfall led to a significant expansion of the state, particularly as it used the revenue to finance an array of public services (especially education) and public works projects (Loveman 1979; Pinto 1970). The state would continue to grow with the adoption of ISI in the late 1930s, to the point where its role in the economy and society was second only to that of Cuba's by the end of the 1960s (Bitar 1986).

The growth of a strong centralized state under civilian authority provided a fertile ground for the early emergence of an institutionalized political party system spanning the ideological spectrum.[3] This was particularly true given the early importance of elections, in which political parties were the natural competitors; they quickly became the principal mechanism for attaining access to state institutions and their resources. By the middle of the nineteenth century, the landed oligarchy—soon to be joined by emerging commercial and industrial interests tied to the export sector—competed for power through two political parties, the Liberals and the Conservatives. The two principal political parties that would represent the middle sectors when they were fully incorporated into the political system in the 1920s, the Radical Party (Partido Radical) and Democratic Party (Partido Democrático), had been formed in 1861 and 1887, respectively. The working-class parties of the Left, the PC, and the Socialist Party (Partido Socialista), similarly trace their origins to radical workers organizations that first emerged in northern mining communities in the latter part of the nineteenth century (Bergquist 1986; Pinto 1970; Angell 1972). In fact, all the principal political parties in Chile in the early 1970s, with the exception of the Revolutionary Left Movement (Movimiento Izquierda Revolucionaria,

MIR), could trace their origins either directly or indirectly (as a result of their formation through schisms in older political parties) to the period preceding the emergence of Chile's first institutions of controlled inclusion in the mid-1920s.

The early emergence of institutionalized political parties had important implications for state-society relations and the nature of citizenship rights. First, with the exception of the Right, political parties were already well established before their main political constituencies actually enjoyed meaningful citizenship rights. As a result, political parties inevitably became the principal vehicles for the incorporation of new social groups under controlled inclusion, often growing in institutionalized strength in tandem with the expansion of state institutions for social inclusion. But this was a very top-down affair, with party elites mobilizing followers. While the effect was to pressure the state for more rights of citizenship, the goal was increasing the power of the parties and party elite behind this mobilization. The parties were quite successful in sinking deep roots into society, but this fell far short of citizenship as agency because such mobilization was carried out in an extremely hierarchical fashion that placed partisan interests at the front of the political agenda. Foremost among those interests, even among much of the Left, was the mobilization for votes and other demonstrations of societal support to increase party access to and control over state institutions. Access to state resources and the exercise of any rights that might result was then conditional on continued loyalty to the party responsible for the mobilization. Political parties became the principal mechanism for placing demands on the state, and their own centralization paralleled that of the state as demands from the local level were channeled up through party hierarchies to eventually arrive at the pinnacle of decision-making power (Valenzuela 1977).

Second, the centrality of institutionalized political parties to Chile's political system resulted in the absorption of civil society, undermining the capacity of actors to define and defend their interests independently of the particular political party responsible for their mobilization (Garretón 1989, 2003; Oxhorn 1995b). While access to state resources in exchange for continued political support was hardly unique to Chile, its channeling through an institutionalized political party system was. Clientelism in Chile took on a decidedly partisan (as opposed to personalist) quality that would ultimately contribute to the polarization of society, as the pragmatism of political parties in the 1930s and 1940s gradually gave way in the 1960s and early 1970s to party platforms based on strong ideological positions that prevented compromise. Virtually all spheres of Chilean society became highly politicized and penetrated by political parties, which served as the principal arena through which social actors were organized and mediated the rights those actors were able to enjoy as part of the predominant citizenship as co-optation model.

While the Left explicitly sought revolutionary changes that would completely overturn the socioeconomic and political order in Chile, it was far from encapsulating a model of citizenship as agency. This is because the Left, like virtually all parties in Chile, was unwilling to accept the autonomy of civil society actors. Indeed, their democratic centralism and insistence on ideological conformity and intolerance of disloyalty epitomized the basic dynamic that defined political party and grassroots linkages in Chile. As Manuel Castells's (1983, 199–209) detailed study of popular-sector mobilization in Chile during the early 1970s clearly shows, "the overpoliticization from the beginning, and the organizational profile of each political party within the [urban squatter] movement undermined its unity and made the autonomous definition of its goals impossible. Instead of being an instrument for reconstructing people's unity, the *pobladores*' [urban poor's] movement became an amplifier of ideological divisions" (209).

Together, both of these consequences of the early emergence of institutionalized political parties contributed to an instrumental view of political democracy. While Chile's democratic regime clearly enjoyed a high level of legitimacy and was consolidated in any meaningful sense of the word, it was viewed by most Chileans as a means toward the end of greater material well-being.[4] While this was most obvious for the supporters of the Left and the Right, it was also true for most middle-sector Chileans who identified with Center parties. Ironically, this instrumental attachment was the result of the concrete gains that political democracy brought in terms of access to state resources and, for the middle sectors and popular sectors, an expanding set of rights or entitlements. Yet this fundamentally reflects the way in which political parties linked access to those rights and resources to continued partisan loyalty. Even for the Left, this quid pro quo of Chilean politics reinforced the limits on citizen agency embodied in controlled inclusion and citizenship as co-optation, at the same time that it undermined normative support for political democracy as a regime type. When political democracy was no longer viewed as the best means toward a better life, it would be abandoned in support of some more promising alternative.

Finally, although the prior existence of institutionalized party mechanisms for representing the interests of new groups and channeling their participation helped preserve general political stability, the hierarchical nature of those parties meant that if political elites found themselves in a stalemate, the resultant political instability was severe. This inevitably meant that the military would prove pivotal for breaking that stalemate. The first major instance of this revolved around the introduction of controlled inclusion and the creation of Chile's Compromise State (Estado de Compromiso) beginning in the mid-1920s (Garretón 1989).[5]

The transition from a state dominated by the oligarchy to controlled inclusion, a new mode of interest mediation, began when Arturo Alessandri was able to take advantage of convulsions in the export sector to win the 1920 presidential elections. Using the miners of the north "as electoral cannon fodder" (Pinto 1970, 16), Alessandri was at the head of what Federico Gil (1966) describes as a "revolt of the middle class." Yet winning elections was not sufficient to overcome the oligarchy's opposition to sharing political power, and the military proved decisive. As Aníbal Pinto (1970, 16) notes, overcoming such opposition would require the intervention of soon-to-be general and "dictator [Carlos] Ibáñez, who counteracted the resistance of the extreme Right by placing the army on the other side of the scale."[6] The military's direct involvement in politics began in September 1924, when a group of military officers issued a series of legislative demands that Congress dutifully approved. These included a package of labor measures, the most important being a new labor code that legalized labor unions for the first time. So began an eight-year period of relative political instability marked by continued military intervention from 1924 through 1932, during which the oligarchy was forced to share its political tutelage with the middle sectors under a new constitution enacted in 1925 (Collier and Sater 2004; Loveman 1979).

The Compromise State was fundamentally based on controlled inclusion, mediated by strong institutionalized political parties that relied on the gradual expansion of citizenship as co-optation to expand their social bases. For this reason, political rights steadily increased during this period, as the right to vote was given to more and more groups of people, culminating in 1970 when suffrage was granted to illiterates and eighteen-year-olds (Loveman 1979, 260). Closely linked with this was a similar expansion of social services. By the early 1970s Chile had one of the highest rates of social security coverage in Latin America. A full 72 percent of the total population was covered by social security in 1971, and with the inclusion of small businesses and the self-employed, expansion reached 80 percent in 1973 (Mesa-Lago 1978, 22–69).

Yet because this expansion of social services was intrinsically tied to processes of controlled inclusion, levels of coverage were notoriously unequal. In contrast to the welfare states of Western democracies, Chile had a system that was best characterized as "stratified universalism" (Filgueira and Filgueira 2002). While undoubtedly cushioning the consequences of social inequality, Chile's social welfare policies also "reproduced the existing distribution of wealth along socioeconomic as well as geographic lines" (Borzutzky 2002, 52; see also Mesa-Lago 1978). Economic inequality remained relatively stable during the period 1958–63, under the right-wing government of Jorge Alessandri, and actually increased during the reformist Christian Democratic Party (Partido Democrática Cristiana, PDC) government of Eduardo Frei (1964–69), since better-organized, more powerful groups received a disproportionate level of state resources. Social welfare policies would positively affect inequality under the Popular Unity (Unidad Popular) government of Salvador Allende, in part through genuinely redistributive policies and in part due to an overheated economy which reduced unemployment to historical lows (Laraña 2001).

This pattern underscores the co-optive nature of citizenship during Chile's Compromise State and the fact that more powerful, better-organized groups were the first to be included. Beginning with the middle sectors in the 1920s, organized labor was gradually incorporated in the 1930s and 1940s. Women were able to vote for the first time in 1952. Controlled inclusion reached a new peak in the 1960s when President Eduardo Frei sought to secure an electoral footing in rural areas and urban slums by mobilizing peasants and the urban poor, unleashing a fierce competition for the support of marginalized groups between the PDC and the various parties of the Left that would culminate in the 1973 military coup. Aside from unleashing a process of social mobilization that would soon escape the capacity of political parties to contain, Frei's so-called Revolution in Liberty (Revolución en Libertad) represented the first assault on a key pillar of the Compromise State by threatening the archaic system of ag-ricultural relations, on which the oligarchy relied for its power, by organizing peasants (Oxhorn 1995b). In other words, Frei, and not Allende, was the first to really test the limits of controlled inclusion.

Because controlled inclusion was mediated by political parties, citizenship as co-optation was tied to party loyalty. The promise of material resources for support was clearly based on partisanship, reflecting the ways in which political parties created and absorbed what would normally be considered the social or-ganizations of civil society. A good example of this is the way in which political parties of the Left, particularly the Communist Party, essentially created Chile's labor movement (Angell 1972; Bergquist 1986). Long before unions were actu-ally legalized in 1924, Left parties had been active in organizing workers, par-ticularly miners in Chile's mineral-rich northern desert. For this reason, within a year of being legalized, a total of more than two hundred thousand workers belonged to 214 different unions. These were working-class organizations, but they were guided by their political allegiances and remained fiercely loyal to the Left until well into the military regime, when repression and other factors allowed the PDC to penetrate the movement.

Such political loyalty, in turn, proved to be relatively quite beneficial for or-ganized labor. As was generally the case for Latin America, organized labor ul-timately served the interests of only a small segment of the popular sectors that were fortunate enough to have jobs in the formal sector of the economy. At its peak in 1972, total union membership was 632,485 and accounted for more than 22 percent of the workforce (Baraona 1974). The strength of their organiza-tions allowed unionized workers, particularly those in the modern industrial and mining sectors, to gain clear advantages over workers in smaller firms and the unorganized informal sector, who together made up the vast majority of the popular sectors. This "privileged group within the popular classes" (Faletto and Ruiz 1970, 234) was able to negotiate higher wages and maintain a generally higher standard of living than the other segments of the popular sectors. Moreover, it was able to maintain its relative position during both inflationary periods—which its own negotiated wage increases contributed to—and subsequent downturns, when restrictive monetary and fiscal policies were implemented to reverse inflationary spirals (Pinto 1970; Faletto and Ruiz 1970; Bitar 1986; Stallings 1978). Equally important, organized workers had privileged access to state social welfare programs and other resources (Borzutzky 2002).

Chile's political parties were acutely aware of the potential limits of socio-economic and political change under the Compromise State, even as they explicitly tested those limits with reforms. This was most obvious for the Left, which openly debated the feasibility of significant reforms in the absence of a true revolution through civil war. For the political Center, however, the goal was to preempt more radical change. As President Arturo Alessandri noted in 1923, on the eve of the creation of the Compromise State, "If we establish some social equilibrium through fair laws that take into account the demands of the proletariat, we will prevent anarchic and subversive elements from predicating their theories. You will see how these theories crash against the wall erected by social justice" (quoted in Borzutzky 2002, 11). Similarly, Eduardo Frei's Revolution in Liberty was explicitly framed as an alternative to a socialist revolution (Fleet 1985; Scully 1992; Garretón 1989). By mobilizing the popular sectors, the PDC hoped to preempt the Left, which largely ignored them to focus its efforts on the formal-sector working class until the PDC starting organizing peasants and the urban poor. The PDC hoped that as a consequence of this mobilization, it would cement the loyalty of the popular sectors and create a new electoral majority that would guarantee PDC political dominance for the foreseeable future—a threat that the Left could not let go unchallenged.

The mediation of controlled inclusion by institutionalized political parties had several important consequences. First, political parties essentially absorbed civil society by severely limiting its autonomy. Unlike other countries where a single political party dominated civil society (see chapter 6 on Mexico), real competition among Chile's various parties had the effect of creating a spiral of mobilization within civil society as political parities tried to expand their electoral base. Social mobilization became a proxy for winning and measuring support as political parties competed against one another by promising to deliver greater access to state resources. This led to increasing demands being placed on the political system, as well as growing levels of inclusion, as political parties had to deliver on those demands to further shore up their own political bases. While the demands were real in the sense that they reflected the material needs of Chile's popular sectors, they were mobilized from the top down, based on party programs developed by Chile's political class. Reforms, however important to their beneficiaries, did not represent solutions demanded by an autonomous civil society from the bottom up. As is typical of controlled inclusion, they were essentially decided by elites in pursuit of their own interests, albeit partisan rather than strictly individualistic. Political parties became the necessary link to the state, cementing their central role in Chile's political system.

By pushing the limits of controlled inclusion too far, this competitive dynamic threatened to overwhelm the democratic regime that made it possible. Instability was avoided during the first decades of the Compromise State in part because Chile began to implement a policy of ISI, which led to the expansion of the state and more employment opportunities for the middle sectors and workers in the formal economy (Pinto 1970). Equally important, the Radical Party—which championed the creation of the Compromise State and dominated Chilean politics until the early 1950s—played a critical role in moderating the destabilizing effects of this dynamic by alternating its political alliances between the Right and Left (Fleet 1985; Scully 1992). Political polarization was avoided with the result that controlled inclusion could expand in tandem with the capacity of the state and the political system to absorb the growing demands placed on them as a consequence of party competition.

The rapid rise of the PDC and its pretensions for creating a third way between socialism and liberal capitalism fundamentally transformed this basic dynamic (Fleet 1985; Scully 1992). In sharp contrast to the Radical Party's political pragmatism in the pursuit of its own electoral fortunes, the PDC identified its potential electoral success with adhesion to a reformist Christian Democratic ideology that distinguished it from the Marxist Left and the economic liberalism of the Right. Such ideological adhesion made it difficult for the PDC to compromise with other parties. This reticence to seek compromise with political opponents was only reinforced by PDC's rapid rise to political predominance. Founded in 1957 by a group of young social Christians who split from the Conservative Party, the PDC eclipsed the Radical Party as the principal representative of Chile's middle sectors when its candidate, Eduardo Frei, came in third behind the winning Jorge Alessandri representing a united Right, and Allende the Left, in the tightly contested 1958 presidential elections. Only six years later, Frei won the presidency in 1964 with 56 percent of the vote—a landslide in Chile's multiparty system.

The 1958 elections proved a turning point in Chilean politics by signaling the emergence of Chile's infamous "three-thirds": an electorate divided into roughly three equal ideological blocs, each of which was capable of winning a plurality in any given electoral competition (Garretón 1989; Valenzuela 1978). With the Radical Party now reduced to a relatively minor political role, the competition that characterized controlled inclusion no longer had any significant moderating influences. At the same time, the cold war was heating up, leading to a radicalization on both the right and left that made it increasingly difficult for them to accept political compromises. This radicalization of party politics actually was the source of the PDC's huge electoral margin in 1964: fearing the growing strength of the Left under Allende and lacking a candidate who could compete, the Right threw its support to Frei as a defensive reaction. But the PDC's victory, much to its chagrin, did not signal an end to the three-thirds deadlock, and, in large part due to PDC's reluctance to compromise with the Right while in power, Allende narrowly won the presidency in 1970 when the Right again ran its own candidate.

Aside from making political compromise increasingly difficult, the growing prominence of ideology in Chilean politics effectively raised the ante for political parties competing for support as it fed rising popular-sector expectations. The liberal economic policies offered by Jorge Alessandri when he won the presidency in 1958 were followed in succession by the ambitious reform goals of Frei's Revolution in Liberty and, finally, Allende's promised socialist revolution. Ironically, this escalation in political promises and popular expectations ultimately came back to haunt the PDC, because Frei's substantial achievements in land reform, urban housing, and other direct gains for the popular sector paled in comparison to both his own exaggerated goals when he took office and the promise of even greater change from the Left.

Ultimately, with the Right, Center, and Left increasingly identifying themselves with rigid ideological projects, political parties equated their own interests with those of the nation. This made compromise all but impossible across blocs and further circumscribed the potential for any autonomous organizational activity on the part of civil society (Garretón 1989, 2003; Oxhorn 1995b). Elite competition led to a spiraling of mobilization based on demands for increasing redistribution. A surge in urban land seizures from 1969, one year before the presidential elections, through 1972 was emblematic of an increasingly destabilizing dynamic (Castells 1983, 200–201). In the space of roughly four years, literally hundreds of thousands of poor people were mobilized by political elites to illegally occupy land to build homes. Compromise among Chile's political elite became progressively more difficult to achieve as the various parties on the left—including the parties that formed Allende's Popular Unity coalition as well as the centrist PDC—mobilized more and more homeless people to exert pressure on the state, demonstrate each party's relative strength, and, at least for the parties still claiming allegiance to the democratic regime, lay the foundation for greater voter support in the next elections.

Both the Center and the Left took advantage of this mobilization to advance their own partisan interests in ways that would unravel the democratic regime at its foundations. For the Left, both within and outside the Popular Unity coalition, this mobilization became a way to demonstrate social support for political parties that openly opposed Chile's bourgeois democracy. While more radical elements found the land seizures to be a mechanism for pushing Allende's hand and forcing a radicalization of his promised revolution, land seizures by more moderate parties in the coalition were an important mechanism for preserving their quota of power within the state, as well as for winning votes in subsequent elections.

While Frei was in power (1964–70), the centrist PDC could not afford to alienate the popular sectors by repressing the land seizures, because they were seen as the key to the PDC's ability to win future electoral majorities. For the same reasons, the PDC was all too quick to enter the fray when Allende assumed the presidency, recognizing that the new government similarly could not afford to repress land seizures and hoping such mobilization would shore up PDC support in the shantytowns for the next elections.

This dynamic played itself out in rural land seizures by peasants and factory seizures by the working class. Increasingly, it was met by countermobilizations by Chile's middle sectors and allied groups, with the backing of the Right. Indeed, as the PDC saw its own middle-sector social base gradually swing to the right in opposition to the Allende government, it felt compelled to follow suit or lose its dominance over the opposition (Garretón 1989; Oxhorn 1995b). Ultimately, social mobilization spiraled out of control as the political elites that instigated it could no longer effectively manage its consequences. With demands on the state growing, along with the defensiveness of the Right, and increasingly the PDC, it seemed only a matter of time before controlled inclusion would be pushed to its limits. At the same time, as elite competition grew more intense, elite cooperation became all but impossible because politics was increasingly seen as a zero-sum game. As political elites divided along increasingly impermeable party lines, compromise was seen as a sign of weakness that would entail high political costs. Instead, legislative obstructionism became more pronounced. Within the executive branch, intense party rivalries meant that effective policy coordination within the public sector became more and more difficult to achieve, further exacerbating problems of governability (Bitar 1986; Garretón 1989; Valenzuela 1978; Oxhorn 1995b).[7]

Lacking any effective counterweight in a strong civil society, the fate of Chilean democracy ultimately rested on the capacity of its political elite to avoid the emergence of zero-sum politics and its consequences in increasingly unrestrained social mobilization. As Garretón (2003, 105) notes, "a latent crisis lingered, for if at any moment the negotiation consensus was undone, the entire society would be rendered defenseless." What this meant in practice became horribly clear on September 11, 1973, when the military, backed by the Right and with the support of the PDC and much of Chile's middle sectors, ended not only Allende's experiment with a "democratic road to socialism," but the Compromise State and Chile's democratic regime.

Laying the Foundations for Neopluralism:
The Military Regime and the Transition to Democracy

The September coup ushered in an unprecedented period of repression (Comisión Nacional 1991). Beyond the sheer horror that was unleashed, the seventeen-year dictatorship of General Augusto Pinochet radically transformed Chile's state and society.[8] In contrast to the period of controlled inclusion, Chile's state-centric "political matrix" was replaced by a more complex system where the economic, political, and state spheres exhibited a new level of autonomy from one another (Garretón 1999). This newfound autonomy held the promise of a return to democratic rule in which democracy became an end in itself because it offered a way of mediating such autonomy. It also opened up new space for a strong civil society to emerge that could more effectively counterbalance the dominant role played by political parties seeking to win control over the state, paving the way for citizenship as agency.

Despite the new political matrix's potential, the military forcefully imposed a neopluralist system of interest mediation that, ironically, would be locked in place by the transition to democracy. While the new political matrix reflected a far more restricted role for the state in both the society and the economy, the rising dominance of neopluralism meant that the logic of markets would increasingly penetrate all spheres of state-society relations. Although most political parties began to emphasize the importance of a new respect for autonomy of civil society in the 1980s, this proved ephemeral at best. Rather than erecting new institutions that would facilitate active state-society synergy in the new democracy, with a few notable exceptions, the transition had the effect of translating this new respect for civil society autonomy into political marginality. More specifically, three aspects of what Javier Martínez and Alvaro Díaz (1996) described as Chile's great transformation are central to understanding the nature of Chile's current democratic period: (1) the impact of massive economic change on Chile's social structure, (2) the loss of the state's capacity to directly influence income distribution, and (3) the paradoxical role of civil society during the military regime and the transition to democracy.

Economic Change and the Emergence of a New Social Structure

Beginning in the mid-1970s, the military government enacted a series of policies that made Chile a leader in adopting market reforms, with profound consequences for the economy in terms of a shift to export-led growth, deindustrialization, a shrinking working class, and unprecedented levels of poverty and inequality (Foxley 1983; Martínez and Díaz 1996; Oxhorn 1995b). Adjustments to the radical reforms of the 1970s in the aftermath of the 1982 economic collapse would ultimately usher in an unprecedented period of growth beginning in 1986. The pattern of development embodied in these policies would become a key pillar of neopluralism with the return to democratic rule. More specifically, the new development model represented an unprecedented redistribution of economic power from the state to large business (Martínez and Díaz 1996). As a result, the logic of markets began to increasingly permeate all aspects of Chilean society and politics.

In effect, this transfer of economic resources amounted to a transfer "from wages to profits, from the poor to the rich" (Martínez and Díaz 1996, 74). Aside from the dramatic surge in poverty during the 1970s and 1980s, there was a significant increase in levels of inequality. Data for the Santiago Metropolitan Area show that the Gini coefficient, which had declined from a high of 0.51 in the 1960s to 0.47 in the period of 1970–73, reached a historical high of 0.59 in the period of 1987–90 (Muñoz Goma 2007, 27). One cause of this was a rise in the share of national income of the richest 10 percent of the population, from 35 percent in 1978 to 42 percent in 1988 (Martínez and Díaz 1996, 124).

Structurally, inequality was further reinforced by two related dynamics. The first was the growing weakness of organized labor, whose leaders were fiercely repressed by the military. While the repression began to subside somewhat in the late 1970s, the ability of workers to organize was undermined because the hardest-hit sectors of the economy (particularly the manufacturing sector) were also the sectors of greatest trade union strength, as well as the principal social bases for the Left (Martínez and Díaz 1996; Oxhorn 1995b).[9] A new Labor Plan (Plan Laboral) was introduced in 1978 that explicitly institutionalized this dynamic. Unions were now legalized, but union strength was severely limited because the law deliberately encouraged fragmentation in the labor movement and placed tight constraints on collective bargaining in favor of employers (Frühling 1984; Ruiz Tagle 1985).[10]

The second dynamic reflects the pattern of job creation established during the military regime. Jobs tended to be created in low-productivity sectors (Oxhorn 1995b). High levels of unemployment and informality in the 1980s, while substantially reduced during the period of democratic rule, reinforced a pattern of high levels of job insecurity. These basic problems continue to this day (OECD 2009; Martínez and Díaz 1996). This economic insecurity makes union organizing much more problematic, at the same time that it limits the advantages of formal-sector employment in terms of access to social benefits and basic workplace rights.

The State's Diminished Capacity to Redistribute

If economic change infused the logic of markets into Chilean politics and society, the legacy of state reform with the return to democracy epitomizes citizenship as consumption. In general terms, the state's redistributive capacity is fundamentally the same as it was when the military regime ended, which is reflected in the continued high levels of income equality. From this perspective, the twin pillars of the reforms were targeting social assistance policies to those most in need and the privatizing health care, education, and the pension system.

While targeting social assistance based on actual need can have important positive effects (Ffrench-Davis and Raczynski 1988), it also severely limits the capacity of the state to use social policy as a redistributive mechanism.[11] Extreme income inequality means that the income level required for the poor to rise above official poverty levels is so low relative to the incomes of other groups that even large declines in poverty will not lead to any appreciable narrowing of income gaps. At the same time, its focus on individuals and their immediate family has meant that social assistance is disconnected from strengthening the collective dimension of civil society (Oxhorn 2003), a major change from the social policies in Chile prior to the coup (Filgueira and Filgueira 2002).

Privatization of public services has further reinforced the importance of individual economic resources in determining access to often vital services, including health care, education, and retirement incomes. Health care, for example, has been stratified into a private system that covers 17 percent of the population and the public system that covers 70 percent.[12] Not surprisingly, the quality of medical care is generally higher in the private sector. This reflects the fact that the private sector is better funded at the same time that its clientele is generally healthier. While a new public insurance plan, Universal Access with Explicit Guarantees in Health (AUGE), was enacted in 2002—the first major reform of the military's health care system—there still are no comprehensive studies of its impact (OECD 2009, 118), and according to a survey conducted by the Universidad Católica, there is a widespread perception among people who had recently used the health care system that it discriminated based on a patient's income (*Santiago Times,* July 24, 2006).

Privatization, however, does not mean that the reduced public sector is free for users. Those who take recourse to the public sector still have to pay for services. For example, co-payments are 50 percent for the public health system, almost 40 percent for public housing, and 10 percent for education (De la Maza 2005, 60).

The Paradox of Civil Society:
Mobilization, Demobilization, and the Transition to Democracy

The paradox of civil society in Chile was that it was arguably stronger during the military regime than after the transition to democracy it helped to achieve (Martínez and Díaz 1996; Oxhorn 1995b; Campero 1987). Within a short period after the coup, civil society organizations began to emerge among the popular sectors, particularly in Santiago. This organizational activity culminated in several waves of a national protest movement in the mid-1980s, only to quickly fade in political significance beginning in 1987, as political parties increasingly focused their efforts on winning the 1988 plebiscite and ushering in a transition to democracy. The nature of the mobilization/demobilization process and its relationship to the transition represent the third aspect of this period that would have important consequences for understanding the nature of Chile's democratic regime.

The harshness of the repression combined with the severity of the economic dislocations caused by the imposition of a new development model led to the emergence of a large number of civil society organizations. Initially, these organizations were essentially survival mechanisms—ways for people to collectively cope with the unprecedented severity of the economic and political situation. The Catholic Church played a critical role in supporting these groups. In particular, it helped shelter them from repression by providing meeting spaces, as well as material support. The church also played an important role through capacity building and advice in helping the poor organize themselves. The church became a catalyst for strengthening civil society that required it to allow organizations a reasonable level of autonomy—something the church was willing to permit in the context of authoritarian rule.

The self-help dimension of many popular-sector organizations remained strong during the period of the dictatorship, but organizations increasingly recognized the important role they could play in opposing the regime. This drew on the importance of human rights organizational activity played out in the *poblaciones* (shantytowns). A turning point came in May 1983, when the Chilean Copper Workers' Union called for a national day of protest. While the protests are noteworthy for the widespread adhesion they enjoyed, a new locus of political activity emerged in the poblaciones, where repression reached levels not seen since the early years of the military regime. The success of this first mass mobilization against the military regime led to monthly protests that grew in size and intensity until a state of siege was declared in November 1984 (De la Maza and Garces 1985).

Although the regime was temporarily put on the defensive by the protests, the most important political consequence of the first wave of protests was that it created a space for political parties to reemerge after almost ten years of repression. Faced with mounting public opposition from within civil society, particularly in the poblaciones, the government could do little to prevent political parties from acting publicly, even though they would remain outlawed until 1987. Within months of the first protest, two new opposition blocs were publicly formed. The Democratic Alliance (Alianza Democrática, AD) was dominated by the centrist PDC and consisted of eight Center-Right or Center parties and the moderate faction of the now divided Socialist Party. On the left, the Popular Democratic Movement (Movimiento Democrático Popular, MDP) was dominated by the

Communist Party and included the more radical faction of the Socialist Party, as well as Revolutionary Left Movement and a number of smaller parties. The two blocs quickly came to dominate opposition politics. Their inability to reach any kind of consensus regarding a post-Pinochet alternative further reinforced the role that the protests and poblaciones played as the principal locus for expressing opposition to the regime. Parties hoped the sheer force of the protests would leave the military regime no alternative other than complete capitulation, even if they could not agree on the kind of government that would replace it.

Although the public reemergence of political parties was made possible only in the wake of the protests, it created new tensions for popular organizations. Political party activists had always played important roles in popular organizations, in part because they frequently had actual organizing experience. Yet the organizations were generally able to maintain an unprecedented (for Chile) level of autonomy from political parties. This reflected the weakness of the political parties in a repressive environment. Parties generally lacked the capacity to assert sufficient control over their activists to be able to capture popular organizations in the way parties had before the military coup. Perhaps more important, this organizational autonomy reflected the popular sectors' lack of trust in political parties, as well as the fact that in most poblaciones no single party was predominant because people identified with either multiple parties or no party at all.[13] Once political parties could openly compete with one another for popular support, civil society autonomy became increasingly precarious as the parties sought to capture an incipient popular social movement as a way to shore up their own political support.

A new protest cycle started again in August 1985, organized around a National Accord for the Transition to Full Democracy (Acuerdo Nacional para una Transición a la Democracia Plena) that had been signed by newly resurgent political parties from the Center-Right, Center, and Center-Left. Infighting among the signatories (mainly members of the AD) and the exclusion of the Left doomed the accord, which was essentially ignored by the regime. Still unable to reach a consensus among all opposition political parties, the parties decided to work behind the scenes by supporting a new civic assembly formally convened by a wide array of civil society organizations, which produced yet another cycle of protests. Culminating in a successful national protest and general strike in July 1986, this wave of mobilizations proved to be the last.

The July protest marked a turning point in opposition strategies for several reasons. It was now clear that protests would not bring the regime down and that the opposition would have to define a clear alternative to the military regime if it hoped to succeed. The brutal repression of the protest was in many ways decisive. Early on the first day of the protest, an army patrol burned two young people alive, one of whom subsequently died. Accounts of his treatment in the severely underfunded hospital lacking even the most basic supplies and his public funeral served to rally opposition support for a regime change, at the same time that it galvanized support for a peaceful transition. Protests no longer seemed appropriate, given both the military regime's lack of restraint and fears of the growing radicalization of pobladores. This started a process of marginal-izing more extreme elements within the opposition, particularly the MDP.[14]

The constitution that Pinochet imposed in 1980 also began to open up new possibilities for achieving opposition consensus. The constitution stipulated that a plebiscite would be held in 1988 to decide who would be the first president with the restoration of civilian rule. The plebiscite entailed a simple vote for or against the military junta's candidate (which was always presumed to be Pino-chet) and offered the opposition an opportunity to defeat the regime accord-ing to its own rules. If the opposition could win the plebiscite, the constitution stipulated that elections would be held within a year, paving the way for a true transition to democracy. Of course, there was no guarantee that Pinochet would accept such a defeat. The opposition assumed (correctly) that the military would not allow him to undermine the constitution by refusing to accept the outcome of the plebiscite. This was because the military increasingly saw the 1980 consti-tution as its principal legacy for legitimating prolonged military rule. Moreover, to give the plebiscite even a modicum of democratic legitimacy, political parties were legalized in 1988 and the opposition parties were able to use the legaliza-tion process (which entailed collecting thousands of signatures throughout the country) to strengthen their ties with civil society. Parties also played an active role in mobilizing voters to register, further reconnecting them with Chileans in the process.

But to take advantage of this unique set of opportunities, the opposition finally had to achieve genuine unity around a viable alternative to continued military rule. The increasing marginalization of the PC helped immensely. The clear goal of defeating Pinochet electorally also helped achieve unity for the first time in decades. Most important, political party leaders now recognized the im-portance of maintaining such newfound unity, with the result that all decisions were increasingly being negotiated by small groups of political elites before they were made public.

From the perspective of civil society, particularly the popular sectors, it also meant that mobilization had to be controlled to avoid provoking either the mili-tary or middle-sector voters wary of popular-sector radicalism. The autonomy of popular-sector organizations seemed to have run its course. Although the growing repudiation of the repression in the 1970s and the complete collapse of the economy in 1982 meant the military regime's lack of legitimacy for the ma-jority was not in doubt, the protest movement and popular-sector organizations that propelled it were necessary for translating the lack of regime legitimacy into regime change. This step was essential for enabling political parties to again assume a public role. Once they reappeared publicly, however, political parties needed time and space to overcome their divisions and reconnect with society after years of repression, and the protests helped ensure that they would have it. With hindsight at least, it is clear that political parties were in no position to govern Chile in 1983.

That had all changed considerably by 1987, and political parties were in a much better position to assert control over popular-sector mobilization, which they quickly did. All efforts were focused on bringing out the vote—first in the plebiscite and then in the 1989 elections. This included directing the activities of the most experienced organizers in the poblaciones to the elections, regardless of whether they had actual party affiliations or not. More important, it resulted in the demobilization of civil society organizational activities that were autonomous of political parties. This process was reinforced by the commitment of party leaders to maintain a consensus, deliberately sidestepping potentially divisive issues and endeavoring to limit the influence of political actors, such as the popular sectors.

The challenge of maintaining unity—now that the goal of defeating Pinochet and the means to do so (first winning the plebiscite, then the subsequent elections) were clear—was daunting given the potential for fragmentation in the opposition. In February 1988 the Command for the No (Concertación por el No) was formed by thirteen opposition political parties, and it eventually grew to include seventeen by the end of 1988. It was dominated by the Christian Democrats (the largest party in the coalition), the moderate wing of the Socialist Party, and the newly formed Party for Democracy (PPD). These same parties would later form the Concertación de los Partidos por la Democracia (Concertación).[15]

Despite what seemed like insurmountable odds, the opposition won the plebiscite with a decisive margin of 54.68 percent voting no compared to 43 percent who voted in favor of Pinochet. In accordance with the constitution, Pinochet presided over what was now a caretaker government for another year, engaging in limited but important negotiations with the opposition regarding constitutional change (Angell and Pollack 1990). Elections were held at the end of 1989, which Patricio Aylwin of the Concertación easily won with 55.2 percent of the vote.

Regardless of the necessity of asserting party control over popular-sector mobilization to safeguard the transition process (O'Donnell and Schmitter 1986), it has proven very difficult to remobilize after the transition. There are a variety of reasons for this, relating directly to neopluralism and citizenship as consumption, but it is also important to note that the transition process established a pattern of state-society relations that neopluralism only reinforced. As Garretón (2003) notes, political parties continued to subordinate their actions to the same dynamics that characterized the transition, creating the illusion of consensus. This distinctly elitist decision-making style, famously characterized as *democracia de los acuerdos* (democracy by agreements), meant that civil society autonomy resulted in political marginalization rather than state-society synergy. The undeniable political and socioeconomic achievements of democracy by agreements only makes substantive reform difficult (Garretón 2007), and any movement toward citizenship as agency that much more problematic.

Citizenship in a Neopluralist Democracy

Chile's return to democracy in 1990 has been exemplary in terms of its political stability, economic performance, and social policy reforms. Indeed, the period from 1990 to 2009 has been the most successful in Chile's modern history and arguably the most successful in a region marked by periodic economic and political crises. The Concertación coalition won every election from 1990 through 2006, and its democracy by agreements meant that political party infighting was kept to a minimum through a consensual process of elite decision making that also included the principal parties of the Right. Political stability meant that Chile could again elect a socialist president, Ricardo Lagos, in 2000, who in turn was succeeded in office by another socialist, Michelle Bachelet—Chile's first woman president and a single mother who had been tortured in the aftermath of the 1973 coup.

Political success was more than matched by economic success. Chile experienced an average annual real economic growth rate of 6 percent through the end of 1998 (when Chile, as well as the rest of the region, entered into recession). This thrust Chile to the highest position (number thirty-four) of all Latin American countries, according on the Index of Human Development (UNDP 1999). More than a million and a half people were able to escape poverty in just seven years, as the poverty rate declined from 46.6 percent in 1987 to 28.5 percent at the end of 1994. Chilean government statistics show that, by the end of 1998, poverty had declined even further, to just 21.7 percent of all families when government financial support is included (*Santiago Times*, June 11, 1999). Not surprisingly, the recession was both relatively mild and short-lived. By 2004 real economic growth was again approaching 6 percent per year. Real GDP per capita increased on average 4.3 percent over the past two decades, and as a result poverty rates hit historical lows (OECD 2009, 15, 54).

These impressive achievements justifiably set Chile apart from most other Latin American countries, but they also belie the existence of the same fundamental challenges faced by all democratic regimes in the region. The strength of Chile's political parties and state institutions has meant that neopluralism has been more subtle in its concrete manifestations and less authoritarian than in other countries. Yet Chile has come to epitomize citizenship as consumption. Neopluralism, even in its more moderate form, is in many ways at the root of Chilean democracy's most important deficits.

The limits of neopluralism and citizenship as consumption can be seen in what the United Nations Development Program in its 1998 Chile Human Development Report (Informe de Desarrollo Humano en Chile) concluded was the "paradox" of Chilean development: "a country with notable economic development where the people do not feel happy" (PNUD 1998, 53). As early as 1997, long before there was any indication that Chile would be heading into a recession at the end of 1998, a survey of human security for the United Nations Development Program found that there was an "important dissonance between [Chile's] objective achievements and the perception of the people" (3). One poll that was part of the larger survey taken in the southern zone of Santiago, for example, found that almost 83 percent of the respondents said they were not happy, regardless of their impression of the country's economic situation. More concretely, this dissonance reflects the same four obstacles to citizenship as agency that are found in all of Latin America: (1) widespread economic insecurity, (2) a segmented educational system, (3) insecurity caused by rising crime rates, and (4) a general crisis of representation.

Pervasive Economic Insecurity

As Oscar Muñoz Goma (2007, 216–17) notes, "the proliferation [of] . . . precarious employment has contributed to the dissemination of a perception of insecurity and lack of confidence among important segments of workers." This problem of economic insecurity is a consequence of several structural characteristics of neopluralism. While Chile has done relatively well in terms of maintaining low levels of unemployment through job creation, the jobs created tend to be of low productivity in a context of poor working conditions (A. Cárdenas 2005; Muñoz Goma 2007; OECD 2009; Reinecke and Velasco 2006). This reflects the fact that almost two-thirds of employment is in the service sector, which means that "Chile's 'deindustrialization' process appears about as advanced as many 'old' industrialized economies" (OECD 2009, 42). The economic slowdown that began in 1998 exacerbated this problem. The number of jobs in the manufacturing sector shrunk until 2000. Although there was again growth in the manufacturing sector from 2000 to 2005, the relative size of the sector continued to decline until 2005–6, when it stagnated at 13 percent (42).

Of course, Chile is far from being an old industrialized economy in terms of its social structure, and the consequences of this are exacerbated by neopluralism. In addition to a relatively large agricultural sector (12 percent of total employment), many of Chile's poor since the democratic transition are working poor, including a sizable percentage of workers in the formal sector (Díaz 1991; León and Martínez 2007). In 2005, for example, 47 percent of the labor force earned less than double the minimum wage, which is only enough to cover basic needs. Again, this trend was exacerbated during the recovery from the recession of the late 1990s, as less than 37 percent of the workforce was earning less than double the minimum wage in 2002 (*Santiago Times*, December 8, 2005). More than 30 percent of the workforce was still in the informal sector as of 2006 (OECD 2009, 42), and they tended to paid the lowest. For example, in 2003, 36 percent of all workers had no contract, up from 33 percent in 1990. This represented 68 percent of all low-paid workers, a percentage that was almost double the 36 percent of low-income workers without contracts in 1990 (Muñoz Goma 2007, 217).

Having a contract, however, is often only marginally better than being in the informal sector. In 2004, 35 percent of employment contracts signed each year had a duration of less than six months, while another 30 percent lasted for less than a year (Muñoz Goma 2007, 217). From 1996 to 2000, 35 percent of workers who were employed during at least one of two trimesters either changed employment or became unemployed from one trimester to the next (Henríquez and Uribe-Echevarría 2004, 41). Not surprisingly, this was markedly worse when unemployment was rising, although the magnitude of the change is startling. From April–June 1998 through October–December 2000, 78 percent of the workforce either changed position or employment status, and almost 40 percent experienced three or more changes during the eighteen-month period (Henríquez and Uribe-Echevarría 2004, 63). Again, the poor were generally most affected. This is particularly clear when looking at the impact of educational levels on job security. A study by Helia Henríquez and Verónica Uribe-Echevarría (2004, 77) found that 60 percent of workers with higher education remained employed for the entire period, April–June 1998 through October–December 2000, compared to 38.3 percent of workers who did not complete primary school, 43.5 percent who had completed primary school, and 35.3 for workers with a secondary education. Workers with secondary and higher education dominated the formal sector, while those with less education tended to be in informal sector.[16]

Employment instability has consequences that go beyond loss of income. For many workers with high credit card debts and mortgages, their inability to keep up on payments can be devastating.[17] More seriously, employment instability has significant long-term consequences for workers' retirement. Approximately half the workforce in 2006 did not participate in the social security system or did not accumulate enough funds to generate a minimum pension ($140/month) (*New York Times*, December 31, 2006; see also OECD 2009, 45).

All of these problems—informality, employment instability, and low wages—impact women and youth more severely than men. Unemployment among youth (fifteen- to twenty-four years old), for example, typically is three times that of adults (De la Maza 2004, 111). Between 2003 and 2005, when the economy was again growing, the level of youth unemployment increased 2.9 to 3.2 times the level experienced by adults (Reinecke and Velasco 2006, 3). For women, relative unemployment increased from 1.2 to 1.4 times the level for men during the same period (Reinecke and Velasco 2006, 4).

Employment insecurity both reflects and reinforces the weakness of organized labor in Chile. Although the Pinochet-era labor law has been reformed several times since the return to democracy, the trade union movement remains weak and fragmented. The percentage of the workforce belonging to unions was 9.7 percent in 1985 and grew yearly until it peaked at 15.1 percent in 1991. Since then, the percentage of the workforce belonging to unions declined each year, reaching a low for the democratic period of 10.7 percent in 1999. It has risen since, reaching 11.6 percent in 2004. At the same time, however, the number of trade unions has increased from 7,707 in 1991 to 9,414 in 2004, resulting in a decline of average union size from ninety-one members in 1991 to seventy-two in 2004 (Salinero B. 2006, 55). The consequences of this fragmentation for the capacity of unions to engage in collective bargaining are exacerbated by Pinochet-era restrictions on interfirm collective bargaining, as well as by various strains in the relationship between the union rank and file and the leaders of the principal peak labor organization, the United Workers Central (Central Unitaria de Trabajadores, CUT) (De la Maza 2004).[18] Various efforts have been made to promote tripartite negotiations between the government, business groups, and organized labor, but such efforts have generally been unsuccessful (Muñoz Goma 2007, 226–32).[19] As Lagos himself explained to the leaders of the developed countries attending the June 2000 Third Way conference convened by German prime minister Gerhard Schroeder in Berlin, "I told them, you have strong unions that negotiate for your workers. But in our (underdeveloped) countries, characterized by weak unions, who can negotiate on behalf of the worker?" (*Santiago Times,* June 6, 2000).

Structurally, economic insecurity in Chile is intrinsically linked to high levels of economic inequality. Prior to the 1972 military coup, the average Gini coefficient for the Greater Santiago Metropolitan Region was 0.48. This increased sharply from 1974 to 1986, as a result of the military regime's economic policies, peaking in at 0.570 in the period 1987–90, just before the return to democracy with its concomitant increases in social expenditures and economic growth (calculated from Laraña 2001, 305).[20] Since then, however, income inequality has remained historically high. Despite the dramatic decrease in poverty rates, income inequality as measured by the Gini coefficient actually increased until 2003, when it dropped below the 1990 level for the first time (see table 4.1). As Altimir (1998, 15) notes, "Seventeen years after the first reforms and seven after the second round of reforms—and after a profound restructuring—income inequalities are still clearly wider than before structural adjustment, and they are not being reduced by sustained growth."

Even when inequality began to demonstrate some improvement, the total net income of the richest 10 percent of households in 2003 was still greater than the

Table 4.1. Income inequality

Year	Gini coefficient	Income share of households			
		Lowest 40%	Next 30%	Next 20%	Highest 10%
1990	0.554	13.2	20.8	25.3	40.7
1998	0.560	13.0	20.4	26.6	40.0
2000	0.564	13.5	20.5	25.3	40.7
2003	0.552	13.8	20.8	25.6	39.8
2006	0.552	14.6	21.6	26.7	37.1

Source: Data from CEPAL (2009b, 56, 8).

total income of the poorest 80 percent (López and Miller 2008). In fact, it was not until 2006 that the per capita income for the poorest 20 percent of families increased at a faster rate than the national average; from 1996 through 2000 it increased at half the national average (*La Tercera,* June 25, 2007). For these reasons, as Garretón (2007, 87) notes, enduring high levels of inequality remain "the principal Achilles heel of Chilean society."

There are several reasons for this, including the weakness of the labor movement (Robinson 2003). Intergenerational social mobility is very low, which reflects, among other factors, inequality in educational outcomes (Nuñez and Risco 2004). More important, however, are the limits to the institutional capacity of the state to directly affect the actual distribution of income. Even the region's most effective social policies are insufficient for reversing high levels of inequality due to their targeted nature. Only 19 percent of Chile's dramatic reduction in poverty levels from 1990 to 2006 can be attributed to the distributive effect of social policies (CEPAL 2009b, 18). This structural problem is only reinforced by Chile's taxation system, which effectively prevents expanding social policies from affecting redistribution. Limited changes to the Pinochet-era tax system mean that personal and corporate income taxes are low and the state has not been able to capture a significant portion of the revenues generated through natural resource exports. As a consequence, Chile has been forced to rely on one of the highest value-added tax rates in the world (19 percent), which tends to be regressive (López and Miller 2008). Yet significant tax reform is not something the Concertación, and much less the parties of the Right, are willing to consider (Garretón 2007). As Cristian Pizarro Allard, then a senior official in Chile's Confederación de la Producción y del Comercio (Production and Commerce Confederation, CPC), a principal representative of business groups, explains,

> Chile must choose between combating poverty and improving the distribution of income. The ideal is to achieve both together, but we do not think it is possible to do so. On an ethical, political, and social level, it is

better to deal with poverty first, then inequality. . . . The country cannot ignore this because it will affect global indicators. . . . In a country like Chile,
the gap between executive salaries and workers will not be so great. More
important is what workers can do with their salary—eat or not eat, have a
roof over their heads or not. . . . This can be achieved through growth and
targeting of social expenditures. When this is resolved, then we can deal
with the distribution issue. . . . The criticism about the distribution is a
means to find problems with the economic model. It is an effort to provide
a bad cure for a disease that might exist. (Personal interview, Santiago,
December 2, 1995)

Given that Chile has enjoyed record lows in poverty rates for some time, and has
had two socialist presidents, one can only wonder when the time will be right to
address issues of distribution.

Privatized Education and the Segmentation of Chile's Social Structure

Changes in the educational system introduced by the Pinochet regime in many
ways represent the quintessence of neopluralism and citizenship as consumption. The system was institutionalized with the Ley Orgánica Constitucional de
Enseñanza (Organic Constitutional Law for Education, LOCE), one of the last
major pieces of legislation enacted by the military regime in 1990. The most important aspects of the new structure were decentralization at the municipal level
and the creation of a three-tiered system composed of private schools, private
schools that receive state subsidies, and public schools. Following the neopluralist norm that market principles should guide the provision of basic public services, the new system was based on the belief that competition would improve
the overall quality of education by rewarding the schools that provided the best
educational outcomes and ensuring that schools unable to meet minimal quality standards would close due to lack of student demand. While this seems logi-
cal in theory, in practice the result has been an unprecedented impoverishment
of public education that both reflects and further reinforces high levels of social
inequality.

State subsidies to private schools are not new in Chile. They were first established in 1951. What is new is that that they are now equal to the amount
spent per pupil in public schools, whereas before subsidies to private schools
had been capped at 25 percent of costs in the public system. This surge in resources to private schools was reinforced when the LOCE was amended to
allow public schools and private schools receiving government subsidies to
charge co-payments, provided a majority of the parents or guardians of the students agreed. A full 72 percent of subsidized private schools now charge such
co-payments, compared to just 6 percent of public schools. As a result of this

combined windfall, enrollment in private schools skyrocketed from 20 percent in 1980 to approximately 50 percent now (Franco 2008, 1–4).[21]

A direct consequence of these changes is that Chile's school system has become stratified by social class, with the private, nonsubsidized schools being attended almost exclusively by the children of the wealthiest segments of society and the poor attending public schools because they are effectively the supplier of last resort. A recent international study of educational inequality carried out by the Universidad de Chile (University of Chile) concluded that "Chile's educational system ranked as the 'top most economically segregated' system among 40 countries." As Juan Pablo Valenzuela, one of the study's authors, explains, this is in large part because "the poorest schools have the highest drop-out rates, lowest parent involvement and least qualified teachers" (*Santiago Times*, April 8, 2008).

This structural inequality is reflected in several aspects of the system that tend to further reinforce the problem. The principal cause is levels of funding (Franco 2008; López and Miller 2008). Although successive democratic governments have increased funding for education fivefold to 3.7 percent of GDP in 2005, Chile still has among the lowest levels of expenditure on a per student basis (López and Miller 2008, 2682–83). Private schools can compensate for this, and in fact spend approximately four times more per student than the public sector (López and Miller 2008, 2693). For example, while both subsidized private schools and public schools can charge co-payments, very few public schools do, and the amount they charge—an average of less than five U.S. dollars per month in 2004—pales by comparison to what subsidized private schools charge, which was more than twenty-six dollars per month in 2004 (Franco 2008, 9). The consequences of this are exacerbated by the fact that the costs entailed in educating children from the poorest segments of society are greater given the lack of resources they enjoy outside the school (Franco 2008).

At the same time, children from lower-income families are largely excluded from the private sector. Geography is important, and subsidized private schools are found in only 6 percent of low-income zones, making transportation an additional barrier to their admission (Franco 2008, 6). But the ultimate barrier for children from lower-income families is that the private schools must agree to admit applicants, and they rarely admit lower-income students. While competition should in theory have led to an increase in equality and quality of educational opportunities, instead it has served to further concentrate economic resources among the relatively well-off.

This inequality is evident in the quality of education received by children in public schools. Studies by the World Bank (*Santiago Times*, July 2, 2008), the Inter-American Development Bank (October, 28, 2008), the Organisation for Economic Co-operation and Development (March 12, 2009), and, most recently, the Universidad Diego Portales (May 18, 2009) all conclude that Chile's public education system underperforms compared to other countries, both in and out of the region. Within Chile, this translates into an extreme skewing of university admissions toward the children of higher-income families. Admission into public and the best private universities in Chile is dependent on a student's performance on the Prueba de Selección Universitaria (University Selection Exam, PSU). Of the fifty-five secondary schools with the highest combined scores on the 2008 PSU, fifty-three were nonsubsidized private schools. The highest-scoring public school, which came in seventh place, was also the country's oldest secondary school, the Instituto Nacional José Miguel Carrera. One other public elementary school, the Liceo Carema Carvajal, came in at number thirty. Not coincidentally, both public schools were also in the relatively well-off Providencia sector of Santiago (*Santiago Times,* May 18, 2009). The findings from a recent survey of students from four hundred high schools illustrate the nature of the problem: "public school students had studied less than 30 percent of the material covered in the language portion of the PSU, while private school students had reviewed 63 percent. In the math exam, public school students had studied 50 percent of the material and the private schools 75 percent. Subsidized school students had scores between these extremes: they had reviewed 50 percent of the language material and 63 percent of the math material" (December 1, 2009).

The ultimate consequences of segmentation can be observed in the rates of school completion since the return to democracy. While there has been a noticeable improvement for all income groups, the poorest 60 percent of the population clearly lags behind the richest 40 percent, particularly regarding higher education, where even the middle quintile's participation rate is less than half the top quintile's and 30 percent lower than the next highest quintile's (see table 4.2). The implications of this for Chile's capacity to lower inequality in the long term are quite serious, given that the return in terms of income is 22 percent for higher education, compared with 10 percent for secondary education and just 3.5 percent for elementary education (Muñoz Goma 2007, 212).

Crime and Citizen Insecurity

Chile is generally considered the among the safest countries in Latin America, yet fear of crime is consistently among the three most important problems Chileans identified in public opinion polls since the democratic transition.[22] It is the number one concern of Chileans since the June–July 2005 poll conducted by the Centro de Estudios Públicos (2010), even during 2009 recession.

While problems of crime are widespread in the region and directly associated with neopluralism, Chile stands out from the rest of Latin America in several respects. The strength of its state institutions means that public confidence in the judiciary and police are relatively quite high (Dammert 2009, 246). The level

Table 4.2.   Levels of education by income

Income quintile	Preprimary education		Primary and lower-secondary education		Upper-secondary education		Higher education	
	1990	2006	1990	2006	1990	2006	1990	2006
First	17.0	38.0	95.6	98.4	73.8	87.7	4.4	19.8
Second	17.6	39.2	96.9	99.0	77.1	90.9	7.7	25.1
Third	20.8	44.3	97.7	99.2	80.6	93.4	12.4	33.3
Fourth	27.0	46.4	97.5	99.6	87.0	97.3	22.0	47.2
Fifth	32.5	52.0	98.9	99.6	94.5	97.6	40.7	67.1
Total population	21.0	42.4	96.9	99.0	80.8	92.4	16.2	38.7

SOURCE: Data from OECD (2009, 51).

of crime has undoubtedly gone up, but the lack of comparable data makes it difficult to know by how much. In sharp contrast to many other countries, criminal violence is quite low (Garro 1999, 237). These differences in comparison to the rest of the region make the similarities that much more important from the perspective of understanding neopluralism's impact on democratic politics and citizenship.

As Lucía Dammert (2009, 240) notes, "fear has become one of the most transcendental public policy problems of the last decade." As early as 1998—before Chile's first posttransition economic recession—there was growing concern regarding of this widespread problem. For example, in the 2006 Encuesta Nacional Urbana de Seguridad Ciudadana (National Urban Survey of Citizen Security, ENUSC), which is carried out by the Interior Ministry, 38.4 percent of households reported that at least one person was a victim of a crime (Dammert 2009, 237). While this is certainly significant, the actual level of public concern with crime seems to be much greater than one would expect. This was clear in the 1998 Chilean Human Development Report (PNUD 1998, 7–8). Almost 80 percent of respondents to the national survey conducted for the report felt it likely that within the next year they would be the victim of robbery in a public space, and 60 percent feared they would be robbed in their home. Such fears, however, seemed far removed from reality in that over the previous twelve months, only 17.4 percent of the respondents reported that they or someone in their household had been robbed in the street without violence, and 6 percent said they or a family member were robbed in a public place in a violent act. Only 6 percent of respondents reported that they or a family member had been robbed in their home. While incidence of crime seemed to be greater in 2006, the reported level of concern in the ENUSC still seemed unusually high. More than 50 percent of Chileans felt that they would be a victim of crime and 59 percent felt it was likely someone would break into their home to rob them. Of even more concern was the finding that 23.3 percent of Chileans felt uncomfortable walking alone in their own neighborhood at night, and 5 percent were too afraid to even go out at night (Dammert 2009, 241–44; see also Dammert and Malone 2003).

While there are many reasons for this exaggerated fear of crime, including the media's sensationalism, it is fundamentally conditioned by neopluralism. Insecurity due to economic change and the privatization of health care and social security, including unequal opportunities to access education and health services—the hallmarks of neopluralist democracy—are among the most important reasons for this problem (PNUD 1998). Similarly, despite Chileans' relatively high level of respect for the police and judiciary, a certain marketization of the rule of law is noticeable, and Chileans have responded to this fear in much the same way as other Latin Americans. On average, less than 40 percent of all crimes are reported (Dammert 2009, 238–39). For those with resources, solutions including alarms, security fences, and private guards have been taken by 37.6 percent of the population, according to the 2006 ENUSC. Propelled by the political Right, there is also substantial support for more police and stiffer punishments (Dammert 2009). This is one reason why Chile consistently has the highest rate of incarceration (318 per 100,000 residents) in Latin America, reflecting a 70 percent rise in the prison population over the past decade to nearly 54,000 (*Santiago Times*, October 13, 2009). The failure of all these efforts to reverse public fear only underscores the tendency for the marketization of the rule of law and repressive police practices to create a vicious cycle. Not surprisingly, the dominance of neopluralism in the political system has also meant that civil society's role in addressing the problem of raising crime rates has been minimal (De la Maza 2004; Espinoza 2004). Of course, this is also part of neopluralism's fourth challenge to citizenship.

Neopluralism and the Crisis of Representation

In comparison to the rest of Latin America, it may appear to be an exaggeration to label the current system of representation as "in crisis." From the perspective of citizenship as agency, this crisis of representation takes place on two levels: (1) political representation at the level of the regime and the political party system and (2) the level of civil society. Both are problematic under neopluralism, and Chile stands out because of the historical strength of its political party system. The fact that political parties are strongly institutionalized and span the left-right spectrum means that Chile has a unique potential in Latin America for fostering state-society synergy and citizenship as agency. Ironically, the very strength of the political parties and the lessons learned from both the breakdown of democracy in the early 1970s and prolonged military rule make it difficult to realize that potential. The "crisis" reflects lost opportunities.

As table 4.3 shows, while the majority of Chileans firmly believe in democracy, this belief belies potentially serious problems with the way Chilean democracy works in practice. Since 1995 a clear majority has been less than satisfied with the governments they elect. While a small minority (16.7 percent) in the surveys agreed that authoritarian governments can be preferable under certain circumstances, a more significant group (28.1 percent) felt it made no difference if the government were democratic or not. More troubling for democracy's long-term future, the country seems roughly split, according to the survey, on the issue of whether an authoritarian government would be justified if it resolved economic problems. Most tellingly, from 2004 to 2008 on average almost three-quarters of the population felt that "the country was run for the benefit of powerful interests." In 2002, for example, Chile was the only country in the Latinobarómetro polls where the majority surveyed felt that the private sector was responsible for economic policy. A 2001 survey conducted by the United Nations Development Program similarly found that "80 percent of the people interviewed felt that politicians did not worry about the problems of the people" (Ortega 2006, 1). Perhaps for this reason, the Latinobarómetro polls in 2008 (the only year the question was asked) found that just 24.7 percent of the population felt that democracy lowered inequality, while 56.9 percent felt it left it unchanged and 18.3 percent felt inequality was actually increased by democracy. Increasingly, eligible voters, particularly among the young, are simply refusing to even register to vote (Navia 2010).

Not surprisingly, a large majority of those surveyed in the Latinobarómetro polls did not trust either political parties or Congress. As shown in table 4.4, using World Value Survey results, both have suffered the steepest decline in levels of public trust of any institution. By way of comparison, the church, the armed forces, and the press enjoyed substantially higher levels of public trust than political parties and Congress in 2000. Even big business enjoyed significantly higher levels of public confidence, despite the fact that Chile was only just beginning to recover from its first recession since the democratic transition.

At least initially, one reason for these problems of political representation was the so-called authoritarian enclaves in the 1980 constitution. People's frustrations were only compounded by a noticeable lack of change after the return to democracy. This stagnation included Pinochet's continued political presence, first as commander in chief of the army and then as senator for life, as well as the veto role played by conservative-designated senators and right-wing political parties, which are overrepresented in the legislature due to Chile's binomial electoral system (Siavelis 2000).[23] Yet these authoritarian enclaves were gradually eliminated, and with the 2005 constitutional amendments, only the binomial electoral system remained as the most significant obviously authoritarian institutional constraint in the constitution.

Table 4.3. Public perceptions of Chilean democracy (%)

Question[a]	1995	1996	1997	1998	2000	2001	2002	2003	2004	2005	2006	2007	2008	Avg.
Support for democracy														
Democracy is preferable	54.4	55.9	62.8	53.6	55.3	48.6	53.2	52.5	58.5	62.5	58.9	47.8	53.8	55.2
Under some circumstances, an authoritarian government can be preferable	19.3	20.0	16.5	16.5	17.9	20.8	15.2	14.6	14.2	11.4	14.0	21.7	14.5	16.7
It does not matter	26.3	24.1	20.7	29.9	26.8	30.5	31.7	32.9	27.3	26.1	27.1	30.5	31.7	28.1
Satisfaction with democracy														
Very satisfied	5.6	3.5	6.3	4.4	6.1	3.9	3.4	4.6	3.5	7.8	4.3	3.8	4.6	4.8
Rather satisfied	28.9	24.9	31.8	28.4	28.2	20.6	25.6	29.6	38.6	37.5	39.6	34.2	35.1	31.0
Not very satisfied	51.1	55.7	46.1	49.4	48.9	50.3	54.5	47.1	45.0	39.3	44.4	47.7	44.4	48.0
Not at all satisfied	14.5	15.9	15.8	17.8	16.7	25.3	16.5	18.7	12.9	15.3	11.7	14.3	15.9	16.3
How the country is governed														
For the benefit of the powerful	...	...	...	...	...	...	...	...	73.8	68.1	71.9	76.5	75.8	73.2
For the good of all	...	...	...	...	...	...	...	...	26.2	31.9	28.1	23.5	24.2	26.8
I would not mind a nondemocratic government if it could solve economic problems[b]														
Strongly agree	...	...	...	...	...	...	11.8	15.9	13.0	...	...	...	19.7	15.1
Agree	...	...	...	...	...	...	42.7	41.5	34.5	...	...	...	35.8	38.6
Disagree	...	...	...	...	...	...	30.8	28.0	37.7	...	...	...	29.9	31.6
Strongly disagree	...	...	...	...	...	...	14.7	14.5	14.8	...	...	...	14.5	14.6

continued

Table 4.3. Public perceptions of Chilean democracy (%)   (continued)

Question[a]	1995	1996	1997	1998	2000	2001	2002	2003	2004	2005	2006	2007	2008	Avg.
Confidence in political parties														
A lot of confidence	4.6	2.7	6.8	3.1	3.1	2.9	1.2	0.3	1.8	0.8	2.6	1.6	0.9	2.5
Some confidence	28.9	25.7	28.8	22.0	18.7	19.8	11.7	13.3	18.4	16.4	21.9	19.0	15.4	20.0
Little confidence	37.3	37.5	38.0	35.6	29.9	38.7	26.2	35.8	42.8	43.7	35.4	38.8	42.7	37.1
No confidence at all	29.2	34.1	26.4	39.3	48.3	38.7	61.0	50.6	37.0	39.1	40.0	40.7	40.9	40.4
Confidence in Congress														
A lot of confidence	10.2	6.4	12.9	7.3	9.5	5.1	3.1	1.1	3.0	4.8	3.5	2.9	1.9	5.5
Some confidence	38.2	36.9	42.0	34.2	29.0	28.1	28.8	21.9	27.7	33.4	27.7	27.7	31.0	31.3
Little confidence	35.7	37.0	34.3	37.6	33.9	43.4	35.0	39.4	44.5	43.1	39.8	41.4	43.9	39.2
No confidence at all	15.9	19.7	10.8	20.8	27.6	23.4	33.1	37.6	24.9	18.6	29.0	28.1	23.3	24.1

SOURCE: Data from Latinobarómetro (2009a).

[a] Questions may be paraphrased.

[b] Question not asked in all years.

Table 4.4.   Trust in institutions

Institution	Percentage of population expressing a high level of trust		
	1990	2000	Change
Church	76	78	+2
Armed forces	40	48	+8
The press	43	48	+5
Unions	47	46	-1
Police	59	55	-4
Congress	63	35	-28
Public administration	49	40	-9
Government	59	58	-1
Political parties	50	28	-22
Big business	53	50	-3

SOURCE: World Value Survey results reported in Segovia (2009, 212).

Without minimizing the importance of the constitutional reforms implemented since the 1988 plebiscite, it is important to recognize that the representational gap reflects how neopluralism has distorted Chilean politics. For example, state reforms and globalization have complicated "things tremendously for political parties because they deliver [results] through the state and not private enterprise. . . . How can one be a senator with a weak state and a lot of demands, but little power?" (Sergio Bitar, former senator, personal interview, Santiago, August 14, 2000).

More important, Chile's so-called democracy by agreements has defined the political process since the return to democracy. Party elites remain responsible for reaching a consensus on virtually all major political decisions before submitting them to public judgment. The moderation and need to subordinate civil society mobilization to preserve elite agreements, a lesson learned in the late 1980s, continues to condition democratic politics. Excessive participation was seen as the problem earlier, and Chile's political elites are still determined to keep it at a minimum (De la Maza 2010). This has disconnected parties from their mass base in unprecedented ways. As former senator Sergio Bitar notes, "political parties are in a crisis because they are not with civil society" (personal interview, Santiago, August 14, 2000). Similarly, as the then leader of the United Workers Central and Christian Democrats, Miguel Vega, recognized relatively early on,

> There we have a problem, and it is not only with the [P]DC, but in general. If there is a social strata that has remained behind [since the transition], it is the political parties. . . . They listen to our critiques of the parties— we've strongly criticized the PDC for its lack of interest in developing

the strength of civil society. A party without roots in society cannot deal with all social problems because it will not know what they are. Intellectual parties are no good. . . . They produce tendencies or sensibilities or "partisan machines" that are not in agreement with what the social base thinks. . . . They are professional politicians. If [labor leaders] were dedicated 100 percent to politics, we would do it better than them! We have ties to society, more legitimacy. All they do is politics. (Personal interview, Santiago, December 27, 1995)

This problem of being disconnected from civil society has not gone unnoticed by the Concertación since 2000. Increasing citizen participation was a major policy objective of Ricardo Lagos, Chile's first socialist president since Allende, and initially was an even more central concern of his successor, Michelle Bachelet, who also is a socialist. Even earlier, the Citizen Council for the Strengthening of Civil Society (Consejo Ciudadano para la Fortalecimiento de la Sociedad Civil) was convened by the government of Eduardo Frei in the late 1990s and concluded in its final report that a new state-society synergy was needed: "a new culture needs to be promoted in the management of government funds and programs that is centered on the creation of strategic alliances between public and private actors, with the goal of expanding the coverage and quality of work of the work of civil society organizations" (quoted in De la Maza 2005, 77).

Yet the actual policies that have been implemented to increase participation have been minimal and largely limited to helping to employ policies decided by the political elite (De la Maza 2010; Navia 2010; Valdés 2010). As Garretón (2003, 177) warns, Chile needs "a considerable shift in the socioeconomic, political, and cultural model to mobilize and harness the social energies of this country. Without these forces, the erosion, banality, and irrelevance of politics will become inevitable, which surely will affect the legitimacy of the country's democracy."

Even if Chile's political elites were willing to share power with civil society, civil society is unable to fill this representational void because it remains weak and fragmented. One reason for this is an exaggerated sense of citizen insecurity (PNUD 1998), as well as the impact of economic insecurity (De la Maza 2005). Both are clear reflections of neopluralism's negative impact on the development of civil society. As Garretón (2003, 175) again warns, the challenge this poses is serious because "what is at stake in the coming years is forming the country into a community worth living in, rather than a territory and a space for individual and family consumption."

The constraints on civil society's development go beyond these general threats to people's sense of security. They reflect more specific patterns of state-society relations that are themselves conditioned by neopluralism and citizenship as consumption. Despite continued declarations by political parties and their leaders on the need for greater autonomous participation by civil society dating back to the mid-1980s (Oxhorn 1995b), the scope for such participation remains quite narrow. In what Julia Paley (2001) describes as the "paradox of participation," Chilean participation has more to do with the execution of programs than with their design or evaluation, and much less with an actual discussion of broader policies or priorities (see also De la Maza 2005; Espinoza 2004). Institutions that would allow for such influence generally do not exist (Garretón 2007). When they are proposed, they generally remain hollow shells, lacking the necessary institutional linkages with actual decision making to be effective. This was the case with the 1999 law mandating new mechanisms for local citizen participation (De la Maza 2005), as well as President Lagos's Citizen Participation Project (Proyecto de Participación Ciudadano) (Garretón 2007).

As part of the Citizen Participation Project, government ministries were requested to provide proposals for increasing citizen participation. Out of the 106 reported initiatives, 23.6 percent did not actually involve citizen participation. The rest generally reflected plans to create the conditions for participation rather than actually increase it, for example, by improving intergovernmental coordination, promoting participation campaigns, and increasing contact with people through the use of information technology. While 50 percent could be characterized as actually involving increased participation, on a 9-point scale (with 9 reflecting citizen control) the highest score was below 4.5. Only 18.9 percent of the proposals dealt with more advanced forms of participation, such as support for organizations, networks, or working groups. Increasing contact with service users was addressed in 17.9 percent of the proposals. Only 10.4 percent considered representation of the users in the formulation, design, or implementation of public policies (Espinoza 2004, 155–57). The severe shortcomings of all of these efforts led President Bachelet to announce her Pro-Citizen Participation Agenda (Agenda Pro Participación Ciudadana) 2006–10, and while she did open some potential new spaces for citizen participation, her initiative largely failed to change the overall pattern of state-society relations in Chile (De la Maza 2010; Navia 2010; Valdés 2010).

These general problems are clearest in the two institutions explicitly designed to allow for citizen participation: neighborhood councils (*juntas de vecinos*) and Community Economic and Social Councils (Consejo Económico-Social Comunal, CESCO). Neighborhood councils were first established in the mid-1960s as part of President Frei's Revolution in Liberty reforms. Although they were increasingly becoming the battlegrounds for political party infighting, particularly in the poblaciones, and directly contributed to polarization of Chilean society as a result (Oxhorn 1995b), the neighborhood councils were important loci for local participation. The military regime changed this by allowing for the organization of multiple neighborhood councils in the same community. This had the effect of diluting each council's available resources and political influence, at the same time that it increased competition among different groups within the same community. This further fragmented civil society and encouraged people to pursue their own narrower personal interests rather than any sense of community public good. This was, of course, precisely the Pinochet government's goal, and when changes were made to the law governing neighborhood councils in 1996, the Constitutional Tribunal declared the ban on multiple neighborhood councils in the same community to be unconstitutional (De la Maza 2005; Posner 2004). At the same time, neighborhood councils have no formal role in local political decision making and few people actually bother to participate in them. An average of less than 2 percent of eligible voters participate in elections for local neighborhood councils (Posner 1999).

Perhaps in recognition of the limited social legitimacy of the neighborhood councils, the CESCO was created in 1992 by the new democratic government. CESCOs are intended to allow grassroots organizations to work with municipal governments by providing an arena for local input on policy. Like the neighborhood councils, they have no formal role and at best serve only an advisory function. While they are supposed to be elected by the communities they represent, CESCOs ultimately are no more representative than the neighborhood councils and their limited influence is dependent on the goodwill of the mayor (Barozet 2005; De la Maza 2005; Greaves 2004; Posner 2004).

Neopluralism is in many ways epitomized by a wide variety of competitions that various Chilean state departments conduct to finance civil society organizations. While this can lead to important innovations, it also has intrinsic limitations consistent with a neopluralist pattern of state-society relations (Barozet 2005; De la Maza 2004, 2005; Espinoza 2004). Limited resources mean that organizations compete with one another for access to them, fragmenting civil society. Because the state sets the terms of the competition, the autonomy of the organizations is limited in terms of their ability to represent the interests and priorities of their members. These competitions also necessarily favor organizations with the capacity to elaborate project proposals, further fragmenting civil society.

Ultimately, participation is "more instrumental than empowering" (Espinoza 2004, 155). More recent programs, like President Lagos's 2001 program for addressing extreme poverty, Chile Solidario (Chile Solidarity), give assistance directly to individual families, sidestepping issues of community organization and the strengthening of civil society (De la Maza 2004). At the same time, access to resources opens the door to new forms of clientelism and dependence on the state, with mayors playing increasingly dominant roles (Barozet 2005; De la Maza 2005, 2004). As the then CUT official Carlos Cantador noted, "pobladores can resolve only small, local problems working with the mayor. There are few opportunities for civil society to influence, to participate, in resolving larger national problems. . . . It is not because civil society does not want to participate, but there are no mechanisms for it" (personal interview, Santiago, June 27, 1996).

Similarly, former director of the Chile Human Development Report, Eugenio Ortega (2006, 6), observes that "the privatization of life is a reality that in some manner affects the gap between politics and society." At best, civil society is "a sum of legitimate particular interests, often contradictory among themselves" rather than a "space for the negotiation of the general interest" (Garretón 2007, 95). Participation in civil society is "purely instrumental, fragmented, without networks, targeted at the poorest and dependent on public funds" (De la Maza 2010). The extreme imbalance "between social organizations, especially the most vulnerable sectors, and the most powerful actors that are active in the economy, the de facto powers, not only appears not to have diminished but has become worse. This means that the weakened social actors are seen as being obligated to adopt as their only task their own particular problems" (Garretón 2007, 89).

While the emphasis here has been on disadvantaged sectors of society, it is also important to underscore the importance of business sectors willing to work with civil society and the state for achieving citizenship as agency. This is central to the dispersion of power that strong civil societies represent and is essential for reversing structural inequality. The absence of such business sectors reflects the nature of neopluralism. As Garretón (2007, 85) stresses, "Chile lacks a business class that is responsible, not for profits at any cost or its non-economic whims, but to the country . . . as an agent of development in permanent cooperation . . . with the state."

The complexity of the shortcomings in state-civil society relations can be seen in the failed attempts to overcome decades of economic stagnation in Arica, a port city on Chile's northern border with Peru and Bolivia. Arica was a classic example of the success that import substitution industrialization provided much of Chile in the postwar period (Bitar 2001). In the late 1950s the port was designated a free port (*puerto libre*), allowing for the importation of products either banned or with high tariffs in the rest of the country, while local production was protected from competition. The result was the growth of the electronics and automobile industries. All of this ended with the coup, when state protection was removed. Given growing tensions with Peru, the military chose to invest resources in Iquique, which was farther down the coast from the border, with the creation of a free trade zone in 1975 (Alfredo Navarrete, personal interview, Iquique, July 22, 2001; see also Bitar 2001). The combination resulted in decades of economic decline in Arica.

As a result of local mobilization in the early 1990s (Julio Olivarez, local CUT president, personal interview, Arica, July 23, 2001), a Plan Arica was adopted by the Chilean legislature in 1996 and modified in 2000 (Bitar 2001). The central idea behind the legislation was to make Arica an international center that could capitalize on its location at the border of three countries—Chile, Bolivia, and Peru—through tax exemptions and credits, as well as a variety of investment subsidies to develop the region through trade (German Lafuente, head of the State Development Corporation office, personal interview, Arica, July 23, 2001; Bronia Castillo, governor of Arica, Arica, July 23, 2001). In particular, the goal was to turn the port into a major gateway for Brazilian exports and imports to and from the Pacific Rim. The plan also attempted to promote tourism, including ecotourism and tourism for the elderly, given the area's mild climate (wedged between the Pacific Ocean and Atacama Desert) and relative security (Jorge Aragón, president of the Tourist Board, personal interview, Arica, July 23, 2001).

Despite the best of intentions, the effort largely failed. The fundamental reason was the fragmentation of interests and the inability of Arica to create a "citizen commitment to the city" (Luis Le Blanc, general manager of the Center for the Promotion and Facilitation of Investment and former national representative for Arica, personal interview, Arica, July 23, 2001). As Le Blanc went on to explain, the law reflected "at least eight different perspectives. The government had to try and satisfy so many interests. . . . If there had been unity and one project, it would have been different. Each [group] had its own. Participation is good, but it must have direction. If everyone goes their own way, you can't satisfy everyone."

Although the state initiated the plan, it ultimately failed to assume sufficient leadership over its execution. As former senator for the region Sergio Bitar (2001, 7) noted, "there was a communications gap between government bureaucrats and social organizations, business groups and local political parties. The expectations of citizens were high, at the same time that bureaucratic inertia was strong." Local government was unable to fill this gap, lacking the resources (Industrial Association of Arica officials, personal interviews, Arica, July 24, 2001) and political will to even try (Jaime Masilla, vice mayor and head of planning, personal interview, Arica, July 24, 2001; Luis Le Blanc, Arica, July 23, 2001).

To succeed, substantial investment was needed. This was particularly true for upgrading the port. Although the port was still publicly owned, the state failed to provide funding, choosing to rely on private-sector investment instead (Industrial Association of Arica representatives, personal interviews, Arica, February 24, 2001). Unfortunately, private investors generally were uninterested (Eusebio Sankán, Port of Arica general manager, personal interview, Arica, July 24, 2001; Luis Le Blanc, Arica, July 23, 2001; Bronia Castillo, Arica, July 23, 2001). For this reason, the local CUT representatives concluded that the lack of development was the "fault of business" (Julio Olivarez, local CUT president, personal interview, Arica, July 23, 2001).

The lack of business investment had several causes, including the unwillingness of banks to make loans (Industrial Association of Arica officials, personal

interviews, Arica, July 24, 2001; Luis Le Blanc, Arica, July 23, 2001). In a kind
of catch-22, the markets were too small to provide sufficient returns, but without additional investments, they remained truncated. As an official from the
Industrial Association of Arica (Asociación de Industriales de Arica) pointed
out, "Not even 5 percent of our members can make due in Arica. The Arica
market does not produce anything for anyone" (personal interview, Arica, July
24, 2001). For this reason, businesses ultimately depended on their investments
outside of Arica for their profits (Jorge Aragón, personal interview, Arica, July
23, 2001; Jaime Masilla, Arica, July 24, 2001). Even when resources were obtained for investing in Arica, business used the funds for a quick profit (Luis
Tapia Rector, personal interview, University of Tarapaca, Arica, July 24, 2001) or
to finance their activities in Santiago (Industrial Association of Arica officials,
personal interviews, Arica, July 24, 2001).

Ironically, the problem also is the result of the legacy of ISI and state protection, which continues to create a business culture of dependence and a short-
term outlook (German Lafuente, head, Arica office of the State Development
Corporation, personal interview, Arica, July 23, 2001). As Le Blanc lamented,
"the locals are broken. They lack innovation and modernization. They do not
change" (personal interview, Arica, July 23, 2001). As the principal author of
the Plan Arica, Bitar (2001, 9) was forced to conclude, "there is not an entre-
preneurial potential, either political or financial, capable of propelling regional
development."

There have been some notable partial exceptions to this general lack of civil
society mobilization in Chile in recent years, particularly among subcontract
workers, some sectors of organized labor, and the Mapuche indigenous movement (De la Maza 2010). The most emblematic was the 2006 secondary school
movement. In many ways, it represented both the promise and limits of citizenship as agency in neopluralist democracy.

In May 2006 six hundred thousand high school students took to the streets
to demand fundamental changes to the Pinochet-era education law (LOCE).
Not only was this the largest mobilization since the transition to democracy, it
enjoyed tremendous support from other sectors of society, including students
from approximately one hundred private high schools—among the primary
beneficiaries of the current system—as well as the major university student associations (*Santiago Times*, various issues). The movement was also the first new
one to emerge since the transition; unlike other movements that were subordinated to political parties, the students became a referent for other social actors
in demanding that the state respond to their demands (Garretón 2007). According to Osvaldo Torres, city council member for the low-income municipality of
Peñalolen, their movement "transformed a fight for the defense of public education into a debate about the right to have quality public education" (*Santiago
Times*, June 13, 2006). The result was a new law, the General Education Law (Ley

General de Educación), which was enacted in 2009, based on recommendations from a special committee convened by President Bachelet.

While the new law added some important changes to the old LOCE system, including the introduction of municipal education boards that would incorporate community members as well as the mayor (*Santiago Times,* April 6, 2009), the General Education Law ultimately fell short in terms of its ability to fundamentally transform Chile's educational system and was widely criticized by both students and teachers alike. There were several reasons for this failure, including the weakening of the student movement after its initial success in forcing the government to commit itself to reform and the necessity of reaching a compromise with the Right in the Congress. More important, however, were the immense costs that any reform would necessarily entail to redress the imbalance between the public and private sectors. As Garretón (2007) stresses, it would require a radical reform of the tax system. Not only would the political Right refuse to support such a change, the students had ultimately lost the support of the average citizen and could not alter the reforms agreed upon by the political elite (De la Maza 2010). It was back to politics as usual and Chile's "democracy by agreements." Ironically, the protests may even have helped to further consolidate neopluralist democracy in Chile, as Patricio Navia (2010, 319) suggests: "The students' protests in 2006 turned public opinion against the idea of popular participation. [Bachelet's] critics found it easy to associate popular participation with protests, destruction and lawlessness. Inevitably, the commendable objective of strengthening civil society was associated with a soft hand that would bring about street demonstrations and would eventually end up undermining democracy."

Neopluralism and the Public Sphere: Chile's New Political Style

As a process of interest intermediation, neopluralism inevitably affects how politics is carried out. Undergirded by the nature of citizenship as consumption and the structural changes first introduced by the military regime, this new political style both reinforces the limits of Chile's democracy, at the same time that it makes overcoming them that much more difficult by diverting public attention away from their fundamental sources. The 1999–2000 Chilean presidential elections were a watershed in this regard.

Ricardo Lagos's electoral victory on January 16, 2000, was historic for a number of reasons, not least of which was the fact that a socialist would again occupy the La Moneda presidential palace. Lagos's victory was the third for the Concertación coalition since it spearheaded the transition to democracy in 1990 in a country historically marked by dramatic swings in governing party alliances from election to election. The 1999–2000 elections also marked the first time that the presidency was decided through a runoff election after no candidate won a majority of the vote in the December 1999 electoral contest. The runoff provision was included in the 1980 constitution as one of several institutional mechanisms established by the military regime in an effort to engineer a new political party system that would be dominated by two electoral blocs, if not parties. The closeness of both elections suggests that the military might have actually succeeded. In the December contest, Lagos narrowly beat the right-wing candidate, Joaquin Lavín, 48 to 47.5 percent. The outcome of the runoff was almost as close, with Lagos receiving 51.3 percent of the vote to Lavín's 48.7 percent. This polarization of the vote itself was also historic. Never before in Chile's modern history had a right-wing candidate received such a high percentage of the popular vote.

In some senses, the narrowness of Lagos's victory is not surprising. Chile had entered into its worst recession since the economic collapse of 1982. Unemployment had again reached double digits. To make matters worse, a prolonged drought had curtailed hydroelectric production, and Chileans were forced to endure blackouts and electricity rationing. The slow response by the Frei government to both problems fed growing perceptions that the government was not only lacking in initiative but also increasingly distant from the average person, given its excessively technocratic, probusiness policy style. For many, it seemed that after ten years in power, the Concertación was running out of new ideas and a change was needed. Lavín recognized this, successfully campaigning on the slogan ¡*Viva el cambio!* (Long live change!).

What is surprising is the swiftness of Lagos's electoral slide. Lagos had dominated national opinion polls as late as just six months before the first-round election. His apparent invincibility was underscored when he resoundingly defeated the PDC's presidential nominee Andres Zaldívar in a national primary election held in May 1999. Despite the PDC's clear organizational advantages over the PS and the PPD, which supported Lagos, 71 percent of the vote went to him. Within a matter of months, the race changed dramatically and became the closest electoral contest since the 1988 plebiscite that began the transition process. Although the personalities and styles of the two candidates certainly played a significant role, the election ultimately solidified a new style of engaging in politics that reflects the impact of neopluralism on Chile's public sphere.

In many ways, perhaps the most important factor is something that took place outside of Chile: Pinochet's detention by British authorities in London on October 16, 1998, for possible extradition to Spain to face trial for human rights abuses. Pinochet's detention and the drawn-out process through which he was eventually allowed to return to Chile in March 2000 put the issue of past human rights abuses squarely on the public agenda, yet had surprisingly little direct impact on the elections, although it led to a spate of judicial activity in defense of human rights.[24]

Given this context, the closeness of the 1999–2000 elections represents the first definitive break in the authoritarian-democracy cleavage that has characterized Chilean politics since at least the 1980s and that crystallized in the 1988 plebiscite, in which 54.68 percent of the electorate voted no (for democracy) and 43 percent voted yes (for continued authoritarianism) on a ballot to accept or reject Pinochet as the military junta's candidate for president. This general voting pattern held, particularly for the presidency, until Lavín broke the ceiling on votes for the Right in December 1999. The fact that this outcome came in the midst of the increasingly public demands for justice regarding past human rights abuses by a majority of Chileans demonstrates that the public has begun to disassociate their electoral choices from their views of the military regime. This is what both candidates sought as they deliberately tried to distance themselves from their pasts and proclaim their desire for human rights issues to be resolved by the courts. It is also consistent with the authoritarian elements of neopluralism.

The apparent consolidation of two voting blocs, the Center-Left Concertación and a Center-Right bloc, which during the Lavín campaign was called the Alliance for Chile (Alianza por Chile), also reflects the declining importance of ideology and party identities in Chilean politics. Even though the two candidates clearly were positioned on opposite ends of the political spectrum, the spectrum ultimately proved to be quite narrow, confirming a centering tendency in Chilean politics since the return to democracy (Scully 1992). The closeness of the election in which together the top two candidates nearly captured the entire vote before the runoff reflects the fact that they both received substantial support from most social stratums in Chilean society. This was not an ideologically charged campaign, and, in the key area of economic policy, the two candidates were not that far apart from one another.

This lack of ideology helps explain why Lagos was quickly able to win the support of a considerable number of Lavín's supporters after the intensely fought elections were over. Lagos consistently enjoyed very high levels of popular approval of 60 to 70 percent during his term of office, making him one of the most popular presidents since Chile's return to democracy. This is one more indicator of the declining level of identification with political parties and any ideological tendency since the return to democracy. By mid-1997 only 53 percent of the population identified with any particular political tendency, a sharp drop from the 68 percent who did so in mid-1990 and an even more marked contrast with the highly partisan nature of Chilean society before the coup (Siavelis 2000, 104). This suggests that the two blocs will remain fluid and ill-defined, with either of them capable of winning electoral majorities depending on the qualities of the individual candidate.[25]

If the substantive differences between Lagos and Lavín were less than might have been expected, the contrast in their campaign styles and the kind of relationship that they sought to establish with the electorate could not have been sharper. This contrast was in part generational, although the differences separating the two candidates in this regard were far greater than their fifteen-year age difference. Fundamentally, the sixty-one-year-old Lagos represented the kind of politics associated with Chile's rich democratic past, whereas the forty-six-year-old Lavín was a new kind of politician much more in tune with Chile's neopluralist democracy. As Gonzalo Cordero, a senior Lavín advisor, succinctly explained, "Lavín is a communicator. Lagos is an academic, more elitist" (personal interview, Santiago, July 19, 2001).

In the earlier period that came to a dramatic end in 1973, politics revolved around a strong centralized state and was orchestrated by equally strong, equally centralized political parties. These parties were closely identified with rigid ideological projects and dominated Chilean civil society, intensifying the dimension of social class in political identities. This system gave rise to Chile's infamous three-thirds voting pattern, in which the principal electoral tendencies were divided into roughly equal Right, Center, and Left tendencies. No single tendency could hope to win a majority, yet their ideological differences made effective coalitions and compromise increasingly difficult to achieve.

The radical reforms of the state and the economy instituted by the military regime, combined with its intense repression of all political activity, irrevocably undermined the foundations for this kind of politics. Global trends, particularly the end of the cold war and processes of globalization, accentuated this and contributed to the rise of neopluralism. The declining importance of political parties and ideologies, as the Chilean case clearly demonstrates, is one clear consequence of the new style of engaging in politics. Thus, even though the Chilean electorate is still divided, the consequences are very different. Instead of political stalemate and confrontation, the dominant political outcome has been, if not cooperation, inertia. Moreover, the largest group of voters by far identifies with no particular tendency, giving Chilean politics an unprecedented fluidity.

The role traditionally played by political parties and ideology has largely been replaced by the candidate's ability to personally connect with the people. The prestige of being chosen to lead powerful, well-organized parties in presidential elections no longer suffices to ensure voter allegiance. Lavín recognized this early on. He launched his national campaign with an unorthodox "Caminata por Chile" (Walk Through Chile) that brought him into direct contact with Chileans from all walks of life across the country's territorial expanse. Throughout the campaign, Lavín adopted an "anti-party and anti-politics stance that is popular with the Chilean right [and] played to a similar mood in a populace disillusioned with the limitations of Chilean democracy and the self-absorbed maneuvers of its increasingly distant political leaders" (Winn 2000, 7). Lavín's own advisor largely agreed, saying that Lavín is a political "actor who is close, in service to people, solving problems in a nonconfrontational style. . . . Lavín is not antiparty—he is a member of the Independent Democratic Union [UDI] and a honorary member of the National Renovation party [RN]—but represents modern politics: efficiency and the right priorities" (Gonzalo Cordero, personal interview, Santiago, August 18, 2000).

As a result of direct connection with the people, Lavín claimed to know their true problems better than Lagos and focused his electoral promises on issues of most concern to them. To buttress his claim to truly know what was on the average Chilean's mind, he announced with considerable fanfare in early June the results of a poll conducted on his behalf, which showed that voters were concerned most about jobs and crime, followed closely by education and child care. Based on this poll, Lavín then introduced a ten-point list of priorities for his government if elected—priorities that mirrored neopluralism's threat to democracy in surprising ways:

1. A job-creation program to be administered by municipal authorities
2. Construction of more secure prisons in isolated areas for the most serious offenders
3. Day-care subsidies for working women
4. Prearranged appointments to avoid lines at public clinics
5. Guaranteed student loans for high school students who achieve a minimum score on the national college entrance exams
6. Measures to eliminate delays in securing major surgery
7. More neighborhood police posts
8. Measures to increase the obligations of private health insurers in cases of catastrophic illness, old age, and periods of high unemployment when people may not be able to pay their premiums
9. More loan money for postsecondary education
10. A democracy tax to create a fund for popular initiatives

The results of Lavín's poll were hardly unexpected. They were very similar to those conducted by the respected Centro de Estudios Públicos in late April and early May of the same year (CEP 2000). What was unexpected is the degree to which Lavín explicitly tailored his platform to the polls—even if he never adequately explained how he would fund these initiatives given his commitment to fiscal restraint. By implication, Lavín was distinguishing himself from ten years of unresponsive Concertación government. His overriding message was that he would listen to the people, whereas the previous government and Lagos had not.

Lavín's approach proved particularly popular, especially among the poor. As Alejandro Herrera, then director of the Indigenous Studies Institute (Instituto de Estudios Indígenas) in Temuco, explained, "The Concertación has a discourse that is so general that it speaks to all of us, but no one specifically. Lavín [on the other hand], says peasants should receive ninety thousand pesos each month, according to the government. Have you received it? Why? Because the money goes to the friends of politicians, NGOs, family, political parties. . . . It appeals to each person in particular, rather than a discourse that talks about democracy, liberty" (personal interview, Temuco, August 23, 2000).

The reaction of the Lagos campaign helped Lavín succeed in getting this message across. Whereas Lavín sought to deal directly with the consequences of neopluralist democracy, Lagos sought to deal with their underlying structural sources at the political level. Lagos was certainly not insensitive to the concrete issues of most concern to the average voter, but his priorities appeared to be different.[26] For example, even though polling data consistently showed that Chileans were largely uninterested in constitutional changes to advance Chilean democratization, this remained a priority for Lagos. Contrasting the Concertación primary process with Lavín's poll, Lagos noted that "these are two different ways of listening to what people are saying. . . . The public is able to separate the wheat from the chaff. But why is it we are told [by Lavín] that we should only fight crime, and should not concern ourselves with the issue of designated senators. Let's get serious!" (*Santiago Times*, June 8, 1999).

Similarly, Lagos's approach to the economy appeared to be the polar opposite of Lavín's promise of change. His campaign slogan, *Crecimiento con igualdad* (Growth with equality), failed to capture the imagination of the average Chilean and seemed more like another iteration of the Concertación's original promise of neoliberalism with a "human face." The appeal of Lagos's promise was, ironically, limited by the legacy of the first Concertación government. Given the years of neglect under the military regime and his clear electoral mandate, the Aylwin government was able to increase social expenditures by 21 percent in real terms between 1990 and 1992 and witnessed a dramatic decline in the poverty rate from 46.6 percent in 1987 to 28.5 percent at the end of 1994. Continued progress under Aylwin's successor would inevitably pale by comparison—especially during a recession. This undoubtedly contributed to the declining popularity of the Frei government and popular perceptions that it was overly "probusiness," creating yet another challenge for Lagos in trying to separate himself from the sitting Concertación president without distancing himself too much from the same coalition he now effectively headed.

Admittedly, Lagos's options were limited in the area of economic policy. This was part of Allende's legacy—the need to prove that a socialist could be fiscally responsible. Indeed, this was perhaps the most successful part of his campaign leading up to the first-round election, achieved through various meetings with Chilean business groups and the representatives of various international economic interests. The problem for Lagos was that it reinforced other aspects of his political style, as he himself recognized in changing his campaign slogan soon after the December elections to *Chile mucho mejor* (A much better Chile).

Lagos was also handicapped by his inability to match the Lavín campaign's immense financial resources. While the absence of campaign disclosure laws makes it impossible to quantify the differences with any precision, it is clear that the lavish support given Lavín by the business community allowed him to significantly outspend the Lagos campaign. Moreover, Lavín used his estimated $50 million war chest to contract U.S. advisors—certainly the most proficient practitioners of this kind of electoral style. Connecting with the people in this sense is very expensive!

The contrast between the two styles was captured well by Peter Winn (2000, 8) when he wryly observed how "in contrast to Lagos's top-down statesman, Lavín offered a bottom-up populist." The best indicator of the permanence of this new style is that Lagos was increasingly forced to emulate it to compete. As Andrés Velasco points out, a defining moment in Chilean politics came on January 7, when both presidential candidates used a popular term equivalent to the word "job" in English, *pega:* "That night . . . both presidential candidates did not promise more employment, more work or even an improved labor market, but more pega" (*La Tercera*, February 27, 2000). With this simple word—something that would be of little importance to an American audience that is long accustomed to its leaders promising more "jobs"—the two candidates' perceived need to reach out to the common person, to speak "in their language," was graphically exposed. Fundamentally, it reflects a shift from Lagos's (and the Concertación's traditional) focus on the structural or institutional causes of Chile's social problems to Lavín's insistence on addressing in a direct way the consequences of those same underlying problems. Beginning with its overwhelmingly successful challenge to the basic institutional impediment to change—the military regime—through Lagos's commitment to constitutional change, this has been an important part of the Concertación's efforts to distinguish itself from the Right. While such changes are fundamental to the long-term prospects for Chilean democracy, the problem is that a commitment to achieving them is no longer sufficient to win elections and may even exacerbate public perceptions of a distant, self-absorbed political class that is unconnected with the people.

This focus on the consequences of Chile's structural and institutional problems also inevitably shifts attention away from issues of democratization. Then Communist Party secretarial general and 1999 presidential candidate Gladys Marin's harsh criticism of Lavín strikes at the core contradiction or paradox of neopopulist democracy: "He was a functionary of the Pinochet dictatorship. He doesn't know what democracy is all about" (*Santiago Times*, June 7, 1999). The authoritarian elements that are an intrinsic part of neopluralism make Lavín's close ties to the military regime irrelevant, even if Lagos's own socialist past conditions his candidacy in substantial ways. More accurately (and independently of Lavín's tainted past), this style of politics, at best, takes political democracy for granted. At worst, it leads to extremes of plebiscitary styles that, in between elections, run roughshod over basic democratic principles of accountability and citizen participation. It plays to the growing economic insecurities of people at the same time that it places a premium on private economic resources for allocating political power, if not actually determining the practical effectiveness of individual rights of citizenship.

The Future of Chile's Neopluralist Democracy

The 1999–2000 elections proved to be a watershed in many ways. Although Chile's two successive socialist presidents enacted a series of important reforms in the areas of health care, education, and labor rights, none fundamentally changed the nature of inequality or citizenship as consumption in Chile's neopluralist democracy. While virtually all of the authoritarian enclaves, with the notable exception of the binomial electoral system, were finally removed by Lagos's constitutional reforms, they were no longer necessary for undergirding the structural changes that were introduced by the military regime. The threats to citizenship posed by neopluralism, combined with a new style of politics, meant they were essentially superfluous. In many ways, the reforms—however important for addressing specific democratic deficits—only made further reform more difficult to achieve by their very, albeit limited, success (Garretón 2007). As Eugenio Ortega (2006, 4), former director of the United Nations Development Programme's Chile Human Development Report, laments, "in focus groups organized for [various Human Development Reports] one observes a kind of 'desertion' from the leaders, winners of the plebiscite that ended the dictatorship in favor of the losers who retained power."

The lack of ideology and the declining importance of political parties today does not mean Chile should return to the rigid ideological positions that characterized Chilean politics in the past. One of the principal political lessons that the parties of the Concertación learned is the need to seek compromise and avoid attempting to equate party ideologies with the national good. Rather than the parties building on this political learning, however, the role traditionally played by political parties and ideology in aggregating interests and attempting to develop long-term projects for national development has largely been replaced by the candidate's ability to personally connect with the people. This new style of politics is perhaps the most insidious obstacle to realizing more profound change. Garretón (2007, 136) best summarizes why: "the increasingly diffused acceptance that political-ideological options are obsolete and that politics

CHILE'S DEMOCRATIC TRANSITION

should revolve around the concrete problems and immediate calculations [of interest] because everything else will only alienate the people."

Politically, economically, and socially, Chile remains the best case in terms of the impact of neopluralism and citizenship as consumption on the quality of democracy. In most other countries, where a potentially representative political party system was never institutionalized and state institutions are weaker, the impact of neopluralism is likely to be much more severe.

THE FAILURE OF CITIZENSHIP:
BOLIVIA'S POPULAR PARTICIPATION LAW

Bolivia is a country rich in paradoxes, if not contradictions. It was the second country in Latin America to undergo a revolution "from below" based on widespread mobilization of peasant and workers (principally miners) in 1952. Yet, unlike the Mexican (1917) and Cuban (1959) Revolutions, the Bolivian Revolution did not lead to political stability in any meaningful sense.[1] Instead, the Revolution contributed to a period of extreme political instability that was unparalleled in the region and has been effectively overcome only in recent years.

One reason for such political instability is that the revolutionary government failed to create strong state institutions. The Bolivian state remained weak in almost every sense, from its inability to effectively penetrate vast parts of the country's territory to its lack of a modern, professionalized bureaucracy that could resist the corrupting influences of extreme politicization and clientelism. From a strictly Weberian perspective, and in sharp contrast to Chile, the Bolivian state remained problematic throughout most of the past century. Even the revolutionary regime's most profound structural reforms—particularly the land reform and nationalization of the tin mines that destroyed the old ruling elite's political and economic power base—reflected the state's inherent weakness. They were not the consequence of a deliberate effort at social engineering by a triumphant new state elite but instead resulted when the (somewhat surprised) government recognized what was essentially a fait accompli at the level of society, as armed peasants and miners seized the land and mines that had provided them with their livelihoods.[2]

These institutional shortcomings of the state are also at least indirectly responsible for the survival of a strong indigenous culture among the majority of Bolivians that is maintained by a network of literally tens of thousands of traditional organizations. Most of these organizations are located in rural areas where the state's presence until 1994 was minimal to nonexistent. The retention of a strong indigenous cultural identity has come at a very high cost, often abetted ironically enough by racism in its various insidious forms: extreme poverty.

In pointing out the "cost" of maintaining strong pre-Columbian ethnic identities and institutions, I in no way wish to imply that cultural preservation is not extremely positive or that poverty was its natural consequence. I want only to underscore the fact that this undeniable success also reflects the unusually weak (by South American standards at least) threat that criollo/mestizo culture posed, because there was no modernizing state capable of imposing it in isolated rural areas where the majority of Bolivians lived. By itself, it does not say much about the actual strength or representative quality of indigenous organizations, much less their relationship to a strong civil society. The survival of such cultural identities does not mean they are static. Cultures do not survive hundreds of years of aggression by simply enduring, however much one might wish to romanticize about them. Their dynamic quality is undoubtedly an important factor in their survival, just as struggles for cultural survival inevitably transform all the cultures involved—criollo/mestizo and indigenous cultures alike.

The problem is that national economic development has left most indigenous people behind, and efforts to integrate indigenous peoples into national structures inevitably raise questions about how and under whose terms. This issue was raised most forcefully by the 1952 revolution's land reforms, which have been interpreted by many as a failed intent to change Bolivia's socioeconomic structure by homogenizing it to conform to Western liberal values. Ironically, traditional organizations of local governance are now seen by reformers as a potential counterweight to the more Western forms of organization along functional or corporatist lines that grew in influence after the revolution and are often portrayed as the source of many of Bolivia's problems—including the failure of the land reforms to generate greater social equity. Either way, the important question is not if indigenous cultures can or should remain in some idealized, pristine form, but whether or not indigenous people will play an active role in shaping the social construction of cultural identities—their own as well as the national identity of the Bolivian people as a whole—which are fundamental to their rights as citizens.

The combined problems of socioeconomic marginality and a weak state are also reflected in the nature of Bolivian civil society. The richness of Bolivia's multiethnic society belies what has historically been a weak civil society precisely because of the way in which different organized groups relate to the state. On the one hand, there are a vast number of organizations that historically have had a subordinate role in national political processes, at the same time that these organizations have remained highly suspicious of state institutions because of the threat of subordination that they represented.[3] Fragmentation and isolation combined to limit not only their actual political incorporation but also their desire for political incorporation. In the mid-1990s, reformers specifically targeted these organizations to serve as the basis for local (and ultimately national) democratization, and they are predominantly territorially based traditional indigenous institutions.

On the other hand, civil society in Bolivia has been historically dominated by functionally based or corporatist bodies, including the powerful civic committees and a radicalized labor movement. These organizations have been associated with many of the worst abuses of political power in Bolivia through the pursuit of narrow, particularistic interests that often result in excessive rent seeking (i.e., corruption and waste), clientelism, and authoritarianism.

In sharp contrast to Chile, where a strong state and relatively successful economic development have tested the limits of neopluralism and citizenship as consumption, Bolivia represents a case where both neopluralism and citizenship as consumption have been most problematic. A weak state and party system, lackluster (at best) economic performance, and the extreme socioeconomic and political marginalization of its indigenous majority have led to growing levels of instability and development failure. After more than twenty years of democratic rule, the limits of state-society synergy and the absence of citizenship as agency amounted to what can be described as the failure of citizenship.[4]

From this perspective, Bolivia's Popular Participation Law (LPP) appears at first glance to be a highly improbable experiment, perhaps doomed to failure from the onset, given the complex and multifaceted problems that have dogged Bolivian politics for much of this century. This radical decentralization of the Bolivian state was enacted through constitutional amendments in 1994 that completely reorganized Bolivia's political landscape around 311 municipal governments, the majority of which were not only new but erected precisely in those areas where the state had been most noticeably absent. These new local governments were also given substantial economic resources according to the number of inhabitants in each municipal jurisdiction, eliminating the extreme concentration of state resources along the three-city axis, La Paz–Santa Cruz–Cochabamba. For the 42 percent of Bolivians who lived in rural areas, mostly members of indigenous communities with little or no prior contact with the state, the state had dramatically arrived—and with unprecedented amounts of money to be spent locally.

To ensure that these new resources would actually be used to the benefit of the community, more than sixteen thousand Organizaciones Territoriales de Base (Base-Level Territorial Organizations, OTBs) were legally recognized by mid-1997 (Galindo Soza 1998, 241). Many of these were the traditional organizations through which indigenous communities had traditionally governed themselves. The OTBs would establish community priorities though participatory planning exercises associated with the elaboration of a Programa Operativo

Anual (Annual Operation Program) in each municipality. The OTBs would also select members for a new institution in each municipal jurisdiction that would be charged with representing community interests through its monitoring of municipal government activities: Comités de Vigilancia (Vigilance Committees, CVs).

In one fell swoop, the LPP offered institutional solutions to begin addressing many of the problems plaguing Bolivia, from state strength and territorial penetration to the development and construction of a multiethnic society. Moreover, the LPP sought to address these problems democratically, at the local level, through the collective participation of citizens and the strengthening of civil society, thereby laying the foundations for social controls over rampant corruption and excessive politicization by a party system driven by rent seeking. Somewhat paradoxically, the state sought to deal with fundamental national problems by rebuilding the political system from the bottom up, retrieving the organizational capacity of long-marginalized traditional indigenous groups for the purpose of creating a modern democratic political system firmly grounded in the respect for human rights.

The LPP represents a deliberate attempt to create state-society synergy and strengthen civil society by imposing a model of citizenship as agency. It is an ideal case study for understanding the limits neopluralism imposes on the social construction of citizenship. If Chile represents the most successful country in the region in terms of the social construction of citizenship, Bolivia in many ways represents one of the least successful, and the LPP was an attempt to reverse this. From a comparative theoretical perspective, Bolivia's experience with LPP promises to provide new insights into the nature of civil society, particularly in rural areas that the literature on civil society tends to ignore; the ways in which local and central government institutions interact in the resolution of long-standing problems of "governability" and weak democratic institutions in Latin America; and the challenge of achieving citizenship as agency under neopluralism.

The chapter is divided into five sections. In the first section, I provide a brief historical overview of Bolivia's 1952 revolution and its aftermath, focusing on the political and economic instability that culminated in major economic and constitutional reforms beginning in the mid-1980s. I then analyze the contradictions in the way the LPP was actually designed and implemented. In the third section I discuss how the LPP has fared in practice, highlighting its principal achievements, limits, and challenges. In the fourth section I look specifically at the issues relating to indigenous groups, focusing in particular on the experience of coca growers in the Chapare region. Finally, in the conclusion I discuss how the LPP may have ultimately been superseded by the same problems it sought to resolve.

Bolivia's Failed Revolution from Below

In many ways, the LPP was the culmination of the national reform processes that began with the 1952 revolution, particularly its land reforms (Carlos Hugo Molina, personal interview, Santa Cruz, July 15, 1999).[5] Ironically, the incomplete nature of the revolution made state decentralization necessary and the LPP, as one particular way of achieving it, feasible. The revolution represented, at best, a protoform of citizenship as agency that quickly degenerated into the predominance of citizenship as co-optation. Yet the severe limits placed on any attempts at controlled inclusion in Bolivia also meant that citizenship as co-optation was precarious at best, and for much of the period 1964–85 it is hard to speak of citizenship in any meaningful sense when describing Bolivian politics. The ultimate consequences of this reflect the revolution's failure to create strong national state institutions to undergird a new social order. Instead, its legacy of political party competition based on clientelism and rent seeking meant that it would take more than forty years before any form of state decentralization could become politically possible. To understand this, it is necessary to analyze the causes and nature of the revolution in some detail.

The revolution was a dramatic response to Bolivia's chronic problems stemming from economic underdevelopment and the lack of national integration of its vast rural areas and indigenous population. Until the late 1880s the country had been dominated both economically and politically by a small criollo oligarchy. They controlled the bulk of the arable land through a semifeudal hacienda system of land tenure in which the vast majority of peasants lived in conditions close to serfdom. The oligarchy's position would be challenged only when Bolivia began to experience an economic boom based on tin mining from the 1890s to roughly 1925. This coincided with a new liberal political order, established after the 1898 civil war. As a result, "the locus of power shifted from southern Bolivia and an elite based on silver and land to northwestern Bolivia and an elite based on tin, bureaucracy, and land" (Malloy 1968, 182).

The shift in political and economic power did not destroy the oligarchy. Instead, Bolivia was effectively divided into two distinct socioeconomic systems: the modern sector based on the tin economy and centered on the national state, and the locally based haciendas scattered throughout most of the country and largely engaged in subsistence agriculture. Linking the oligarchy and tin interests was a new political elite that sought to ensure its own position by acquiring land and adopting the values of the oligarchic elite, at the same time that it successfully monopolized its hold on political power. For the 60–70 percent of the population who were (largely indigenous) peasants and lived on the haciendas, their dependence on the oligarchy was total. Indeed, "politically, the peon was ruled not by the national state but by the direct will of his *patron*" (Malloy 1968, 185).

The stability of this new system was tied to the tin economy and relatively short-lived. By 1925 international tin prices began to decline at the same time that Bolivia's mines were becoming exhausted. Tin production peaked in 1929, and increasingly became labor intensive due to the decapitalization of the mines. With continued economic prosperity undermined, political discontent grew. A new reformist movement emerged among university students and young professionals to challenge the legitimacy of the system, as organized labor, particularly miners, began to show the first signs of growing strength and radicalization. In the meantime, two-thirds of the population still lived in the countryside, where little had changed since independence. The highly stratified nature of rural society only sharpened as the situation of the peasantry deteriorated, leaving most Bolivians landless and living in conditions of bare subsistence. As late as 1940, as much as 64 percent of the population was completely outside the money economy (Klein 1969, 163).

Faced with a growing economic crisis, increased opposition from the middle sectors, and rising leftist mobilization, particularly among workers, Bolivia's political elite sought to rally support by going to war with Paraguay in 1932. The Chaco War lasted three years and ended with a humiliating defeat for Bolivia. A total of 25 percent of Bolivian forces were killed, deserted, or died in captivity, and almost all were young indigenous soldiers who "had little will for fighting and dying for their country, or even understanding why they were in the Chaco in the first place" (Klein 1969, 187). Moreover, because the war was funded by internal borrowing and the printing of money, Bolivia's economic crisis only worsened.

Although "the overwhelming majority [of peasant soldiers] quietly returned their weapons and resumed their former place in the social and economic system without protest" (Klein 1969, 189), the loyalty of the middle sectors to the political system was severely shaken, and divisions were becoming more severe among the political elite. Political instability continued, as reformist governments (generally including the military) alternated with reactionary right-wing governments.[6] Continued economic decline, growing political violence, and the progressive radicalization of workers contributed to deepening middle-sector alienation.

The Movimiento Nacionalista Revolucionario (Nationalist Revolutionary Movement, MNR) was formed in 1941 in the midst of this downward political spiral. At the time, the MNR was "less a party than a parliamentary and electoral cabal . . . playing upon middle-class dissatisfaction" (Klein 1969, 191). It made few efforts to establish any organizational links with a mass base until after 1946, when the reform military government it participated in was overthrown in a right-wing coup.

The working class had become increasingly well organized and radicalized during this period. For the MNR, organized labor was an essential ally for gaining power, although the party retained its middle-sector reformist outlook and was suspicious of labor's growing radicalism. Organized labor was open to the MNR as its political representative, given the MNR's role in earlier reformist efforts, but it retained its own independent organization and hoped to radicalize the party from within after the MNR came to power. In large part due to labor's support, the MNR won a plurality in the 1951 elections, leading the military to stage yet another coup to prevent the MNR from assuming office.

The 1951 coup galvanized the opposition around the MNR. This exacerbated the growing division within the MNR between middle-sector reformists and radical elements connected with the labor movement. The party leadership, in exile, adopted a pragmatic position as it tried to secure the most effective coalition possible. Significantly, no efforts were made to establish alliances with peasant groups until after the revolution.

Events quickly came to a head in 1952. An uprising started on April 9, led by elements of the MNR in conjunction with the national police. When key elements of the army allied with the government toward the end of the first day, the uprising floundered. Then, on April 11, armed railway and factory workers joined the uprising. When armed miners captured a munitions train and surrounded potential army reinforcements, the military crumbled. After three days of fighting with six hundred dead, the MNR returned to power.

Despite its intentions, the MNR now found itself dependent on the armed labor movement for remaining in power. Within days, a system of workers' militias was in place and the Central Obrera Boliviana (Bolivian Workers Central, COB) was formed. It demanded co-government, which the new government conceded, giving the COB the right to name key government ministers. The COB increasingly mobilized popular pressure for the nationalization of mines, agrarian reform, and universal suffrage.

To deal with the growing pressure from the COB, the new president, Víctor Paz Estenssoro, and other MNR leaders adopted what James Malloy (1968, 200) calls a "pragmatic nationalist position." Recognizing the need to rely on the armed workers' movement to fend off potential counterrevolutionary challenges, the MNR formed a Center-Left coalition in which it hoped to neutralize the radical leftist tendencies within the COB. The revolutionary government limited the power of the military (but would not eliminate it), nationalized the three big tin companies (but not all tin producers, and without any threat to private property in general), and instituted universal suffrage.

The issue of agrarian reform proved to be the most difficult issue for the new government, and the way it was ultimately resolved provides important insights into the nature of the revolutionary process itself. With support from organized labor, there were increasing numbers of peasant uprisings and land seizures.[7] This led a number of the original MNR leaders to stage a coup, with the support of elements from the army and police, on January 6, 1953. The coup was quickly quashed, but the next day COB militia poured into La Paz demanding a right-wing purge of the government. Paz was forced to agree, although it proved to be "a most mild purge" (Malloy 1968, 201)—there was no bloodshed, and the complicity of many was covered up, although the known leaders were sent into exile.

At this point, the government appointed a commission to draft an agrarian reform program, although peasant uprisings continued. On August 3, 1953, agrarian reform was officially instituted, "but it was clear that in heavily populated key areas . . . the document merely ratified a *fait accompli*. In the meantime, well-organized and armed peasant unions were formed throughout the country." The MNR leaders were "at best reluctant revolutionaries" (Malloy 1968, 202). Or, as Susan Eckstein (1982, 60) puts it, "land distribution depended on the outcome of localized struggles, initiated 'from below' and resisted 'from above.'" In this way, "the MNR core had presided over (rather than directed) a profound drama of revolutionary destruction" (Malloy 1968, 203). Whatever the MNR's intentions, "the latifundia class was literally wiped out" (Klein 1969, 404). The 6 percent of Bolivian landowners who owned 92 percent of the farmland generally lost that land.

Even though it hung on to power, the MNR government failed to construct new state institutions that could successfully govern the country, much less integrate Bolivian society into a cohesive whole. As Malloy (1968, 208) argues, "the issue was one of internal sovereignty, that is, the ability of a central authoritative decision center effectively to overrule local nonauthoritative centers." The state had lost its legitimate monopoly of force to militias and private armies at the regional and sectoral levels. Workers' militias had been organized under the COB, although the COB's control over them was also tenuous. In rural areas the agrarian reforms created a void with "extreme atomization and the breaking of rural control" that neither the MNR nor the COB could fill. As Malloy stresses, "in many parts of the country the peasants simply withdrew from the national existence into an atomized state. In other regions, the peasants were united (often by force) into regional federations dominated by powerful unions" (211). The MNR, with its core support based in the urban middle sectors, could not hope to unite the nation, yet it was dependent on the support of armed peasants and workers over whom it had little control. Ultimately, "national institutions became epiphenomenal to the forces which actually held sway" (209). This militarization of society represented the antithesis of a strong civil society. Bolivia's revolution thus left in its wake both a weak state and a weak civil society, making meaningful synergy between the two all but impossible.

In the meantime, the economy was running out of control. Per capita income fell 20 percent from 1952 to 1958, inflation was soaring, and the newly nationalized mines were in decline. Inflation, in particular, was turning the middle sectors against the MNR, while efforts to control it only alienated other important groups, particularly miners.

To garner support, the MNR increasingly had to literally buy it, and "the party became an instrument through which various sectors could legitimately assault the system's meager collective surplus" (Malloy 1968, 214). This, in turn, engendered a rent-seeking mentality that "was institutionalized as a style of public life. Organizations proliferated, as each sector sought to build a solid front with which to protect what it had, while it assaulted the system for more" (215). The result was only further political instability and the undermining of national institutions based on a very weak model of citizenship as co-optation.

The MNR leadership shifted to the right with the election of Hernán Siles as president in 1956. Siles began to rebuild the military to counter the workers' militias and purged leftists from the government. He also appealed to peasants, trying to split them from the labor Left. In 1960 Paz again assumed the presidency and continued the MNR's rightward drift. With U.S. backing under its new Alliance for Progress program, Paz put himself on a collision course with organized labor and the Left. The economic and political problems unleashed by the revolution remained unresolved, and the Paz government found itself increasingly isolated. Appeals to peasants—the beneficiaries of the land reforms enacted during Paz's first term in office—to support the increasingly beleaguered government were to little avail. Political violence and clashes with the Left and workers were on the increase. When Paz indicated that he planned to succeed himself, the now powerful and professional armed forces moved against him on November 3, 1964. Paz again tried to mobilize peasant support, but when it did not materialize, he left for exile in Peru, ushering in decades of military rule and continued political instability.

Clientelism, rent seeking, and authoritarian structures were not created by the revolution. The institutional void that it left, however, exacerbated their impact and contributed to continued processes of institutional decomposition. The weakness of both the state and civil society meant that it was difficult to identify any meaningful sense of citizenship during this period, even one as inherently limited as citizenship as co-optation. Instead, Bolivia became an extreme example of patrimonial politics—virtually a free-for-all in which the behavior of political parties and other actors was driven by access to patronage and other rents (Gamara and Malloy 1995) rather than to any appeals to a broad base of citizens. Even the period of military rule following the 1964 coup was increasingly undermined by this rent-seeking, patrimonial dynamic so that by the mid-seventies, the military itself was behaving as if it were "little more than an armed political party" (408). Increasingly, the officer corps was competing with civilian politicians, who often cut opportunistic deals with them over control of state patronage; thus, state institutions were undermined from within. This led not only to institutional decay, but to increasing levels of political instability despite military rule. The transition to democracy would take five years, from 1978 to

1982, and was punctuated by seven military and two weak civilian governments. The first elected civilian government was even forced from office a year early, in 1985, because of its inability to deal with Bolivia's hyperinflation.

A semblance of political order was restored with the return of Paz Estenssoro to the presidency in 1985, and the way it was achieved is illustrative of Bolivia's institutional problems (Gamara and Malloy 1995). Political order was accomplished, first, by bringing the economy under control. This was done through Nueva Política Económica (New Economic Policy) policies, developed in secrecy and implemented by decree. Opposition from the Left was quashed, with its leaders sent into temporary exile. The second ingredient for political stability was then put in place in October 1985: the Pacto por la Democracia (Pact for Democracy) between the MNR and Acción Democrática y Nacionalista (Nationalist Democratic Action, ADN), the political party formed by former military dictator General Hugo Bánzer in 1979. The key to the pact's success was the ADN's agreement to support Paz's government in the legislature, in exchange for guarantees of access to state patronage positions. Stability was restored by minimizing conflict between the executive and the legislature. It allowed Paz to then ratify the Nueva Política Económica in the legislature and permitted him sufficient autonomy to both organize an effective administration for governing the country and isolate his economic team from the pressures of patrimonial rent seeking. Yet the pact did not resolve the fundamental political problems that gave rise to it. Instead, it "reduced the legislature to rubber-stamping an essentially authoritarian policy-making process . . . [and] reinforced the patronage logic of the system" (415). Political rights were restored, but citizenship was tightly constrained by limited elements of co-optation and more extensive patterns of exclusion that belied any sense of controlled inclusion. Even before the large-scale adoption of neoliberal economic policies, both neopluralism and citizenship as consumption were already beginning to predominate.

The pact's success led to similar pacts undergirding the next three presidencies. While the pacts may have laid a foundation for consensual politics and democratic stability that helped consolidate Bolivian democracy (Mayorga 1997), they did so at the expense of needed institutional reforms at the level of the state and political parties, as well as the strengthening of civil society. The state still was highly politicized, even if Bolivia was now governable as a result of pacts. Rather than curb rent seeking, the pacts helped to further institutionalize it. For example, Bolivia consistently ranks among the most corrupt countries in the world in the various surveys of corruption. For example, the annual survey on global competitiveness published by the World Economic Forum declared Bolivia to be the most corrupt country among the fifty-nine across the globe included in its study (El Nuevo Día, July 15, 1999). In particular, the World Economic Forum found that Bolivia's politicians ranked as the most corrupt and least trustworthy, and noted that Bolivia (along with Mexico and China) were the only countries among the twenty countries ranked lowest that showed an increase in illegality, corruption, and violence over the previous year. Any semblance of civil society remained, at best, at the margins of political processes as they unfolded.

Political parties shouldered most of the responsibility, as they were increasingly "disconnected from the interests of Bolivian society" (Gamara and Malloy 1995, 411). As noted by the respected Bolivian social scientist Carlos Toranzo, political parties showed great skill in making political pacts, but the downside of this pact making was that parties did so to achieve power, without any concern for who was in the pact or what its programmatic base might be. Instead, "political parties had become machines for taking power" without long-term vision, exacerbating problems of clientelism and rent seeking (personal interview, La Paz, July 2, 1999). ADN senator Walter Soriano, part of the governing pact headed by the former dictator, President Bánzer, echoed a common sentiment by suggesting that the roots of Bolivia's patrimonial dynamic are in its highly personalist politics: "the political culture in the country is one of *caudillismo*," which undermines democracy and the prospects for needed reforms (personal interview, La Paz, July 1, 1999), as well as the potential emergence of a civil society sufficiently inclusive to be able to work with the state to address pressing developmental challenges.

These problems are not lost on the Bolivian public. A national survey of political culture in Bolivia (Seligson 1998), for example, found that only one in ten Bolivians supported the political system and expressed political tolerance, while more than half held values that would support the breakdown of democracy. The legitimacy of the political system was actually lowest among people with a university education. Regarding tolerance, the survey found that "Bolivians are especially intolerant of the right of free speech and the right to run for political office" (Seligson 1998, 11). Not surprisingly, political parties scored particularly low. Another poll, conducted in the early 1990s, found that while 78 percent of Bolivians supported democracy, only 5 percent felt political parties represented their interests, and 71 percent felt that the current government represented the interests of the wealthy and of politicians. Political parties and Congress received the lowest approval rating of all institutions (Gamara and Malloy 1995, 418–19). The LLP was intended to address these perceptions, yet they only tended to grow in intensity as Bolivia was rocked with a new wave of political instability at the turn of the century.

The weakness of political parties has also been reflected within civil society through the growing influence of different corporatist or functionally based organizations, which often bypassed the legislature to attempt to deal directly with the executive. *Comités cívicos* (civic committees) in particular grew in influence by replacing political parties in the articulation and aggregation of regional interests and became the principal overseers of congressional activity. This was also reflected in their high level of legitimacy among Bolivians at the time the LPP was promulgated. For example, an opinion poll conducted in the early 1990s found that civic committees ranked second to the Catholic Church in terms of public respect (Gamara and Malloy 1995, 419). At the same time, the COB (and the entire radical Left) had lost considerable influence in Bolivian society. One sign of this was that popular support for the declaration of states of siege was directed against them. Bolivian civil society also was not immune to the demobilizing impact of democratic transitions and neopluralism in Latin America. As Oscar Coca, a former COB advisor, wryly noted, "we were united under the dictatorship, but under democracy we destroyed ourselves! We have not had the capacity to propose alternatives" (personal interview, Cochabamba, July 13, 1999).[8]

The socioeconomic consequences of weak central state institutions with their patrimonial political dynamic and civil society's inability to fill the void are easily identifiable. While the land reform effectively destroyed the oligarchy as a social class, its long-term effects on the rural population have been far more ambiguous. The percentage of farms of fewer than five hectares, *minifundias* that are insufficient even for family subsistence farming, changed only marginally from 59.3 percent of all farming units in 1950 to 56.6 percent in 1967 (Eckstein 1982, 54). Moreover, the combined number of peasants who were either landless or owned minifundias, after an initial drop due to the land reform, actually increased later (58). More than 70 percent of all Bolivians lived in poverty in 1992, with an astounding poverty rate of 95 percent in rural areas (Grupo de Trabajo 1998, 13–14). These poverty rates placed Bolivia among the poorest countries in the world in terms of the United Nations Development Program's human development scale, just above Haiti, Honduras, and Nicaragua in this hemisphere. In rural areas, the level of development is more on par with sub-Saharan Africa. This reflects, among other things, the lack of access to potable water, sufficient health care and housing, and adequate educational opportunities (particularly for women). It also reflects high levels of income inequality, particularly between men and women. As Roberto Laserna (2003, 5) sadly points out, the 1950s land reforms created "sham landowners" who could sell their property only to family members and "after three generations, 'peasants with land' are the poorest group in the country."

Bolivia thus represents an interrelated variety of development shortcomings, if not failures. The immense poverty and limited life chances of the vast majority are the end result of decades of political and institutional decay, which invariably took their toll on civil society. The LPP was a bold and extremely creative effort to deal with all of these structural problems democratically, by trying to impose a model of citizenship as agency in a country where citizenship of any type has been shallow at best.

The Popular Participation Law: An Attempt at Revolution from Above

By any measure, the changes ushered in by the LPP were monumental (see table 5.1). They were a unique combination of state decentralization and participatory democracy designed to address problems of institutional development, rent seeking, and national integration from the bottom up. With the LPP, the entire country was placed under the jurisdiction of 311 municipal governments, including 187 new municipal governments covering almost two-thirds of the nation's territory.[9] These municipal governments would now have responsibility for administering health care, education, and infrastructure services, as well as other areas of social investment. To cover these new responsibilities, a new revenue-sharing scheme, *coparticipación,* was instituted. The state would double the percentage of its revenues that it shared with municipal governments to 20 percent, and distribution would be exclusively on a per capita basis. The result was a windfall for the new city governments and many of the old ones as well. Prior to the change, only 61 city governments received state revenue sharing, and 90 percent went to the three largest cities—La Paz, Santa Cruz, and Cochabamba. Now, half of the funds went to rural districts. The municipal governments' share of public investment rose from 11 percent to 39 percent, total social investment doubled, and investment in education tripled. Municipal governments administered almost $3 billion, involving more than seventy thousand projects over ten years, contributing directly to the reduction of poverty from 70.9 percent in 1992 to 58.3 percent in 2003 (Aliendre España 2004, 53).

This dramatic decentralization was accompanied by an innovative scheme for democratizing local governments. Each municipal government would be governed by a popularly elected city council and mayor. CVs were created to serve as the principal link between local government and the literally tens of thousands of OTBs that would now be legally recognized. The OTBs, which in rural areas included traditional indigenous governing organizations, were considered the authentic representatives of the interests of Bolivian civil society, and they would elect the members of the CVs to articulate and represent their priorities in new participatory planning processes to be carried out in each municipal jurisdiction. The CVs would also serve as a mechanism for exercising social control over the portion of municipal budgets financed through coparticipación.

From the perspective of the social construction of citizenship, the LPP epitomized an attempt to institutionalize state-society synergy based on a model of citizenship as agency. The reform explicitly sought to ensure government accountability and transparency by creating a hybrid form of democracy, incorporating Western traditions of representative democracy with local, indigenous traditions of community self-government—"individual liberty and a communitarian symbiosis" (Secretaría Nacional 1997, 10). The LPP's goal, according to then vice president Víctor Hugo Cárdenas—one of the most prominent political

Table 5.1. Impact of the Popular Participation Law

Socioeconomic impact	Pre-LPP	Post-LPP
Recognition of OTBs as legal entities	Fewer than 100 communities	19,000 communities
Number of municipalities receiving coparticipación funds	61	311
Percentage of fiscal resources subject to municipal coparticipación	10%	20%
Mechanism for fund distribution	Based on legal residence of taxpayers	Based on total population
Municipal share of total public investment	11%	39%[a]
Social investment	1.72% of GDP in 1993 (US$90 million)	3.62% of GDP in 1995 (US$180 million)
Investment in education[b]	US$10 million in 1993	US$30 million in 1995

SOURCE: Data from PNUD (1998, 119).

[a] This number later declined dramatically as a result of new funds freed for central government investment by Bolivia's participation in the Heavily Indebted Poor Countries (HIPC) initiative.

[b] The LPP also coincided with a major reform of the educational system, which is now administered at the local level.

leaders of indigenous descent in Latin America at the time—was "municipal governance without homogenizing social representation" (24). In contrast to past state policies of social integration that were seen as overly Westernizing, integration would now be achieved by accepting difference (Arias and Molina 1997). The LPP also specifically set as one of its objectives guaranteeing equal opportunities for men and women. Ultimately, as the then president Gonzalo Sánchez de Lozada explained when introducing the LPP to parliament, through the LPP "we will end both the exclusion of the great national majorities and the squandering of the little that we have" (1997, 19–20).

For the 42 percent of the population living in rural areas, the state not only arrived for the first time in decades or longer, it brought unprecedented resources. Despite initial widespread skepticism and in many cases outright opposition by the law's presumed beneficiaries, five years after its enactment the overwhelming consensus was that the Bolivian people had legitimated the LPP and the institutional changes it brought were therefore irreversible.[10]

The key to this success was undoubtedly the coparticipación resources. As the intellectual author of the LPP and the first national secretary for Popular Participation, Carlos Hugo Molina, explained, "the fundamental success for the consolidation of popular participation was the existence of resources. People linked popular participation directly with the resources" (personal interview,

Santa Cruz, July 15, 1999). In fact, a central aspect of the government's campaign to raise support for the new institutions was to publicize how much money was arriving to local governments so that people would have an incentive to start exercising some control over its expenditure. As ADN senator Walter Soriano noted, even when all other aspects of the LPP were not living up to the previous government's expectations, "what is good is that the Finance Ministry has to deliver the money—it is delivering it late, but it is delivering it (personal interview, La Paz, July 1, 1999). The rapid legalization of so many OTBs reflected their desire—and in many instances the desire of political parties linked with them—to gain access to these resources (Booth, Clisby, and Widmark 1997, 23–24).

This centrality of financial resources in the legitimation of LPP institutions raises important questions in terms of civil society and its relationship to the state. As Senator Erika Brockmann, then chair of the Senate Committee on Popular Participation (Comité del Senado sobre Participación Popular) from the MIR, noted, this ran the risk of creating an impression that access to resources does not entail responsibilities, further contributing to a rent-seeking mentality (personal interview, La Paz, June 30, 1999). More fundamentally, the legitimation of institutional reforms embodying citizenship as agency was sought through recourse to a model of citizenship as co-optation. This basic contradiction has serious long-term implications for the ability of the LPP reforms to achieve state-civil society synergy and citizenship as agency. Its negative impact would only be exacerbated because the distance between the state and civil society in the past had generated a conflictual relationship that the LPP would have to reverse to succeed (Molina Saucedo 1997, 33; Ardaya Salinas 1998, 15–17). Civil society would have to learn how to use the democratic spaces the LPP opened up, as well as possess both the capacity and the will to use those spaces. Given Bolivia's stratified social structure and the widespread skepticism toward state institutions, these steps were problematic. Moreover, while a majority of Bolivians felt the LPP increased both the representative quality of local government and its efficiency, more than two-thirds felt that it did not make any difference in terms of poverty reduction and that the capacity of municipal governments for overcoming poverty remained unchanged (PNUD 1998, 27, 120). If material benefits are the ultimate source of the LPP's social legitimacy, the laws cannot be considered truly consolidated or irreversible until these perceptions change.

The architects of the LPP deliberately sought to sidestep the issue of state-civil society conflict by basing the LPP on territorially based organizations. Functionally based or sectoral organizations were explicitly excluded from participating in the institutions established by the LPP. The logic behind this decision was both philosophical and based on Bolivia's particular experiences. Philosophically, the LPP represents an effort to "recover the concept of citizenship in the face of corporatism," which has traditionally served as the basis for incorporating individuals into the Bolivian political system (Carlos Hugo Molina, personal interview, Santa Cruz, July 15, 1999). Corporatism in this sense refers to an organizational dynamic based on economic activity or specific group interests. Class organizations such as the union movement and employers groups are classic examples, and other corporatist organizations include civic committees and women's organizations—two kinds of nonterritorially based organizations explicitly excluded from the LPP. The corporatist basis for organizing the Bolivian political system has been predominant at least since the 1952 revolution and its mobilization of workers and peasants in union structures.[11] Even political parties are organized sectorally as opposed to territorially, which is the norm in Western democracies (PNUD) 1998, 128).

In many ways, corporatism is the antithesis of the liberal, pluralist model for organizing polities on which the LPP is based (Schmitter 1974). As Carlos Hugo Molina explains, this is due to corporatism's collectivist nature: "There is often an excessive emphasis on the community and the individual as a member of it. This vision can definitively strengthen the corporatist logic that is very much present in Bolivian society. To speak of citizens implies speaking about subjects, those who have no rights, but only individual and public responsibilities. The dimension of responsibilities is important, since organizations or the community cannot lose responsibilities, only the individual. In the same way, satisfaction is essentially individual" (Molina Saucedo 1999).

This very liberal view of citizenship rights and the fundamental critique of corporatism it implies seems at odds with the non-Western basis of traditional organizations—a tension found in the LPP. But it highlights what has been a predominant feature of Bolivian politics for many decades: the lack of responsibility and concern for public (as opposed to personalist) interests. The LPP seeks to redeem politics by refounding it on the basis of individuals as members of their respective communities defined exclusively in terms of the territorial unit in which they live. The per capita distribution of coparticipación is intended to reinforce this understanding of rights (C. H. Molina, personal interview, Santa Cruz, July 15, 1999). It is a view of citizenship very similar to the classic exposition on the topic by T. H. Marshall (see chapter 1), who also saw the evolution of citizenship in terms of the evolution of individual rights that closely corresponded to the economic development of England.[12]

This negative view of corporatism corresponded to recent Bolivian experience as well. For many prominent Bolivian policy makers, corporatism went hand in hand with authoritarianism, exclusion, and rent seeking (see, for example, V. Cárdenas 1997, 25; Molina Saucedo 1997, 35). Corporatism was seen as breeding dependency on state resources and opening up more opportunities for corruption (PNUD 1998, 115). The dominance of corporatism also implied for its critics the need to make space for more popular participation by reducing the influence of corporatist actors, particularly labor (63).[13] In sharp contrast to the narrow interests represented by corporatist organizations, communities

were seen as being inherently more inclusionary by their very nature: "Corporatist, trade union, sectoral organizations—they only represent a sector of the
population. They defend the interests of a specific group. OTBs have greater
scope. They often represent all the groups [in a community]. It is the primary
organizational form. . . . The neighborhood council represents everyone who
lives there, independently of who they are" (Roberto Barbery, personal interview, Santa Cruz, July 16, 1999).

Regardless of whether this idealist view of community organizations is accurate, there is nothing intrinsic to either territorially or functionally based organizations that makes them inherently good or bad for promoting democratization.
An important determinant of whether general patterns of organizational activity in civil society will reinforce clientelism, corruption, and authoritarianism
or more democratic processes of accountability and the pursuit of public (as
opposed to private) interests is the nature of the state. States inevitably structure
opportunities and incentives for different types of collective action (Skocpol
1985). States also have played a decisive role in strengthening or even creating important collective actors in civil society—including corporatist actors in
Bolivia beginning with the 1952 revolution. The kind of narrow rent-seeking
behavior often associated with functionally based actors in Bolivia is one consequence of extremely weak politicized state institutions, and the same would be
potentially true of territorially based organizations. This is especially important
for understanding the LPP, given that it is an explicit attempt to overcome state
institutional weakness by relying on different societal organizations. The danger
is that negative dynamics associated with corporatist actors stemming from the
problems in the central state apparatus that the LPP is intended to address will
distort the new local democratic institutions and the nature of their links with
civil society. In other words, narrow partisan-based politicization, corruption,
and other authoritarian tendencies at the national level may constrain local democracy as much as, or even more than, local democratic institutions can effectively democratize national state and political party structures.

One of the consequences of the LPP was that it displaced another social organization that had grown in importance as an alternative to Bolivia's corrupt
political party system: civic committees. As sectoral organizations that largely
represented regional economic elites, the civic committees could not formally
participate in the institutions established by the LPP. Moreover, with the notable
exception of the more self-sufficient Santa Cruz civic committee, the LPP's pro-
hibition of municipal funding for civic committees pushed them into financial
crisis (PNUD 1998, 127). Overall, regional economic elites were "clear losers in
Popular Participation" (Grindle 2000, 21). Yet the principal demand for decentralization from within civil society was coming from the civic committees.[14]
The rest of civil society was relatively silent on the issue before the LPP was
announced.

From the perspective of state-civil society relations, the LPP seemed to come out of nowhere. It was conceived and designed with virtually no input from civil society (Grindle 2000; Van Cott 2000). The then president Sánchez de Lozada was actively involved, working closely with his key advisers. Even his vice president, Víctor Hugo Cárdenas, one of the most prominent political leaders of indigenous descent in Latin America, played almost no role. Yet, the success of the LPP was dependent on civil society actors who not only had not participated in its elaboration but were historically suspicious of state institutions.[15] Indeed, many traditional organizations feared that the proposed LPP would create new OTBs that would be manipulated by the state in much the same way that the corporatist organizations associated with the revolution were manipulated in the 1950s (Maydana 2004, 201).

The architects of the new policy made critical assumptions about a very autonomous part of civil society in terms of its willingness and ability to work within the new institutions being established. While most OTBs had not been engaged in a conflictual relationship with the state, with the partial exception of the *sindicatos campesinos* (peasant unions), they generally had not been engaged in any meaningful relationship with it. Their autonomy reflected their marginalization from larger political and economic processes.[16] This is the exact opposite of a model of the social construction of citizenship.

As a result of this elite process, the government had to enact the LPP with little or no social support. The government then had to win over public opinion after the law was already in place and had begun transferring resources to the new municipal governments. Moreover, the government had to do so in the face of a very effective opposition campaign against the *leyes malditas* (damned laws) that was able to mobilize substantial opposition from a variety of sources, including political parties, corporatist organizations (especially organized labor), and the nongovernmental organizations that had come to play an important role in sustaining a variety of forms of social organization within Bolivian civil society. For many, the LPP was thus seen as "a gift . . . and they do not feel that it is a right" (Jose Luis Nuñez, personal interview, La Paz, July 5, 1999). This same attitude was also the hallmark of controlled inclusion and citizenship as co-optation.

The team responsible for the design and implementation of the LPP claimed this top-down, insular approach was necessary to prevent vested interests from undermining the law. While this is obviously a legitimate concern, it shows a remarkable lack of confidence in the very groups who were supposed to be the principal beneficiaries of the laws. Rather than work with civil society to counter elite opposition, the government chose to exclude its potential allies along with its opponents, demonstrating a particular elitism and a new source of disconnect between the political class and the most disadvantaged groups in Bolivian society. The design and implementation of the LPP reflected an attempted state-led "democratic revolution" that emulated some of the same problems in Bolivian politics it sought to reverse—citizenship as co-optation, a lack of transparency, and a clear hierarchy that was anything but democratic. Distrust was unnecessarily increased, making the LPP's survival more dependent on citizenship as co-optation. Even if trust and legitimacy could later be attained, the danger was that the LPP's potential to create citizenship as agency would be overwhelmed by its reliance on citizenship as co-optation.

This top-down process also meant that a vital opportunity was lost for improving the quality of the institutional design of the LPP. The tension between the essentially liberal view of citizenship embodied in the LPP and the alternative views reflected in many OTBs would now have to be reconciled after the law was put into effect rather than through a more appropriate institutional design at the reform's onset. While such a reconciliation might be possible, the strategy ran the risk that OTBs would see the LPP as yet another attempt to impose a homogenizing Western formula, seriously limiting the LPP's capacity to achieve its stated objectives.

The task was further complicated by the fact that even within the same communities from the same indigenous groups, there were competing forms of citizen participation and development objectives (Arias 2004). Assuming the local actors involved could reach a consensus, there was no guarantee that the new institutions would prove flexible enough to adapt to any alternative views the OTBs might want to offer, especially given the intensity of the political struggles entailed in implementing the law. By deliberately avoiding a political dialogue consistent with an inclusionary process of the social construction of citizenship, the hoped-for hybrid would be much more difficult to achieve than would have been the case if alternative views been taken into account earlier. In other words, the most fundamental flaw of the LPP may prove to be a contradiction created when a law intended to maximize citizen participation at the local level was designed and implemented at the highest reaches of the state with little input from civil society.

The LPP in Practice: Neither Popular nor Participatory?

Creating almost two hundred new municipal jurisdictions, primarily in poor rural areas, is a monumental task. The law's central concern with respecting indigenous communities and their organizations further complicates the task. A number of problems are technical in nature, including the severe lack of skills necessary to run effective municipal governments (and the related challenge of getting people with the appropriate skills to live in isolated rural communities), the administrative challenges created by population dispersion and the scale of rural municipal jurisdictions, as well as very low levels of voter registration.

These problems have been addressed in a number of detailed studies (Secretaría Nacional 1997; UIA 1998b; Booth, Clisby, and Widmark 1997; ILDIS 2004) and are beyond the scope of this book.

One problem that is of both a technical and political nature relates to setting jurisdictional boundaries, particularly in areas with large indigenous populations. Deciding the appropriate municipal authority for particular communities, identifying indigenous districts within municipal jurisdictions, and more general problems of administratively dividing up huge expanses of often sparsely populated territory is always problematic. In particular, there is a danger of disempowering communities, including ethnic ones, through excessive atomization and fragmentation. The crux of the problem is that there are no uniform formulas that can be applied in any objective fashion. One cannot even assume, for example, that a particular jurisdiction with a large indigenous population would even want to be labeled an indigenous district, regardless of the benefits such a designation might imply under the LPP (Ayo 1998). Critics have argued that municipal boundaries established by the LPP were often created in a haphazard way "without taking into account fundamental aspects, such as geographic characteristics, uses, customs, traditions, accessibility and other territorial references" (Luizaga 2004, 412), an accusation supported by continued jurisdictional disputes among municipal jurisdictions more than a decade after LPP was implemented. At the same time, the sheer number of municipalities created has contributed to the fragmentation and atomization of Bolivia instead of helping to create "a country that is integrated and interconnected, that recognizes itself" (Ameller 2004, 315; Gray-Molina 2003).

The only viable solution to such jurisdictional problems requires negotiations between the affected communities and appropriate government authorities. It is a very specific example of the importance of the social construction of citizenship. Their resolution will be mediated by various political factors: (1) the impact of the patrimonial dynamic of national politics on municipal governments, (2) the ability of the OTBs to represent the various groups in civil society, (3) the success of participatory planning, and (4) the effectiveness of CVs as the primary interlocutor between territorially organized civil society and local state institutions.

Before turning to each of these four factors, it is important to recognize that the success of the LPP in terms of generating governability at the local level and effective citizen participation has varied greatly from one municipality to the next. Surprisingly, the prior strength of existing OTBs does not appear to be a factor (Iván Arias, personal interview, La Paz, July 6, 1999). Much more important is the preexisting sociopolitical dynamic (Rojas Ortuste and Thévoz 1998; UIA 1998a; Thévoz and Velasco 1998). In communities where there was a dynamic of confrontation among different actors, including between the state and civil society, the LPP's impact was minimal and tended to exacerbate the preexisting tendencies in a kind of vicious cycle.[17] In contrast, where the dynamic was more one of state-society synergy, the result was a more virtuous cycle in which the institutions and resources associated with LPP contributed to a marked increase in local democracy and development. As Gonzalo Rojas Ortuste and Laurent Thévoz (1998, 20) conclude, "it is the LPP, along with all of the entities responsible for its implementation, that are in a situation of dependency in the face of these municipal dynamics and not the reverse." Oscar Coca went so far as to suggest that "popular participation is nothing new. It is the legitimation of something that already existed" (personal interview, Cochabamba, July 13, 1999). So strong was this influence that it helped mitigate the negative consequences of political party competition in those communities were state-society synergy predated the LPP.

Surprisingly, no systematic study has been conducted to try to understand the sources of this preexisting yet powerful political dynamic. While such a study is beyond the scope of this chapter, one plausible explanation might be found by looking at the differentiated impact of local struggles connected with the 1952 revolution. As suggested earlier, the revolution reflected very weak central institutions in which local communities acted with considerable autonomy from the state, political parties, and even peak labor and peasant organizations at the national level. This vacuum at the center was filled to differing degrees and in a range of ways according to various factors that reflected the preexisting nature of the economy, the strength of different local actors, and even the relative strength or weakness of local actors' ties to central institutions. This underscores why institutional reforms like those in the LPP cannot be imposed if their goal is to generate social change, particularly in those areas where the preexisting level of trust in central state institutions is low. Moreover, it is precisely in those areas where a conflictual relationship exists between the state and civil society that the model offered by the LPP is most needed. This is why an inclusive process of state-society synergy is necessary so that the state can work with civil society to build new sources of consensus and more legitimate institutional mechanisms, allowing citizenship as agency to flourish.

The LPP has had very little impact in urban areas. For example, 80 percent of the recognized OTBs by the end of 1995 were in rural areas (Booth, Clisby, and Widmark 1997, 24). Similarly, a national survey of Bolivian political culture found that people in small towns and rural areas were two and a half to three times more likely to participate than people in cities with populations greater than twenty thousand (Seligson 1998, 14). One comprehensive study of the LPP chose not to even include urban areas (Booth, Clisby, and Widmark 1997). This in part reflects central government policies targeting rural areas. More important is the fact that in the areas where LPP has had the greatest impact, the state has been largely absent, and, as a result, significant political party activity was also noticeably lacking. Relying on preexisting organizations and substantial coparticipación funds, the LPP has been most successful in areas with an institutional vacuum. Conversely, larger cities are characterized by "the persistence of practices and customs of corporatist representation in the principal institutions and organizations," which also explains lower levels of political participation (Molina Saucedo 1999). Larger cities also have substantial sources of revenue independent of coparticipación funds, weakening that incentive for people to become involved in LPP mechanisms. This reflects a real limit to the LPP's underlying goal of "reconciling the formal state with the real state" (Barbery Anaya 1997, 56). The formal state in urban areas, corrupted and weakened as it is by rent-seeking and patrimonial political parties, was too formidable an obstacle to be easily displaced by the LPP reforms. The challenge for local democracy in rural areas is to resist these same tendencies, transforming the formal state in the process.

Municipal Governments and the Threat of National Patrimonial Politics

The contradiction between national-level political processes, with their corruption, inefficiency, and partisan extremes, and the ideal of local participatory democracy is a stark one. The hope behind the LPP is that the local ideal, if fully realized, will force democratizing changes up through the state structure. The obvious danger is that the direction of causality will go in the opposite direction, with national political tendencies undermining local democratic experiments. National politics does not offer much of a model for civic spiritedness, at the same time that effective decentralization and local democratic accountability threaten the prerogatives of powerful political actors. For this reason, political parties insisted that only they be able to compete in local elections—a monopoly that was safeguarded in the national constitution and that political parties refused to give up in passing a new Political Party Law (Ley de Partidos Políticos) (*El Diario,* July 28, 1999).[18]

The central institutional role this provided political parties at the local level suggests that "one of the greatest dangers confronting Popular Participation in the longer term is that it provides no more than a basis for a systematic extension of the less acceptable features of Bolivian national politics down to the grassroots" (Booth, Clisby, and Widmark 1997, 48–49). This was particularly serious because as a direct assault on the power and impunity of established interests, the LPP threatened "a conspiracy [that] exists between political parties and the bureaucracy in the three branches of the state—the Legislature, Judiciary and Executive—where traditional elitist, centralizing, authoritarian and racist conceptions of politics predominate" (Ardaya Salinas 1998, 36). Ironically, one way to undermine this potential of the LPP is to use its institutions as a means for increasing party bases, so municipal governments lose their autonomy to the patrimonial dynamic of political parties. The newness of the local governments and other institutions created by the LPP may make them particularly susceptible to such pressures (Vargas R. 1998, 39).

Increasing evidence suggests that traditional political party logics undermined the democratic potential of the LPP (Armando Ortuño, personal interview, La Paz, June 29, 1999; Vargas R. 1998; Ardaya Salinas 1998; Booth, Clisby, and Widmark 1997; Albó 1999). At the same time, undemocratic political party structures did not change and represented a "powerful entry-barrier for the poor and disenfranchised" (Gray-Molina 1998, 16). In some cases, even NGOs working with local governments were captured by political parties (Booth, Clisby, and Widmark 1997, 50), and a number of OTBs linked with political parties were the first to seek legal recognition to gain access to new resources.

The negative consequences of political party penetration at the local level emerged early on: by the end of 1997, eight municipal governments had their funds frozen due to budget abnormalities and seventy-eight had been investigated by the central government (Gray-Molina 1998, 6). The length of investigations, which could take years, undermined public confidence in local institutions and may even have contributed to a sense of impunity that threatens the legitimacy of those institutions (Armando Otuño, personal interview, La Paz, June 29, 1999; PNUD 1999). At least one public opinion poll found that people generally considered "municipalities the worst instances of corruption in the country" (UIA 1999, 38).

Party penetration of local government politics was also facilitated by the constructive censure vote (UIA 1999; Rojas Ortuste 1998; Luján Veneros 2004). This measure was promulgated through a 1995 constitutional amendment, when the mayor's term in office was extended from two years to five. After one year in office, a mayor could be removed by a three-fifths vote of the members of the municipal council. In practice, this amounted to a simple majority of councilors in 95 percent of municipalities, where there were only five or seven councilors on the municipal council. The result was an extremely high level of political instability. In 1996, one year after the 1995 municipal elections, 39 percent of all mayors were removed from office by this means. In 1997 another 39 percent lost their posts so that 80 percent of all mayors had been removed from office between 1995 and 1997.[19] While the number of mayors who were removed in later years declined significantly to 19.11 percent of all mayors in 2000–2001 (Luján Veneros 2004, 175), continued reliance on the "'destructive censure vote' . . . has ominous results in Bolivia, destabilizing the municipal organizational culture" (Roca 2004, 172).[20]

The effect of this has generally been to impose national political alliances on local governments, frequently displacing local leaders and local interests, as the political parties used municipal elections to enhance their national electoral prospects and power (PNUD 1999; Luján Veneros 2004). Local political dynamics "have responded fundamentally to [national] political interests and personal graft" (UIA 1999, 42). People's skepticism toward local government only increased (Erika Brockmann, personal interview, La Paz, June 30, 1999; *La Razon,* April 4, 2006) and electoral participation declined (Luján Veneros 2004), further undermining the legitimacy of political parties rather than democratizing them.

Equally serious, this politicization of municipal governments further undermined their limited administrative capacity. The high turnover among elected officials invariably led to the high turnover among city employees, as partisan and particularistic interests prevailed over professional qualifications (Aliendre España 2004; Galindo Soza 2004; Lastra Vía 2004; García Salaues 2004). The lack of a permanent civil service and low levels of training for municipal employees was too fragile to bear the burden of excessive politicization. Yet labor laws also ensured that dismissed employees received compensation, creating another drain on limited municipal resources (García Salaues 2004).

The political abuse of the constructive censure vote disproportionately affected indigenous people and women. For example, although the proportion of indigenous mayors removed from office through the constructive censure vote was basically the same as the national average, in both 1996 and 1997 there was a 10 percent reduction in the number of indigenous mayors because not all of their successors were indigenous. This meant that there were only sixty-six indigenous mayors in 1998, compared to seventy-nine in 1995. For women mayors, seven out of the nine who were elected in 1995 had been removed from office by 1998—a total of 78 percent! In contrast to the situation of indigenous mayors, however, they were usually succeeded by other women (UIA 1999).[21]

The lure of power (personal and partisan) also had the effect of seriously fragmenting electoral politics, as increasing numbers of parties competed for power (Gray-Molina 2003). This dispersed votes and weakened the social base of candidates who actually won elections. For example, in the 1999 elections, only 7.31 percent of the mayors were elected by absolute majority, down from 13.5 percent in 1995 (Luján Veneros 2004, 174). In many cases, municipal councils had as many parties in them as there were counselors, raising serious obstacles to the emergence of strong local governments. Despite the undisputed democratic quality of the elections themselves, this fragmentation raised fundamental questions about representation because under these circumstances, "counselors no longer represent the interests of the electorate, but political parties or their own" (153).

The situation ultimately became intolerable. Popular pressure and repudiation of traditional political parties forced traditional parties to remove their constitutional monopoly over political participation for the 2004 municipal elections. For the first time, citizens groups and indigenous people not linked to a particular political party could run for election.

While political parties had resisted this change to guard their own interests, the long-term impact of opening electoral competition may have been to
paradoxically further undermine the democratic potential of LPP, because it
further exacerbated problems of excessive political fragmentation. The organization that captured the most votes was Evo Morales's Movement Toward Socialism (Movimiento al Socialismo, MAS), with a mere 18.48 percent of the total
national vote. The second biggest vote winner, the Fearless Movement (Movimiento sin Miedo), had just 8.74 percent of the vote. Indeed, the fragmentation
reached such an extreme that different ethnic groups in the same rural communities competed against one another at the local level, further dividing the indigenous movement (Gisselquist 2005).[22] Although local electoral success may
have contributed to Morales's success at the national level in winning the December 2005 presidential elections, weak, fragmented local government meant
that challenges of integration and successful state-society synergy could not be
effectively addressed at the local level. This raises important questions about the
relevance of LPP for dealing with these challenges.

OTBs as the Interlocutors for Civil Society

OTBs form the foundation upon which the LPP rests. In basing the LPP's most
innovative participatory mechanisms on the OTB, the architects of the law assumed that the OTBs enjoyed relatively high levels of participation and social
inclusiveness. Initially, due to misunderstandings about what the LPP entailed
and a general distrust of all state institutions, there was much resistance to the
LPP precisely in those areas where there was a history of local organization.
Conversely, the LPP was most widely accepted where there was little history of
local organizations, making it very difficult to construct interlocutors to work
with municipal governments (Archondo 1997, 279–80).

As noted, most of this opposition was eventually overcome and tens of thousands of OTBs quickly received legal status. Once this was achieved, however,
there generally has been little effort to mobilize organizations or citizens to get
people to actually participate in local politics (Grebe López 1997, 181; Booth,
Clisby, and Widmark 1997, 86). This was particularly true for the young: a national survey conducted by the United Nations Development Programme
(PNUD 1998, 117–18) found that 73.7 percent of people twenty-one to thirty
years of age had no contacts with local organizations, and this was especially
pronounced among women.

One factor explaining this low level of participation is demographics and
migration from depressed rural areas (Booth, Clisby, and Widmark 1997, 76). As
Ramiro Bocal explained, "agrarian unions had not been renewed. Many leaders had left and only women and old people remained. So when the LPP was

adopted, nothing changed. . . . The unions were practically abandoned" (personal interview, Cliza, July 8, 1999). In other cases, organizations were formed simply to channel new funds or work with state institutions but without any real connection to society. Instead, these organizations were viewed as "imposed, artificial" (Ana Maria Lema, personal interview, Santa Cruz, July 15, 1999).

This was in sharp contrast with important functional organizations, particularly committees formed to secure irrigation and potable water. The reason for the dynamism of such committees, according to Bocal, is that they had something concrete to offer their members. Successful committees often did not disband once irrigation or potable water was obtained for their members, and they have shown the capacity to move into other areas of activity related to community development.[23] Yet because they were not territorially based, they were excluded from the LPP.

These problems are particularly acute in urban areas, where neighborhood councils are the principal form of OTB. A PNUD study (1998, 17, 125–26) found that fewer than 30 percent of residents participated, and that the principal participants were men over thirty from privileged socioeconomic classes. Political party influence was also quite noticeable. This is one reason why the LPP has had such a limited impact in urban areas, as Rafeal Archondo (1997, 279) explains, "the ideals of participatory democracy fall through the floor when one sees close up how the majority of neighborhood councils function. All of the vices associated with rent-seeking and the usurpation of the general will are found in them. For the same reason, mayors are able to manipulate their members so that the resulting vigilance committees are mere appendices of the municipal executive."

The lack of a solid social foundation among many OTBs makes them particularly vulnerable to the problems of rent seeking and corruption that plague Bolivian politics. From the perspective of state-civil society relations, the weakness of civil society actually is a primary source of extremes of self-interest, simply because civil society is incapable of providing an effective countervailing force. This can be seen clearly in the rather pessimistic conclusions of Humberto Vargas R. (1998, 38):

> Given the traditional characteristics of political actors and the way they govern with the greatest concentration of power possible, this assures the survival of clientelist relations in their dealings with the leaders of base organizations. These leaders are like prisoners given that, if they want to legitimate their leadership, they have to obtain benefits for their community; and as the formula established by the authorities is through the negotiation of favors, a mandatory structure has been created that constrains them. . . . The stronger political will (that of the authorities because of the power they are given) will always impose itself on the weak.

Beyond the inability of the OTBs to represent civil society in general, the LPP has had a significant negative impact on female participation at the local level. This is despite the LPP's formal commitment to ensuring equal opportunities for men and women. As already noted, female mayors were much more likely than their male counterparts to be removed from office through recourse to the constructive censure vote. This is particularly troubling given that the number of women mayors had actually fallen in the aftermath of the 1995 elections (the first under the LPP), from nineteen to eleven. The drop in the percentage of female counselors was even greater, falling to only 8 percent compared to the 27 percent achieved under the previous system. Yet the number of municipalities for which mayors were elected in 1995 had increased by 150 percent, and there was a concomitant increase in the number of women candidates for counselor.

The situation was sufficiently alarming that in 1997 a quota was established requiring that 30 percent of all candidates be women. Yet the reluctance of political parties seriously undermined the impact of this change. Most women candidates had to run as alternates, and they accounted for 70 percent of people running as alternates in 2000. There were even cases of men running with women's names who were discovered by authorities only after they already had been elected. As a result, the number of women mayors increased to only twenty in 2000 (one more than under the old system). While the number of female counselors doubled, this was a far cry from what they had achieved prior to the introduction of the LPP.[24] At the same time, women who did find themselves serving on municipal councils tended to be passive and less active than their male counterparts, further reinforcing the traditional gender stereotypes that have kept women out of the municipal councils in the first place (Kudelka 2004, 535–58).

The decision to exclude sectoral organizations from participating in the LPP also had a negative impact on the potential for women's participation to improve (Dianna Urioste, personal interview, La Paz, July 5, 1999; Booth, Clisby, and Widmark 1997, 26). OTBs have traditionally been run by men, while women have tended to participate much more actively in groups such as mother's clubs, handicraft cooperatives, and women's sections in labor organizations that are not territorially based. One survey, conducted in 1999, showed that the rate of male versus female participation in OTBs was twenty-four to one, while it was eight to one in CVs (Kudelka 2004, 534). The result, according to Vargas R. (1998, 18–19), is "a structural bias in the LPP" against women's political participation, which has meant that "women are paying the price of the Law's creators' preoccupation with excluding [corporatist organizations] like the COB and its union affiliates."

A virtual explosion of opportunities for women to participate paradoxically resulted in fewer women in positions of political power. A number of factors were involved. Cultural biases against female political participation, in both traditional indigenous society and Bolivian society at large, worked to discourage female participation (Roberto Barbery, personal interview, Santa Cruz, July 16, 1999; Gloria Aguilar, La Paz, July 5, 1999).[25] Now that the LPP gave real power and resources directly to municipal governments, and indirectly to OTBs, men quickly came to dominate positions that in the past were less attractive to them (Kudelka 2004).[26] High rates of female illiteracy (especially in rural areas) and lower levels of female educational achievement were also important handicaps (Gloria Aguilar, personal interview, La Paz, July 5, 1999; Booth, Clisby, and Widmark 1997, 26). Women's own lack of self-confidence also prevented them from trying to assume more responsible roles in their communities (Dianna Urioste, personal interview, La Paz, July 5, 1999).

The specific example of women's participation and the more general problems of representation associated with OTBs underscore how efforts at social engineering are fraught with complexities that can lead to unanticipated consequences. Decisions, such as excluding corporatist organizations, can be seen as quite arbitrary if the perspective is changed to look at the impact of those decisions on the groups directly affected. At the same time, the LPP's limited impact on improving the participation and representation of disadvantaged groups highlights the ambiguity of cultural distinctions between the West and traditional indigenous cultures. In reality, there is much overlap, both positive and negative. Efforts to create institutional mechanisms that allow them to co-exist democratically must recognize this and harness the inherent dynamism of all cultures in constructive ways. These inherent difficulties can be rectified only through a more inclusive process of state-society synergy that prioritizes citizenship as agency from its inception. The experience of women, in particular, demonstrates quite forcefully the importance of negotiating and ensuring that all affected parties are somehow included before institutions are enacted by fiat.

The Limits of Participatory Planning

The problems of weak state institutions and extreme poverty combine to complicate the challenge of successful participatory planning. Indeed, one of the principal challenges of participatory budgeting is "to convert the planning process into a vehicle for state-civil society relations, given the critical state of other institutions, such as political parties for example. In this way, there would be a very strong vehicle, with better direction and power that is very versatile in the generation, coordination, application and control of public policies, something that would evidently build a nation" (Galindo Soza 2004, 139).

The most immediate effect of extreme poverty is that it skews local investment of coparticipación funding away from productive investments that would create employment and additional sources of municipal income toward social expenditures that address the more immediate needs of the community (Archondo 1997; PNUD 1998; Booth, Clisby, and Widmark 1997; Gray-Molina 1998). One study found that 67 percent of the resources in twenty-seven municipalities went to social expenditures (health care, education, and housing), and only 7.5 percent went into productive investments. The rest went into transportation and commercialization. And even when there is recognition of the need to build infrastructure and fund large-scale projects, people still prioritized their own neighborhoods because of a lack of strategic vision (Galindo Soza 2004). As Archondo (1997, 276–77) concludes, if it has to rely on participatory budgeting, "the municipality will not be able to convert itself into a productive engine [for growth] or have an income or employment policy."

From the perspective of the poor, there may be a trade-off in addressing immediate needs and long-term strategic planning, and they "opt for the easy way" (Erika Brockmann, personal interview, La Paz, June 30, 1999). This tendency is exacerbated by other factors, including the symbolism and visibility of building plazas or parks, as well as the fact that such investments are easier to implement (Carmen Barragán, personal interview, La Paz, July 3, 1999; Archondo 1997). Barragán also noted that high levels of political instability provided mayors with few incentives to engage in strategic long-term planning.

Equally important, PNUD (1998, 61) concluded that the lack of municipal resources was a further impediment to change. This is particularly important in rural communities, where the lack of resources independent of the coparticipación funds severely restricted the scope of participatory budgeting and required difficult decisions regarding priorities for the use of scarce funds. Conversely, in the few larger cities that generate almost 85 percent of municipal revenues independent of coparticipación funding (principally La Paz, Santa Cruz, and Cochabamba), the scope of participatory budgeting is severely limited by the relative lack of importance of coparticipación funding (Galindo Soza 2004; Lastra Vía 2004).

At the same time, participation by OTBs generally was limited to setting priorities for expenditures and making demands, rather than actually participating in the planning process (Archondo 1997; Vargas R. 1998; Booth, Clisby, and Widmark 1997; Galindo Soza 2004). This was partly due to the nature of the planning process itself, which was not designed for more active inputs from civil society, particularly given the time constraints of annual budgeting processes. But it also reflects past patterns of a more paternalist and, at times, conflictual relationship, in which civil society looked to the state to resolve its problems. As Thomas Reilly of the USAID's Democratic Development and Citizen Participation Program noted, referring specifically to the period of military rule, there has yet to be a "transition from protesting to making proposals" (personal interview, La Paz, July 1, 1999).

The noticeable lack of productive investment has attracted increasing concern. Without job creation and productive economic development, the redistributive advances of the LPP from urban to rural areas are undermined. The
larger productive base and more developed administrative capacity for tax collection in the larger cities (the nine department capitals and El Alto) give them a
relatively large autonomous source of revenue that minimizes the impact of coparticipación funds on municipal expenditures.[27] In 1996 coparticipación funds
represented just 27 percent of their total revenues, compared to 68 percent for
the other 301 municipalities. Yet because of their large populations, these ten
cities received 70 percent of the increased revenue sharing from the central state
between 1995 and 1996. Unless the other municipalities can begin to develop
their own productive base, the relative redistribution of state resources in favor
of rural areas will eventually be reversed (Porcel and Thévoz 1998, 98–99; Rojas
Ortuste and Thévoz 1998, 18). There is even the danger of a vicious cycle if migration to the larger urban areas is not slowed. Indeed, one reason for enacting
the LPP was to reverse such trends, given that projections showed urbanization
would reach 80 percent of the population by 2000, compared to 58 percent in
1992 (Secretaría Nacional 1997, 12). Moreover, the absence of public policies will
likely increase income inequality in rural areas as better-off farmers pursue private means to increase their own productivity (Gray-Molina 1998).

The importance of productive investment is becoming increasingly clear to
Bolivian citizens as well, and there has been a noticeable increase in demands
for productive projects (Carmen Barragán, personal interview, La Paz, July 3,
1999). Unfortunately, municipal governments do not seem to listen. A study of
ninety-four municipalities found that only 36 percent of community demands
were actually incorporated into municipal plans. In particular, elected governments favored social investments with visible, rapid payoffs for beneficiaries
over longer-term productive investments (Archondo 1997, 289–90). By 2000
this number had fallen to just 23 percent (Galindo Soza 2004, 112–13).

To address this problem, mechanisms for cofinancing productive investments were established by the central state through its various national investment funds, the Programas Nacionales de Inversión Pública (National Public
Investment Programs) and departmental governments at the regional level (Archondo 1997, 290; Grindle 2000). Similarly, as part of the 2000 National Dialogue Law (Ley de Diálogo Nacional, LDN), it was stipulated that 45 percent
of community demands be incorporated into municipal plans (Galindo Soza
2004, 112–13). Both national policies underscore the ways in which competing
developmental goals and priorities can constrain local decision-making autonomy in the participatory budgeting process. This is an important recognition
of the limits of local development efforts, highlighting the need for national
development policies to catalyze those efforts by providing appropriate incentives and additional resources beyond the capacity of municipal governments to

mobilize. There is a clear need for more comprehensive policies that focus on the source of these discrepancies, particularly between community expectations and national development goals, if new contradictions are not to be introduced into the institutions of LPP. Even this small gain in the percentage of community demands included in municipal plans was stipulated centrally and contrasts sharply with other experiences of participatory budgeting.

National development policies, such as the LPP itself, should be designed and implemented with local participation. Centrally mandated policies promoting productive investments introduced new tensions in state-society relations that could have a long-term detrimental impact on Bolivia's democracy. The requirements for cofinancing have often disrupted local planning processes, creating the perception that municipal governments had lost their own initiative due to impositions from higher levels of government in line with major national development programs such as the Programa de Apoyo Solidario a las Escuelas (Program of Support in Solidarity with Schools) and the Seguro Materno Infantil (Maternal-Child Health Program). Moreover, when development projects had to be revised to receive funding, this was rarely done in consultation with civil society. Even relatively successful programs have had their impact limited because they were enacted without input from the affected communities (Galindo Soza 2004). In some cases, local governments have also been forced to include projects in their budgets that were the priorities of funding agencies to get assistance with their own priority projects. Bolivia's participation in the Heavily Indebted Poor Countries (HIPC) initiative of the World Bank and the International Monetary Fund has led to a further recentralization of key social policies, particularly in education and health care (Ameller Terrazas 2002). Together, these various interactions demonstrate the unequal relationship between municipal governments and other levels. This further delegitimizes participatory mechanisms, "consolidating the population's lack of trust in their authorities and opinions that 'in any case, they do what they want'" (Porcel and Thévoz 1998, 102).

This problem was further exacerbated by preexisting centralist tendencies at the national level and a tendency not to take local governments into account in national decision-making processes (Vargas R. 1998, 33–34; Casanovas Sainz 2004). As Gloria Aguilar, a member of the La Paz Consejo Municipal (Municipal Council), noted, the LPP provided only for "halfway decentralization" (personal interview, La Paz, July 5, 1999). Traditional paternalist policies—the mere distribution of goods and services—are still pervasive (Vargas R. 1998, 31). There may even be a tendency toward making "stereotypical demands" that do not necessarily reflect the real necessities of people, but what people feel central state institutions are promoting at any particular time (Erika Brockmann, personal interview, La Paz, June 30, 1999). More recently, particularly under policies adopted for Bolivia to gain access to resources freed up by HIPC, the share of municipal investment in total public investment declined to 20–22 percent in 2002–3 (Galindo Soza 2004, 105n20).

Of course, central, regional, and local governments must also be up to the task of promoting local (as well as national) development. The institutional weaknesses at all three levels have contributed to diminishing important aspects of the LPP. For example, budgeted programs frequently are not implemented. In the study of municipal budgets reported by Archondo (1997, 277), only 33 percent of approved projects were actually undertaken. In the larger study by Porcel and Thévoz of 151 representative municipal governments (1998, 103–14), only slightly more than 50 percent of budgets were actually executed. This reflected the weakness of municipal administrations, particularly in elaborating projects and following through. But it also reflected the dependency of local governments on higher levels of government, which did not always follow through on their own obligations. This put local governments in an unsustainable situation: "they are responsible to their electors for the execution of municipal projects, when in reality they do not control the factors that are most influential" in determining their success (105). This was particularly true in the area of productive investments, which Porcel and Thévoz characterized as examples of "catastrophic execution" (109). Overall, according to Porcel and Thévoz, "in terms of the rural reality, we can confirm that the actual system of co-financing does not permit the satisfaction of social demands identified through participative mechanisms at the municipal level" (113). The lack of national and regional programs is also a problem because it "makes it radically impossible for municipal governments to place a priority on many demands of the productive sectors" (102).

Of particular concern is the institutional weakness of the departmental governments.[28] The Ley de Descentralización Administrativa (Administrative Decentralization Law) increased the power and resources of the prefecture so that it could fill the role of coordinating the activities of all three levels of government—municipal, regional, and central. Departmental governments retain control over important parts of the health care and education sectors, and also administer the Fortalecimiento Municipal (Municipal Strengthening) program that plays an important role in supporting municipal planning processes.

In practice, strong opposition to the LPP has come from this level, which David Booth, Suzanne Clisby, and Charlotta Widmark (1997, 99–100) describe as an example of "oligarchic decentralization." The new powers and resources at the prefects' disposal have created strong temptations to use them for political ends, with the result that presidential appointments have been determined by national party logics. This has created serious problems of limited technical capacity, at the same time that regional governments have been taken over by the rent-seeking and clientelist logics that dominate national politics. For local governments, relations with regional governments have often been problematic, blocking access to needed resources. According to Gloria Aguilar, a municipal council member in La Paz, the departmental governments have become ends in themselves rather than the means for greater democratization that they were intended to be, further circumscribing the autonomy of municipal governments (personal interview, La Paz, July 5, 1999).

In this context, it is not surprising that participation has been low and declining, particularly in large urban areas where it is really only a formality.[29] In both rural and urban areas, municipal development plans are often written with little or no community consultation, and in rural areas they are frequently prepared by consultants with limited background or expertise. Issues of representation are compounded by the even more limited role played by women, youth, and indigenous people. The intrusion of partisan dynamics and interests, as well as clientelism and rent seeking, raise further questions about the legitimacy of community demands. These problems are only exacerbated by the shortcomings associated with the LPP that make it harder to motivate disadvantaged groups to even attempt to engage in the process. From this perspective, the real danger for Bolivian democracy may ultimately be that by not fulfilling its promise to provide democratic institutional mechanisms for finding solutions to the problems the disadvantaged majority confronts, the LPP will pass on into irrelevance and disuse as people increasingly seek political recourse outside of state institutions.

Linking Civil Society with Local Government: The Role of the CVs

If OTBs are the foundation on which the LPP rests, then the CVs are its central pillars. One CV is elected by the OTBs in each municipal jurisdiction. The CV's tasks include articulating OTB demands in municipal planning processes and protecting community interests through the oversight of the expenditure of coparticipación funds. Ideally, CVs also serve as schools for learning citizenship and prepare local leaders for assuming other positions of responsibility (Molina Saucedo 1999). They have a de facto monopoly in exercising social control at the local level (Maydana 2004; Guzmán Boutier 1998) and ultimately are the principal channel for popular participation under the LPP. Their success is directly related to their legitimacy and ability to represent civil society's full spectrum. If they do not succeed in fulfilling their role, the democratizing promise of the LPP will be seriously undermined.

Creating 311 CVs was a slow process. By December 1995, only 163 had been formed. Then the government issued a decree on December 12, stating that CVs had to be formed by December 31 to be in compliance with the LPP—and be eligible for coparticipación funds. The result: "in 15 days all the political parties that governed municipalities created Vigilance Committees" (Ardaya Salinas 1998, 25). This process, aside from raising obvious questions about who

CVs actually represent, underscores how local civil societies did not value the role CVs potentially could play in empowering them. As creations of the state, CVs suffered from legitimacy problems that undermined their ability to serve as a link between civil society and the local municipal government. According to Raúl Maydana (2004, 204), "in the majority of cases they had only formal relations; the base makes demands, but does not support" the CV.[30] Even the minimal success that CVs are able to achieve is dependent on external support, from both the central government and international cooperation, rather than civil society (2004).

This lack of mobilization behind their creation is just one of a number of problems CVs have had to confront. As a result, CVs are only rarely able to fulfill their assigned role. In one study of eleven CVs (Guzmán Boutier 1998), only two were functioning, with important qualifications in both cases. The finding is consistent with other studies and found that the relatively few successful CVs were able to perform their assigned role due to the presence of strong indigenous and peasant organizations. This further underscores the difficulties CVs face in urban areas, where such an organizational infrastructure is lacking, highlighting the importance of a strong civil society. Even members of CVs share this negative assessment. At the Fourth National Meeting of Vigilance Committees (Cuarto Encuentro Nacional de Comités de Vigilancia) held in 2002, social actors expressed their dissatisfaction with the exercise of social control, given the way CVs were manipulated by municipal governments and co-opted by political parties (Maydana 2004).

A basic confusion over the actual role CVs are supposed to play in the LPP, particularly their role in exercising social control over the expenditure of co-participación funds, only exacerbates these problems. Neither the members of OTBs who elect the CVs nor the elected members of the CVs actually understand what it means or how to achieve it. While the LPP specifically empowers only CVs to perform a social oversight role, other institutions, including the municipal councils, also have an oversight role and the LPP does not clearly delineate what is distinct about CVs (Booth, Clisby, and Widmark 1997; Guzmán Boutier 1998; Vargas R. 1998; Maydana 2004). Nine different institutions, each with its own procedures and jurisdiction, can receive complaints of abuse, allowing citizens to bypass CVs completely (Maydana 2004, 226). And this is exactly what tends to happen. For example, of the forty-two complaints lodged with the Contraloría General de la República (Office of the Comptroller General) in 1995–96 for not respecting the LPP's budgeting guidelines, only ten (24 percent) were made by CVs. The rest came from the mayor's office (sixteen, or 38 percent), the municipal council (five), neighborhood councils (four), individuals (four), civic committees (two) and OTBs (one) (Guzmán Boutier 1998, 142–43). Similarly, of the fifty-two cases the *defensor del pueblo* (ombudsman) decided favorably on in 2002, only two came from CVs in predominantly rural municipalities (Maydana 2004, 227). This is clearly not in the spirit of the LPP, and it directly limits the effectiveness of one of its principal institutional innovations.

There are also major obstacles to effective financial oversight at both the national and municipal levels. At the national level, the process of lodging complaints is fragmented with little coordination, given that such complaints are received by three different bodies: the Department of Finance (Ministerio de Hacienda), the Comptroller (Contraloría), and the Senate. Follow-up is often very slow, with the result that municipal budgets can be frozen for long periods of time (Erika Brockmann, personal interview, La Paz, June 30, 1999; Guzmán Boutier 1998). The process also is not transparent and is vulnerable to political intervention (Maydana 2004). Moreover, priority is given to addressing complaints from larger cities, undermining the role of CVs in the rest of the country (Guzmán Boutier 1998, 146).

At the municipal level, CVs depend on the municipal government for vital information, and the local government often simply refuses to provide it. This can create a vicious cycle of distrust and conflict between municipal governments and the organizations empowered by the LPP: "The many questions that . . . CVs have with respect to the execution of municipal works often remain unanswered and instead generate/feed vulnerabilities and conflicts among municipal actors. This disinformation, in turn, feeds the lack of transparency or the local conflicts surrounding municipal financial management" (Porcel and Thévoz 1998, 111; see also Ardaya Salinas 1998).

Other serious problems relate to the autonomy of CVs. A variety of factors contribute to the distancing of the CV from its social base. The vast physical distances in many rural jurisdictions require that CV members spend substantial periods of time away from their local communities. Much of the actual work of CVs therefore takes place "where local moral pressure is weakest, costs of living are high and the temptations of office are not insignificant" (Booth, Clisby, and Widmark 1997, 31). This is particularly true for the CV president, who has come to dominate CV activities, exercising control as if the CV were almost a personal fiefdom (Maydana 2004).

The LPP deliberately did not provide for financing the activities of the CVs, in part to avoid turning them into a source of patronage and out of fear of co-opting them, but also because the LPP is founded on the liberal ideal that community service should be voluntary (PNUD 1998, 132). Moreover, the task of fiscal oversight is a very technical one. Few CV members have the necessary skills to fulfill these tasks, which also increases their vulnerability to political pressures from the municipality. The result is that the members of CVs, particularly the CV presidents, are increasingly exposed to the patrimonial and rent-seeking dynamic of Bolivian politics in general. This is particularly true in the larger cities, where political parties and clientelism are generally stronger (133).

All of these issues compound the problem CVs confront in trying to gain social acceptance for their oversight role, particularly when the municipal government is very popular (Booth, Clisby, and Widmark 1997). It also undermines the ability of CVs to mobilize society in their support, making them even more vulnerable to co-optation by municipal governments and political parties (Porcel and Thévoz 1998, 111). In some cases, the problem is so acute that there is real doubt as to whether the CV even understands the true nature of community demands (Guzmán Boutier 1998).

In an effort to address some of these problems, a Social Control Fund (Fondo de Control Social) was established to give CVs more independence from the municipal governments they are supposed to oversee. The effect may actually have been to make matters worse (Maydana 2004). The creation of the fund has only increased dependence on municipal governments responsible for transferring monies to the CVs and the prefects, who are responsible for overseeing how they are spent. At the same time, the lack of transparency has contributed to the political manipulation of funds by the municipal governments, while they have increased the power of CV presidents who manage the funds once they are received. With hindsight, the LPP's architects may have been right not to provide CVs with funding, for the ultimate consequence of the fund has been to further delegitimate CVs, as their perceived distance from civil society increased.

As the example of the Social Control Fund demonstrates, as CVs in effect become more distant from civil society, they become even more dependent on the municipal governments they are supposed to oversee and influence on behalf of civil society. This further diminishes the ability of CVs to perform the role they have been assigned in the LPP, ultimately "causing a weakening of citizen participation in municipal management" (Guzmán Boutier 1998, 138). The problem has become so acute that some even are calling for the abolition of CVs, particularly now that OTBs can compete in municipal elections (Galindo Soza 2004).

Rather than promote citizenship as agency and state-society synergy, in practice the LPP accentuates the logic of "civil society versus the state." At best, CVs become channels for making demands on state resources, to the exclusion of a "logic of complementarity between civil society and the state" (Maydana 2004, 234–35). At worst, they are little more than new sources of patronage and a mechanism for introducing divisive partisan dynamics that increase the abuse of power and co-opt some segments of civil society at the expense of the same disadvantaged groups the LPP was originally intended to empower. Rather than state-society synergy, the CVs represent a unique hybrid, combining elements of citizenship as co-optation and controlled inclusion with institutions intended to promote participatory democracy and social inclusion, adding yet another level of contradiction in the LPP's institutional design.

Indigenous Groups and the Quest for Democratic National Integration

One of the principal dynamics behind the LPP is the incorporation of indigenous communities into Bolivian politics and society, while recognizing their cultural distinctiveness. The LPP explicitly pledges to respect the *usos y costumbres* (practices and customs) of local communities in recognizing OTBs and in operationalizing various other aspects of the law. The LPP is a conscious effort to avoid the homogenizing thrust of previous reform efforts, including the agrarian reforms of the 1950s, which were often perceived by indigenous communities as poorly disguised efforts to impose Western structures on their cultures and societies. As already discussed, the LPP's ultimate goal is to create a hybrid system that combines the best of Western representative democracy with the more communitarian aspects of indigenous social organization.

Rather than a mere attempt to integrate indigenous communities into Bolivian politics and society, indigenous cultures and practices are seen as source of fundamental change for the entire political system. The vast majority of OTBs—the foundation of the LPP—are indigenous organizations. Their organizational style, based on consensus building and culturally determined democratic forms, is seen as the key not only to building stronger state institutions but to curbing abuses of existing institutions that result from individual self-interest at the expense of the public good (PNUD 1998). The assumption behind the LPP, which was developed without input from indigenous people, was that their traditional organizations were in fact compatible with the specific structures entailed in the LPP and that their members would be interested in participating in the LPP for reasons that transcended access to economic resources. To a lesser extent, there also may have been certain assumptions about the authenticity and democratic nature of indigenous culture embodied in these organizations that may not be entirely accurate, as the previous discussion of OTBs and women's participation makes clear. There certainly was an assumption that indigenous cultures were far more homogeneous that is in fact the case; even within communities representing the same indigenous group there are multiple forms of citizen participation and competing visions of development (Arias 2004).

The tension between the liberal, individualist philosophy that underlies the LPP and the collectivist nature of the indigenous community organizations that the LPP seeks to incorporate into local governance reflects the way the LPP was designed and implemented, not any irreconcilable cultural differences. Both individualist and collectivist visions of civil society are consistent with a concept of civil society in which its strength is determined by a multiplicity of self-organized groups demanding incorporation into larger political processes. A false dichotomy was created because the process by which the LPP transformed the Bolivian state prevented the successful mediation of the two perspectives through an inclusive process of the social construction of citizenship. Despite the best intentions of the reformers, the LPP in practice only made any potential contradiction worse.

Because of agrarian reforms and the weakness of central state institutions, civil society was arguably strongest in rural areas, and there was little overt demand for incorporation due to a deep distrust of modern or foreign institutions. In contrast, civil society was much weaker in urban areas—the usual locus of civil society activity—because the state and political parties curtailed its autonomy by undermining independent organizations. This situation is not unique to Bolivia, but in most other Latin American cases domination by the state or oligarchy over rural collective action is even more intense. Not surprisingly, particularly after sindicatos campesinos were recognized as OTBs, the impact of the LPP on rural communities has been mixed as the state's arrival threatened civil society's former autonomy.

This is clear in four in-depth case studies summarized by Booth, Clisby, and Widmark (1997, 68–94). All four cases were from rural municipalities with high concentrations of indigenous people. In the first case is Moxa, a municipality marked by a long history of conflictual relations and the continued dominance of criollo ranchers aided by the state even after the land reform. Here, the LPP has led to no change in power relations. Indigenous communities did not even consider the possibility of choosing indigenous candidates to run in municipal elections. There was no evidence of participatory planning and the CV was essentially not functioning.

In contrast, in the altiplano municipality of Corque, the traditional local governance institution of the *ayllu* was still very strong, largely because this was not an area historically dominated by haciendas. As a result, the land reform had little impact and sindicatos campesinos never developed any independent identity. With the LPP, there was the widespread perception that political parties were taking control of decision-making processes in the local government, at the same time that individuals started to seek public office for personal gain rather than out of a commitment to public service: "Elections were means by which people were 'tricked by the whites,' by the people with money, by the foreigners" (Booth, Clisby, and Widmark 1997, 79). Although much progress had been made in formally institutionalizing the LPP in Corque, the study concluded that "much of what had been achieved was superficial from the point of view of an authentic rural democratisation. . . . It still felt like an alien imposition; people might accept it with their minds but they had not taken it to their hearts" (79–80). The CV was not even meeting because it was perceived to be duplicating traditional practices of accountability rather than building on them.

The other two cases both come from the Chapare region of the department of Cochabamba, where the Asamblea para la Soberanía de los Pueblos (Assembly for the Sovereignty of Indigenous Peoples, ASP) has been very successful. The ASP is a political movement formed principally by coca producers (*cocaleros*) and their allies in the regional sindicato campesino movement. Out of forty-four municipalities in the department, the ASP won eleven mayorships, including all of those in the Chapare region, and elected forty-eight consejeros (Booth, Clisby, and Widmark 1997, 53). Formed in March 1995, the ASP is clearly one of the most successful examples of how indigenous groups have used the LPP to increase their political power—in this case, the coca producers who, according to Xavier Albó (1995), had become one of the best organized and most highly mobilized groups in Bolivia in the past decade. They also served as the foundation for Morales's electoral victory in 2005.

In sharp contrast to the general pattern in which the LPP was most successful in areas where the predominant political dynamic was much closer to state-civil society synergy, in the Chapare, organizations were strengthened as a result of the increasingly repressive state policy of coca eradication (Oscar Coca, personal interview, Cochabamba, July 13, 1999). For the cocaleros, it was a conflict revolving around their ability to survive economically, although they successfully incorporated ethnic and cultural elements into their discourse (Albó 1995). Their principal demand was not the right to sell coca for profit but rather the right to subsistence, and they stressed the need for the state to provide economic alternatives through regional development (Albó 1995; Herrera 1997). While official government policy was not crop eradication but crop substitution, the state's failure to provide successful economic alternatives while continuing to destroy coca crops only contributed to growing hostilities and the militarization of the coca-growing regions in the high security so-called red zones.

The first case in the Chapare analyzed by Booth, Clisby, and Widmark (1997) is Independencia. Agrarian reform had a big impact here, which corresponded with the emergence of a powerful peasant union movement. Due to a disciplined drive to get out the vote by the unions, the ASP won the majority of council positions and the mayor's office. Significantly, candidates were selected on the basis of the "practices and customs" of the union movement, and all had recently occupied senior union leadership positions. For the authors of the study, this was a clear example of the "empowerment of the formerly disempowered, and thus rural democratisation" (85). Yet the members of the new local government faced daunting problems, given their lack of education and their inability to contract needed technical assistance due to the absence of economic resources. Because of the delay in establishing a CV, the municipal budget was also temporarily frozen. Moreover, the study found that there was virtually no mobilization of OTBs to support either the local government or OTBs own interests. The study concluded that "little changed to raise the *quality* of the democratic participation of community members" (87).

The last case was Puerto Villarroel, where the population is mostly indigenous colonists who had arrived only within the past twenty years. Like Independencia, there was a well-organized union movement. Puerto Villarroel was also designated a "red zone," and the state was widely perceived as an intruder, threatening local residents' means of subsistence and culture. This served as the basis for an electoral campaign in which the ASP elected the mayor and four out of five council members. Indeed, the study found that the intensity of the conflict with the state gave the movement high levels of solidarity and coherence. Because of the ASP's success, the LPP is now portrayed as a social conquest as a result of the movement's struggles. Still, the municipal government suffers from a lack of funds and problems of project execution. There were also noticeable problems in programming productive investments because of the limits in the planning process, in which popular participation consists largely of only setting budget priorities. In this context of antagonism toward institutions established by the central state, it is not surprising that the CV "is largely a dead letter" (Booth, Clisby, and Widmark 1997, 93).

What all of these four cases underscore is that even the successful implementation of the LPP still suffers from many basic shortcomings. The limited developmental alternatives available through participatory planning and the more or less inoperative CVs stand out. At the same time, where successful, both traditional organizations and the rigid institutions proscribed in the law have evolved through their interaction or a process of state-civil society synergy. Democratic spaces have been opened up in the process. Where such evolution on both sides has been lacking, so too has any effective process of democratization.

This experience also underlines the fact that the problem confronted by the LPP in rural areas is not strictly cultural. As Diego Ayo (1997, 335) points out, it would be wrong to characterize Bolivia as consisting of two parallel political systems because the logic and codes of the Western world have penetrated rural areas. Sadly enough, this is one reason for widespread problems of low self-esteem (Jose Luis Nuñez, personal interview, La Paz, July 5, 1999)—the flip side of entrenched racism and discrimination. What is at stake is the process of how citizenship rights are constructed. The top-down approach to promulgating the LPP prevented this from happening in the earliest, formative phases of the reform. Instead, the LPP was often viewed with skepticism, as a formula for homogenization that makes all peoples conform to the same set of rules and institutions.

At the same time, the choices for indigenous peoples may be quite stark: complete autonomy is not acceptable if it comes at the cost of extreme rural poverty. Tellingly, 74 percent of the approximately 150 indigenous municipal districts (DMI) established as part of the LPP to further target indigenous communities have poverty rates of between 85 and 100 percent (Arias 2004, 437). Poverty and racism allow for, if not require, an almost opportunistic use of indigenous identity as "the demand for the creation of DMI is a response to the *lack of attention* from the municipal government to a specific canton or community and not the need to strengthen, increase the cohesion and protect a socio-cultural unit from a process of fragmentation. This has produced, in some communities, an almost artificial re-indigenization with the objective gaining access to more rights" (Arias 2004, 462–63).

Once again, racism and neglect can reinforce models of citizenship as co-optation, belying the existence of a more positive form of agency that can contribute to greater democratic inclusion. For many indigenous organizations, adapting to the practices and institutions of the LPP may entail adopting the pernicious logics the LPP was intentionally designed to control.

Pristine qualities of indigenous cultures should not be romanticized. The flip side of racism, exclusion, and extreme poverty is that some of the most insidious aspects of any culture are sometimes overlooked by well-meaning outsiders, at the same time that the concomitant weakness of civil society allows such shortcomings to go relatively unchallenged by those who are marginalized even within their own cultural communities. This is particularly true for women, and is undoubtedly one reason why their levels of participation showed a marked decrease with the introduction of the LPP. As one Bolivian researcher, Ana Maria Lema, sadly pointed out, "if by 'practices and customs' you mean incest, rape, and abuse," then the introduction of Western values may not be such a bad idea (personal interview, Santa Cruz, July 15, 1999).

The ultimate challenge is to create the kind of democratic hybrid originally envisioned by the LPP's architects through a process of the social construction of citizenship that includes citizens rather than imposes institutional innovations. Innovation and creativity on the part of all concerned actors are essential, and the LPP is an unprecedented, albeit flawed, attempt to achieve this. But for the LPP to realize its full potential, indigenous groups representing all segments of the indigenous population (not to mention other segments of Bolivian society) will have to have a role to play in determining the LPP's institutional evolution. It will require their sustained mobilization and more effective participation than has been the case to date. This is the only way to ensure that such a hybrid form of democracy, mixing Western and non-Western culture and practices, is socially constructed in an inclusive way and legitimated. In other words, indigenous groups will have to be actively involved in (re)defining Bolivian national identity and citizenship rights.

Opportunity Lost? Confronting the Challenge of Citizenship and the Growing Irrelevance of the LPP

The urgency of this challenge has become all too clear with growing levels of social mobilization and political instability, starting with the so-called water wars in Cochabamba in early 2000. The wave of mobilization that was unleashed ultimately led to the 2003 resignation of Sánchez de Lozada—ending the second presidential term of the same person who was responsible for the LPP's imple-mentation. After more than five years of political instability, the December 2005 electoral victory of Morales—as both Bolivia's first indigenous president and the first president to win a clear majority of votes since the democratic transition in 1982—has at least temporarily restored a semblance of political calm.

Both the wave of protests and Morales's political career began at the local level, raising important questions about the role the LPP may have played in the unfolding of these events. Given that the LPP represents an effort at social en-gineering designed to restructure Bolivian political institutions democratically from the bottom up, with the goal of achieving national integration not only for the first time but in a way that respects the pluricultural nature of Bolivian society, one would expect it to have played a decisive role, particularly in un-derstanding Morales's spectacular rise as a national leader. Yet the LPP was also intended to reverse many of the same socioeconomic and political dynamics that fed the growing social unrest and Morales's personal appeal, suggesting that it was, at best, irrelevant to recent political events or, at worst, one of the causes of a growing crisis of Bolivian democracy. Solving this puzzle is important not only for understanding the challenges for the LPP but for achieving citizenship as agency through state-civil society synergy.

Many of the problems that have prevented the LPP from achieving its stated goals are the same ones that it sought to resolve—corruption, the politicization of state institutions by political parties, excessive centralization, hierarchy, the lack of transparency, and so on. Above all, the LPP sought to reconnect those who governed with the people they governed. After ten years in practice, these problems had not gone away, and in many ways were perceived to have wors-ened. For example, Latinobarómetro data show that in 2003 only 6 percent of Bolivians had confidence in political parties, compared to an average of 16 per-cent during 1996–2001, while only 16 percent were satisfied with democracy in 2004, compared to 25 percent in 1996. Similarly, Bolivia has one of the highest levels of corruption in the world, with a ranking of eighty-four out of the ninety-one countries surveyed by Transparency International in 2001 (Barr 2005, 76). Even before the significance of the waves of social protest was apparent, these various problems led prominent analysts to even ponder the viability of Boliv-ian democracy (Whitehead 2001). When the significance of the social mobiliza-tion had become obvious, it was equally clear that the LPP did not live up to its promise. As Luis Verdesoto (2004, 43), explains, "the fundamental problem in Bolivia today is the disconnection between a civil society that has created power in the streets, repudiating the political system, and a political society whose par-ties cannot find an agenda for linking themselves with those who they claim to represent." What went wrong?

The fundamental problem underlying social discontent is economic, reflect-ing the consequences of neopluralism. Just thirty thousand jobs were being produced a year in Bolivia, even though 120,000 people entered the labor market ("Fragile States," 40), and most jobs were short-term or in the informal sector (Cisneros Merino 2004, 292). While poverty as measured by Unsatisfied Basic Needs (Necesidades Básicas Insatisfechas) in 2001 was down from 70.9 percent, in 1992 it was still at 58.6 percent. Much of this reduction was due to urban migration, which increases people's ability to meet their basic needs. The lack of employment creation has meant that the level of poverty as measured by the poverty line has not changed (Toranzo Gutiérrez 2004, 358). Poverty actually increased in eighty municipalities (Ameller 2004, 306–8). The lack of employment creation was most acute in rural areas, driving urban migration and underscoring how much of the investment in infrastructure through the LPP was underutilized, effectively wasting those resources.

Only a national development policy can address this economic problem. While the institutions created by the LPP could help implement such a policy, the LPP's record was particularly poor in creating employment. For this reason, as well as the fact that the government of Hugo Bánzer (who succeeded Sánchez de Lozada in 1997) opposed the LPP in favor of a regional decentralization model supported by civic committees, new antipoverty policies further marginalized municipal government in promoting development.

National policies for alleviating poverty since the 1990s have been centered on Bolivia's participation in the HIPC. National Dialogues were held in 1997 and 2000 to meet international requirements and were formally institutionalized by the National Dialogue Law (LDN) in July 2001. At first glance, the National Dialogues appeared to strengthen the LPP by integrating its institutions at the municipal level into the new Bolivian Strategy for Poverty Reduction (Estrategia Boliviana de Reducción de la Pobreza). With access to the HIPC, Bolivia received an average of US$105.1 million a year for poverty reduction through international debt relief. The same institutions that were the backbone of the LPP would participate in a national process to determine how that money should be spent.

While the National Dialogues raised hopes and further institutionalized the LPP, its actual effect was to undermine the LPP in practice. As Vladimir Ameller Terrazas (2002, 90) explains, one of the great losers under National Dialogues was the decentralization process "because, even though it still benefited from the extraordinary conditions for deepening [decentralization] and the will of a government technical team, a centralizing myopia ended up winning out, reaching its maximum expression in the Ministries of Education and Health, the ones that ignored the process of decentralization from the beginning."

Moreover, the new processes associated with the HIPC funds suffered from many of the same problems that limited the success of participative planning. Diego Ayo noted that the decision to spend HIPC resources in infrastructure, health care, and education was made because it was felt that the resources associated with coparticipación under the LPP had been squandered, so it was better "to say that we, the technocrats, would decide what the resources would be spent on. In the end this was counterproductive because it is inflexible. There is no basis for generating jobs, for example" (personal interview, La Paz, June 20, 2002). More concretely, only 11 percent of national public investment in 2002 was assigned to the productive sector as a result (Cisneros Merino 2004, 290).

Recentralization was complemented by the marginalization of popular-sector actors. Instead, politicians (especially mayors) and civic committees closely associated with economic elites dominated the process (Laserna 2003; Van Cott 2000). The result, as Julia Toranzo (2004, 347–48) explains, was that HIPC resources did not lead to poverty reduction because of "the lack of representation of the poor in the 2000 National Dialogue process. . . . An external model for generating strategies for reducing poverty that did not reflect the needs of local actors [was implemented], but was based on the necessity of formulating strategies for reducing poverty as an element of conditionality for obtaining external resources."

At the same time, popular expectations were raised by the promise that National Dialogues would lead to new, more effective policies. The limited impact participation had on those policies—"participation without empowerment"—dashed those expectations, contributing to the further delegitimation of participatory institutions. For many, it was another example of the "sickness of permanent consultation with civil society without making decisions" (Galindo Soza 2004, 116).

These rising expectations could not have come at a worse time in terms of the state's ability to meet them, as basic issues of governance became increasingly problematic. The growth of organized crime and criminal violence, combined with high levels of police corruption, undermined state institutions already weakened by pervasive corruption (*Economist*, May 2, 2002). The political system became increasingly fragmented as traditional actors continued to suffer a crisis of legitimacy and people sought alternatives, further undermining the ability of any actors to represent large segments of the population (Verdesoto 2004).The creation of new municipal governments (Ameller 2004; Mendoza 2004), as well as the creation of economically nonviable indigenous municipal districts (Arias 2004) and reforms allowing citizens groups to participate directly in municipal elections, all reinforced fragmentation (Arbona 2005). The LPP was specifically intended to address this basic problem of governance, not make it worse. Rather than simple protests, Bolivia was increasingly wracked by "social explosions" (Verdesoto 2004, 47), as the poor, largely indigenous majority, sought some redress for their endemic poverty that successive nonresponsive governments could not or would not provide.

Tellingly, these social explosions were ignited by fundamentally local issues, yet they took place largely at the margins of LPP institutions. The first social explosion began over the privatization of water provision in Cochabama in early 2000 and they reached a climax in October 2003, when Sánchez de Lozada became the first of two presidents forced to resign due to widespread popular protest.[31] Throughout this period, the level of violence associated with social mobilization seemed to spiral out of control, "surpassing the capacity of the government to control," leading to only more violence (Laserna 2003, 7). The spiral of violence was also fed by the central government's decision to enforce an already suspect rule of law through confrontation rather than reconciliation or negotiation (García Orellana, García Yapur, and Quitón Herbas 2003). While the LPP had its greatest impact in the rural areas where poverty was also most concentrated, the social explosions that began in 2000 were urban phenomena in which more conservative civic committees and regional elites played a central role in reaction to protests in which "the poorest groups in the country did not mobilize. [Instead] youth on the urban periphery, who aspire to greater levels of consumption and participation, mobilized in their name" (Laserna 2004, 15; see also Verdesoto 2004).

As Laserna (2000, 15) notes, the water wars of Cochabamba provided an opportunity for "rehearsing other battles . . . [in] one of the most participative and spontaneous mobilizations in recent times."[32] Cochabamba, Bolivia's third largest urban area, had long been notorious for the lack of an adequate water supply system and the disproportionate impact this has had on the poor. While the problem had been ongoing for decades, political tensions began to grow in the early 1990s when the city sought alternative sources of water. In 1999 a decision was made by the municipal government and its allies—the Comité Cívica de Cochabamba (Cochabamba Civic Committee) and regional economic elites—to award control over the collection and distribution of water to a private consortium dominated by foreign capital. The privatization of the city's water services was also strongly backed by the Bánzer administration in La Paz, which rushed legislation through the national legislature to allow the concession to take effect after the contract had already been signed locally, without public consultation and despite the project's high costs.[33]

The project met with immediate protests from farmers and peasant organizations whose members depended on well water they no longer would be able to obtain for free. When water rate increases of more than 100 percent were announced in January 2000, opposition grew to include people who had access to the city's water system. An umbrella organization, the Departmental Coordinating Committee for Water and Life (Coordinadora Departmental del Agua y la Vida) was formed by the various neighborhood groups and potable water committees mobilizing against the water privatization scheme. A twenty-four-hour strike was called for January 11, at the same time that a three-day roadblock was organized (Assies 2003). Over the next few months, the confrontation escalated until the week of April 4–10, when protests paralyzed Cochabamba and the municipal government was forced to recognize the coordinating committee as the legitimate interlocutor for civil society, nullify the contract with the private consortium, and repeal associated changes in the municipal code: "Having lost control of the city despite the mobilization of armed forces that could not deal with the barricades in the streets. Overwhelmed by the social pressure, [the government] accepted the demands of the citizenry" (García Orellana, García Yapur, and Quitón Herbas 2003, 51).

This victory was in many respects a Pyrrhic one. While it is true that civil society organized autonomously to successfully challenge government policies that seemed illegitimate, it was far removed from a successful exercise in citizenship as agency and state-civil society synergy. Instead, the water wars ultimately served to underscore the deep cleavages and inequalities that inevitably weaken civil society, at the same time that they highlighted the lack of institutions that could serve as a basis for state-civil society synergy. Society was polarized between the economic and political elites on one side, and a wide array of civil society actors on the other whose interests in the mobilization were often quite contradictory. The people most directly affected by privatization were not the poor, but relatively well-off urban and rural groups who had access to piped water through the municipality and for irrigation. While the poor played a crucial role in the mobilizations, it was not because the water privatization directly increased the cost of their water or their ability to farm. In fact, the victory did little to improve the plight of the poor, even though the new public body overseeing municipal water supplies was run by members from the coordinating committee. Instead, five years after the wars had ended, "the excluded continued to be condemned to consume little water, of poor quality, and that was very expensive" because they continued to depend on unregulated private firms to distribute their water (Laserna, *Los Tiempos*, May 25, 2005). For the poor and disadvantaged, the dominance of foreign capital and the political fait accompli, with the strong ethnic overtones that water policy came to represent, served as a new focal point for venting popular frustration with neopluralism—a powerful combination that would continue to catalyze popular-sector mobilization for the foreseeable future.

The institutions associated with the LPP also played no role, although the mayor of Cochabamba was a key player whose own vacillation between support for the official position he adopted at the start of the crisis and sympathy for the opposition belies any effort at negotiated compromise in favor of his own populist political future.[34] Instead, the Cochabamba civic committee that was deliberately excluded from the LPP played a dominant role, along with the central government. The local institutional vacuum was to some extent filled by the Catholic Church (García Orellana, García Yapur, and Quitón Herbas, 2003), in a way that is more reminiscent of the role the Catholic Church played under authoritarian regimes when democratic channels for resolving social conflict are deliberately shut down. In the end, socioeconomic exclusion and political manipulation continued to define the predominant model of citizenship as consumption: "Those who wanted to take advantage of the necessities and aspirations of the people in order to start an unsustainable project started this war, and it was ended by those who were able to take advantage of the anger and protests in order to recuperate or win positions of power, or conserve small privileges" (Laserna 2000, 15).

The social tensions exacerbated by a model of citizenship as consumption and neopluralism—extremes of poverty and social exclusion, the growing crisis of representation—continued to produce escalating social explosions in the aftermath of this citizens' victory in Cochabamba. Like the water wars, essentially local issues spawned growing levels of social mobilization that were at best at the margins of the institutions established by the LPP and had national repercussions. As local concerns and organizations became enmeshed in larger issues of economic development, foreign exploitation, and the sociopolitical exclusion of Bolivia's indigenous majority, these mobilizations came to challenge the legitimacy of Bolivia's ruling elite and, ultimately, the very meaning of Bolivia's national identity. Like Cochabamba's water wars, the apparent victory of citizen mobilization often belied the existence of citizenship as agency, threatening the foundations of Bolivia's political system.

The social mobilization in El Alto that began in September 2003 in many ways epitomized all these contradictions.[35] El Alto rapidly grew to become the country's third largest city, just on the outskirts of La Paz, as hundreds of thousands of poor, largely indigenous people migrated in search of jobs. While their poverty continued to haunt them, the city's rapid growth meant that urban infrastructure could not even begin to keep pace. The corruption and hierarchy associated with traditional political actors, as well as the general distrust of state institutions and political parties, was endemic. A social explosion would seem to be inevitable, particularly after the example of Cochabamba's water wars.

The immediate cause of the mobilization was an increase in municipal taxes. The mobilization quickly gained momentum in early October and spread to other areas of the country as it came to be associated with a variety of other demands that included a rejection of the national government's endorsement of plans to export natural gas through Chile by international energy companies. The violence of the state's response to the protests, ultimately claiming more than seventy lives, culminated in the demand for the resignation of President Sánchez de Lozada, who had been reelected the year before.

The mobilization succeeded on many fronts: Sánchez de Lozada was forced to resign, the plan to export gas was suspended with the promise to hold a national referendum on nationalizing Bolivia's vast gas reserves, and the monopoly enjoyed by political parties in local elections was broken.[36] Moreover, the mobilization reflected the emergence of a variety of new community organizations and local networks of both old and new organizations, suggesting a possible resurgence of civil society.

As in the water wars of Cochabamba, however, the potential of this victory for promoting citizenship as agency remained in doubt. While protest and social mobilization continued—forcing the resignation of Sánchez de Lozada's successor, Carlos Mesa, in 2005—the organizations and networks that emerged in October "practically disappeared, ceding political power to the 'old' structures" after the president's resignation (Arbona 2005, 11). Corruption, clientelism, and political parties reasserted themselves at the local level. Political fragmentation only increased as the legitimacy of traditional actors declined and citizens groups began to multiply to fill the new spaces created with the opening up of municipal elections to nonparty actors. This demonstrates how "a strategy for legitimizing the movement also results in the co-optation and fragmentation of the social power won through the mobilizations" (Arbona 2005, 13).

In the end, the institutions associated with the LPP failed to contain the mobilization, which took place largely outside them, raising further questions about their relevance, if not legitimacy, for addressing citizens' most pressing concerns.[37] This experience highlights the general problem of weak institutions and the need to "establish institutional channels for processing differences" that can end the tendency for social mobilization to overwhelm the state (Verdesoto 2004, 44). In their absence, the growing marginalization characteristic of neopluralism and citizenship as consumption threaten to generate new forms of populism (Laserna 2003; Verdesoto 2004). The combined weakness of democratic institutions and civil society make both state-society synergy and citizenship as agency elusive goals. The LPP was intended to address both weaknesses. Its failure to do so is at the heart of the wave of social explosions that have wracked Bolivia since 2000, providing a dramatic testament to the complexity of the challenges facing Bolivia as it seeks to not only restore political stability but reverse literally centuries of exclusion for its indigenous majority. While it is beyond the scope of this chapter to analyze Morales's government, the experience of the LPP demonstrates that problems are daunting. His unprecedented electoral success, repeated with his reelection in 2009 with an even larger margin of victory, and a new constitution are promising in this regard, but as the LPP experience also makes clear, good intentions can have unanticipated consequences as a result of day-to-day struggles over how new institutions function in practice.

THE PROMISE OF CITIZENSHIP: CIVIL SOCIETY AND MEXICO'S TRANSITION TO DEMOCRACY

With the election of Vicente Fox of the National Action Party (Partico Acción Nacional, PAN) in 2000, Mexico became the most recent entrant into the club of Latin American democracies. After a seventy-year period of one-party rule by the Institutional Revolutionary Party (Partido Revolucionario Institucional, PRI) and a transition that lasted well over a decade, an opposition candidate was able to assume the office of the presidency for the first time in modern Mexican history.

Fox's victory represented, among other things, a concerted effort by important civil society actors to ensure that the 2000 elections would be free and fair. Even more so than in Chile, and in sharp contrast to Bolivia, Mexico's transition reflected the culmination of a process of citizen mobilization that helped force reluctant elites to share power. Yet despite this important mobilization, the process was dominated from the beginning by political parties that, while willing to share power among themselves, were even more reluctant than Chile's political parties to share power with civil society. The ability of political parties to succeed belied the existence of a strong civil society in many fundamental aspects.

This success on the part of political parties reflects both the nature of Mexico's prolonged period of controlled inclusion and the impact of neopluralism. Elections became the central catalyst for civil society mobilization during most of the 1990s in large part because this was the only space available. Such limited space reflected the continued strength of the basic institutions of controlled inclusion and the repercussions of extremes of economic instability beginning in the early 1980s, as well as the market-oriented policies implemented to address that instability. Ironically, the 1917 revolution—won through the active mobilization of peasants and workers and proclaiming social justice for all—is at the heart of this conundrum. As a direct result of the successful institutionalization of the revolution in the 1930s, the ability of civil society to engage in the social construction of citizenship remains stunted to this day. Despite fleeting promises of citizenship as agency, neopluralist democracy represents an uneasy mix of citizenship as co-optation and as consumption, with dramatic consequences for the quality of democratic rule.

To understand this unique intertwining of revolutionary and democratization processes, this chapter first discusses the nature of the revolution and its key institutions for achieving controlled inclusion. The chapter then examines Mexico's first transition toward a more open, liberal economy, underscoring how this epitomized the authoritarian aspects of neopluralism. In the third section, Mexico's second transition toward political democracy is discussed, emphasizing how it exemplifies the electoral dimension of neopluralism. Finally, in the last section, the chapter explores the nature of neopluralist democracy, particularly the ambiguous role of civil society, through two case studies: (1) the various mobilizations against criminal violence and impunity that began in 1997 and (2) the 2006 mobilizations of the Popular Assembly of the Peoples of Oaxaca (Asamblea Popular de los Pueblos de Oaxaca, APPO).

The Revolutionary Foundations of Controlled Inclusion

One of the fundamental distinctions of the Mexican experience is that, rather than trying to prevent a revolution, institutions of controlled inclusion were designed to ensure that the mobilization responsible for the Mexican Revolution and its subsequent consolidation would be severely constrained. The institutions that resulted from the revolution were legitimated and strengthened by their close association with progressive social change and Mexican nationalism, particularly during the government of Lázaro Cárdenas (1934–40). In sharp contrast to Bolivia, where the 1952 revolution did not result in either the creation of strong institutions or political stability (see chapter 5), the strength of key institutions associated with Mexico's revolution was responsible for an unprecedented degree of political stability, despite its authoritarian nature and ultimate incapacity to actually create the inclusive and socially just society that the revolution promised in its 1917 constitution. Indeed, the regime's ability to endure despite this glaring performance gap and in the face of increasingly daunting challenges is a sad testament to the very strength of those institutions.

The Structural Roots of Revolution

Given its history and socioeconomic structures, Mexico (like Cuba) was an ideal candidate for revolution. As the heart of one of the two principal indigenous civilizations at the time of the conquest and later the principal seat of the Spanish Empire in the Americas, the colonial experience and war of independence were particularly harsh in Mexico, resulting in a huge death toll. While the former represented an overt and concerted effort to destroy the indigenous society, the latter devastated the entire colonial society and economy.

When Mexico finally won its independence in 1821, the country was dominated by caudillos—the generals who had actually fought the war and maintained their own private armies now dominated politics as they fought among themselves over the spoils. The result was extreme political instability for decades. From 1821 to 1860, Mexico had no fewer than fifty separate presidents, each averaging less than a year in office. The principal means for taking power was military coups, and thirty-five of the fifty presidencies were led by military officers (Skidmore and Smith 2005, 257). The political vacuum created by extreme instability was largely filled by the Catholic Church, which was the biggest landowner in the country and closely allied with the landed oligarchy.

Political instability was only exacerbated when the United States invaded northern Mexico and, with the 1848 Treaty of Guadalupe, took possession of approximately half of Mexico's national territory. Civil war broke out between Liberal and Conservative factions of the elite, and Mexico even experimented with empire when the Conservatives were able to impose the reign of the Austrian Maximilian von Hapsburg (1864–67) with the support of France.

After more than four decades of political instability, some semblance of political order was finally created when the Liberals overthrew Maximilian and Benito Juárez assumed the presidency, ushering in Mexico's first experiment with liberalism during the period known as the Reform. Despite their democratic connotations, one of the primary impacts of Juárez's liberal reforms was increased land concentration, coming largely at the expense of the church and the indigenous. The Catholic Church saw its lands expropriated and sold. More important, indigenous communities lost their communal property rights dating back to the colonial period when their land was divided among its inhabitants and declared transferable. The result was that many indigenous people quickly became landless as new landowners gained control of their formerly communal properties.

The period of liberal political stability was short-lived, lasting just five years. Juárez's sudden death in 1872 ushered in a new period of political instability that ended only when Porfirio Díaz imposed a thirty-five year period of dictatorship known as the Porfiriato (1876–1911).

Abandoning any pretext of democratic politics, Díaz intensified Juárez's economic liberalism (Hamilton 1985, 44–55). Free trade policies fully integrated Mexico into the world economy by increasing foreign ownership, particularly of the mineral resources that were the main source of Mexico's foreign exchange, and growing commercially dependent on the United States. The privileged position enjoyed by foreign interests increasingly alienated virtually all domestic interests outside Díaz's small clique, including commercial landowners, ranchers, mine owners, small farmers, and small and medium businesses. Workers' wages remained low, while labor mobilizations were repressed and the regime attempted to co-opt potential labor leaders. The growth of commercial agriculture coexisted with hacienda systems, resulting in a decline in agrarian wages as both sectors exploited workers, with commercial plantations amounting to a form of "neo-slavery" (54).

Despite the growing penetration of foreign capital, peasants still constituted 70 percent of the population and were largely excluded from the market economy. Land concentration reached new extremes as the remaining community-held indigenous land was seized and public land was granted or sold to surveying companies and foreign contractors. By the end of the Porfiriato, most agricultural land was held in approximately 8,245 estates (and even fewer families since many owned more than one). In 1910 eight individuals owned one-eighth of total land in Mexico, while 90–95 percent of the rural population remained landless (Hamilton 1985, 55).

The Institutions of Revolution and Controlled Inclusion

The Porfiriato ended when civil war broke out over Díaz's refusal to step down in 1911, and he fled the country in 1912. This unleashed a protracted period of struggle that ended in 1917 and culminated in the 1917 constitution adopted by the victors of the first successful revolution in the hemisphere. While it is beyond the scope of this chapter to recount in any detail the nature of the revolutionary struggle, it is important to note that it involved virtually every segment of Mexican society, with 1.5 to 2 million people—more than 10 percent of Mexico's population at the time—losing their lives (Hamilton 1985, 60).[1] In particular, peasants, and to a lesser extent workers, played a central role in ensuring both the initial victory by the winning coalition and the subsequent consolidation of the revolution.

Given the conservative outcome of the revolution—it was neither anticapitalist nor associated with the wide array of social rights of citizenship associated with other revolutionary regimes such as Cuba's—its actual significance is often underestimated. The widespread mobilization of armed groups resulted in the replacement of one set of elites with another, who subsequently created a new state designed to preserve their interests. In particular, a myriad of formal and informal institutions were constructed that would condition the development of civil society in fundamental ways until the present day.

First, the new state was based on the 1917 constitution, which declared that "the state was the representative of the revolutionary classes, and would implement their goals" (Hamilton 1985, 62). This meant it would mediate any class conflict based on an "ideology of inclusion" (Shefner 2008, 71). That such inclusion was rarely realized in practice serves to underscore the importance of ideas and ideology in legitimating the new state independently of how they are actually put into practice. Given the significance of foreign—particularly U.S.—interests during the Porfiriato, a cornerstone of the new state's legitimacy also was nationalism and anti-imperialism (Middlebrook 1995). The 1938 nationalization of the oil industry represented the height of revolutionary nationalism and "was unquestionably the most popular act of the Cárdenas government and probably of any Mexican government since the revolution" (Hamilton 1985, 229).

The power of legitimating ideas was enhanced by the lack of alternatives. On the right, the main threat came from the Catholic Church, which historically had allied with the landed oligarchy and was able to exert considerable influence over the peasantry through its cultural importance and control over education. That challenge was neutralized when the revolutionary regime put down the Cristero Rebellion in 1929 with the help of the still mobilized, armed peasantry (Hamilton 1985). The Left, on the other hand, found itself in the unenviable position of trying to oppose a revolutionary regime. Not only was such opposition necessarily "counter-revolutionary" (Middlebrook 1995, 28), it often fell prey to the PRI's ability to co-opt its most promising leaders. While small leftist mobilizations would take place periodically, particularly beginning in the 1960s, the Left was able to mount a credible challenge to the regime only in the late 1980s; the principal opposition until that time had been the right-wing PAN, which was formed in the 1930s.

The prolonged armed conflict preceding the revolution, just like the extended war of independence before it, sowed the seeds for subsequent political instability due to the emergence of numerous powerful caudillos, particularly within the military. As a prerequisite for stability, the new state had to subordinate them to its authority. This process began with the defeat of Adolfo de la Huerta's military insurrection in 1924. In addition to purging dissidents within the military, the regime began to encourage military officials to seek personal benefit through political appointments and private enterprise as a way to increase their stake in the status quo (Middlebrook 1995).

Beginning in the mid-1920s "the process of self-enrichment became 'peacefully regularized' and 'revolutionary capitalists' became one of the most dynamic sectors of the dominant class" (Hamilton 1985, 86). After excluding economic groups from the formal institutions of the revolutionary state, the new ruling elite sought to co-opt them informally, with the result that "particularism and patrimonialism were institutionalized in the relations between the state and business groups" (Olvera 2003d, 43). Lower-class groups were dealt with in a similar fashion, even if the rewards were far less lucrative (Levy and Walton 2009a, 19–21). The capacity of the regime to engage in this type of politics was a "calculated weakness of the state" (Escalante Gonzalbo 2009, 95), in which co-optation and corruption ensured political stability by absorbing potential threats in an unequal and segmented way. Actual and potential leaders of autonomous civil society actors were specifically targeted, further undermining the potential for a leftist challenge to the PRI's dominance for decades.

The situation of the peasantry and workers was particularly important for the new regime.[2] Both, but particularly an armed peasantry, had been mobilized to not only win the revolutionary struggle but to deal with specific threats to its consolidation. The peasantry was crucial for both defeating de la Huerta's insurrection and ending the Cristeros Rebellion. Throughout the 1920s various attempts were made to co-opt and subordinate peasants and workers institutionally, but with little success (Hamilton 1985; Middlebrook 1995). As Nora Hamilton (1985, 183) notes, "the state had to control these groups, or their continued mobilization would enable them to control the state, or even undermine its basis of existence" by radicalizing the revolution more than the new elite desired.

Looking specifically at the peasantry, the revolution had brought little change in their quality of life. The vast majority of Mexicans still resided in the countryside, yet 70 percent of them together owned less than 1 percent of the land. Conversely, just twelve thousand large landowners held four-fifths of rural property (Hamilton 1985, 109). While the working class was much smaller than the peasant class, it held strategic importance due to its role in key sectors of the economy (for example, mineral extraction, ports, and transportation). Moreover, given the revolutionary elite's desire to promote industrialization, labor would inevitably grow in importance, both economically and politically. Yet the immediate impact of the revolution was no better for workers than for peasants, as their working conditions did not noticeably improve. Organized labor remained weak and fragmented. In fact, the size of the industrial workforce actually shrank from 17.2 percent of the economically active population in 1910 to 15 percent in 1930 (Middlebrook 1995, 110). The collapse of the world economy during the Great Depression made the situation more volatile by further alienating "peasants who were dissatisfied with the slow pace and the threatened termination of agrarian reform, and workers fed up with ineffective and corrupt union leadership" (Hamilton 1985, 115).

In this context, Lázaro Cárdenas became president in 1934 and launched the most radical phase in the revolutionary process since it began in 1911. Recognizing that the only way to overcome conservative opposition within the new ruling elite to needed reforms was to yet again mobilize peasants and workers, Cárdenas seized the moment to create centralized, hierarchical organizations that were dependent on the state and would allow it to effectively curtail future mobilizations. He succeeded where past efforts had failed by ensuring that for the first time mobilizations would be directly linked with appreciable improvements in the quality of life for workers and peasants. Such improvements were channeled through the new institutions Cárdenas created and were substantial enough to create the expectation that future improvements would be forthcoming through allegiance to those institutions, even among the many who did not directly benefit materially from Cárdenas's reforms. The legitimacy of these new institutions would be further cemented in the collective psyche by their association with the government that dramatically challenged U.S. dominance by nationalizing its oil companies in 1938.[3] The end result was the birth of Mexico's institutions of state corporatism.

More specifically, the National Peasant Confederation (Confederación Nacional Campesina, CNC) and the Confederation of Mexican Workers (Confederación de Trabajadores Mexicanos, CTM) were formally created in 1938 at the head of a wave of mobilizations pushing through important reforms. In the rural sector, "the agrarian reform destroyed the power of the large landowners and succeeded in its goal of eliminating or at least significantly reducing 'feudal' relations of production" (Hamilton 1985, 178). Land reform, much of it based on a traditional form of collective ownership, the *ejido*, meant that 47.4 percent of all cultivated land in 1940 was collectively owned, compared to just 15 percent in 1930, including 57.3 percent of all irrigated land. The number of landless rural workers was reduced by more than half a million, from 2,479,000 in 1930 to 1,912,000 in 1940—a significant number that by no means resolved the underlying structural problem (177–78). For most workers, wages and working conditions generally improved as well. Labor leaders in particular were offered political power through new access to their state and a variety of subsidies for unions (Middlebrook 1995, esp. 95–105).

These new benefits came at the price of rigid constraints on the capacity of workers and peasants to organize autonomously. In the rural sector, for example, beneficiaries of the land reform were dependent on access to credit, training, and technology, all tightly controlled by the state. The result, as Fernando Escalante Gonzalbo (2009, 94) observes, was that "the new agrarian entities were, since their foundation, incorporated in a political and institutional structure that might have been more or less corrupt, authoritarian and inefficient for promoting development, but was nonetheless real. This is not to say there was no rural violence, but that it was always intertwined with the revolutionary political order and state institutions."

The state similarly retained important legal controls on the formation of unions, as well as union membership and internal affairs. In particular, the state exercised tight control over strike activity (Middlebrook 1995, 207). The state also retained ultimate control over the subsidies given to unions, including access to social security benefits, to further reinforce its capacity for ensuring labor discipline and allegiance. For both labor and peasants, the coercive strength of the state was also always in the background, adding to the chilling effect that corporatist institutions had over autonomous social mobilization.

The CTM and the CNC were two central pillars of controlled inclusion, but by the very nature of Mexico's economic underdevelopment, they could never be sufficient for maintaining political stability. The large informal sector and landless peasants—even after Cárdenas's land reforms—meant that, at best, the CTM and CNC could constrain mobilization of a relatively small segment of the popular sectors, albeit a strategically important one. Traditional corporatist institutions also could not mediate elite conflict, a real problem in Mexico dating back to the caudillo wars in the first half century of independence. To fill this void, a different kind of political institution was required and the PRI soon became the critical mechanism for mediating not only intra-elite conflict but state-society relations in general.[4]

The PRI's roots trace back to the National Revolutionary Party (Partido Nacional Revolucionario, PNR), which was formed in 1929 to fill the leadership vacuum created when the designated president, Alvaro Obregón, was assassinated before he could assume office. It quickly became a centralized, authoritarian institution that was the only channel for career advancement for politicians and civil servants—the principal occupation for the middle sectors. The governing party's lock on political advancement for individual politicians was firmly institutionalized in 1934 when, upon assuming the presidency, Cárdenas ordered former president Plutarco Elías Calles (1925–28) into exile. Until that time, Calles had been the real political power behind the scenes, exercising control through a series of puppet presidents. With Calles's forced exile, Cárdenas firmly established the office of the president as the institutional locus of political power.

Designated by the incumbent, each new president would assume virtually complete control over the state for six years—the so-called *sexenio*—but would then marginalize himself from politics, allowing an effective rotation of political elites. One study done in the 1960s found that the rotation associated with a new sexenio included eighteen thousand elected offices and more than twenty-five thousand appointed offices (Eckstein 1988, 26). In practical terms, this meant that if politicians accepted the hegemony of the dominant party and played by its rules, career advancement—and personal enrichment—was assured. This would also create an extremely effective means for co-opting political and civil society leaders who might emerge as future potential challengers to the PRI's hegemony, because the growing rewards of cooperation over one's political career were virtually guaranteed while the consequences of dissidence were obvious and absolute. Mexico's noncompetitive elections thus resolved a central problem of all nondemocratic regimes by creating an institutional mechanism for assuring a smooth succession, at the same time that they helped generate a generally homogeneous political class and offered some form of legitimation for incoming administrations.

The governing party helped maintain political stability in other ways as well. Reorganized and renamed the Party of the Mexican Revolution (Partido Revolucionario Mexicano, PRM) in 1938, the party directly incorporated the CNC and CTM into its hierarchical, centralized structure. This not only helped solidify the party's claim to encapsulating the revolution's legacy and monopolizing political ideas and ideology, it further limited the CNC's and CTM's autonomy by reinforcing their political subordination and authoritarian tendencies. At the same time, the PRM created new institutional barriers to collaboration between workers and peasants given the party's carefully segmented, vertical structures, creating yet another obstacle to potentially more radical change.

From the perspective of the popular sectors, patronage and clientelism were the principal mechanisms for political inclusion and citizenship as co-optation (Filgueira and Filgueira 2002). The growing influence of the centralized state in the economy and society ensured "the institutionalization of particularism and clientelism as the dominant model for relations between the state and society" (Olvera 2003d, 43–44). While access to services and resources were not guaranteed by cooperation with the PRI, it was clear that those who refused to support it would not receive anything.

Clientelism affects the potential for civil society to emerge in numerous ways. In addition to undermining any meaningful sense of civil society autonomy, clientelism meant "that politics was kept local, fragmented, and focused on material needs" (Shefner 2008, 72). This was deliberately far from the kinds of structural changes that would support a more equal, democratic society. The strength of civil society was further undermined because clientelism created a dynamic in which different organizations, particularly their leaders, competed with one another for the spoils of access (Eckstein 1988). This only contributed to civil society's fragmentation and ultimate marginalization from actual decision making.

The success of Mexico's variant of controlled inclusion—combining corporatism, political dominance by a revolutionary political party, and clientelism—included maintaining relative political stability in a context of growing levels of inequality. Controlled inclusion actually contributed to the rise in inequality because in practice any rights of citizenship were intentionally limited, segmented, and politically contingent. From the 1940s to the end of the 1960s—a period of relatively high growth rates and rapid urbanization coinciding with the heyday of Mexico's experience with ISI—virtually all relevant indicators demonstrated that Mexico was becoming more unequal, despite the fact that Mexico already was one of the most unequal countries in the region and that inequality was a primary structural factor explaining the 1917 revolution. For example, one study found that the poorest 70 percent of the population saw its share of national income fall from 31.6 percent in 1950 to 27.46 percent in 1963 (Eckstein 1988, 19). Similarly, another study found that the income share of the bottom 20 percent of the population declined from 4.7 percent in 1950 to just 4 percent in 1969. Conversely, the richest 5 percent of the population earned twenty-two times what the poorest 10 percent earned in 1958, and this rose to fifty times the income of the poorest 10 percent by 1977 (Bruhn 1997, 57). One reason for this was labor's declining share of the national income, despite rapid industrialization and a growing working class. In 1940 labor's share of the national income (including wages, salaries, and benefits) was 52.1 percent. By 1947 it was down to only 40.2 percent and it would not regain the 1940 level until 1966 (Middlebrook 1995, 215–16). Of course, labor's share of national income also entailed other forms of inequality given the negative impact of corporatism on income distribution. Workers in the formal sector were a privileged, yet relatively small, group who garnered the lion's share of national income compared to the peasantry and growing informal urban sector. Conservative estimates by Alejandro Portes (1985, 22–23, table 2) show that formal sector workers accounted for only 15.9 percent of the economically active population in Mexico in 1972, underscoring how the vast majority of Mexicans were outside corporatist structures and considerably worse off given their lack of even minimal labor rights and social welfare benefits.

This is not meant to suggest that there was no autonomous civil society mobilization in Mexico during this period. Particularly beginning in the late 1960s and through the 1970s, the Mexican regime was challenged on a variety of fronts; it was anything but a situation in which the state was able to suppress all opposition. Rather, the success of controlled inclusion in Mexico was reflected in the way the state was able to adapt to such threats while maintaining relative stability. This adaptability, often achieved through various forms of co-optation, with violent repression generally playing only a secondary role, distinguishes controlled inclusion in Mexico from other cases in the region (Brachet-Márquez 1996; Favela Gavia 2006).[5] At the same time, it highlights the limits, rather than total absence, of social movement gains.

There were three important crossroads in the evolution of civil society prior to the 1990s. Each represented an instance when popular-sector mobilization could potentially lead to significant changes in the nature of the regime. In each case, however, the regime successfully adapted to the threat, with the subsequent demobilization and co-optation of the actors involved.

The first was the 1968 student movement and its violent repression in the infamous Tlatelolco Massacre, named for the sector of Mexico City where government forces killed hundreds of unarmed students demanding the democratization of the Mexican regime (Olvera 2003d; Brachet-Márquez 1996). The killings underscored the extent to which the regime would go to ensure political stability, as well as the impunity that it enjoyed (those responsible have yet to be investigated, much less held accountable for their actions). The chilling effect this had on political activity in general meant that, apart from a small group of radical students who would proceed to join guerrilla groups, there would be a small effervescence of civil society activity at the grassroots level, as student activists began to seek alternative forms of engagement that were less overtly political. Significantly, they were aided by a new source of ideological legitimacy through the spread of liberation theology within some segments of the Catholic Church.[6] While a significant number of organizations emerged in cities and in the countryside, their effectiveness was quite limited due to the PRI's stranglehold on the state and its ability to use that to constrain civil society. As Alberto Olvera (2003d, 48–49) points out, "the lack of connections between these emergent groups and political society, still monopolized by the official party, prevented their expansion and the development of alternative political projects, keeping the movements at the local level and [ensconced] in social particularism." When such organizations became too large for the state to ignore, they were co-opted. For example, the National Union of Autonomous Peasant Regional Organizations (Unión Nacional de Organizaciones Regionales Campesinas Autónomas), an important independent peasant movement, eventually supported the constitutional reforms in the early 1990s that put an end to land reform and allowed individuals to sell their stake in the communal ejido lands—two key pillars of the revolution's promise for social change (Bizberg 2003).

The second important crossroads was the so-called labor insurgency of the 1970s (Middlebrook 1995, 222–54). This challenge to state corporatism emerged largely in manufacturing, particularly the new automobile sector, as a reflection of the challenges corporatist unions faced in high-tech, high-productivity sectors of the economy. Worker frustration with traditional leaders' inability or unwillingness to successfully address their grievances led to new demands to democratize union structures as a way to increase workers' capacity to engage in collective bargaining. While the consequent democratization of new independent unions did not necessarily end union corruption, it did lead to increased strike activity and alliances among more autonomous union organizations that promised to challenge the dominance of the CTM. This in turn led to important advances in terms of promotion procedures and employment conditions, including better job security.

The ability of insurgent labor to actually challenge the state's control over organized labor ultimately proved to be minimal, in part because the economic crisis of the 1980s undercut workers' bargaining position dramatically. But more than simply bad timing was to blame. As Ilán Bizberg (2003, 155) cogently remarks, while the surge in independent worker and peasant organizations in the 1970s "was short-lived and did not contribute much to actively dismantle the old regime, it was crucial because it showed the limits of the capacity of independent movements to organize in Mexico." Corporatist institutions in Mexico, aided by their subordination to a centralized state, were simply too robust to be undermined from the margins.

The final crossroads revolved around the September 19, 1985, earthquake that leveled large swaths of Mexico City, particularly among low-income dwellings.

Almost six thousand buildings were damaged, of which 65 percent were homes. Officially, the government claimed that 9,089 people died and 5,638 went missing and unaccounted for, while unofficial estimates put the death toll at almost 20,000 or more (Favela Gavia 2006, 169).[7] Largely in response to perceived government indifference, the result was "the enormous activation of the urban popular movement in the City of Mexico" (Olvera 2003b, 354).

Initially, the mobilization helping victims cope with the immediate aftermath of the earthquake in a demonstration of "spontaneous, disinterested solidarity" (Favela Gavia 2006, 194) soon transformed itself into formal organizational structures for negotiating with the state. On September 27—just over a week after the earthquake—sixty-seven organizations formed the Popular Committee for Solidarity and Reconstruction (Comité Popular de Solidaridad y Reconstrucción). Two weeks later, continued government inaction led to the formation of the Unitary Committee of Earthquake Victims (Coordinadora Única de Damnificados, CUD) by forty-two organizations representing thirty thousand people. The CUD would quickly become the principal representative of those most affected by the earthquake.

The mobilization was fundamentally a reaction to the state's negative response to the disaster. While the army was ostensibly sent in to help, its true purpose was to contain popular mobilization. Similarly, although the president tried to be "discretely compassionate" (Favela Gavia 2006, 200), his aides responsible for addressing residents' demands were anything but compassionate and were at best indifferent. In particular, government officials were concerned with relocating people from valuable property in the city center to make way for more lucrative business ventures, destroying communities, and distancing people from their only sources of employment. When people refused to leave their damaged homes, the government even cut off services in a vain attempt to force them to leave. Not surprisingly, government officials initially refused to deal directly with the CUD and instead attempted to work with official organizations dependent on the state or create new organizations that were obviously clients of the PRI rather than representatives of the affected communities.

The CUD's demands centered on the right of people to rebuild their homes in the same neighborhoods they had lived in before the earthquake, state assistance in doing so, and judicial investigations to determine the responsibility of government officials and private contractors for the extent of the damage. Mobilization was a primary tool that the CUD employed in its attempt to force the government to negotiate, and in late 1985 twenty thousand to fifty thousand people took to the streets in one of the largest unauthorized mobilizations since the revolution to try to force the government's hand.

Ultimately, the CUD succeeded in pressuring the government to accept its principal demands, with the important exception of the demand for a judicial investigation to determine any culpability on the part of government officials.[8]

This success was formalized in the signing of the Pact for Democratic Cooperation for Reconstructing Housing (Pacto de Cooperación Democrática para Reconstrucción de Viviendas) by state representatives and the myriad of groups involved in the aftermath of the earthquake. While these included organizations controlled by the PRI, for the first time the PRI was forced to recognize the legitimate claims of a major autonomous civil society organization by allowing the CUD to also sign the agreement, which it did. Less surprisingly, the CUD was subsequently marginalized from all activities relating to the agreement's implementation. The government also took advantage of the public relations opportunity that the signing of the accord represented when the then president Miguel de la Madrid proclaimed that the "PRI is still the Party of the Revolution, an assertive party that is close to the courage of the people and far from the demagogy and systematic protest. This belongs to a bitter minority" (quoted in Favela Gavia 2006, 215).

"Success," once again, came at the expense of civil society. Despite the critical role autonomous civil society mobilization played, the cost was either the loss of that autonomy or forced political marginalization that sharply curtailed the space for future success. As Eckstein (1988, 276) cogently argues, "The residents succeeded because they defied the public order in ways that did not attack the state 'frontally.' . . . People . . . never challenged the state's right to rule: they sought justice from the state, not its demise. . . . The defiant groups only gained what they wanted when they agreed to play by state-imposed 'rules of the game.'"

The example of the CUD and other instances of autonomous civil society's organizational activity underscore how in Mexico, more than in any other country in the region with the telling exception of revolutionary Cuba, civil society has been boxed in by the predominance of state institutions intentionally designed to restrict its growth. Even human rights movements—the spearhead for civil society throughout Latin America in the 1970s that enjoyed unprecedented international support and legitimacy—were noticeably constricted in their ability to mobilize (Keck and Sikkink 1998). The paradoxical nature of Mexico's first transition from its ISI development model to one more firmly based on market principles further underscores the almost insurmountable barriers autonomous civil society activities had to confront.

Mexico's Economic Transition and the Perseverance of Corporatism

In many ways, Mexico's transition to a market-oriented economic model represents the mirror image of the revolution's foundational premises. Not only did the transition's capstone, the North American Free Trade Agreement (NAFTA), represent an unprecedented formal intertwining of the Mexican and U.S. economies (along with Canada's), but as part of the preconditions for its signing, land reform was ended and the ownership of the communal ejido landholdings—one of the revolution's principal achievements in the country-side—reverted to the individuals who farmed them so that the land could then be sold. Indeed, one reason why the treaty was deemed necessary was to ensure that the market-oriented economic reforms that were being implemented in the aftermath of the 1980s economic crisis would not be reversed as a consequence of Mexico's unpredictable political dynamics (Moreno-Brid 2009). Significantly, there was no requirement in the NAFTA accords for a future democratic tran-sition and certainly no intention on the part of the president of Mexico at the time, Carlos Salinas de Gortari, to even contemplate one. In this way, Mexico's first transition epitomized the authoritarian aspects of neopluralism.

Paradoxically, the ability of the regime to successfully navigate this 180-degree ideological turn in policy was dependent on the continued strength and adapt-ability of the same institutions that were firmly consolidated with the revolu-tion's radicalization in the 1930s. Not only did the turn to a market-oriented development model have significant negative consequences for the popular sec-tors, but corporatist institutions, particularly the CTM, were essential mecha-nisms for ensuring a relatively smooth yet radical change in economic policy.[9] Rather than ushering in their demise, neopluralism reconstituted an essentially economic role for institutions such as the CTM, further constraining the devel-opment of a strong civil society.

It is important to appreciate the magnitude of the economic impact of the 1980s economic crisis and the policies implemented to address it. As can be seen in table 6.1, growth was at best lackluster for most of the period 1980–2000, and even when it picked up considerably in 1995–2000, it was still significantly lower than it had been in the 1970s. Although real GDP per capita growth was higher in the period 1995–2000, it really is an example of too little, too late: at $3,537 in 1998, it was only marginally higher than the 1980 level of $3,424 (Alarcón 2003, 451), providing, at best, little direct improvement for most Mexicans after almost two decades.

The impact of slow growth was born disproportionately by the popular sec-tors. As can be seen in table 6.2, Mexico's Gini coefficient is high and gener-ally worsened during the period 1981–2000.[10] This reflected several convergent trends. First, there was a marked decline in high-paying manufacturing posi-tions. Compared to 1980, there were 22 percent fewer jobs in the manufacturing sector in 1993, and by 1995 there were 30 percent fewer manufacturing positions (Alarcón 2003, 453). This is despite the fact that Mexican manufacturing exports were increasing at a rate of more than 10 percent per year, 1993–2006, which was one of the fastest rates in the world (Moreno-Brid 2009, 69).[11] For workers lucky enough to have a job in the formal sector, wages fell 26.6 percent in the period 1991–98, which is considerably better than the almost 50 percent drop

```

**Table 6.1.**  Economic growth rates

| Year | 1970–80 | 1980–85 | 1985–90 | 1990–95 | 1995–2000 |
| --- | --- | --- | --- | --- | --- |
| Avg. real GDP growth/year | 6.7 | 1.9 | 1.8 | 1.5 | 5.4 |
| Avg. real GDP per capita growth/year | 3.2 | -0.5 | -0.3 | -0.4 | 3.8 |

SOURCE: Data from Alarcón (2003, 451).

**Table 6.2.**  Gini coefficients

| Year | 1981 | 1984 | 1989 | 1992 | 1994 | 1996 | 1998 | 2000 |
| --- | --- | --- | --- | --- | --- | --- | --- | --- |
| Gini coefficient | 0.429 | 0.429 | 0.469 | 0.475 | 0.477 | 0.456 | 0.476 | 0.481 |

SOURCE: Data from Boltvinik (2003, 394).

experienced by the self-employed (largely in the informal sector) during the same period (Salas and Zepeda 2003, 529–30). Looking at the period 1982–2000, real wages in general fell 38.4 percent (Bensusán 2005, 250).

For the 60.9 percent of the labor force in the informal sector (Levy 2009, 206), the evolution of the legal minimum wage is more relevant. From 1983 through 1988, the real minimum wage fell 40–50 percent (Bruhn 1997, 118), and many in the informal sector did not earn even that amount. Another study, looking specifically at the period 1982–2001, concluded the real minimum wage fell an astounding 74.6 percent (Bensusán 2005, 250). To put this in perspective, a low-income worker is generally considered someone who earns three times the minimum wage or less. In 2005 this was the case for half the workers in the formal sector and a staggering 85 percent in the informal sector (Levy 2009, 206).

The impact of the crisis and policies implemented to address it can be also understood in terms of the percentage of Mexicans who could not afford to purchase even basic necessities (the Normative Basket of Essential Necessities / Canasta Normativa de Necesidades Esenciales). After falling from 56 percent to just 3 percent between 1963 and 1977, the percentage stabilized for a brief period until it rocketed up to 50 percent from 1982 to 1987 (Brachet-Márquez 1996, 208). For these reasons and others, the UN's Economic Commission for Latin America and the Caribbean found that income poverty in Mexico in 1998 was almost the same as it was in 1989, the end of the infamous lost decade of development, and actually higher than it had been in 1969 (Boltvinik 2003).

Given the depth of the economic crisis and the lack of any meaningful political regime change, the relatively smooth economic transition is even more remarkable. As Viviane Brachet-Márquez (1996, 19) eloquently explains, starting
```

in 1982, "Mexico entered into the deepest and most enduring economic crisis in its history. . . . The reach and nature of state intervention in society was fundamentally transformed, leaving in its place a much reduced and partially decentralized state apparatus. At the same time, almost all investment in public services . . . was cut to pay the immense external debt. In any other Latin American country, this massive crisis would have led to political disturbances and a violent change of regime. In Mexico, surprisingly, nothing has changed in terms of the . . . formal configuration of power."

The reason for this reflects the central role played by Mexico's corporatist institutions of controlled inclusion, particularly the CTM and its affiliated unions in the public sector.[12] As Francisco Zapata (1998, 156) succinctly points out, "one can only explain the absence of massive resistance to technological modernization, layoffs, revision of collective contracts, and restructuring of businesses if the existing power of the corporatist control exerted by labor leadership is considered."

Mexico's corporatist institutions facilitated the economic transition principally through wage restraint.[13] In other words, labor's official "representatives" were largely responsible for the deterioration in wages since the 1980s. This began with the debt crisis in early 1982 and was institutionalized with the first Pact for Stability and Economic Growth (Pacto para la Estabilidad y el Crecimiento Económico) in 1987—a tripartite agreement negotiated among representatives of business, the state, and organized labor that soon became the hallmark of Mexico's de facto incomes policy. While the initial justification for this was to control inflation (and employers, for their part, agreed to controls on prices and interest rates), it soon became the basis for achieving a low-wage comparative advantage to promote the export of manufactured goods.[14]

There are a number of reasons why the CTM and its affiliates accepted such policies, despite their negative impact on workers. At least initially, inflation was an important source of worker complaints, so it was viewed as a simple trade-off: lower wages to protect the buying power of workers so that their existing salaries would go further. For union leaders, an essential quid pro quo was that there be no significant changes to Mexican labor law—a condition respected by successive PRI and, post-2000, PAN governments (Bensusán 2005; Burgess 2004; Middlebrook and Zepeda 2003b; Zapata 1998). This ensured that union leaders would retain key sources of power, including a monopoly over worker representation and the collection of dues, which gave them tremendous resources that are largely unaccountable, as well as the power to decide who works and who is fired. Union leaders also retained the power to assign union members to special union duties that allowed them to avoid actually working for the firm that hired them. According to government statistics, this amounted to almost eighteen thousand positions (Mayer-Serra 2009, 185–89). Such power also meant that established union leaders could punish union dissidents as a way to prevent the democratization of union structures (Middlebrook 1995), as well as (illegally) supplement their incomes by selling positions. At the same time, the leadership of all corporatist institutions, including the CTM and CNC, retained direct access to positions of power in the state and PRI, including elections to the legislature that, in turn, provided even more resources to expand their patronage networks and personal powerbase (Heredia 1992).

Of course, workers did realize some important benefits as well. Despite wage restraint, public-sector workers in the petroleum, telecommunications, and teaching sectors still received significantly higher wage increases than other groups (Guerrero, López-Calva, and Walton 2009). Moreover, workers have benefited from the provision of social welfare benefits and job security; in fact, their contractual situation has not changed and even the reforms of such key sectors of the economy as education and energy have been designed to minimize their negative impact on union members (Levy and Walton 2009a).

This continued role of corporatist labor organizations is often welcomed by the private sector. Given the newly competitive economic environment associated with free trade, private business sees the advantage of working with the CTM and its affiliated unions as a source of labor discipline. In sectors such as automobile manufacturing, firms have even allowed the CTM to recuperate the space it had lost to independent unions in the 1970s (Bensusán 2005). As Richard Roman and Edur Velasco Arregui (2006, 96) aptly note, corporatist labor organizations have been able to take advantage of the opportunities opened up for them by Mexico's new development model to occupy "a new-old niche as agents of labor control." Of course, an important "new" aspect of this niche is how economics has replaced politics in labor control. It is a good example of how neopluralism replaces the political criteria underpinning controlled inclusion and citizenship as co-optation with the market criteria for inclusion that defines citizenship as consumption.

The National Educational Workers Union (Sindicato Nacional de Trabajadores de la Educación, SNTE) offers a dramatic example of the consequences of the continued influence of corporatist unions. With 1.4 million members, it is the largest union in Latin America (*Economist,* July 19, 2007). While states are responsible for the administration of public education, the SNTE negotiates salaries and working conditions with the federal government (World Bank 2006). With an estimated at least 2 billion Mexican pesos (more than 175 million U.S. dollars) a year from union dues, the SNTE has considerable economic clout (Mayer-Serra 2009, 185–86). The political influence it enjoys through its direct relationship with the state is supplemented by its control over a block of deputies and senators, both through the SNTE's own political party and through its members in other political parties. As a result, "it is hardly surprising that the SNTE has been able to legislate in its own favor" (186). The 2002 Education Law Reform (Reforma de la Ley de Enseñanza)—adopted after the PRI lost the presidency in 2000—is a good example of this. The reform mandated that the federal government spend 8 percent of GDP on education in 2006. The target was equal to the combined value of federal income and value-added taxes, yet the SNTE was not required to commit to any improvements in teacher performance. While only 5.4 percent of GDP was actually spent on education in 2006, it still accounted for 25 percent of the federal budget (186). The SNTE also controls the supervision of teachers through the Ministry of Education, "which effectively means that the administration of a school has little control over what happens in its school" (186–87). Not surprisingly, teachers' base salary increased 52.4 percent and their fringe benefits went up by 9.1 percent from 1998–2001, with real salaries for teachers having increased more than the rate of GDP growth since 1993 (187–88). In fact, most of the increases in educational expenditure in recent years has gone to teacher salaries (World Bank 2006) and 77 percent of unionized teachers had incomes that placed them in the top income quartile nationally (Guerrero, López-Calva, and Walton 2009, 121–22).

This blatant abuse of power is accentuated by the fact that improved teacher salaries in Mexico have not lead to better educational outcomes (World Bank 2006). Student performance on standardized tests in Mexico is the worst in the Organisation for Economic Co-operation and Development (OECD) and among the three lowest in Latin America (Guerrero, López-Calva, and Walton 2009, 139; Mayer-Serra 2009). Among other things, this reflects the near absolute insulation of teachers from local- or even state-level accountability. But in sharp contrast to Chile, "the system is surprisingly egalitarian." Controlling for socioeconomic status and school infrastructure, "public school students actually perform slightly better overall" (Mayer-Serra 2009, 168, 171).

There are several reasons for this outcome, which at first glance seems to contradict a basic premise of neopluralism and citizenship as consumption since privileged groups would be expected to use their economic resources to ensure a better educational outcome for their children. One reason this has not happened is that the SNTE has monopoly over teacher training for public- and private-sector teachers. There also are no national examinations that parents could use for comparing schools. Perhaps more important (and more consistent with the preponderance of market criteria under neopluralism), the decision to send children to private schools reflects parents' desire to ensure that their children are in appropriate social circles that will provide them with the contacts that they need to earn higher incomes later. Because "the job market seems to depend much more on whom one knows than on merit" parents are satisfied when their children find good jobs (Mayer-Serra 2009, 171).

Few analysts would have predicted this outcome for corporatist institutions. The retreat of the state from its economic role under ISI and the dominance of market principles in determining state-society relations was presumed to make corporatism a relic of the past (Oxhorn 1998a). Moreover, the size of unions has been dramatically shrinking throughout Latin America. The CTM was no exception as its membership fell by half from 1997 to 2005 (Roman and Velasco Arregui 2006, 98). Yet size is not everything and statistics can be misleading. With 16.1 percent of workers in unions in 2005 (Guerrero, López-Calva, and Walton 2009, 122), the relative size of the unionized portion of the workforce was more or less the same as it had been in 1978, when 16.2 percent of the workforce belonged to unions (Bensusán 2005, 272). The control that corporatist unions exercised in key sectors of the economy where union membership has always been much higher has not changed substantially and may have actually increased as part of the political compromises made to ensure a relatively smooth transition to a new economic model.

The continued influence and strength of corporatism has had important negative consequences for the development of civil society. The resistance of the leaders of corporatist institutions to the democratization of their own internal structures meant that they opposed a transition to democracy; this was a major reason why the transition would take more than a decade to complete (Middlebrook 1995). The CTM's continued strength has also made it even more difficult for alternatives to emerge, within both the union movement and the political party system (Zapata 1998).

Most important, corporatism distorts the labor market by decreasing economic and productivity growth rates, further entrenching inequality. While a relatively large and permanent informal sector is a defining characteristic of Latin American economies, this is especially true for Mexico. As Santiago Levy (2008, 90; italics in original) points out, *"over the last decade and a half, informal employment has accounted for more than half of the labor force despite positive economic growth in most of those years—and in absolute terms it has increased."* The reason for this is the existence of parallel social welfare programs: a system of social security for formal-sector workers that is the legacy of controlled inclusion and a newer system of social protection targeting people not in the formal sector (2008).

In the social security system, nonwage costs amount to 34.7 percent of total wage costs, of which government subsidies finance only 15 percent (Levy 2008, 26, 18). This creates a substantial de facto tax that affects workers' salaries because of the burden imposed on firms. It also diverts funds away from investments needed to spur higher economic and productivity growth rates, which remain low not only in comparison to Mexico's earlier experience under ISI but also in relation to most other economies in the region.

Social protection, on the other hand, is almost fully subsidized by the state, which in effect amounts to subsidizing informality. By encouraging the growth of the informal sector in this way, productivity and GDP growth are depressed even more. In terms of their relative sizes, during the period 1998–2007, social protection funding increased more than 110 percent, or twice the rate of funding for social security programs, which increased less than 50 percent during the same period. In 2003 health services through social protection programs received more funding than health services in social security (Levy 2008, 27–29). This has had minimal impact on income distribution since social protection has been funded largely by oil rents rather than taxes on more privileged segments of Mexican society (Levy 2008; Levy and Walton 2009a). Its distributional impact is further limited because the actual value of the benefits each individual person or family receives is quite low, despite the impressive aggregate statistics. Because expenditures also " bolster the government's political legitimacy . . . this practice has been [largely] invariant to the party in power" (Levy and Walton 2009a, 13).

This dual system for social provision further segments society because the poor bear the brunt of the negative consequences. First, even though the non-wage tax applies to all formal-sector workers, actual access to the basic elements of the benefits package—retirement pensions, day-care facilities, housing assistance, and health care—are all dependent on one's income (Levy 2008, esp. 54–80).[15] For poorer workers in the formal sector, these labor rights are more apparent than real, making the fully subsidized social protection system more attractive. For this reason, fewer than 2 percent of eligible workers in the informal sector take advantage of their legal right to opt into the social security system (Levy 2008, 61). Conversely, higher-income workers can either take advantage of social security benefits or find alternatives in the private sector. For firms, their effective savings are higher if low-paid workers remain in the informal sector because the cost of social security benefits to the firm is the same regardless of the employee's actual salary, yet low-paid workers' direct contribution to overall company earnings is much lower than it generally is for higher-paid workers, which allows the company to recoup more of the cost.

The consequences of this are multifaceted. First, there is a high rate of volatility as workers move between the informal and formal sectors of the economy, affecting the poor disproportionately. One study found that 26 percent of unskilled workers, compared to 9 percent of skilled workers, left their jobs every six months, much of it reflecting shifts between the formal and informal sectors (Maloney 2009, 253). As a result, the poor's access to basic benefits is further undermined. Data for the period 1997–2005 show that the average low-wage worker who was enrolled in the public security system in 1997 remained in the formal sector for 4.3 years, or 48 percent of the period. High-wage workers, however, remained in the formal sector for an average of 6.5 years, or 72 percent of the period. Since the right to receive a pension and other benefits requires twenty-five years of contributions, this means a low-wage worker would have to work for fifty years to be eligible (Levy 2009, 207). As Levy (2008, 106; italics in original) points out, *the problem for low-wage workers is not entering a formal job, it is staying in a formal job.*

Second, social protection policies do not solve the problem of poverty and actually may perpetuate it. It is important not to romanticize the quality of these programs, particularly given the decision not to make them redistributive. While the absolute levels of funding for them may be high and they are growing, social protection policies are the last resort for the vast majority of Mexicans who do not have stable formal-sector employment. Moreover, social protection programs have only a minimal impact on actual social mobility out of poverty.[16] As Levy (2008, 82; italics in original) argues, it is not a coincidence that social protection policies seem to better serve the poor than social security programs: "*It is the result of decades of government program design and service provision policies that have proceeded, de facto, under the assumption that nonsalaried workers are poor and salaried workers are non-poor. Those program design and service provision policies contribute to trapping the poor in poverty.*"

Finally, this duality exacerbates the tendency for neopluralism to undermine civil society. Labor market volatility represents an extreme form of economic insecurity that has serious implications for the possibility for autonomous organizational activity within civil society. For the poor in particular, the imperative of remaining employed makes it that much more difficult to devote energy and time to any kind of autonomous organizational activity. Corporatism's power is only enhanced by the challenges this creates for organizing independent unions.

While corporatism continues to have a lasting and largely negative influence on Mexican politics and society, it is a shadow of its former self in one particular sense: corporatism no longer has the capacity to effectively ensure the PRI's monopoly on political power. Urbanization has shifted the locus of political power away from the countryside, where PRI dominance through corporatist institutions and clientelism remains largely intact. However important corporatism remains economically, it can no longer mobilize sufficient votes to deliver electoral majorities for the PRI. Civil society has been unable to fill the resultant organizational void, in part because of corporatism's legacy and, in the 1980s and 1990s, because the state was not yet willing to tolerate significant widespread autonomous civil society mobilization. Instead, the market—or neopluralism—began to supplant many of the political roles formerly undertaken by corporatism. In particular, citizenship as consumption increasingly began to displace citizenship as co-optation, although the latter continues to play an important role even after Mexico's transition to democracy. For example, many aspects of social security delivery and administration were privatized in 1995, "creating a market-driven system for those who could afford to pay" (Laurell 2003, 333; see also Evangelista Martínez 2001). Specifically in the area of health care, 52.9 percent of expenditures were out of pocket, despite Mexico's dual system of health care provision. By comparison, only 16.6 percent of such expenditures were out of pocket in the United States (Barraza-Lloréns et al. 2002, 49). The only solution to citizenship as consumption is universal social welfare rights (Barraza-Lloréns et al. 2002; Evangelista Martínez 2001; Levy 2008). But without more effective citizenship as agency, it is hard to imagine this happening.

President Carlos Salina (1988–94) recognized the limits of corporatism better than anyone else. Not only was he a principal architect of Mexico's new economic model, he ambitiously attempted to implement a strategy for the "modernization of traditional corporatism" (Olvera 2003d, 55). First, he set out to reduce—but not eliminate—the influence of labor and peasant leaders in the PRI to make it more commensurate with their role in society (Bruhn 1996). For example, Salinas set in motion a process that saw the proportion of PRI deputies coming from the labor sector of the party fall from 31.4 percent in 1979 to just 8.6 percent in 2003 (Bensusán 2005, 254). Salinas also targeted labor leaders who were judged ineffective or refused to follow the party policies, such as the head of the oil workers, who was actually imprisoned on corruption charges (Brachet-Márquez 1996; Burgess 2004).

The cornerstone of this effort to reshape Mexican corporatism was a new social welfare program, the National Solidarity Program (Programa Nacional de Solidaridad, PRONASOL). Through PRONASOL, Salinas attempted to circumvent traditional PRI leaders and establish a parallel system of patronage and clientelism that focused on the popular sectors as poor people rather than as members of the traditional working class and peasantry (Bruhn 1996; Shefner 2008; Dresser 1994). Its close link to neopluralism and citizenship as consumption could not be more explicit, as Denise Dresser (1994, 147), explains, "PRONASOL redefines the members of the traditional corporatist coalition essentially as consumers, and creates majorities by slicing the social spectrum in a horizontal fashion." Local solidarity committees were formed ostensibly for the purpose of local oversight and participation. In practice, they were composed largely of PRI activists with little autonomous grassroots participation to establish new clientelist networks through the disbursement of PRONASOL funds. Communities where the Left had done well in the 1988 presidential elections were targeted, while a number of people involved in the PRONASOL program were nominated by the PRI in the 1991 congressional elections.

PRONASOL ultimately failed to achieve most of its goals. Evidence suggests that while the poor were willing to accept PRONASOL funding, they did not shift their votes from the Left to the PRI (Bruhn 1996). Although the PRI was able to win the 1994 presidential elections, Salinas failed to build a new majority coalition and the PRI went on to lose the next two successive presidential elections. At the same time, poverty increased during the Salinas sexenio from 64 percent of the population in 1989 to 66 percent in 1992 (Brachet-Márquez 1996, 216).

Despite this failure, PRONASOL represents a turning point in social policy, and the lessons learned have played an important role in the development of social protection policies under all subsequent Mexican presidents. Salinas's successor, Ernesto Zedillo (1994–2000), replaced it with a new program, Progresa, in 1997. It was renamed Oportunidades in 2002 by President Fox and was continued by his successor. Like PRONASOL, Progresa/Oportunidades (Progress/Opportunities) targets poor people rather than members of any particular class. It also bypasses the traditional corporatist organizations associated with the PRI. Unlike PRONASOL, Progresa/Oportunidades is strictly a needs-based program specifically targeting people living in extreme poverty. To further insulate it from political interference, no new beneficiaries can be added six months prior to presidential and congressional elections (Levy 2006). The program grew steadily from its initial budget of $58.8 million, providing assistance to three hundred thousand families. By the end of 2005, the budget for Oportunidades was $2.8 billion and it provided assistance to more than 5 million families, which was roughly the number of households living in extreme poverty according to government calculations (1–2). The average amount of assistance in 2005 was $35 per month, which was the equivalent of 25 percent of average poor rural household income and 15–20 percent of poor urban household income. Assistance increases with the number of children in the household and their grade levels, although the maximum is capped ($153 per month in 2005) to not create incentives for larger families. To avoid making families dependent on assistance, more than 50 percent of program benefits are temporary (Levy 2006, 22–25). In exchange for receiving these benefits, children must attend school and various workshops on such topics as health and nutrition, and receive regular medical care, among other things.

The results from Progresa/Oportunidades, verified by external evaluations, have been overwhelmingly positive, with numerous international organizations, including the World Bank and the United Nations Children's Fund, lauding it as a model program (Oportunidades 2008). As Levy (2006, 77), one of the principal architects of the original Progresa program rightfully notes, "families are eating more and have better diets, they are using more preventative health services, and children and young people are going to school more often and probably performing better."

Without denying the importance of Progresa/Oportunidades to its beneficiaries, it is important to underscore important limits on its capacity for substantially altering Mexico's highly unequal social structures. First, it deliberately targets only those in extreme poverty, which is approximately 2.8 percent of the population, according to calculations by the Mexican government (Levy 2006, 25). Yet in 2005, 35.5 percent of all Mexicans lived below the poverty line, according to the UN's Economic Commission for Latin American and the Caribbean (ECLAC 2007, 300). Progresa/Oportunidades also uses a very conservative calculation for determining extreme poverty, and alternative definitions suggest a considerable gap in actual coverage for even this group (Boltvinik and

Cortés 2000). For example, the Economic Commission for Latin America and the Caribbean (ECLAC 2007, 300) calculated extreme poverty for Mexico in 2005 at 11.7 percent of the population, or more than four times the population covered by Oportunidades. At the same time, the small size of the program, amounting to less than 0.4 percent of GDP, cannot have any significant redistributive effect. The impact of even this relatively small amount was limited even more by the fact that, as a condition for its adoption, no new revenues were collected and the gradual expansion of Progresa/Oportunidades was paid for by phasing out generalized food subsidies. Moreover, unless the definition of the target group changes, the percentage of GDP will only decline in the future because full coverage has officially been achieved. As Levy (2006, 77) explains, "from the point of view of the poor, it is a substantial redistribution. From the point of view of the country as a whole, it is not." Even the program's potential longer-term contribution to greater social mobility is unlikely to have an effect on actual incomes and income inequality, given the structural problem of a vast informal sector. Elsewhere, Levy (2008, 4) laments, "under current conditions, poor youth who enter the labor force in the coming years after benefitting from Progresa-Oportunidades will be very unlikely to find jobs in the formal sector . . . and . . . few firms will be willing to invest in training them and gradually raising their productivity. Those youngsters, while healthier and more educated than their elder peers, will end up in low-productivity jobs in the informal sector. Under current conditions, Progresa-Oportunidades is unlikely to break the inter-generational transmission of poverty."

There are limits of Progresa/Oportunidades in terms of its potential for strengthening civil society, as it is essentially an innovative form of citizenship as consumption. As Levy (2006, 99) notes, the deliberate decision to limit the political manipulation of the program meant that it could include no community participation. Civil society's development is constrained because "social welfare will be identified as an individual achievement and a personal and family responsibility" (Evangelista Martínez 2001, 164), completely unrelated to civil society organizational activity. This further limits the institutional space for achieving citizenship as agency by constraining the state's ability to work with collective actors (Laurell 2003). The incentives to even attempt to engage in state-society synergy are significantly reduced as needs-based targeting "makes political participation irrelevant. . . . The net effect of these changes has been to increase the cost of targeting the state while making it less likely that political action will be successful" (Holzner 2007, 104). In the end, civil society is likely to become more atomized.

Progresa/Oportunidades also risks dividing communities (Teichman 2008; Holzner 2007). The obvious division between recipients and nonrecipients is exacerbated by the conservative definition of extreme poverty, which in practice can appear to be arbitrary given the pervasiveness of poverty and inequality in Mexico. Findings from public opinion surveys in poor communities suggest this problem will only be exacerbated because "a higher value is placed on being treated 'equally' than on 'equity'"—a normative judgment that is fundamentally at odds with the rationale used for rationing scarce program resources (Adato 2000, 349). Finally, despite the intention of being totally apolitical, there is a real danger that the program will be used to further partisan interests because of its reliance on community facilitators. They are chosen by mothers participating in Progresa/Oportunidades to provide information and help administer the program without any consideration of their own party loyalties, potentially introducing an indirect mechanism for partisan manipulation of the program at the grassroots, despite careful targeting criteria (Schteingart 2000).

Although there had been a growing gap between what the revolution's promise of a more just, inclusive, and sovereign society and its actual achievements before the economic collapse of the 1980s, that collapse and the policy response to it created a huge chasm. This unique combination of policy failure and the market-oriented response to it proved to be the necessary conditions for ensuring Mexico's second transition, this time to democracy. With this second transition, Mexico's shift toward neopluralism would be complete.

Mexico's Democratic Transition and the Civil Society Moment

If Mexico's transition to a market-oriented development model accentuated the authoritarian aspects of neopluralism, Mexico's second transition to democracy underscores that nature of its democratic potential. The resiliency of the key institutions associated with seventy years of PRI hegemony meant it would necessarily be a "protracted transition," in which elections played a central role (Labastida Martín del Campo and López Leyva 2004). While the transition technically began with the electoral reforms of 1977, the PRI remained firmly in control during the first years of this so-called transition and sought to use reforms to legitimate its continued rule by expanding the role for opposition parties while maintaining its absolute dominance.[17]

Beginning in the early 1980s, however, the PRI's ability to retain control over the reform process became increasingly tenuous as growing segments of Mexican society began to contemplate the possibility of an alternative to the PRI's monopoly of political power. For the Right, including large portions of the economic elite and middle sectors, the economic crisis and resultant nationalization of the banking system in 1982 seriously undermined their confidence in the PRI's capacity to govern effectively. For a growing portion of the popular sectors, any sense of social pact was broken by the economic dislocations associated with the crisis and the reaction of the PRI government. For example, as demand skyrocketed when unemployment and poverty exploded, per capita social expenditures during the period 1986–88 were just 30 percent of what they had been during the period 1971–81 (Bruhn 1996, 154).

Through the course of the 1980s, the process of regime change inevitably came to focus exclusively on elections, which had been held regularly since the 1930s. As "Mexican political-cultural elites . . . decided to accept the electoral route as a civilized and peaceful way to propel a regime change," the Right saw elections as a way to impose their conservative values on society (Olvera 2003d, 53). Conversely, the failure of the radicalism spawned in the aftermath of the 1968 Tlatelolco Massacre to change the system, combined with new levels of economic deprivation among the popular sectors, suggested that elections could be the potential Achilles heel of the regime. As Olvera (2003b, 356) argues, "From the idea of the revolution put forth by popular collective actors there was a movement to the acceptance that democratization of public life and participation in electoral politics were the only practical path for resolving national problems in the long term." This focus on elections was reinforced by progressive Catholic Church and liberation theology (Chand 2001).

The 1988 presidential elections were a key turning point in the transition process. In elections wracked by electoral fraud and intimidation on the part of the PRI, Carlos Salinas was declared the victor after officially winning just 50.3 percent of the vote. Growing and widespread discontent had found a new champion in the candidacy of Cuauhtémoc Cárdenas, son of the revolution's own champion, former president Lázaro Cárdenas. His emergence as a credible challenger to the PRI came as a surprise to most observers, who thought the Right would ultimately benefit from growing discontent with the PRI given its increasing strength and organizational resources.[18] Cárdenas had publicly broken with the PRI only months earlier along with a number of other former high-level PRI officials who had formed a dissident group, the Democratic Current (Corriente Democrática, DC), within the PRI in 1986. When the DC left the PRI in 1987, it formed a broad, loosely organized electoral alliance, the Democratic National Front (Frente Democrático Nacional, FDN), with a number of smaller leftist parties and civil society groups. And they almost won.[19] Tensions within the coalition and the trauma of its near win quickly led to its dissolution and, in 1989, the DC, along with some elements of the 1988 alliance, formally became Mexico's third major political party, the Party of the Democratic Revolution (Partido de la Revolución Democrática, PRD).[20]

As Kathleen Bruhn (1997, 2) notes, Cárdenas's success was in large part due to an "unprecedented alliance with popular movements that historically resisted electoral cooperation," yet that alliance virtually had disintegrated by 1991. While there are many reasons for this, including the inability of the PRD to build durable party structures (Bruhn 1997; Wuhs 2008), it fundamentally reflected the way in which controlled inclusion and citizenship as co-optation continued to condition state-society relations, even as they were being displaced by neopluralism and citizenship as consumption. The space for autonomous organizational activity within civil society was essentially limited to mobilization in favor of free and fair elections, because of the enduring nature of corporatist institutions, as well as the ongoing reluctance of civil society organizations to engage with political parties and the state, given the very real threat that they would be absorbed by them as a result. Even in 1988 civil society played a secondary, albeit very important, role in getting out the vote. It only became involved once Cárdenas declared his candidacy, and much of its involvement was spontaneous and the result of unstructured grassroots initiatives rather than organized mobilization led by civil society leaders (Bruhn 1997). Even more than in Chile, political parties (however weak PRD may have been institutionally) dominated the transition, negotiating the new rules of the game and controlling mobilization (Eisenstadt 2004; Olvera 2003a; Schedler 2000). As Olvera (2003a, 19–20) concludes, this ultimately would severely constrict the role of civil society when the transition to neopluralism was complete: "The parties not only monopolized the direction of the mobilization, but also created institutions and rules that gave them a financial, organizational and legal autonomy with respect to civil society. [This] . . . destroyed earlier links and intermediations between the political system and society, but did not construct new ones, which explains why the alternation in power has not yet meant a real reform of relations between the state and society."

The importance of the initial split within the PRI over how to respond to the growing economic crisis and the role of dissent within the governing party as a catalyst for change cannot be underestimated. Not only did this place the party's continued dominance in doubt by publicly exposing its own divisions, it opened up the possibility for a challenge from a Left that claimed to be the true bearer of the revolution's legacy once dissident party members defected. This was a mantle that Cuauhtémoc Cárdenas personally could assume more effectively than any other politician in Mexico at the time. It was essential for garnering widespread popular support for Cárdenas's insurgency given the depth of Mexico's economic crisis. But rather than ensuring any revolutionary change, the unprecedented popular-sector support that Cárdenas's campaign galvanized reinforced the growing belief that the PRI was not invincible and that the most effective way to take advantage of its vulnerability was to demand free and fair elections.

In the context of corporatism's continued perverse influence on civil society and with the legacy of controlled inclusion still all too fresh in the popular sectors' daily encounters with the state, the intrinsic neutrality of elections made them the most viable way of opposing the PRI's continued rule; mobilizations around elections quickly came to eclipse other manifestations of civil society organizational activity . Electoral mobilization is neutral from the perspective of the popular sectors for two reasons. First, such participation could remain explicitly nonpartisan, avoiding the threat of both clientelist entanglement with any party, as well as the risk of becoming entangled with the wrong party should another party prove victorious. Given the extreme uncertainty and continued political dominance of the PRI, the importance of this should not be underestimated. Second, electoral mobilization offered an alternative to actually working with the state. While this also meant that any meaningful state-society synergy would be undermined—with lasting consequences for civil society's future development—it was an attractive alternative to many because it insulated popular-sector organizational activity from the corporatist trap. Rather than work with the state, civil society increasingly strove to create a parallel state in the electoral arena by creating new mechanisms for holding the state and elected officials accountable by ensuring that elections would actually be relatively free and fair.

This electoral dynamic was reinforced by a series of events in 1994. By the end of that year, virtually all of the principal social and political actors viewed elections as the safe and preferred way to engage in the politics of demanding a political opening. With the economy growing, poverty rates declining, and future economic well-being seemly assured after NAFTA went into effect in January of that year, Mexicans increasingly turned their attention to politics in the context of an unprecedented level of political instability. The PRI's designated heir to the presidency, Luis Donaldo Colosio, was assassinated before the elections, which was followed by the assassination later in 1994 of the party's secretary general, José Francisco Ruiz Massieu. Even earlier, the Zapatista Army of National Liberation (Ejército Zapatista de Liberación Nacional, EZLN) began a violent insurrection in January 1994 that literally caught the world's attention. The EZLN would soon renounce its militaristic pretensions, but by raising military confrontation as an alternative to a peaceful transition, its example strengthened the commitment of political elites to achieving a transition to democracy through increasingly competitive elections (Cadena Roa 2008; Bizberg 2003). The institutionalized nature of elections made them the most attractive way to restore at least a modicum of political stability. The result was the adoption of key electoral reforms in 1994, including the creation of the Instituto Federal Electoral, that ultimately paved the way for the transition's completion in 2000. In the longer term, the centrality of political parties in elections further ensured the dominance of parties during the transition, adding yet another constraint on the subsequent development of civil society once the transition was completed in 2000.

The year 1994 was also the defining moment for civil society with the formation of the Civic Alliance (Alianza Cívica, AC) in April. The AC was arguably one of the most effective autonomous civil society organizations in modern Mexican history. Tracing its roots back to the mobilizations associated with student radicalism and the progressive Catholic Church in the late 1960s and

1970s, the AC was formed by the country's principal prodemocracy civil society organizations to ensure that there would be no repeat of the 1988 electoral fraud. Drawing on its diverse networks, it soon organized what would be "one of the largest experiments in integrated electoral monitoring that had been carried out in the world at the time" (Olvera 2003b, 352). The AC developed a representative sample of twenty-four hundred stations for the 1994 elections, which were "invigilated by an army of 18,000 citizens (of which 12,000 were legally registered as observers) mobilized in a civic action without precedent in the country" (360).[21] This allowed the AC to set the agenda for electoral reform by insisting on the creation of autonomous institutions for monitoring elections and a more or less level playing field for party competition. By 1996 the AC had an estimated two thousand official members, could mobilize between sixteen thousand and forty thousand people for electoral observation, and could convene anywhere from four hundred thousand to one million people in a series of "public consultations" (Rea Rodríguez 2001, 168–69n5).

The success of the AC reflected more than the legitimacy of the civil society organizations that created it. The AC's appeal was gauged in terms of citizenship rights: "the causes that it defends are profoundly [those of the] citizens" (Ramírez Sáiz 1997, 353). This was reinforced by the AC's deliberate decision not to openly oppose the regime, insisting instead on the right of Mexican citizens to free and fair elections (Bizberg 2003), a sharp contrast with prodemocracy movements in other countries, including Chile.

The AC example also sharply contrasted with the Chilean experience in that the AC remained steadfastly nonpartisan.[22] The importance of this stance was particularly clear in the 1994 elections. While the AC did find significant examples of vote buying and coercion in rural areas, as well as unfair competition given the PRI's media exposure and access to state resources, it concluded that the PRI's Ernesto Zedillo had in fact won the elections. When Cárdenas (who launched his second attempt at the presidency) and the Left ignored the AC's findings, claiming that the election was stolen by the PRI, the AC's credibility and perceived impartiality only grew. The AC realized the importance of its nonpartisan approach to mobilization because, left to themselves, it was now apparent that the opposition parties still did not have sufficient credibility to beat the PRI in fair elections (Olvera 2003b, 361–62).

However important its activities were for ultimately ensuring that elections would be free and fair, the AC was unable to achieve a similar level of success in other endeavors.[23] This was clearest in the AC's decision to launch a series of national consultations in December 1994. The first was held in February 1995 to gauge public opinion regarding the possible prosecution of former president Carlos Salinas, who abandoned the country in disgrace after the economy collapsed in 1994; whether to accept the U.S. credits offered to save the banking system; and the perceived need to restart government dialogue with the

EZLN. Although 626,525 people participated, the consultation had no noticeable political impact. While a second consultation held at the EZLN's request
focusing on the EZLN's future and the inclusion of indigenous rights in the
constitution drew more than a million participants, subsequent consultations
were more noticeable for their lack of adhesion. A three-month consultation
on government economic policies, September–November 1995, attracted only
428,345 signatures, underscoring the inability of the AC and its allied organizations to mobilize people outside the electoral arena. The AC would try again in
December 1996, this time organizing the First National March Condemning the
Government's Economic Policy (La Primera Jornada Nacional de Condena a la
Política Económica del Gobierno), but only 182,366 people participated, again
demonstrating its lack of mobilizational capacity between elections. This initiative also included presenting a formal proposal for lowering the value-added tax
in the legislature. When the proposal was simply ignored, the AC's leadership
began to realize that the consultations were unproductive, although that did not
prevent them from organizing a final consultation in June 1997—on the eve of
the midterm elections—in support of a citizen agenda. The fact that it mobilized
only 156,000 people and received little media coverage only demonstrated, once
again, the limits of the AC's political influence when it was not focused specifically on elections. Parallel to these consultations, the AC launched a campaign
to hold elected officials accountable in between elections, but this also failed to
generate important results.

In the end, the AC was a victim of its own success. Recognizing the perhaps
irreplaceable role it played in ensuring that elections would eventually be free
and fair, once that goal was met, the AC's importance quickly evaporated. The
movement's success was assured in 1996, when electoral reforms guaranteed the
autonomy of the IFE and guaranteed more equal media access to Mexico's three
principal parties. The fact that the reforms had been negotiated by the leader-
ships of the PRI, PAN, and PRD without any participation by the AC highlighted how the movement's time was coming to a rather sudden, albeit largely
happy, end. The importance of the 1996 electoral reform was confirmed in 1997,
when the PRI lost its majority control over the legislature for the first time. The
AC entered into a period of internal crisis and with the 2000 elections, "the
movement in its earlier form had arrived at its end, giving way to an NGO that
would have to become more specialized and look for its niche for action in the
new historic circumstances" (Olvera 2003b, 388–89).[24]

Neopluralist Democracy and the Poverty of Civil Society

It is ironic that perhaps the most enduring legacy of Mexico's 1917 revolution
is a peculiar form of neopluralist democracy. The perseverance of corporatist

institutions and citizenship as co-optation in the context of a market-oriented economy, a sharply reduced role of the state, and the growing importance of citizenship as consumption has created unique political dynamics that further accentuate neopluralism's authoritarian characteristics. With few alternatives, civil society mobilization focused on the demand for free and fair elections with impressive success, yet civil society faded from importance even though elections could not solve many of the fundamental challenges that Mexico needs to overcome to create state-society synergy and citizenship as agency. As José Woldenberg (2009, 98), who headed the IFE during the critical years of the transition from 1996 to 2003 sadly observes, "after a successful democratic transition . . . one finds the democratizing process is eroded and exhausted because in other areas of social life the reality is darker. The democratizing transition has been accompanied by deficient economic growth, a persistent social inequality and the phenomenon of exclusion associated with it, a notorious growth in crime, a fragile and counterfeit rule of law, a public life that is raucous and unintelligible."

The perseverance of corporatism is one important source of these democratic deficits. As already noted, there has been no significant change in labor relations legislation as a result of either transition, and this has allowed labor unions to retain important prerogatives. Perhaps one of the most surprising continuities post-2000 is the continued loyalty of the old corporatist organizations to the PRI (Bizberg 2003; Ramírez Sáiz 2002). One reason is that victories by both the PAN and PRD generally did not improve the situation of workers (Bensusán 2005). Given the important role corporatist unions continue to play in maintaining economic stability, in practice PAN and even PRD governments need to reach an accommodation with them (Muñoz Armenta 2006; Roman and Velasco Arregui 2006).

At the same time, the disconnect between the union leadership and the rank and file, which independent unions challenged in the 1970s, also remained unchanged. As Roman and Velasco Arregui (2006, 99) argue, "the few unions that were democratic continued to be so, while the fundamentally corrupt and authoritarian cultures of officialist unionism persisted even in some unions that claimed to be dissident and rhetorically challenged some of the tenets of the neoliberal project." Unions have often assumed a kind of hybrid character compared to the past as they now work with both the state and employers to ensure worker discipline on an economic level, compared to the period of controlled inclusion when they worked more exclusively with the state and political control was far more important. Political parties, particularly the PRD, have further undermined the potential for the emergence of alternative labor organizations by continuing to absorb labor leaders into party structures and clientelist networks.

Even if these corporatist groups have not been able to ensure a PRI electoral majority since at least the mid-1980s, neopluralist democracy has paradoxically increased their political and economic clout, along with that of other special interests. They continue to be represented directly in the Congress and Senate (Guerrero, López-Calva, and Walton 2009). Informal agreements established under the PRI's rule continue to remain in place, seemingly out of inertia (Olvera 2010). This inertia reflects the diminished power of the executive branch in relation to the legislature, as well as the renewed strength of local officials and, in particular, state governors. Political power is more fragmented than in the past as more actors are able to exert political influence compared to the authoritarian period, when so much political power was concentrated in the office of the president. This creates new spaces for influence that labor, business, and other special interests are able to capitalize on at the expense of majority interests. In particular, they have effectively blocked legal reforms that would negatively affect their interests (Mayer-Serra 2009), while regulatory agencies (with the exception of the Central Bank), lack the necessary autonomy from the sectors they oversee to effectively fulfill their function (Guerrero, López-Calva, and Walton 2009). Even the IFE's autonomy from political influence has been questioned in recent years (Olvera 2010). Ironically, an authoritarian president could coordinate and control the access of these de facto powers more effectively than a democratically elected one. As Santiago Levy and Michael Walton (2009a, 14) note, "a nomenklatura from all political parties shuffles and balances the interests of those in business and labor who are able to exercise voice and power as often as needed to maintain and reproduce their hold on power, while the population at large is able only to exercise its vote when scheduled in formal elections."

It comes as no surprise that most Mexicans have not been satisfied with the quality of the democratic regime once the transition ended in 2000. As table 6.3 shows, Mexicans generally view democracy as preferable to any other system of government, yet there is a sizable group—the majority, in fact, for three of the nine years for which data are available—that would consider nondemocratic alternatives. Less than a quarter of those surveyed expressed any level of satisfaction with the elected government in nearly two out of every three years since the transition. While levels of confidence in the government are somewhat higher, on average almost 70 percent of those surveyed in 2002–8 expressed no confidence in their elected government. Political parties fared even worse in the public eye. On average, slightly more than 20 percent of those surveyed in 2000–8 expressed any confidence in political parties. Former IFE head José Woldenberg (2009, 101) best summarized the public mood: "While it is certain that there is no alternative model that enjoys sufficient social support, the disenchantment with democracy . . . appears in every sphere: in the schools and in employment centers, in the media and circles of friends; and, of course, it is captured in the polls. Once again, the great illusion appears to be a fraud."

Table 6.3.   Public opinion and the evaluation of Mexican democracy

Year	2000	2001	2002	2003	2004	2005	2006	2007	2008	Avg.
Democracy is preferable to any other kind of government	45.9	48.3	65.3	54.9	56.5	61.4	61.8	52.3	48.1	54.9
"Very satisfied" and "relatively satisfied" with democracy	37.4	27.4	17.9	18.2	19.1	24.3	34.0	31.9	24.6	26.1
"A lot" and "some" confidence in government	...	...	19.1	23.5	20.1	31.6	46.7	36.7	36.2	30.6
"A lot" and "some" confidence in political parties	34.3	21.4	12.3	10.3	14.8	20.2	29.6	23.7	17.3	20.4

SOURCE: Data from Latinobarómetro (2009a).

In many ways, civil society has borne the brunt of these various dynamics. The consequences of corporatism's perseverance have limited the growth of civil society and exacerbated economic insecurity for the vast majority of Mexicans.[25] As a community organizer in Guadalajara complained, today "it is very rare to see . . . the mobilization of people for their needs. . . . Now people were not uniting because they had to work. Now when you return to your house, you do so tired. So, you don't have any energy to fight. So if you have been spending two, three years fighting for something that is not won, you get tired" (quoted in Shefner 2008, 188).

The rapid decline in the AC's effectiveness as a key representative of civil society also created a vacuum that has not yet been filled (Olvera 2010). Instead, there has been a fragmentation of civil society. Although the number of civil society organizations in Mexico has grown to approximately twenty thousand—500 to 1000 percent more than existed in the 1970s—they remain very small by international standards (Coordinación Presidencial 2002, 37). Most, like the AC after 2000, are not really autonomously organized civil society organizations at all, but NGOs with their own agendas and funding, and few roots in society (Olvera 2010).

As Claudio Holzner (2007) notes, the weakness of civil society is directly related to its perceived lack of relevance for most Mexicans. After peaking in 1997, the year the PRI lost its majority in the legislature, political participation began to decline sharply because of decreasing confidence that it would actually result in any meaningful outcomes. Even before the transition ended, the AC's own research for the period 1997–2000 confirmed how "the high electoral participation contrasts with the low participation of citizens in the design, execution, supervision and evaluation of public policy, as well as with their modest incorporation in the activities of political, social and civil organizations, and other non-profit activities" (Coordinación Presidencial 2002, 26).

Expectations that the new democratic government would open up spaces for public participation never materialized (Olvera 2010; Coordinación Presidencial 2002). For the victorious PAN, civil society had no political role because the PAN saw politics as the exclusive responsibility of political parties. The PRD also failed to open significant new channels for state–civil society synergy, despite its pretensions to the contrary. This was clear in how it governed the federal district after winning the first elections to head the capital in 1997.

Rather than new forms of citizen participation, Mexico's democratic regime has been characterized by older practices of clientelism, patronage, and corruption. The PRI's loss of its monopoly on political power seems to have led to the same practices being carried out by all the major political parties (Hilgers 2008; Montambeault 2009; Olvera 2010; Shefner 2008). Although there have been some notable democratic reforms, particularly the 2003 Transparency and Access to Public Information Law (Ley Federal de Transparencia y Acceso a la Información Pública), their overall impact has been limited due to the continued control exercised by political parties over the institutions of the state, to the near complete exclusion of civil society participation (Olvera 2010).

The ambiguous role that civil society plays in Mexico's democracy becomes particularly clear when analyzing two important examples of recent civil society mobilization: the protests against criminal violence that began in 1997 and the Popular Assembly of the Peoples of Oaxaca, May–November 2006.[26]

Mobilizing Against Criminal Violence

Mexico began to experience significant increases in crime in the mid-1990s, which the transition to democracy has failed to contain. As figure 6.1 shows, crime rates generally remained stagnant at an elevated level and then increased beginning in 2006. Half of the reported crimes involved violence and firearms (Rayelo 2004), and women have been particularly vulnerable (Olivera 2006). While reported kidnappings showed a significant decline through 2005, they then skyrocketed (see figure 6.2). In fact, the levels of criminal violence have reached such an extreme that Mexico now finds itself confronting "elements of extreme social disorder and a breakdown of political and legal institutions and practices that make questions about representation and democratic participation almost irrelevant" (Davis 2006, 82).

Not surprisingly, the top concerns of Mexicans since the late 1990s have consistently included crime, corruption, and injustice (Shirk and Ríos Cázares 2007). The 2002 National Survey of Public Insecurity (Encuesta Nacional Sobre

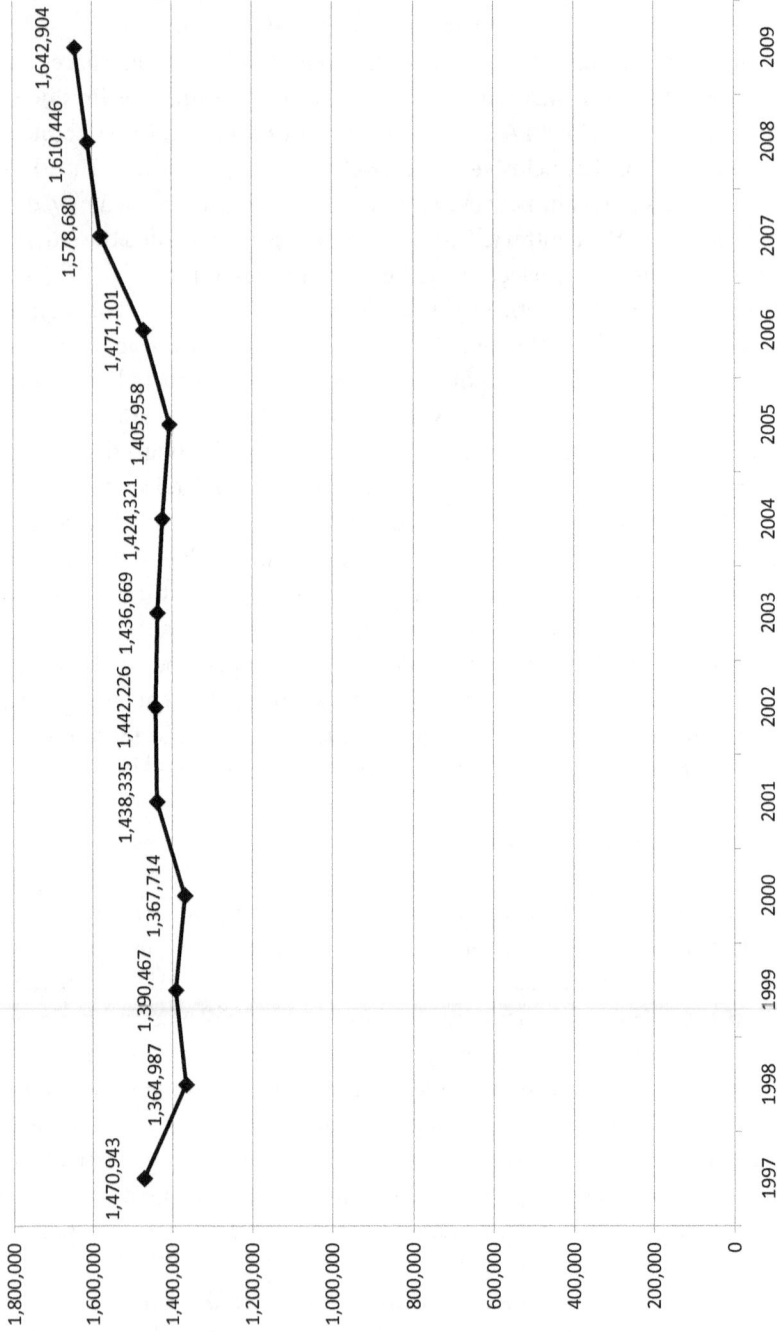

Fig. 6.1 Total crimes: preliminary findings, 1997–2009. Reproduced with the permission of México Unido Contra la Delincuencia (MUCD 2010).

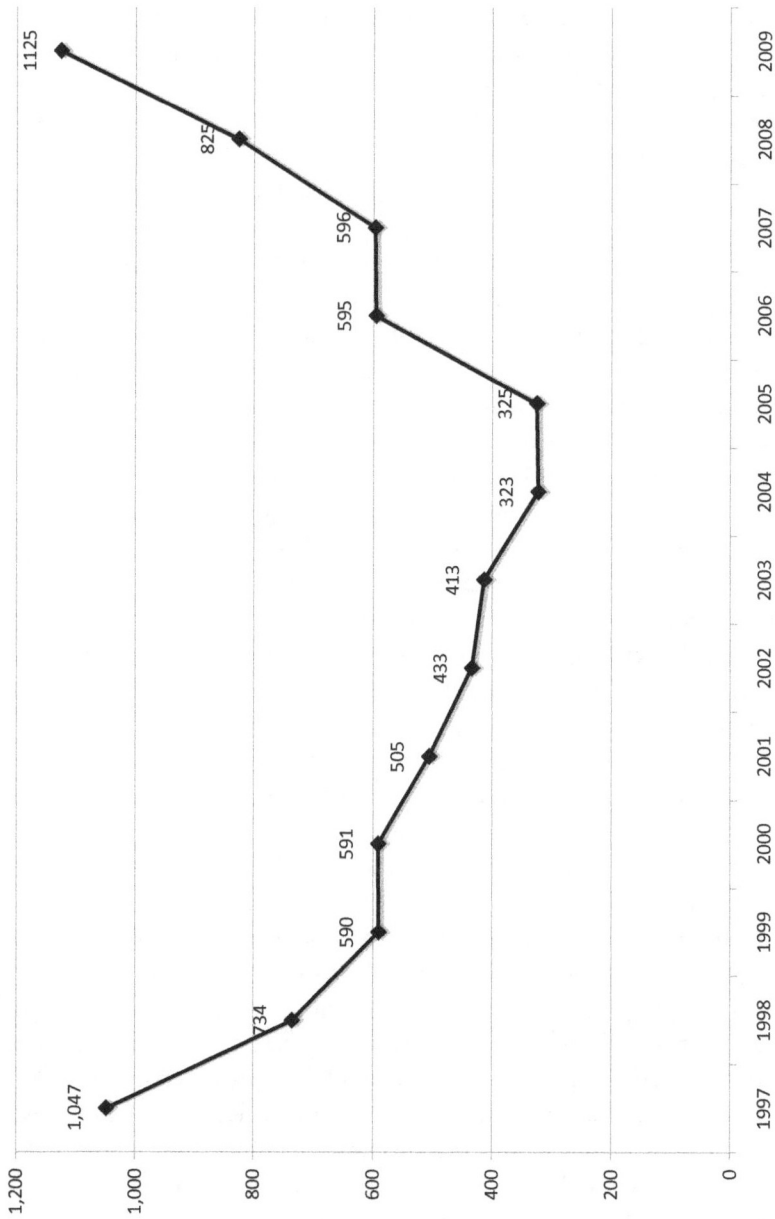

Fig. 6.2 Kidnappings: preliminary findings, 1997–2009. Reproduced with the permission of México Unido Contra la Delincuencia (MUCD 2010).

Inseguridad Pública) found that 47 percent of respondents felt somewhat or
very unsafe (Zepeda Lecuona 2007, 134). A 2004 poll uncovered that 47 percent
of the respondents had been victims of a crime during the previous year (López
Leyva 2009, 4). This has affected how a significant number of Mexicans live.
According to the 2002 survey, 44 percent of Mexicans no longer carried cash in
the street, 37 percent stopped wearing jewelry, and 27 percent stopped visiting
friends and family who lived far away (Rayelo 2004, 23).

The empirical reality of criminal violence is compounded by a sensationalist press that accentuates feeling of insecurity (Escalante Gonzalbo 2009). For
example, a 2008 opinion poll found that 77.1 percent of those interviewed feared
being kidnapped, while 67.8 percent were afraid of being robbed—probabili-
ties far higher than would be suggested even by Mexico's rates of crime (López
Leyva 2009, 5). As Jorge Tello Peón (2009, 21), notes, "The great quantity of
information that 'influences' perceptions of security in Mexico, crime, violence
and impunity, is assimilated as a risk to personal security and is transformed
into fear, confusion, anger and frustration among the population."

Given the urgency of the situation and its impact (both perceived and real) on
virtually all aspects of people's lives, civil society's response to criminal violence
underscores the challenges that neopluralism creates for citizenship as agency.
Three marches were held, focused mainly in Mexico City but with important
parallel mobilizations in other cities across the country. The organizers and
participants described them as citizens' initiatives: "Citizens demand that the
authorities end insecurity and impunity" (*Reforma,* August 31, 2008). The first
march took place on November 29, 1997, and brought 15,000 to 50,000 people
onto the streets. The second and by far the most important occurred seven years
later, on June 27, 2004, with between 250,000 and 500,000 people protesting.
The last march, on August 30, 2008, had between 80,000 and 200,000 march-
ers. The marches showed little actual organizational continuity, yet they shared
a number of important characteristics that together help explain their lack of
long-term impact.[27]

Perhaps the most notable aspect of all three marches was the prominent
role that relatively privileged groups played. This included middle- and upper-
middle-class protesters, prominent business groups and the Right, along with
representatives from all the major political parties and the popular sectors. At
least for the few hours that they lasted, the marches represented a true micro-
cosm of a strong civil society in terms of its breadth and depth. As one observer
noted with enthusiasm, the 2004 march demonstrated that "civil society now is
no longer from the left and lives" not only in poor neighborhoods "but can be
antipolitical" and include rich ones (Mejía 2004, 25).

With a few noticeable exceptions, however, this is not how the diversity of
participants was interpreted by many observers. For at least some in the press,

the marches' gravitas seemed to be undermined by the more expensive clothing of the protesters: "at times the march appeared like a fashion show" or "this is definitely another 'civil society'. . . the Calvin Klein Society" (*El Universal*, June 28, 2004).

More seriously, the association of business interests and the political Right with the marches was often seen as divisive, as if their mere presence in civil society somehow distorted its true essence, regardless of the shared concern for an effective state response to crime and impunity. This division was not because there was any noticeable difference on how to address the problem; regardless of their social class, the consensus among protestors in all three marches was for more repressive policing policies. Juventino Castro y Castro, a former national supreme court justice, emphasized how the 2004 march represented a call to increase the penalties for criminals and even establish the death penalty, rather than demands for an effective response that would improve economic and social conditions for important sectors of Mexico's population (Gil Olmos 2004a). Instead of representing the unity of civil society, the presence of society's haves and have-nots created a tension between two groups of self-perceived "victims," as each group's attempt at "prioritizing its perception of injustice" polarized the march (Mejía 2004, 26). Business groups and their right-wing representatives were also seen as hijacking the marches by imposing a very conservative political agenda (Delgado 2004). As social critic Carlos Monsiváis warned with reference to the 2004 march, the worst thing to do would be to "repeat the error, extremely costly, useless, self-destructive, to award the march to the ultra-right" (quoted in *El Universal*, June 28, 2004). Doing so permitted political elites to deflect their potential influence.

These are concrete manifestations of the increasing marketization of the rule of law, which was exacerbated by the transition to democracy that left the authoritarian nature of the preexisting system of public security largely intact (Benítez Manaut 2009). The mobilizations reflect very low levels of public confidence in the judiciary and police force (Guerrero, López-Calva, and Walton 2009; Benítez Manaut 2004), as well as the de facto impunity of those guilty of human rights abuses prior to the democratic transition (Aguayo Quezada and Treviño Rangel 2006).

Ironically, the demand of the protestors for more repressive public security policies reflects such policies' ineffectiveness more than a lack of government responsiveness (Benítez Manaut 2004, 2009; Davis 2006). Successive governments since the mid-1990s have been increasing the severity of policies toward criminals and suspected criminals and militarizing policing. More recently, President Calderón called on forty-five thousand federal troops and police to deal with organized crime when he assumed office in 2006 (*Economist*, January 12, 2008). The presumption of innocence until proven guilty has been effectively denied in practice given that "a suspect is guilty of committing a crime until it is proven that he is innocent; in other words, the police detain in order to investigate and do not investigate in order to detain" (Benítez Manaut 2004, 103).

The impact of such policies is dramatically unequal. Businesses and individuals with resources are able to purchase some insulation from criminal violence, as the number of private security firms mushrooms, employing tens of thousands of security guards (Benítez Manaut 2004; Davis 2006). Rather than connecting the police with communities, decentralization of policing at the municipal level has undermined police professionalism due to abuse by local governments and a lack of resources (Benítez Manaut 2004, 2009). The lack of professionalism is reinforced by the proliferation of policing authorities, with more than 1,600 existing at the local, state, and federal levels. Low professionalism, in turn, offers more opportunities for corruption and buttresses perceptions of impunity. Less than 20 percent of reported crimes actually result in an outcome that can be considered satisfactory, while in the vast majority no conclusive outcome is ever achieved (Zepeda Lecuona 2007, 142). In fact, someone is apprehended in only 11 percent of reported cases (Rayelo 2004, 23). Not surprisingly, approximately two-thirds of crimes are never even reported (Rayelo 2004; Zepeda Lecuona 2007).

For the poor, the consequences of the marketization of the rule of law are much more insidious. Even though the crimes they suffer lack the kind of public drama that was the direct catalyst for the 1997 and 2008 marches, their daily experiences are much more severe. Not only are the poor more likely to be the actual victims of criminal activity (Mejía 2004), the criminal justice system is overwhelmingly biased against them. A 2002 study of thirty-five thousand prisoners in Mexico's largest prisons was quite revealing (Rayelo 2004). Corruption and inefficiency meant that the most dangerous criminals were not actually imprisoned. Instead, prisons were overwhelming populated "by the poorest, whose capture implied less effort" (19). And the majority of even these criminals were in prison for only minor offenses. Tellingly, 70 percent of those convicted of robbery indicated that they would have bribed the appropriate authorities, but lacked the money![28] The survey revealed numerous problems with due process and coercion of inmates, including the use of torture.

Ultimately, the marketization of the rule of law both reflects and further weakens the precarious state of civil society in Mexico. While the marches may at first glance appear to represent a strong civil society reaction to an increasingly intolerable situation, their divisions and lack of projection belie the existence of a strong civil society. Not only does civil society remain fragmented, but the fear of co-optation prevents many NGOs that might offer more effective solutions for criminal violence from attempting to work with the state and political parties (Davis 2006). But even if they did, the state is likely to be unreceptive and has actually worked to demobilize civil society as part of its approach to public security problems (Martínez Sánchez 2009). Misguided policies, however, mean that civil society continues to be wracked by the high levels of economic insecurity that are the root cause of growing levels of criminal violence (Benítez Manaut 2004, 2009; Cervantes 2004).

Most Mexicans had few expectations about the ultimate outcome of the marches. A poll taken before the 2004 march found that 47 percent of those interviewed felt the march would have little or no impact on the crime rate. For the 2008 march, the same poll found that 62 percent of respondents felt that way—an increasing level of pessimism undoubtedly related to the perceived lack of government responsiveness and the deterioration of the situation. A number of other polls showed similarly high levels of skepticism regarding the impact of the marches (López Leyva 2009, 5–6). Ultimately, there is the risk of a vicious cycle as criminal violence grows because people attempt to take justice into their own hands (Davis 2006; Gil Olmos 2004b).

The Popular Assembly of the Peoples of Oaxaca (APPO)

In much the same way that the three marches against criminal violence belied a strong civil society, APPO is also symptomatic of the challenges neopluralist democracy creates for the development of a more inclusive civil society and the realization of citizenship as agency. APPO was undeniably a "true popular uprising" (Olvera 2010) that directly challenged both the Oaxacan state and the federal government from June 2006 until November 2006, when it was brutally repressed. Its emergence reflects one of the paradoxes of a weak civil society: the venting of accumulated social frustrations can create unique outbursts of social mobilization that appear to reflect a remarkable level of civil society agency, but whose dynamics and composition in practice demonstrate how neopluralism ultimately places severe constraints on their capacity to generate structural change.

As Carlos Sorroza (2008, 24) notes, "the conditions were given for producing a social crisis of great depth in Oaxaca." With a rich history of social mobilization (e.g., see Rubin 1997), APPO represented the "accumulation of an earlier process of resistance to a tyrannical regime that exceeded endurable limits and that knew no other way to impose itself other than through violence" (Rendón 2008, 67–68).[29] Rich in natural resources, Oaxaca is one of the three poorest states in Mexico in terms of socioeconomic indicators. One reason is that the state has the largest percentage of rural and indigenous populations. Both groups are generally among the poorest in Mexico, and this is particularly important for understanding the origins of APPO, because declining agricultural production was leading to increasing rural poverty in the years preceding its emergence in 2006.

Politically, Oaxaca had been dominated by the PRI, although its dominance was coming under increasing pressure, particularly from the PRD. After winning 73 percent of the vote for state deputies in 1992, the PRI won only 47 percent in 1998. This put the PRI on the defensive, increasing its reliance on corruption, patronage, and, in particular, violence to maintain its stranglehold on power.[30] José Murat, who was elected governor in 1998, is emblematic of this deterioration. Murat used the state budget at his discretion, increasing the already high levels of corruption. Repression reached new heights because he was "criminalizing anyone who did not double under his decisions" (Sorroza 2008, 24). Social leaders and even private-sector leaders were arrested if they did not obey him. Murat also tried to reduce the increased level of autonomy that indigenous communities had won earlier.

Murat's increased authoritarianism divided Oaxaca's elite, resulting in a tightly contested election in 2004 that was narrowly won by Ulises Ruiz of the PRI. Ruiz continued the pattern set by Murat, with high levels of corruption and repression. Human rights groups reported that three people were killed and that six hundred political prisoners were jailed in the first eighteen months of his administration (Beas 2006, 237).

On May 15, 2006, the regional teachers' union, section 22 of the SNTE, staged its annual protest in celebration of the Day of the Teacher (Día del Maestro). Along with traditional complaints against the federal and state governments, as well as the national leadership of the SNTE, the union's principal demand was for a rezoning that would raise teachers' salary levels to those of teachers living in the most expensive areas of Mexico. The federal government (which is responsible for setting teachers' wages) simply chose to ignore the salary issue, and the state government's refusal to meet this demand led the teachers' union to organize a tent city in the state capital's central plaza starting on May 22. Teachers went on strike, suspending classes across the state. On June 14, the governor sent in the state police in a violent but unsuccessful attempt to clear the plaza.

Despite the obvious irony of a teachers' union demanding the highest salary rate in the country in one of the poorest states in Mexico, support by Oaxacan society was immediate and overwhelming. On June 15 the first of seven "megamarches" took place as more than one hundred thousand people brought the state capital to a standstill, demanding the resignation of Governor Ruiz. Subsequent protests would mobilize as many as eight hundred thousand people, even though fewer than a million people actually lived in the city of Oaxaca (Beas 2006, 238–39). Two days after the first megamarch, APPO was formed.

This impressive mobilizational capacity reflected a groundswell of popular frustration on many levels and the adhesion of a wide array of social organizations. APPO was formally created by 365 organizations, most of which had never cooperated with one another before. APPO itself recognized this in an early statement: "For years, social, political, and human rights organizations; NGOs; ecologists; gender organizations; student organizations; unions; indigenous communities; and so on, the thousands of Oaxacans that believe in the need for a genuine change, we always look for a unifying process . . . but for different reasons there has not been one, until [June 14]" (quoted in Velasco n.d., 10n2).

With the noticeable influence of indigenous groups, APPO was also an experiment in participatory government (Beas 2006; Esteva 2008; Rendón 2008). Yet such a disparate movement, including many people who did not belong to any particular organization, inevitably lacked any pretense of a formal or even informal leadership. This made it difficult for APPO to exercise control over the people and organizations that formed it (Beas 2006).[31] The collective demand that Ruiz be removed from office was APPO's only source of unity (Velasco n.d.; Sorroza 2008).

Tellingly, section 22 of the SNTE, whose violent repression gave birth to the movement, never joined APPO. For the teachers' movement, the salary demand remained their only real concern, a point driven home in October when the union leadership accepted an economic package worth approximately $16 million (considerably more than the estimated cost of meeting the initial salary demand) and immediately called off the strike (Sorroza 2008, 26). Simultaneously, negotiations with APPO were ended. In response, APPO stiffened its own resolve, and on October 24 called for a "peaceful popular insurrection" to start on December 1 (Sorroza 2008, 26).

Although central to its success in mobilizing hundreds of thousands of people, APPO's diversity and weak organizational structure, not to mention its problematic relationship with the teachers' union, reflect its fundamental limitations as a civil society actor. While this was less apparent when the movement dramatically burst onto the scene in June, its weakness meant that the political party dynamics APPO could not control determined its fate, from its inception until its dramatic demise in November 2006.[32] As APPO itself recognized, the unity it achieved had proven impossible before the decision was made by Ruiz to attempt to violently expel the striking teachers from the state capital's central square. Yet that decision and the ability of the strikers to resist being evicted were a result of party dynamics. With presidential elections scheduled for July 2006, Ruiz felt emboldened to take dramatic action against a group he felt was being manipulated to undermine him. Not surprisingly, the PRI was concerned with a possible further deterioration of its influence in Oaxaca should a PRI governor be forced to resign, especially since it feared a PRD candidate would be elected to replace Ruiz. The ruling PAN was most concerned about the challenge it faced from the PRD's presidential candidate Andrés Manuel López Obrador in the upcoming July presidential elections. To openly side with Ruiz by intervening on his behalf could only favor López Obrador, which was particularly risky given the tightness of the presidential race. President Fox initially took an ambiguous stance toward the conflict in Oaxaca and chose not to intervene, in particular by not sending in federal forces when it became clear Ruiz would not be able to dislodge the strikers. Siding with the strikers was also out of the question since it would alienate the PRI, whose support the PAN needed in the upcoming election.

Party dynamics began to change dramatically after the July 2 elections. Official results showed that the PAN's Calderón had won with just 35.89 percent of the vote, compared to López Obrador's 35.31 percent. López Obrador immediately challenged the legitimacy of the official results. When the Federal Electoral Tribunal certified Calderón's victory by a margin of 233,831 votes on September 5, López Obrador refused to accept the decision and declared himself the legitimate winner, pledging to prevent Calderón from taking office as scheduled on December 1—a position APPO supported.

As the inauguration date approached, the Fox administration gradually increased its support for Ruiz. Given the closeness of the election and López Obrador's intransigence, the PAN's alliance with the PRI only grew in importance to help ensure as smooth a transition as possible. On October 29 federal police effectively took control of the city of Oaxaca. Through arrests and other efforts, APPO was demobilized by the end of November, just in time for the presidential inauguration. The underlying causes of the mobilization remained unchanged. Ruiz was even able to serve out his six-year term, despite being found guilty of human rights abuses during the confrontation with APPO by the national Supreme Court, whose decision was only advisory.

The Poverty of Civil Society in Mexico's Neoliberal Democracy

In many ways, civil society remains trapped by the legacy of the Mexican Revolution, particularly the perseverance of corporatist institutions and a pattern of state-society relations based on a uniquely pervasive pattern of clientelism that undergirded institutions of controlled inclusion. This legacy only exacerbates the pernicious effects that neopluralism and citizenship as consumption have had on civil society's development throughout most Latin America. The limits of what appear at first glance to be instances of citizenship as agency, such as the marches against criminal violence and APPO's experience in Oaxaca, are the most dramatic examples.

At the same time, the experience in Mexico underscores why citizenship as agency and state-society synergy, however difficult it may be to realize them in practice, offer the most promising alternative. The inequalities reflected in the capacity of different actors to influence state policies in their favor at the expense of the majority need to be counterbalanced by a strong, inclusive civil society. As Carlos Elizondo Mayer-Serra (2009, 191) cogently points out, "The government will always be limited in its ability to confront the country's most powerful actors. What is really needed is to involve society by making people understand that they are the ones who are actually paying for these privileges." Throughout Mexico's modern history, it is precisely this kind of involvement that has been noticeably absent or ineffective beyond the short term.

7 LATIN AMERICA'S DEMOCRATIC CROSSROADS: THE CHALLENGE OF MAKING CIVIL SOCIETY RELEVANT

Never before has Latin America been so democratic. Meaningful universal political rights are now the norm in virtually every country in the region, and democracies have survived periods of economic and political instability that in the past would have signaled their downfall. If democracy could ever be truly consolidated in Latin America, the conditions today would seem more propitious than ever before in the region's history.

As the dramatic 1973 collapse of democracy in Chile attests, one should not take democratic consolidation for granted. If any Latin American country could have claimed to have a consolidated democracy in the early 1970s, it would have been Chile. With its strong party system, decades of peaceful alternation of power on the basis of electoral victories and expanding citizenship rights, in many ways it seemed to mimic the ideal path to citizenship described by T. H. Marshall in the 1950s. Yet high levels of inequality and the increasingly clear limits to how far democratization could progress meant that democracy in Chile was ultimately not sustainable—and it would take almost two decades of military rule before Chile could again embark on a very different path toward democratization.

The pervasiveness of neopluralism and citizenship as consumption has changed the prospects for democracy in the region in fundamental ways. Neopluralism's close association with universal political rights opens important new opportunities for altering entrenched structures of inequality in favor of more inclusionary democratic regimes. Citizenship as agency is also now more closely associated with political democracy, laying a foundation for achieving state-society synergy that never existed before in Latin America.

Yet neopluralism's equally close association with precarious civil rights and diminishing social rights of citizenship threatens to undermine this potential in important ways, as the social fabric of society is often torn apart by fragmentation and atomization. This raises the same fundamental questions so dramatically posed by Chile's democratic collapse in the early 1970s: What kind of democracy is being consolidated? How likely is it to endure over time?

This book has argued that civil society and its relationship with the state are central to understanding the sociopolitical dynamics that define the region's democratic potential. More specifically, the theory of civil society developed here demonstrates how it contributes to creating more equal societies where citizenship rights and democratic inclusion can reach their fullest potential. By focusing on the social construction of citizenship, it becomes evident why a strong civil society as defined by the breadth and depth of self-constituted actors is associated with West European welfare states: they are the conquest of strong civil societies in which a myriad of groups contribute directly to defining what it means to be a citizen and the rights associated with citizenship. As the success of both organized labor and women's movements across the globe has shown, unless groups are represented through their participation in the public sphere in the negotiations that define citizenship, at best their interests will be ignored and at worst they will be undermined. In other words, it matters who participates and how in defining what it means to be a citizen. Participation in the public sphere is how the classic rights of citizenship—civil, political, and social—are defined and won, just as this is the only way new rights relating to culture, ethnicity, gender, and the environment, among others, can be added to the panoply of rights identified by Marshall more than a half century ago.

Although strong civil societies are relatively rare and largely limited to Western Europe, Canada, and the United States, this is not because they are culturally determined. Civil society should be understood as requiring only a *thin* rather than *thick* societal consensus, as explained in chapter 1. This shift in definitional focus is not meant to imply that a strong civil society is relatively easy to achieve. It shows how a strong civil society is compatible with a variety of cultural values and is not limited to just one unique (and rare) set of historical circumstances. The potential strength of civil society is conditioned by the nature of the economy and development model being pursued, as well as a country's social structure and state institutions. As these factors change over time, so too does the potential for a strong civil society to emerge. Unfortunately for Latin America, the concentration of power resources associated with high levels of inequality has historically undermined that potential.

Defined as a rich social fabric that simultaneously demands inclusion and resists subordination to the state, civil society as a concept does not change when there is a change of regime or development model; civil society was still civil society when ISI was replaced by an export-oriented, market-driven development model, just as the transition from authoritarian rule to democratic rule did not reflect a fundamentally different understanding of what civil society is. While the specific challenges that a given civil society must confront at any particular point in time obviously change, it is civil society's ability to confront those challenges successfully that will vary. This is why, paradoxically, it was often easier for civil society to mobilize against a repressive authoritarian regime than a democratic one.

A second paradox is that the fate of civil society is inextricably tied to the state, and civil society is able to reach its fullest potential only by working closely with it in the pursuit of common goals. The autonomy of civil society needs to be understood not in terms of its lack of ongoing relations with the state but in terms of the capacity of its various actors to define and defend their interests in such interactions. The lack of relations with the state results in political marginalization, and the risk of approaching the state—particularly in Latin America— is co-optation. The strength of civil society ultimately determines whether and how marginalization or co-optation might be avoided in favor of a synergistic relationship with the state in the pursuit of common goals.

The state also has an important role to play in nurturing the growth of civil society. First, the state must create appropriate institutional spaces that allow civil society to actually work with it. In this way, the state creates opportunities and incentives for different potential actors to organize (Skocpol 1985). On a less obvious, but no less important, level the state must play a critical role in directly supporting the growth of civil society through the provision of various forms of assistance. This is a common practice in countries that now have the strongest civil societies (Skocpol 1996; Schmitter 1974), but it remains a challenge in Latin America.

State assistance can be a double-edged sword from the perspective of civil society. Too much assistance can create dependency—a problem that many NGOs in the region must overcome. It also creates opportunities for abuse through citizenship as co-optation, a real danger in Latin America given its history. Yet under the right circumstances, the state can help civil society uphold its half of the partnership that state–civil society synergy represents. While this is common even in the United States, arguably the country that most closely approximates a liberal ideal of civil society, the most relevant example is much closer to home: the Catholic Church. As discussed earlier, the Catholic Church played a vital role in nurturing civil society's growth under the inauspicious circumstances of violent authoritarian rule throughout the region in the 1960s and 1970s. Such a role did not come naturally to the church, whose track record of working with civil society in Latin America since the conquest was arguably historically worse than the role played by Latin American states. Indeed, it is hard to imagine a more hierarchical and patriarchal institution that is hardly known for its tolerance of dissent. Yet as a result of the Second Vatican Council's reforms in the late 1960s intended to make the church more relevant to the increasingly secular societies in established democracies, the church found itself compelled in many instances to support civil society's development in contexts in which the state not only abdicated this role but directly targeted autonomous civil society organizations for repression. The result, not without tensions, was direct assistance to organizations supporting views on such issues as gender, reproductive rights, and religion often directly at odds with well-known church policies.

Political will is obviously important, although not sufficient, as the example of Bolivia's Popular Participation Law (LPP) demonstrates. Civil society mobilization can be an important factor in generating such will by obliging reluctant political elites to share power and work with civil society. This, in turn, requires that people see participation in civil society as worth the effort.

Making Civil Society Relevant—Again

As the case studies and general discussion in this book make clear, people participate if they feel such participation is meaningful, even if the possibility of actually succeeding seems remote. This was clear in mobilizations for democracy in both Chile and Mexico, and it was also true, for example, in the various mobilizations surrounding public services and natural resources in Bolivia starting in 2000. Given this relatively recent history, one would think that mobilization should be easier under democracy than has generally been the case. Although neopluralism and citizenship as consumption remain important obstacles to continued civil society mobilization, the fact that people participate when they think it is important enough remains an important source of optimism for civil society's future.

Significantly, many of the most pressing concerns of Latin Americans actually require the kinds of collective solutions made possible through state-society synergy. For example, there is ample evidence that when communities work with the state to address pivotal issues relating to the quality of education (Ackerman 2003; Espínola n.d.; Londoño 1996) and the control of criminal violence (Ackerman 2003; Arriagada and Godoy 1999; Tello Peón 2009), the outcomes are much better than when the state monopolizes policy making. For education, the problem in the region has less to do with the absolute level of resources than with how they are actually used. Communities not only understand this but recognize that their future is dependent on the quality of education received by their children, and this is reflected in the positive outcomes that greater accountability creates in how education is delivered.

Similarly, community involvement in addressing issues of rising crime seems inescapable, if only because people must have sufficient confidence in the police and judiciary to report crimes in the first place. Going beyond what is obvious, community involvement is essential for preventing crime and can play a vital role in helping to mediate conflict before it escalates to the point that a crime is actually committed.[1] As the most recent Latinobarómetro (2009b, 64) opinion survey found, Latin Americans appreciate this fact, and 68 percent of respondents said it was good or very good to participate in neighborhood anti-crime groups.

To take advantage of this potential, as Bolivia's experience with LPP shows, the state must be willing to work with civil society, starting with policy design and continuing once new participatory institutions are created. This is the only way that genuine synergy can be achieved. In many respects, this kind of synergy and its potential for promoting citizenship as agency is epitomized by participatory budgeting in Porto Alegre, Brazil.

Citizenship as Agency and Participatory Budgeting in Porto Alegre

Participatory budgeting (PB) was first initiated in 1989 in Porto Alegre, a medium-sized city in southern Brazil, with a population of 1.2 million. While far less ambitious than the LPP in Bolivia, it similarly sought to create new institutions for realizing state–civil society synergy and citizenship as agency at the local level, but with considerably greater success. Indeed, its resounding success led to the adoption of similar programs in more than a hundred cities in Brazil, as well as in many others throughout the world. By contrasting the relative success of PB with the LPP, important dynamics become apparent that help explain why citizenship as agency is often so problematic.[2]

The impetus for PB came from the national level. In sharp contrast to the insulated, secretive process through which the LPP was designed, PB in Brazil was made possible by the 1988 constitution that was crafted with considerable input from civil society. The new constitution achieved this by granting greater authority to local governments to design new policy-making processes and by recognizing the legitimacy of participatory institutions (Wampler and Avritzer 2004). Rather than mandate a single institutional design for the entire country, Brazil's constitution facilitated local experimentation. Porto Alegre took up the challenge.

Several local factors heavily influenced the direction new reforms would take. Porto Alegre had a particularly vibrant civil society, which grew in opposition to Brazil's military dictatorship (1964–85). This experience was ultimately eclipsed by the 1986 electoral victory of the Democratic Labor Party (Partido Democrático Trabalhista, PDT), a left-wing populist party that demobilized civil society to reimpose a more traditional clientelist government. The initial proposal for some form of participatory budgeting actually originated within civil society, largely to allow organizations to renew their own sagging legitimacy in the face of the pervasive clientelism of the PDT government (Avritzer 2002; Baiocchi 2002; Wampler and Avritzer 2004).

The left-wing Workers' Party (Partido dos Trabalhadores, PT) won the 1988 municipal elections, mainly because of public repudiation of the PDT. It had yet to become established as a strong party in Porto Alegre. Despite divisions within the PT (Goldfrank 2003), the party decided to make PB the cornerstone of its municipal policies (Baiocchi 2002; Avritzer 2002). Central to this decision were the close relations between the PT and the various civil society actors demanding greater popular participation in municipal government. Indeed, this combination of party commitment and close ties to autonomous (albeit sympathetic) social movements proved key to the success of PB (Heller 2001).

Despite these favorable circumstances, the PB got off to a rocky start. Participation was initially relatively low and actually declined during its first two years (Goldfrank 2003). The PT responded by working with civil society organizations, negotiating, and perfecting its institutions. Funding levels were increased along with the scope of PB so that by the late 1990s 100 percent of all discretionary municipal expenditures were decided through PB (Wampler and Avritzer 2004, 307). Deliberate efforts were also made to encourage local participants to think beyond their immediate communities, and PB effectively began to address city-wide concerns (Baiocchi 2002).

PB operates on a yearly cycle. It begins in March, when assemblies are held in each of the city's sixteen districts. Delegates are elected to represent their local communities in subsequent phases of the cycle. A forty-two-member Participatory Budgeting Council (Conselho do Orçamento Participativo) is also elected to negotiate the final municipal budget with the local government and review budgets and projects from the previous year. Delegates subsequently meet in intermediary meetings to determine regional priorities and discuss more general city-wide concerns according to designated thematic groupings. The council is also responsible for balancing competing demands, setting priorities, and distributing funds among regions in accordance with larger city-wide priorities. After negotiating the final municipal budget, the council monitors actual expenditures (Avritzer 2002; Baiocchi 2002).

The end result of PB has been "a profound transformation of civil society itself" (Baiocchi 2002, 23). The level of public participation continually increased, from just 976 in 1990 to 26,807 in 2000 (Wampler and Avritzer 2004, 302). In contrast to the LPP, participation is open to all. A deliberate decision was made not to base participation exclusively on prior membership in any organization, often inviting people to participate for the first time. Moreover, the number of social organizations has increased markedly as a result of the PB process. Conservative estimates suggest that the number of neighborhood organizations increased from 180 in 1986 to 540 in 1998 (Baiocchi 2002, 25). Ultimately, PB is an example of how "civil society organizations challenge old practices, such as clientelism and patronage, while simultaneously offering concrete alternatives" (Wampler and Avritzer 2004, 291).

Most significantly, growing levels of participation and organization tend to concentrate in poorer areas, and people with lower incomes and levels of education tend to predominate in the PB process. This, plus the fact that municipal expenditures have been deliberately redistributed toward poorer areas of the city, underscores the empowerment PB offers for disadvantaged groups. More precisely, citizens can see how their collective activities contribute to policy making in positive ways, creating a potentially virtuous circle of growing civil society strength, dispersion of economic and political power, and more inclusive democratic governance.

Civil Society, the State, and the Quest for Citizenship as Agency

The obstacles to achieving citizenship as agency posed by citizenship as consumption and neopluralism seem at times insurmountable. Yet the experience of Participatory Budgeting in Porto Alegre suggests the direction to take for achieving citizenship as agency in Latin America today. Political will, while necessary, is not sufficient for achieving citizenship as agency. This was the goal of the designers of the LPP, but in cutting themselves off from civil society, the institutions they boldly created could not live up to their own promise. The exclusionary, top-down means they chose made it all but impossible to achieve the more inclusionary, bottom-up vision of democracy that guided their efforts. Rather than creating cumulative processes through which citizen participation and the autonomous organization of civil society would increase, the opposite occurred as initial skepticism toward the state was exacerbated by how the LPP was implemented and by its own limits that reflected elite visions and (mis)understandings more than the needs and aspirations of Bolivian citizens.

The contradiction at the core of the LPP ultimately proved fatal in terms of strengthening civil society and creating citizenship as agency. Overshadowing the LPP's lofty pretensions was the inescapable presence of important elements of citizenship as co-optation in the form of coparticipación revenues and the lack of effective mechanisms for ensuring that the public good would prevail. This contrasts sharply with the experience of PB in Porto Alegre. Working with civil society, a clear and powerful alternative to citizenship as either co-optation or consumption was created, literally from the bottom up. The synergistic interchange between the PT as a political party, civil society, and the local state created a process that strengthened civil society and the quality of citizenship.

It is important not to exaggerate the success of PB in Porto Alegre. It is clearly the most successful example out of more than a hundred similar experiments in a country with more than five thousand city governments. Moreover, when the PT lost control of the Porto Alegre city government in 2005, the scope for state-society synergy was narrowed dramatically, resulting in a significant decline in participation since PB was no longer sufficiently relevant for many people (Gugliano n.d.). However important it was for the citizens of Porto Alegre, PB at its height under the PT controlled just 10–15 percent of municipal expenditures, amounting to a meager per capita level of slightly more than two hundred U.S. dollars (Wampler and Avritzer 2004, 307). While it is unquestionably an important right of citizenship for people to actually decide where a school will be built, more fundamental decisions about school staffing and curriculum, for example, are made elsewhere. The ultimate challenge is to scale-up PB processes in the determination of national policies and to further decentralize decision-making authority to local governments so that larger issues can be addressed. Institutionalizing these processes would better insulate them from any particular electoral outcome.

As emphasized throughout this book, civil society and state-society relations are anything but static. Even if structural problems of inequality and circumscribed models of citizenship seem to persist, or get worse, the changing nature of state-society relations and the strength of civil society open new possibilities for greater social inclusion, particularly when people enjoy the right to vote in relatively free and fair elections. At the same time, the accumulated frustrations caused by neopluralism and citizenship as consumption can create a fertile terrain for new variants of popular-sector defensive forms of populism. The majority can fall prey to the manipulations of self-serving elites whose siren song promising a better society at best only leads to short-term gains for the majority that are eventually erased because of the backlash they generate or because they were simply not sustainable. In many ways, this dichotomy between populism and more progressive, sustainable social change represents the region's new crossroads.

This is most apparent when looking at the Latin America's much discussed turn to the left. Beginning with the election of Hugo Chávez in Venezuela in 1998, the region has experienced an unprecedented number of electoral victories by candidates claiming to represent the Left. These include presidents in Argentina (twice), Bolivia, Brazil (twice), Chile (twice), Ecuador, Nicaragua, and Uruguay (twice), as well as the conversion of deposed Honduran president Manuel Zelaya, who had won the election representing the Right. Yet at the level of specific policies, as well as how they actually practice democratic politics, these leaders have little in common apart from their ability to promise to improve the quality of life for their supporters. While it is still too soon to predict what this turn to the left will ultimately mean for Latin American democracies—including the extent to which some of its representatives are willing to respect the minimal requirements for the meaningful exercise of universal political rights—the theory of civil society developed here provides useful guideposts for anticipating its likely outcome in each case.

First, to facilitate at least the possibility of state-society synergy, presidents and their followers must adhere to the thin consensus that characterizes civil society. They must be self-limiting in their demands and willing to respect the right of others to express their dissent.

Second, state-society synergy requires new institutions that provide the space for an active partnership between civil society actors and the state in the pursuit of common goals. This necessitates not only consultation at the beginning of any process of institutional reform, but a continual process of negotiation between civil society actors and representatives of the state. Moreover, civil society participation must be autonomous in the sense that actors are able to define and defend their interests in competition with one another and in their relations with the state. Top-down, hierarchical patterns of consultation by national leaders, unmediated by civil society organizations, represent the foundation stone of populism, not an inclusive process of the social construction of citizenship.

Finally, such political processes need to be founded on universal citizenship rights that include civil, political, and social rights of citizenship as defined through the active negotiation between the state and the myriad of actors that compose a strong civil society. Unless this condition is met, not only will the inclusiveness and depth of those rights be suspect, but other rights—including rights based on gender, culture, ethnicity, age, and other, still undefined categories—will only be ephemeral at best.

The perspective on civil society and state-society relations developed here offers the hope that the vicious cycles of the past can be replaced by virtuous ones that not only build on the strength of civil society but increase that strength in a cumulative fashion. In many ways, this was the key to the ideal path to democratic citizenship in Britain that T. H. Marshall (1950) sketched out so long ago. The rejection of neopluralism and citizenship as consumption in Latin America offers the possibility that this is the path that Latin America may well be entering. But such rejection is no guarantee either that neopluralism will be replaced in the foreseeable future or, if it is replaced, that the alternative will produce more inclusive democratic regimes. The region's history is too full of examples of where change—even well-intentioned change—has serious unintended consequences. In such cases, it has been the popular sectors, and civil society, that have paid the price. To appreciate this and avoid history repeating itself, it is important to adopt an appropriate understanding of civil society and the unique role that it can play in helping to build more just and inclusive societies.

notes

chapter 1

1. Eighteen elected presidents were unable to complete their mandated terms in office in the midst of crises and popular repudiation. Democratic institutions were largely respected in the succession process. This pattern dramatically changed when the military forcefully removed Honduran president Manuel Zelaya from office in June 2009—the first successful military coup in the region in more than thirty years (see Latinobarómetro 2008, 8).

2. Important exceptions include Dagnino (2002), Olvera (2003b), Panfichi (2002), and Feinberg, Waisman, and Zamosc (2006).

3. The liberal predispositions of Ferguson (1966) and Tocqueville (1969) obviously influenced how they interpreted what they observed as well. I only wish to emphasize the explicitly inductive nature of their endeavor.

4. Indeed, the relative balance of liberal and collectivist elements are a defining characteristic of any particular civil society (see Black 1984).

5. Interestingly, Ferguson (1966), the first to equate civil society with the spread of the market, actually lamented the destruction of these collectivist values!

6. In a similar vein, civil rights allowed for the collective representation of workers through the organization of trade unions (see Bendix 1964).

7. This emphasis also contrasts with approaches stressing the importance of deliberation and discourse for understanding civil society's contribution to democratization processes (Avritzer 2002; Cohen and Arato 1992).

8. The existence of resources that the state does not control and the experience of centrally planned economies have often led analysts to conclude that civil society is possible only under capitalism. From the perspective offered here, nonmarket economies tend to concentrate economic resources, which by definition constrains civil society's emergence. But this is not sufficient to prevent an incipient civil society from challenging state domination, as became clear in the transitions in the former Soviet bloc. Moreover, all centrally planned economies historically have been under the control of political regimes intent on retaining power by preventing the emergence of any autonomous civil society activity.

9. For these reasons, the complete separation of the economy and civil society in Cohen and Arato's (1992) exhaustive examination of the concept is inappropriate and misleading. For a similar critique of this artificial separation, see Keane (1998, 17–19).

10. This is not to say that the organization of subaltern groups will necessarily contribute to the emergence of civil society, let alone political democracy. Revolutionary groups seeking to capture the state, for example, are antithetical to civil society. The organization of subaltern groups also has frequently led to an authoritarian backlash.

11. Habermas (1992) tends to limit his analysis to economic status and social class, although his general point is equally applicable to other kinds of social actors (see Calhoun 1993).

12. The term *synergy* was originally coined by Peter Evans (1997b, 3) to describe how "civic engagement strengthens state institutions, and effective state institutions create an environment in which civic engagement is more likely to thrive." His goal was to bridge the literature on social capital and work on the importance of state institutions in economic development. I go beyond this to focus on particular patterns of state-society interactions.

13. Evans (1995) neglects this role for civil society when discussing state-society synergy. While he notes that the state has an important role to play in strengthening civil society, he suggests that if state institutions are characterized by high levels of rent seeking, the likely result of closer state relations will be corruption. By not acknowledging the role civil society can play in resolving this problem, he can offer few insights into how to overcome it.

14. A clear distinction between civil society and the private sphere is important. To subsume the latter into civil society, as Cohen and Arato (1992) do, makes it impossible to fully understand the nature of critical political debates and diminishes the usefulness of the concept of civil society for comparative analysis.

15. For example, civil society often plays an important role through the public sphere in building societal consensus and moderating social conflict without involving the state (see Karl and Schmitter 1991).

16. Marshall (1950, 10–11) defines civil rights as "the rights necessary for individual freedom—liberty, of person, freedom of speech, thought and faith, the right to own property and to conclude valid contracts, and the right to justice."

17. For Marshall, political stability under capitalism requires democratic citizenship and is synonymous with democratic stability.

18. For a similar argument, which also discusses the possibility of elite strategies for expanding citizenship rights, see Rueschemeyer, Stephens, and Stephens (1992) and Collier (1999).

19. Of course, this synergy was anything but democratic, because the overall strength of civil society was limited. The clearest example of was the state's enforcement of the enclosure, which destroyed the peasant class by forcing it off the land.

20. The converse is found in localities where the working class was weak in Britain and civil rights were not enforced (see Somers 1993).

21. Moore also argues that France and the United States ultimately followed the same path as Britain. While Moore's interpretation of all three paths has been extensively criticized (see Femia 1972 and Skocpol 1973), such criticisms are not inconsistent with the perspective I am developing here. My focus on the relative concentration of power resources within society and the subsequent pattern of state-society relations that emerges avoids the problems of Moore's more theoretically deterministic approach by providing a more fluid and contingent understanding of these processes. For example, while the nuances of labor-repressive agriculture and the politically coercive characteristics of labor markets are sources of contention, it is clear that power resources were generally much more concentrated in those cases that Moore characterizes as labor repressive, at the same time that the state's role in commercializing agriculture is not problematic from the state-society perspective developed here.

22. The subsequent success of democracy in both cases is also more consistent with my approach. Relatively high levels of industrialization served as the foundation for a more vibrant civil society that could undergird successful democratization after the Allied occupation ended.

23. An important study by Rueschemeyer, Stephens, and Stephens (1992) builds on Moore's work by emphasizing the importance of working-class mobilization in European and Latin American democratization processes in the twentieth century. The authors also stress the importance of the ability of dominant classes to safeguard their fundamental interests if democracy is to survive. In terms of the arguments developed here, this insight reflects something that is often neglected in the study of civil society: the important role that civil society organizations representing the interests of the middle class and, in particular, the upper or dominant class play in the rich social fabric defining a strong civil society. Given that the challenge, particularly in Latin America, is to prevent their dominance of civil society, researchers frequently forget that

civil society consists of more than subaltern groups. Rueschemeyer, Stephens, and Stephens also underscore the relative weakness of organized labor in Latin America compared to Western Europe. The present study builds on these insights in several ways, including by providing a focus on the limits imposed on lower-class inclusion in the highly unequal societies of Latin America. This, in turn, reflects the shared interests of middle and upper classes in maintaining a status quo from which they benefit disproportionately. By focusing on the social construction of citizenship and civil society more broadly, my study offers a more complete understanding of the recent wave of democratic transitions in Latin America, including their shortcomings and potential for generating the kind of structural changes needed to create more equal societies like those found in Western Europe.

24. My discussion of civil society's emergence in Europe draws from Bendix (1964), Black (1984), Keane (1988a), Schöpflin (1990), C. Taylor (1990), and Brenner (1976).

chapter 2

1. The popular sectors consist of the disadvantaged groups in highly segmented, unequal societies. They are characterized by their limited life chances and consumption opportunities and include formal- and informal-sector workers, groups outside the market economy, and the peasantry (see Oxhorn 1995b).

2. This is not meant to deny the importance of working-class mobilization for forcing reluctant elites to cede such rights, especially in countries such as Argentina and Chile; it only underscores the subordinate nature of this mobilization.

3. While the following refers specifically to the Spanish colonies, the same social conservatism was even more entrenched in Brazil, where independence from Portugal was achieved with the establishment of a Brazilian empire under the tutelage of a member of the Portuguese monarchy. The Brazilian monarchy was dissolved in 1889.

4. In the order of their level of social modernization, these countries were Argentina, Uruguay, Chile, Panama, Costa Rica, Brazil, Peru, Ecuador, Honduras, and Bolivia. Excluding Argentina and Uruguay, the regional average was 31.5 percent (see CEPAL 1989, 31–34). Subsequent reassessment of the data suggests that the CEPAL study may have overstated the extent of this social mobility, but it is unclear by how much; it does not affect the substance of the argument made here (Gurrieri and Sáinz 2003).

5. I want to thank Bryan Roberts for reminding me of the importance of this relationship.

6. The opposition of these business interests to later economic liberalization throughout the region was overcome by military rule or the weakening of their economic clout by the debt crisis in the 1980s.

7. Collier and Collier's (2002) classic study of the political incorporation of workers is an important complement of this study. Our approaches, however, are distinct. Whereas Collier and Collier offer an alternative to political economy by focusing on social and political factors at the elite level, the framework developed here combines both methods to examine the factors conditioning the development of civil society and its relationship with the state. While their focus on critical junctures is compatible with the historical perspective developed here, my research focuses more on the defining characteristics of key periods in the development of civil society, as well as fundamental similarities across periods; identifying and analyzing specific key turning points is only a secondary concern. For the same reason, the Colliers' focus on two modes of incorporation (through political parties or the state) is not central in the development of a theory of civil society but becomes more relevant when applying that theory to case studies.

8. In Brazil, Getúlio Vargas's preemptive incorporation of labor as part of his Estado Novo (New State) in the 1930s prevented the emergence of a strong, independent labor movement until the mid-1970s, when industrial workers organized to challenge the military government in new industries spawned by its ISI policies.

9. This section draws on Oxhorn (1998b). See also K. Roberts (1995) and Weyland (1999, 2001).

10. Rather than distinguish populism during this period from its more recent incarnations by labeling the latter "neopopulist," it is useful to characterize different forms of populist mobilization in terms of how they reflect the situation of the popular sectors. I discuss the more recent popular-sector defensive variant in chapter 3.

11. A final characteristic of populism is its instrumental use of ideology. The heterogeneity of the populist coalition is masked over by ambiguous and amorphous ideological appeals.

12. The United States also played a key role in supporting processes of controlled inclusion, as well as authoritarian alternatives when controlled inclusion broke down. Given the structural nature of the threat that popular-sector mobilization could entail, U.S. policies are best understood as an enabling factor (albeit often a decisive one), not the principal cause of the authoritarian backlashes against civil society mobilization.

13. Coerced marginalization is similar to O'Donnell's (1979a) concept of exclusion under bureaucratic authoritarian regimes. Unlike O'Donnell, the link here between levels of development and this form of authoritarian rule is mediated by the strength and nature of civil society. This explains why countries have abandoned controlled inclusion and ISI without recourse to this kind of regime. Moreover, this extreme level of political violence can be understood only in political terms, even if they are a reflection of economic inequality.

14. As Bowman (2002) notes, the reluctance of Costa Rican elites to accept democratic rule was quite intense. Bowman argues that it took ten years to consolidate democracy in Costa Rica, an outcome that was possible only because the early dissolution of the military meant that elites could not violently overthrow elected governments.

15. Chávez used the opportunities for change that elections represent to offer an alternative to a delegitimated political elite. It is also very likely that Chávez and many of his supporters have a very different conception of democracy, in which core elements of political democracy are replaced by the direct relationship with the leader associated with populism (Latinobarómetro 2009b).

16. Cuba is obviously the most important exception. Bolivia's 1952 revolution was a partial exception (see chapter 5).

chapter 3

1. Several factors accounted for this shift, including the fact that the Left had been a principal target of unprecedented levels of political repression. The rights associated with free and competitive elections, particularly civil rights and the right to dissent, took on new value. The end of the cold war reinforced this tendency.

2. Differences were not limited to ideology. Women, poor people, workers, peasants, and middle-sector professionals, among others, were important actors in these mobilizations. Their conflicting priorities were generally secondary to their shared interest in ending dictatorial rule.

3. There was also a proliferation of nongovernmental organizations throughout the region. While they often work with the poor, their dependent relationship with funding agencies and the state (Foweraker 2005; Roberts and Portes 2006) and small size limit their ability to represent the poor in the social construction of citizenship. At best, NGOs can facilitate the growth of civil society, much like the Catholic Church did during authoritarian rule, by providing groups with resources to organize.

4. There were important exceptions, particularly among segments of organized labor and human rights organizations. Yet their ability to mobilize support beyond their immediate membership generally remained limited compared to the period of authoritarian rule. Movements of indigenous people are the most important exception from the perspective of the social construction of citizenship, although their concrete successes, beyond the very important symbolic level of identity, have often been limited (see chapter 5 and Yashar 1998, 2005).

5. The spread of conditional cash-transfer programs has changed this focus in important ways, although without a significant impact on inequality (see chapter 6).

6. While the impact on overall poverty rates from the 2008 recession was relatively mild and is expected to be reversed in 2010, this is not true of extreme poverty. In fact, the number of people living in extreme poverty in 2009 increased by 3 million—a number equal to the total increase in poverty. Similarly, even though the overall number of people living in poverty is expected to return to the same level as in 2008, projections show 1 million more people living in extreme poverty in 2010. This only serves to underscore how the poorest are disproportionately affected by economic downturns in the region.

7. When asked where they believed their children would be in terms of income level, on a scale of 1 to 10 with 1 indicating the poorest segment of the population, the average response was 7.5 in 2000 compared to 5 in 2009.

8. The PNUD report also notes that prison conditions in Latin America are generally quite poor.

9. This concentration also means that the "movement of poor people through the city makes them possible criminals, or at least suspicious" (Carrión 2003, 59).

10. A telling example of popular justice took place in June 2004 in an Andean village in Peru, when an angry mob beat the mayor to death. As an indigenous leader explained, "The government only pays attention to those who have power. Rights are not for the poor. They are for the rich, by the rich, and so the people here have gotten tired" (*New York Times*, June 24, 2004).

11. A typical example of the poor's vulnerability was a street vendor in Santiago, Chile, in 1986. He was barely able to make ends meet selling periodicals near a central downtown metro station—a choice spot located near offices and the University of Chile. When he was robbed in his own shantytown, he could no longer purchase material to sell, putting him out of business for several months while he rebuilt his capital. When he finally did, his choice spot was long gone.

12. Just five years later, the press release from Latinobarómetro (2003, 3) emphasized the existence of "a notable consensus [that] has emerged in a continent with scarce areas of consensus," when 80 percent of respondents agreed that the region was characterized by significant levels of socioeconomic exclusion.

13. This percentage is a significant improvement from earlier surveys from 2001 to 2006, which averaged around 25 percent.

14. Venezuela stands out as the only country where there is a secular upward trend in institutional legitimacy (Lagos 2003b). Lagos suggests that this is consistent with growing democratic legitimacy (145–46), but it actually highlights the increasingly problematic nature of democracy in the region. The rise in institutional trust coincides with the presidency of Chávez, who centralized power in the office of the presidency at the expense of virtually all other institutions associated with political democracy. Findings like this led Latinobarómetro (2009b, 16–17) to recognize a fundamental ambiguity in what people actually consider democracy to be when signaling their support for it in opinion surveys.

15. The Latinobarómetro survey (2009b, 33) notes that the increased trust in the police represents the strengthening of the police in response to growing public concern with crime. It also probably reflects the public clamor for more repressive policing rather than a better relationship between the police and civil society.

16. Ecuador received the highest score on this question, at 17 percent. It was subsequently wracked by political instability that saw the forced resignation of two presidents and a short-lived military coup.

17. Polls such as the Latinobarómetro provide important insights into compelling political challenges. The problem lies in recognizing their limits and appropriate use. Polls can supplement policy debate by providing useful information but should not supplant participation or debate. A pertinent example of this problem is how the preoccupation of citizens with criminal violence has been used to justify the de facto criminalization of poverty and marketization of the rule of law.

18. This percentage had improved in 2009, when 39 percent of respondents agreed that progress had been made in combating corruption in the previous two years.

19. I am indebted to Bryan Roberts for reminding me of this factor.

20. This study updates Portes's 1985 study discussed in chapter 2. The availability of more detailed data for the current period makes direct comparisons between the two difficult, but the emphasis here is on general patterns of change rather than the absolute size of any particular class. Moreover, difficulties in disaggregating data for distinct social classes generally led Portes and Hoffman (2003) to overstate the size of the dominant classes, while underestimating the size of the informal proletariat. For another study of Latin America's class structure that found even more asymmetry, see Gurrieri and Sáinz (2003).

21. This percentage includes self-employed professionals and microenterprises employing five or fewer people and unpaid family members, as well as the category of informal petty bourgeoisie from the earlier study.

22. Fujimori used his political power to impose a radical program of economic liberalization and state reform, while Chávez has emphasized a more traditional populist platform of expanded state intervention and largesse financed by oil rents, which he helped raise after winning the presidency by orchestrating a hike in oil prices through OPEC.

chapter 4

1. From 1830 to 1973 Chile experienced only thirteen months of unconstitutional rule—a record unrivaled in most of the West (see Valenzuela 1999, 192).

2. In 1925, just as Chile was about to enter into a period characterized by controlled inclusion, not even 7.5 percent of the population was registered to vote (see Loveman 1979, 260).

3. My discussion of state formation and the emergence of Chile's political party system draws on Garretón (1989), Scully (1992), Valenzuela (1977), Gil (1966), and Loveman (1979).

4. After a period of political instability, Chile held regular presidential elections since 1936, in which power alternated among the political Right, Center, and Left.

5. An earlier example of military intervention with less long-term significance was the brief 1891 civil war.

6. Ibáñez was prominent among a group of junior officers whose insistence on reform ultimately led to the military's direct involvement in politics, including two military juntas. Ibáñez dominated Chilean politics for most of this period, particularly after he won the presidency in 1927, until his abrupt resignation in 1932 as a result growing protests in the midst of a deepening economic crisis precipitated by the Great Depression. Ibáñez would return to the presidency—this time as a civilian—after he won the 1952 elections.

7. As Borzutzky (2002) shows, this same dynamic undermined Chile's vaunted social security system. As the Center and Left expanded benefits to appease their bases, they were reluctant to reform the system, given that such reforms would undermine their support. At the same time, business groups were able to avoid paying for the reforms, exacerbating the system's financial crisis.

8. For more on this period, see Drake and Jaksic (1995) and Huneeus (2007).

9. This contributed to a major reconfiguration of the political Left's social base, as the more moderate Left remained cut off from any mass base among the popular sectors, and the radical Left, particularly the Communist Party, saw its support base shift from the formal working class to the urban poor (see also Kenneth Roberts 1998).

10. While there have been some important reforms to the military-era labor law, particularly in 2006, the same fundamental problem of union fragmentation and lack of collective strength persists more than thirty years later (OECD 2009).

11. For example, Chile has the most progressive distribution of social expenditures among seventeen Latin American countries included in a study by CEPAL (see López and Miller 2008, 2680–81).

12. My discussion of Chilean health care draws on OECD (2009, 117–19), M. Taylor (2006, 184–87), and Huber (2002a, 463).

13. Regardless of why people felt the military coup took place, few doubted that political parties were at least part of the problem that led to Chile's political crisis.

14. The PC adopted a strategy of popular rebellion in 1980, which recognized the legitimacy of all forms of struggle. This was a principal source of division between the MDP and the AD, and the violence of the July protest, even though the military was responsible, made the strategy politically nonviable. Yet the PC refused to officially abandon it and was increasingly marginalized as a result of subsequent events, including an unsuccessful attempt to assassinate Pinochet and the discovery of arms caches in the Atacama Desert, as well as growing internal divisions.

15. Although the PC would eventually support the No vote after initially refusing to participate in the plebiscite, the Left in general was excluded from both the Command for the No and the Concertación. The Socialist party reunified in 1989.

16. Worker mobilization led to a 2007 labor law reform that attempted to address this problem of employment instability by regulating subcontracting and temporary workers. The actual impact of the reform, however, is still unclear and may actually lead to an increase in informal employment. The law also is being challenged in court by business groups (see OECD 2009, 19–20).

17. The leader of the United Workers Central (CUT, the principal peak trade union organization), Manuel Jiménez, felt that "union leaders have sold their union prerogatives to be able to pay debts!" (personal interview, Santiago, December 21, 1995). More recently, Arturo Martínez, CUT president, noted that mortgages and credit card debt were "the new chains of the workers" (*Economist*, September 20, 2007).

18. For example, Moises Labraño, then a member of the CUT board of directors, felt that "the CUT does not understand its role in relation to the government. Its commitment to fight for democracy against the dictator led to mistakes after the political system opened up. . . . We are for democracy, a defender of the rule of law and democracy. For some, this meant defend the government. They behaved more like ministers than the Ministers. . . . The CUT continued to construct itself as a party movement. It must connect with the rank and file so that the CUT becomes a leading force, the strength that the labor movement needs" (personal interview, Santiago, December 14, 1995).

19. The principal exception was during the Aylwin presidency, when tripartite bargaining led to some labor reforms and, most important, an increase in the value-added tax to fund new social programs (see Weyland 1997).

20. Prior to the 1990 transition to democracy, data for Chile as a whole are unavailable. While national Gini coefficients are not directly comparable to those for the Greater Santiago metropolitan area, the differences are not great and they are indicative of the same overall trends.

21. The LOCE was replaced by a new education law in 2009 as a consequence of widespread student mobilizations in 2006. I return to this when discussing civil society's influence under the current democratic regime.

22. This trend has been reflected in highly respected polls conducted by the Centro de Estudios Públicos (2010) and is also consistent with other surveys of public opinion (see Dammert 2009).

23. Elections of both houses of Congress are organized around two-seat districts, and all candidates must run on two-person slates, even though each voter has just one vote per district. For both candidates on a slate to win, the combined total of votes cast for both must be more than twice the combined total received by the second-place slate. Otherwise, the top vote winner in each of the two slates receiving the most votes would win. This means that the Right (or any minority party or coalition) would need to win only one-third of the vote in a given district to be assured of winning one of the two seats by preventing the dominant slate from passing the required threshold.

24. Scores of retired and even several active service military officials were brought to trial for human rights abuses during the military regime after Pinochet's detention. Pinochet was also in danger of being convicted, if not of human rights violations, of corruption stemming from a

U.S. Senate investigation that found Pinochet had $8 million in secret bank accounts. Pinochet died in 2006 before legal processes could run their course.

25. These general tendencies prevailed in the next two presidential elections, with the socialist candidate Michelle Bachelet narrowly winning the runoff election in 2006 and the Center-Right Sebastián Piñera winning in a close runoff election in 2010.

26. In fact, Lagos instituted policies to directly address many of the same issues Lavín tried to monopolize during the election. For example, the Lagos government virtually eliminated waiting lines at public clinics. Through constitutional reform, he also succeeded in eliminating most of the remaining authoritarian enclaves.

chapter 5

1. The Nicaraguan Revolution (1979) is also unique. It lasted only approximately ten years and was subjected to intense U.S. intervention. It also ended through democratic elections, in which the Sandinista government accepted its defeat.

2. For this reason agricultural land was redistributed very rapidly in practice, but the actual legalization of the new land tenure was extremely slow (Eckstein 1982).

3. Of course, a subordinate role is not the same as complete political marginalization. At least since the Chaco War (1932–35) and later with the 1952 revolution, indigenous people have not been completely marginalized from national politics, especially in comparison to other countries where they constitute sizable segments of national populations, such as in Peru and Guatemala (see Peeler 2003).

4. The election of Evo Morales in 2006 represents the last best hope for addressing this failure of citizenship by promising to incorporate all Bolivians into a new process of social construction of citizenship.

5. My discussion of the Bolivian Revolution is based largely on Malloy (1968) and Klein (1969).

6. There were at least six unconstitutional changes of government in this period before the MNR seized control of the government in April 1952.

7. As a result, one of the most important legacies of this period was the formation of sindicatos campesinos throughout the countryside. The successful melding of this Western form of social organization with indigenous culture and practices was central to the LPP's success in rural areas.

8. The election of Evo Morales as president in 2006 may represent civil society's ability to overcome these challenges, although it is still too soon to know if Morales will ultimately succeed in this endeavor.

9. Over the years additional municipalities were created, bringing the current total to 337 in 2011.

10. A number of the people interviewed indicated that the best proof of the LPP's irreversibility was the inability of then president and former military dictator, Hugo Bánzer, to make any major changes in the law, or even kill it by neglect.

11. Postrevolution union structures also represent a hybrid form of organization combining Western trade unionism with "the indigenous-communal participative logic" (see Maydana 2004, 191–92). Similarly, a single union model for the entire country was perceived as an "effort to homogenize local community institutions" (Yashar 2005, 159)—a process that the LPP sought to reverse through the legalization of OTBs.

12. This liberal perspective on citizenship is one reason why the LPP was part of a series of market-based state reforms by the Sánchez de Lozada government (see Chávez Corrales 1998). Those reforms also had the effect of weakening corporatist institutions, particularly organized labor.

13. Carlos Hugo Molina made the same point in a personal interview, Santa Cruz, July 15, 1999.

14. Civic committees also wanted to focus decentralization by holding direct elections on the

level of the prefecture or regional government. Some elements of this were later implemented as part of the separate Ley de Descentralización Administrativa, which created a hybrid regional government composed of a prefect selected by the president and a departmental council with membership determined by the municipal governments.

15. For example, to publicize the LPP, the Secretaría Nacional de Participación Popular (National Secretariat for Popular Participation) had to rely on small community radio transmitters, because indigenous communities did not trust urban radio stations (Gaston Zamora, personal interview, Santa Cruz, July 16, 1999).

16. Sindicatos campesinos were also initially not recognized as OTBs, which was a source of much opposition and led to a modification of the law.

17. An important exception is the coca-growing region of the Chapare, where the ongoing conflict between the central state and coca farmers catalyzed a strong indigenous political movement that was able to use the LPP to its advantage.

18. Later reforms and a new constitution eliminated the parties' monopoly.

19. Because mayors cannot be removed from office during the last year of their term, only two mayors were replaced in 1998 in anticipation of the upcoming 1999 municipal elections.

20. The decline is due to reforms that limited the choice of new mayors after a censure vote to the two councilors who had received the highest votes in the preceding election, limiting the political parties' room for maneuver as well as the personal ambitions of individual councilors (see UIA 1999 and Rojas Ortuste 1998).

21. Women counselors were also disproportionately targeted by political parties; after winning elections, various forms of pressure were applied to ensure that they would be replaced by party activists.

22. Another indicator of fragmentation is the number of new actors that actually participated in the 2004 elections. In the department of La Paz alone, ninety-five citizen groups were registered, along with seventeen indigenous peoples groups. The department of Cochabamba came in second in terms of new actors, with eighty citizens groups and two indigenous peoples groups (Corte Nacional Electoral 2004, 8–9).

23. The specific example Bocal gave was a committee that successfully undertook a project to supply drinking water in Cliza. The municipal government gave it assistance after it was denied funding from the central government's Fondo de Inversión Social (Social Investment Fund). Committee members went on to form a variety of other organizations, including a committee that has started the construction of a new school.

24. The electoral code was changed in 2001 to address this by requiring that candidacies for both regular counselors and alternates be rotated between men and women.

25. Maria Eugenia Choque of the Taller de Historia Oral Andina (Andean Oral History Workshop) also emphasized this, pointing out how North American anthropologists often overestimate the actual influence women have in traditional Andean indigenous cultures (personal interview, La Paz, July 1, 1999).

26. Elected women counselors have even been subject to violence by their male counterparts (see Ardaya 2001 and Kudelka 2004).

27. This source of revenue also limits the ability of the CV to oversee government budgeting in the largest cities, because only coparticipación funds fall under its purview.

28. My discussion of departmental governments is based principally on personal interviews with Armando Ortuño, Gloria Aguilar, and Carlos Toranzo in La Paz during July 1999.

29. My discussion of declining participation is based on Galindo Soza (2004). See also Van Cott (2000) on the limited role of women.

30. Reforms in 1999 created Vigilance Committee Consultative Councils (Consejos Consultivos de los Comités de Vigilancia), in which functional organizations could participate. For a number of reasons, including the lack of legitimacy that CVs had for functional organizations, these councils were constituted only rarely (see Maydana 2004).

31. Sánchez de Lozada's successor as president, Carlos Mesa, resigned in June 2005, paving the way for presidential elections in 2006.

32. My discussion of Cochabamba's water wars draws largely on García Orellana, García Yapur, and Quitón Herbas 2003; and Laserna 2000.

33. The first phase of the project was estimated to cost $70 million, not including an additional $200 million for water treatment and distribution or $70 million required to finance planned electricity generation associated with the project (García Orellana, García Yapur, and Quitón Herbas 2003, 22, 34).

34. The mayor's ability to escape political damage as a result is a testament to his skills as a populist leader more interested in political power than political empowerment of the popular sectors.

35. My discussion of the El Alto protests draws on Arbona (2005) and Verdesoto (2004).

36. The Morales government eventually nationalized the gas industry.

37. This separation occurred despite the fact that many of the organizations involved in the protest were the same OTBs that gained state recognition under the LPP (see Maydana 2004).

chapter 6

1. There is an ample literature on the Mexican Revolution (e.g., Knight 1986; Womack 1968).

2. For more information on organized labor, see Collier and Collier (2002).

3. When oil companies refused to respect a decision by the Mexican Supreme Court relating to a 1936 union dispute, Cárdenas had few alternatives other than abandoning any pretext of national sovereignty (see Hamilton 1985). The affected oil companies reacted by boycotting Mexican oil exports and transferring their investments to Venezuela, which became a major oil exporter at Mexico's expense (see Karl 1997).

4. The following discussion of the PRI draws on Favela Gavia (2006), Hamilton (1985), Middlebrook (1995), and Olvera (2003d).

5. This adaptability allowed Mexico to avoid the military governments associated with intermediate levels of socioeconomic development in Argentina, Brazil, Chile, and Uruguay—the so-called bureaucratic authoritarian regimes (O'Donnell 1979a). When guerrilla insurgencies began to emerge in the late 1960s, the regime used violence to quash threats but avoided the extremes of the Southern Cone countries. In some ways what is most remarkable about this was the ability of the regime to resist efforts by reactionary groups, including the military, to exaggerate the threat of such insurgencies to try to justify the suspension of regular elections and even a cursory respect for rule of law.

6. The spread of liberation theology, and the progressive church in general, always remained relatively limited in Mexico compared to other countries in the region. While it would have a significant impact in a number of localities, including Chiapas, especially after the emergence of the Zapatista National Liberation Army in 1994, the church's overall impact on the emergence of civil society was also constrained by the institutions of controlled inclusion, as well as its own conservatism. This is one reason why human rights movements were relatively slow to develop in Mexico (Olvera 2003d; Brachet-Márquez 1996; Shefner 2008).

7. My discussion of the impact of the 1985 earthquake on civil society draws on Favela Gavia (2006) and Eckstein (1988).

8. All investigations were halted and expert reports were falsified to accelerate the demolition process and destroy any possible evidence of government responsibility (Favela Gavia 2006, 211).

9. See Kurtz (2004) for a detailed analysis of the neoliberal transformation of Mexico's countryside.

10. Ironically, the depth of the 1995 banking crisis actually improved income distribution due to the disproportionate losses of Mexico's elite.

11. This rate reflects the capital-intensive Mexican manufactured exports, as well as their limited impact on other economic sectors (see Boltvinik 2003).

12. For a detailed discussion of state-labor relations during the period of economic transition through the early 1990s, see Collier (1992).

13. My discussion of the role played by unions in restraining wages is based on Bensusán (2005), Griffin and Ickowitz (2003), Maloney (2009a), Middlebrook and Zepeda (2003b), Moreno-Brid (2009), and Zapata (1998).

14. Any low-wage comparative advantage Mexico might have achieved has since been eroded as Mexico lost export markets and investment to China (see Gallagher and Porzecanski 2008).

15. In fact, 17.6 percent of the labor force in 2005 illegally avoided paying social security taxes (see Levy 2009, 206).

16. This is particularly true of Mexico's principal social welfare program, Oportunidades.

17. See Méndez de Hoyas (2006) for a detailed discussion of the electoral reform process from 1977 to 2003.

18. They were ultimately proven right when Vicente Fox became Mexico's first elected president in 2000.

19. Most observers conclude that Cárdenas probably won but was denied the election through electoral fraud.

20. For a detailed analysis of the CD and the PRD, see Bruhn (1997).

21. As part of the 1994 electoral reforms, the government agreed to allow citizens to monitor polling sites (see Olvera 2003b, 357–58).

22. Remaining nonpartisan was not always easy to achieve at the grassroots level, given that many local organizers saw electoral mobilization as a way to advance their own partisan interests, particularly among the popular sectors where there seemed to be a natural affinity with the PRD. But efforts to link partisan interests with mobilizations for free and fair elections often created irresolvable tensions within grassroots organizations that led to their demobilization. This is one reason why the PRD's earlier alliance with civil society actors was so short-lived; rather than any genuine partisan allegiance, Cárdenas's electoral success was a response by the popular sectors to the unique circumstances of the 1988 elections.

23. My discussion of the AC's nonelectoral activities draws principally on Olvera (2003b, 369–76). See also Ramírez Sáiz (1997).

24. The AC, and civil society in general, were weakened as activists went into government after opposition victories, first at the local and state levels and then at the federal level. While this also happened in Chile, its impact in Mexico was more damaging given the relative scarcity of experienced civil society activists after decades of PRI rule.

25. Mexico did experience an improvement in its Gini coefficient after the transition to democracy. At 0.501 in 2000, it fell to 0.473 in 2006. The reasons for this decline are less than encouraging for the quality of Mexican democracy. The most important cause was the remittances sent home by Mexican emigrants. The poor's participation in the dramatic growth in narcotrafficking was another important reason (see Jusidman 2009, 192–95, in particular).

26. The EZLN was excluded from this study for several reasons. As the most important indigenous movement in Mexico's modern history, its complexity falls outside the scope of the present volume. At the same time, the EZLN's own weaknesses ultimately reflected some of the same problems affecting Mexican civil society at large. After 2000 it faded in importance compared to the period of democratic transition in the 1990s because of its inability to assume the leadership over a national indigenous movement when the issue of constitutional reform was placed on the political agenda by President Fox (Olvera 2010). As Bizberg (2003, 164) explains, "its violent origin and its reduction to a military character (by its encirclement by the federal army) dramatically reduced its capacity to extend to civic society and become an open social and political movement."

27. Tellingly, the first and last marches were organized after the sensationalist kidnapping and murder of the children of prominent Mexicans. The largest march in 2004 was actually noticeable for its lack of organization (*El Universal,* June 28, 2004).

28. A full 90 percent of all robberies were for fewer than seven hundred pesos, adding a new dimension to the adage that crime does not pay (see Mejía 2004, 26).

29. My discussion of Oaxaca's socioeconomic context draws primarily on Beas (2006), Sorroza (2008), and Velasco (n.d.).

30. Local caciques openly used their hirelings to enforce their will when the police proved inadequate for the task (see Beas 2006).

31. This disparateness also put APPO in a difficult position when guerrilla groups expressed their allegiance, detonating six bombs in Mexico City as a sign of their support. While APPO tried to distance itself from armed groups, the guerrillas' public support was made much of by APPO's opponents (see Velasco n.d.).

32. This discussion of how party dynamics determined APPO's success is based on Olvera (2010), Sorroza (2008), and Velasco (n.d.).

chapter 7

1. As discussed in chapter 1, mediating conflict is a defining characteristic of civil society, so it is important for addressing criminal violence.

2. Although the challenges posed by PB in Porto Alegre were much less daunting, the LPP failed at the local level, given the central government's ability to introduce radical changes by fiat. The same national-level dynamics (corruption, excessive political party influence, and pervasive clientelism) also were very much a potential threat to the success of PB.

references

Ackerman, John. 2003. "Co-governance for Accountability: Beyond 'Exit' and 'Voice.'" *World Development* 32 (3): 447–63.

Adato, Michelle. 2000. *The Impact of Progresa on Community Social Relationships*. Washington, D.C.: Food Consumption and Nutrition Division, International Food Policy Research Institute.

Aguayo Quezada, Sergio, and Javier Treviño Rangel. 2006. "Neither Truth nor Justice: Mexico's De Facto Amnesty." *Latin American Perspectives* 33 (2): 56–86.

Alarcón, Diana. 2003. "Income Distribution and Poverty Alleviation in Mexico: A Comparative Analysis." In Middlebrook and Zepeda 2003a, 447–86.

Albó, Xavier. 1995. "And from Kataristas to MNRistas? The Surprising and Bold Alliance Between Aymaras and Neoliberals in Bolivia." In *Indigenous Peoples and Democracy in Latin America*, edited by Donna Van Cott, 55–81. New York: St. Martin's Press.

———. 1999. *Ojotas en el poder local: Cuatro años después*. La Paz: Centro de Investigación y Promoción del Campesinado / Promoción al Desarrollo Económico Rural.

Aliendre España, Freddy. 2004. "La Ley SAFCO y la Ley de Participación Popular: La revolución administrativa y la revolución política." In ILDIS 2004, 1:21–61.

Almond, Gabriel A., and Sidney Verba. 1963. *The Civic Culture: Political Attitudes and Democracy in Five Nations*. Princeton: Princeton University Press.

Altimir, Oscar. 1998. "Inequality, Employment, and Poverty in Latin America: An Overview." In *Poverty and Inequality in Latin America: Issues and New Challenges*, edited by Victor E. Tokman and Guillermo O'Donnell, 3–35. Notre Dame: University of Notre Dame Press.

Alvarez, Sonia E., Evelina Dagnino, and Arturo Escobar, eds. 1998. *Cultures of Politics, Politics of Cultures: Re-visioning Latin American Social Movements*. Boulder: Westview Press.

Ameller, Vladimir. 2004. "El mito del desarrollo en municipios inviables." In ILDIS 2004, 1:301–26.

Ameller Terrazas, Vladimir. 2002. *Diálogo para la descentralización: Provocaciones, avances, y desengaños*. La Paz: Agencia Suiza para el Desarrollo y la Cooperación.

Angell, Alan. 1972. *Politics and the Labour Movement in Chile*. Oxford: Oxford University Press.

Angell, Alan, and Benny Pollack. 1990. "The Chilean Elections of 1989 and the Politics of Transition to Democracy." *Bulletin of Latin American Research* 9:1–23.

Arbona, Juan Manuel. 2005. "Los límites de los márgenes: Organizaciones políticas locales y las Jornadas de Octubre de 2003 en El Alto, Bolivia." *Nueva Sociedad* 197:6–15.

Archondo, Rafeal. 1997. "La aplicación de la Ley de Participación Popular." In Secretaría Nacional 1997, 273–302.

Ardaya, Gloria. 2001. *Participación política y liderazgo de mujeres en Bolivia*. La Paz: Centro de Información y Estadísticas de la Mujer / Colectivo de Investigación, Desarrollo, y Educación Entre Mujeres/Programa de Formación de Líderers Públicos para la Democracia/ Banco Interamericano de Desarrollo.

Ardaya Salinas, Rubén. 1998. *El comité de vigilancia al auxilio de la democracia municipal.* La Paz: Instituto Latinoamericano de Investigaciones Sociales de la Fundación Friedrich Ebert Stiftung.

Arias, Iván, and Sergio Molina. 1997. "De la nación clandestina a la participación popular." In Secretaría Nacional 1997, 59–74.

Arias, Jorge. 2004. "Planificación participativa en distritos municipales indígenas." In ILDIS 2004, 2:427–67.

Arriagada, Irma, and Lorena Godoy. 1999. *Seguridad ciudadana y violencia en América Latina: Diagnóstico y políticas en los años noventa.* Serie políticas sociales. Santiago: División de Desarrollo Social, Comisión Económica para América Latina y el Caribe.

Assies, Willem. 2003. "Water Rights, Neoliberalism, and the Revival of Social Protest in Bolivia." *Latin American Perspectives* 30:14–36.

Avritzer, Leonardo. 2002. *Democracy and the Public Space in Latin America.* Princeton: Princeton University Press.

Ayo, Diego. 1997. "Indígenas en el poder local." In Secretaría Nacional 1997, 333–43.

———. 1998. "Los distritos municipales." In Unidad de Investigación y Análisis 1998b, 27–65.

Baiocchi, Gianpaolo. 2002. "Synergizing Civil Society: State–Civil Society Regimes in Porto Alegre, Brazil." *Political Power and Social Theory* 15:3–52.

Baraona, J. 1974. "La evolución del movimiento laboral." In *Los actores de la realidad chilena,* edited by Dagmar Raczynski et al., 101–71. Santiago: Pacifico.

Barbery Anaya, Roberto. 1997. "Una revolución en democracia." In Secretaría Nacional 1997, 45–57.

Barozet, Emmanuelle. 2005. "Los nuevos patrones del clientelismo en las urbes chilenas: Reflexión acerca el uso político de las organizaciones comunitarias en Santiago Centro e Iquique." In *Introducción a la teoría y práctica del análisis de redes sociales,* edited by Vicente Espinoza and José Ignacio Porras, 361–400. Santiago: Universidad Bolivariana / Universidad de Santiago.

Barr, Robert R. 2005. "Bolivia: Another Uncompleted Revolution." *Latin American Politics and Society* 47 (3): 69–90.

Barraza-Lloréns, Mariana, Stefano Bertozzi, Eduardo González-Pier, and Juan Pablo Gutiérrez. 2002. "Addressing Inequity in Health and Health Care in Mexico." *Health Affairs* 21 (3): 46–56.

Barrera, Manuel. 1999. "Political Participation and Social Exclusion of the Popular Sectors in Chile." In Oxhorn and Starr 1999, 81–102.

Bates, Robert. 1981. *Markets and States in Tropical Africa: The Political Basis of Agricultural Policies.* Berkeley and Los Angeles: University of California Press.

Baumann, Renato. 2002. "Trade Policies, Growth, and Equity in Latin America." In Huber 2002b, 53–80.

Beas, Carlos. 2006. "Oaxaca: Una rebelión plebeya." *Observatorio Social de América Latina* 7 (21): 231–44.

Bendix, Reinhard. 1964. *Nation-Building and Citizenship: Studies of Our Changing Social Order.* New York: Wiley.

Benítez Manaut, Raúl. 2004. "México: Seguridad ciudadana, conflictos, y orden público." *Nueva Sociedad* 191:103–16.

———. 2009. "La crisis de seguridad en México." *Nueva Sociedad* 220:173–89.

Bensusán, Graciela. 2005. "A New Scenario for Mexican Trade Unions: Changes in the Structure of Political and Economic Opportunities." In *The Dilemmas of Political Change in Mexico,* edited by Kevin J. Middlebrook, 237–85. Washington, D.C.: Brookings Institution Press.

Bergquist, Charles. 1986. *Labor in Latin America: Comparative Essays on Chile, Argentina, Venezuela, and Colombia.* Stanford: Standford University Press.

Bickford, Louis. 1999. *Strengthening Democracy: Stakeholder Institutions, Public Policy, and Democratic Quality: The Case of Chile, 1990–1998.* Montreal: Department of Political Science, McGill University.

Bickford, Susan. 1999. "Reconfiguring Pluralism: Identity and Institutions in the Inegalitarian Polity." *American Journal of Political Science* 43 (January): 86–108.

Bitar, Sergio. 1986. *Chile: Experiment in Democracy.* Philadelphia: Institute for the Study of Human Issues.

———. 2001. "La ley Arica: Una batalla contra el centralismo desde el senado." Unpublished manuscript. Santiago.

Bizberg, Ilán. 2003. "Transition or Restructuring of Society?" In *Mexico's Politics and Society in Transition,* edited by Jospeh S. Tulchin and Andrew D. Selee, 143–75. Boulder: Lynne Rienner.

Black, Anthony. 1984. *Guilds and Civil Society in European Political Thought from the Twelfth Century to the Present.* London: Methuen.

Boltvinik, Julio. 2003. "Welfare, Inequality, and Poverty in Mexico, 1970–2000." In Middlebrook and Zepeda 2003a, 385–446.

Boltvinik, Julio, and Fernando Cortés. 2000. "La identificación los pobres en Progresa." In *Los dilemas de la política social: ¿Cómo combatir la pobreza?,* edited by Enrique Valencia Lomelí, Mónica Gendreau, and Ana María Tepichín Valle, 31–61. Mexico City: Universidad de Guadalajara / Instituto Tecnológico y de Estudios Superiores de Occidente / Universidad Iberoamericano.

Bonner, Michelle. 2003. "Defining Democracy: Women and Human Rights Organizations in the Process of Argentine Democratization." Ph.D. diss., Department of Political Science, University of Toronto.

Booth, David, Suzanne Clisby, and Charlotta Widmark. 1997. *Popular Participation: Democratising the State in Rural Bolivia.* Stockholm: Swedish International Development Cooperation Agency.

Borzutzky, Silvia. 2002. *Vital Connections: Politics, Social Security, and Inequality in Chile.* Notre Dame: University of Notre Dame Press.

Bowman, Kirk S. 2002. *Militarization, Democracy, and Development.* University Park: Pennsylvania State University Press.

Brachet-Márquez, Viviane. 1996. *El pacto de dominación: Estado, clase, y reforma social en México (1910–1995).* Mexico City: Centro de Estudios Sociológicos, El Colegio de México.

Brenner, Robert. 1976. "Agarian Structures and Economic Development in Pre-industrial Europe." *Past and Present* (February): 30–75.

Bresser Pereira, Luiz Carlos, and Yoshiaki Nakano. 1998. "The Missing Social Contract: Governability and Reform in Latin America." In Oxhorn and Ducatenzeiler 1998, 21–42.

Bruhn, Kathleen. 1996. "Social Spending and Political Support: The 'Lessons' of the National Solidarity Program in Mexico." *Comparative Politics* 28 (2): 151–77.

———. 1997. *Taking on Goliath: The Emergence of a New Left Party and the Struggle for Democracy in Mexico.* University Park: Pennsylvania State University Press.

Buchanan, Paul. 1997. "Counterhegmonic Strategies in Neoliberal Argentina." *Latin American Perspectives* 24 (November): 30–75.

Burgess, Katrina. 2004. *Parties and Unions in the New Global Economy.* Pittsburgh: University of Pittsburgh Press.

Bustillo, Inés. 2003. Presentation at the Fourth Forum of Hemispheric Experts. Canadian Foundation for the Americas, Ottawa, June 19.

Cadena Roa, Jorge. 2008. "Evaluación del desempeño de los movimientos sociales." In *Acción colectiva y organización: Estudios sobre desempeño asociativo,* edited by Cristina Puga and Matilde Luna, 265–301. Mexico City: Instituto de Investigaciones Sociales, Universidad Nacional Autónoma de México.

Calhoun, Craig. 1991. "The Problem of Identity in Collective Action." In *Macro-Micro Linkages in Sociology,* edited by Joan Huber, 51–75. Newbury Park: Sage.

———. 1993. "Civil Society and the Public Sphere." *Public Culture* 5 (Winter): 267–80.

Campero, Guillermo. 1987. *Entre la sobrevivencia y la acción política: Las organizaciones de pobladores en Santiago.* Santiago: Instituto Latinoamericano de Estudios Transnacionales.

Cárdenas, Ana. 2005. *El sujeto y el proceso de transformación en las condiciones de trabajo en Chile: Elementos teóricos y empíricos para la discusión.* Santiago: Oficina Subregional para el Cono Sur de América Latina, Oficina Internacional del Trabajo.

Cárdenas, Víctor Hugo. 1997. "El rescate de los viejos postulados." In Secretaría Nacional 1997, 21–26.

Cardoso, Fernando Enrique. 1973. "Associated Dependent Development: Theoretical and Practical Implications." In *Authoritarian Brazil: Origins, Policies, and Future,* edited by Alfred Stepan, 142–76. New Haven: Yale University Press.

Cardoso, Fernando Enrique, and Enzo Faletto. 1970. *Dependency and Development in Latin America.* Berkeley and Los Angeles: University of California Press.

Cardoso, Ruth Corrêa Leite. 1992. "Popular Movements in the Context of the Consolidation of Democracy in Brazil." In *The Making of Social Movements in Latin America,* edited by Arturo Escobar and Sonia E. Alvarez, 291–302. Boulder: Westview Press.

Carrión, Fernando. 2003. "De la violencia urbana a la convivencia ciudadana." In *Entre el crimen y el castigo: Seguridad ciudadana y control democrático en América Latina y el Caribe,* edited by Lilian Bobea, 51–84. Caracas: Facultad Latinoamericana de Ciencias Sociales–República Dominicana / Woodrow Wilson International Center / Nueva Sociedad.

Casanovas Sainz, Mauricio. 2004. "Cadenas productivas y municipio." In ILDIS 2004, 1:247–71.

Castells, Manuel. 1983. *The City and the Grassroots.* Berkeley and Los Angeles: University of California Press.

Centeno, Miguel Angel. 2002. *Blood and Debt: War and the Nation-State in Latin America.* University Park: Pennsylvania State University Press.

Centro de Estudios Públicos. 2000. "Estudio nacional de opinión pública, Marzo-Abril 2000." Accessed March 8, 2011. http://www.cepchile.cl/dms/lang_1/doc_2905.html.

———. 2010. "La perspectiva del tiempo: Percepción problemas." Encuestas CEP. Accessed December 10. http://www.cepchile.cl/graficos_EncCEP/graficos_PersTiempo.htm.

CEPAL (Comisión Económica para América Latina y el Caribe). 1989. *Transformación ocupacional y crisis social en América Latina.* Santiago: Comisión Económica para América Latina y el Caribe, Naciones Unidas.

———. 1991. *Magnitud de la pobreza en América Latina en los años ochenta.* Santiago: Comisión Económica para América Latina y el Caribe / Programa de las Naciones Unidas para el Desarrollo.

———. 1996. *América Latina y el Caribe: Quince años de desempeño económico.* Santiago: Comisión Económica para América Latina y el Caribe / Programa de las Naciones Unidas para el Desarrollo.

———. 1999. *América Latina y las crisis.* In conjunction with Programa de las Naciones Unidas para el Desarrollo, Banco Interamericano de Desarrollo, and Facultad Latinoamericana de Ciencias Sociales. Serie políticas sociales. Santiago: División de Desarrollo Social, Comisión Económica para América Latina y el Caribe.

———. 2003. *Panorama social de América Latina, 2002–2003: Síntesis.* Santiago: Comisión Económica para América Latina y el Caribe, Naciones Unidas.

———. 2009a. *Panorama social de América Latina, 2009: Síntesis.* Santiago: Comisión Económica para América Latina y el Caribe, Naciones Unidas.

———. 2009b. *Panorama social de América Latina, 2009: Versión preliminar no sometida a revisión editorial.* Santiago: Comisión Económica para América Latina y el Caribe, Naciones Unidas.

———. 2009c. *Panorama social de América Latina, 2010: Versión preliminar.* Santiago: Comisión Económica para América Latina y el Caribe, Naciones Unidas.

Cervantes, Jesusa. 2004. "Crece la pobreza . . . y el odio." *Revista Proceso,* July 4, 20–21.

Chambers, Simone, and Will Kymlicka, eds. 2002. *Alternative Conceptions of Civil Society.* Princeton: Princeton University Press.

Chand, Vikram K. 2001. *Mexico's Political Awakening.* Notre Dame: University of Notre Dame Press.

Chávez Corrales, Juan Carlos, ed. 1998. *Las reformas estructurales en Bolivia*. La Paz: Fundación Milenio.

Cisneros Merino, Rodrigo. 2004. "Creación de empleo en los municipios." In ILDIS 2004, 1:273–97.

Cohen, Jean. 1985. "Strategy or Identity: New Theoretical Paradigms and Contemporary Social Movements." *Social Research* 52 (Winter): 663–716.

Cohen, Jean, and Andrew Arato. 1992. *Civil Society and Political Theory*. Cambridge: MIT Press.

Collier, David, ed. 1979. *The New Authoritarianism in Latin America*. Princeton: Princeton University Press.

Collier, Ruth Berins. 1992. *The Contradictory Alliance: State-Labor Relations and Regime Change in Mexico*. Berkeley: International and Area Studies, University of California.

———. 1999. *Paths Toward Democracy: The Working Class and Elites in Western Europe and South America*. Cambridge: Cambridge University Press.

Collier, Ruth Berins, and David Collier. 2002. *Shaping the Political Arena: Critical Junctures, the Labor Movement, and Regime Dynamics in Latin America*. Notre Dame: University of Notre Dame Press.

Collier, Simon, and William F. Sater. 2004. *A History of Chile, 1808–2002*. 2nd ed. Cambridge: Cambridge University Press.

Comisión Nacional de Verdad y Reconciliación. 1991. *Informe de la Comisión Nacional de Verdad y Reconciliación*. Santiago: Nación.

Conaghan, Catherine M. 2005. *Fujimori's Peru: Deception in the Public Sphere*. Pittsburgh: University of Pittsburgh Press.

Cook, Maria Lorena. 1998. "Toward Flexible Industrial Relations? Neo-Liberalism, Democracy, and Labor Reform in Latin America." *Industrial Relations* 37 (3): 311–36.

Coordinación Presidencial para la Alianza Ciudadana. 2002. *Programa nacional de participación ciudadana en políticas pública*. Mexico City: Coordinación Presidencial para la Alianza Ciudadana.

Corrales, Javier. 2003. "Market Reforms." In Domínguez and Schifter 2003, 74–99.

Corte Nacional Electoral. 2004. *Democracia local en Bolivia: Elecciones municipales 2004*. Documento de Información Pública 2. La Paz: Corte Nacional Electoral.

Crozier, Michel, Samuel P. Huntington, J. Oji Watanuki, and Trilateral Commission. 1975. *The Crisis of Democracy: Report on the Governability of Democracies to the Trilateral Commission*. New York: New York University Press.

Dagnino, Evelina, ed. 2002. *Sociedad civil, gobernabilidad, y democratización en América Latina: Brasil*. Mexico City: Fondo de Cultura Económica.

———. 2005. "'We All Have Rights but . . . ': Contesting Conceptions of Citizenship in Brazil." In *Inclusive Citizenship: Meanings and Expressions of Citizenship*, edited by Naila Kabeer, 147–63. London: Zed Books.

Dahl, Robert. 1961. *Who Governs:Democracy and Power in an American City*. New Haven: Yale University Press.

Dammert, Lucía. 2009. "¿Falsa alarma? Temor, crimen y opinión pública en Chile." In *La sociedad de la opinión: Reflexiones sobre encuestas y cambio político en democracia*, edited by Rodrigo Cordero, 225–50. Santiago: Diego Portales.

Dammert, Lucía, and Mary Fran T. Malone. 2003. "Fear of Crime or Fear of Life? Public Insecurities in Chile." *Bulletin of Latin American Research* 22 (1): 79–101.

Davis, Dianne E. 2006. "Undermining the Rule of Law: Democratization and the Dark Side of Police Reform in Mexico." *Latin American Politics and Society* 48 (1): 55–86.

De Ferranti, David, Perry Guillermo E., Francisco Ferreira, and Michael Walton. 2004. *Inequality in Latin America: Breaking with History?* Draft ed. Washington, D.C.: International Bank for Reconstruction and Development / World Bank.

De la Maza, Gonzalo. 2004. "Políticas públicas y sociedad civil en Chile: El caso de la políticas sociales (1990–2004)." *Política* 43:105–48.

———. 2005. *Tan lejos tan cerca: Políticas públicas y sociedad civil en Chile*. Santiago: LOM.

———. 2010. "La disputa por la participación en la democracia elitista chilena." Special Issue, *Latin American Research Review* 45:274–97.

De la Maza, Gonzalo, and Mario Garces. 1985. *La explosión de las mayorias: Protesta nacional 1983–1984.* Santiago: ECO.

Delgado, Álvaro 2004. "La infiltración ultraderechista." *Revista Processo,* June 20, 24–27.

Díaz, Alvaro. 1991. "Nuevas tendencias en la estructura social chilena: Asalarización informal y pobreza en los ochenta." *Proposiciones* 20:88–119.

Di Tella, Torcuato. 1965. "Populism and Reform in Latin America." In *Obstacles to Change in Latin America,* edited by Claudio Veliz, 47–74. Oxford: Oxford University Press.

Domínguez, Jorge I., and Michael Schifter, eds. 2003. *Constructing Democratic Governance in Latin America.* Baltimore: Johns Hopkins University Press.

Drake, Paul W. 1996. *Labor Movements and Dictatorships: The Southern Cone in Comparative Perspective.* Baltimore: John Hopkins University Press.

Drake, Paul W., and Ivan Jaksic, eds. 1995. *The Struggle for Democracy in Chile.* Rev. ed. Lincoln: University of Nebraska Press.

Dresser, Denise. 1994. "Bringing the Poor Back In: National Solidarity as a Strategy of Regime Legitimation." In *Transforming State-Society Relations in Mexico: The National Solidarity Strategy,* edited by Wayne A. Cornelius, Ann L. Craig, and Jonathan Fox, 143–76. La Jolla, Calif.: Center for U.S.-Mexican Studies; San Diego: University of California.

Duce, Mauricio, and Rogelio Pérez Perdomo. 2003. "Citizen Security and Reform of the Criminal Justice System in Latin America." In Frühling, Tulchin, and Golding 2003, 69–91.

Eckstein, Susan. 1982. "The Impact of Revolution on Social Welfare in Latin America." *Theory and Society* 11 (January): 43–94.

———. 1988. *The Poverty of Revolution: The State and Urban Poor in Mexico.* Princeton: Princeton University Press.

———, ed. 1989. *Power and Popular Protest: Latin American Social Movements.* Berkeley and Los Angeles: University of California Press.

Eckstein, Susan, and Timothy Wickham-Crowley, eds. 2003. *What Justice? Whose Justice? Fighting for Fairness in Latin America.* Berkeley and Los Angeles: University of California Press.

ECLAC (Economic Commission for Latin America and the Caribbean). 1994. *Social Panorama of Latin America.* Santiago: Economic Commission for Latin America and the Caribbean.

———. 2007. *Social Panorama of Latin America, 2007.* Santiago: Economic Commission for Latin America and the Caribbean.

Ehrenberg, John. 1999. *Civil Society: The Critical History of an Idea.* New York: New York University Press.

Eisenstadt, Todd A. 2004. *Courting Democracy: Party Strategies and Electoral Institutions.* Cambridge: Cambridge University Press.

Escalante Gonzalbo, Fernando. 2009. "¿Puede México ser Colombia? Violencia, narcotráfico y estado." *Nueva Sociedad* 220:84–96.

Escobar, Arturo. 1995. *Encountering Development: The Making and Unmaking of the Third World.* Princeton: Princeton University Press.

Escobar, Arturo, and Sonia E. Alvarez, eds. 1992. *The Making of Social Movements in Latin America: Identity, Stategy, and Democracy.* Boulder: Westview Press.

Espínola, Viola. n.d. *Autonomía escolar: Factores que contribuyen a una escuela más efectiva.* Washington, D.C.: Banco Interamericano de Desarrollo.

Espinoza, Vicente. 2004. "De la política social a la participación en un nuevo contrato de ciudadanía." *Política* 43:149–83.

Esteva, Gustavo. 2008. "The Asamblea Popular de los pueblos de Oaxaca: A Chronicle of Radical Democracy." *Latin American Perspectives* 34 (1): 129–44.

Evangelista Martínez, Elí. 2001. "Emergencia e institucionalición de nuevos actores en el desarrollo de las políticas sociales en México." In *La política social en la transición,* edited by

Carlos Arteaga Basurto and Silvia Solís San Vicente, 154–72. Mexico City: Escuela Nacional de Trabajo Social, Universidad Nacional Autónoma de México.

Evans, Peter. 1995. *Embedded Autonomy: States and Industrial Transformation.* Princeton: Princeton University Press.

———. 1997a. "Government Action, Social Capital, and Development: Reviewing the Evidence of Synergy." In *State-Society Synergy: Government and Social Capital in Development,* edited by Peter Evans, 178–209. Berkeley: International and Area Studies, University of California.

———. 1997b. "Introduction: Development Strategies Across the Public-Private Divide." In *State-Society Synergy: Government and Social Capital in Development,* edited by Peter Evans, 1–10. Berkeley: International and Area Studies, University of California.

Fajnzylber, Fernando. 1990. *Unavoidable Industrial Restructuring in Latin America.* Durham: Duke University Press.

Faletto, Enzo, and Eduardo Ruiz. 1970. "Conflicto político y estructura social." In *Chile, hoy,* edited by Aníbal Pinto, 213–54. Santiago: Siglo Veintiuno.

Favela Gavia, Diana Margarita. 2006. *Protesta y reforma en México: Interacción entre estado y sociedad, 1946–1997.* Mexico City: Centro de Investigaciones Interdisciplinarias en Ciencias y Humanidades, Universidad Nacional Autónoma de México.

Feinberg, Richard, Carlos H. Waisman, and Leon Zamosc. 2006. *Civil Society and Democracy in Latin America.* New York: Palgrave Macmillan.

Femia, Joseph V. 1972. "Barrington Moore and the Preconditions for Democracy." *British Journal of Political Science* 2 (January): 21–46.

Ferguson, Adam. 1966. *An Essay on the History of Civil Society.* Edinburgh: University of Edinburgh Press.

Ffrench-Davis, Ricardo, and Dagmar Raczynski. 1988. *The Impact of Global Recession and National Policies on Living Standards: Chile, 1973–87.* Santiago: Corporación de Estudios para Latinoamérica.

Filgueira, Carlos H., and Fernando Filgueira. 2002. "Models of Welfare and Models of Capitalism: The Limits of Transferability." In Huber 2002b, 127–58.

Fleet, Michael. 1985. *The Rise and Fall of Chilean Christian Democracy.* Princeton: Princeton University Press.

Foweraker, Joe. 2005. "Toward a Political Sociology of Social Movement Mobilization in Latin America." In Wood and Roberts 2005b, 115–35.

Foxley, Alejandro. 1983. *Latin American Experiments in Neoconservative Economics.* Berkeley and Los Angeles: University of California Press.

"Fragile States in the Andes: Pressure Builds Again in Bolivia." 2005. *Economist* 375 (April 23): 38–40.

Franco, Rolando. 2008. *Educación en Chile: Masificación y problemas de calidad.* Santiago: Facultad Latinoamericana de Ciencias Sociales.

Frühling, Hugo. 1984. "Repressive Policies and Legal Dissent in Authoritarian Regimes: Chile 1973–1981." *International Journal of Sociology of Law* 12:351–74.

———. 2003. "Police Reform and the Process of Democratization." In Frühling, Tulchin, and Golding 2003, 15–44.

Frühling, Hugo, Joseph S. Tulchin, and Heather A. Golding. 2003. *Crime and Violence in Latin America: Citizen Security, Democracy, and the State.* Washington, D.C.: Woodrow Wilson Center Press; Baltimore: Johns Hopkins University Press.

Fukuyama, Francis. 1989. "The End of History?" *National Interest* 16 (Summer): 3–18.

Galindo Soza, Mario. 1998. "La participación popular y la descentralización administrativa." In Chávez Corrales, 1998, 223–82.

———. 2004. "Diez años de planificación participativa en el proceso de la participación popular." In ILDIS 2004, 2:85–144.

Gallagher, Kevin P., and Roberto Porzecanski. 2008. "China Matters: China's Economic Impact in Latin America." *Latin American Research Review* 43 (1): 185–200.

Gamara, Eduardo A., and James M. Malloy. 1995. "The Patrimonial Dynamics of Party Politics in Bolivia." In Mainwaring and Scully 1995, 399–433.

García Orellana, Alberto, Fernando García Yapur, and Luz Quitón Herbas. 2003. *La "Guerra del Agua," Abril 2000:La crisis de la política en Bolivia*. La Paz: Fundación para la Investigación Estratégica en Bolivia.

García Salaues, Alfonso. 2004. "Deuda municipal." In ILDIS 2004, 1:63–100.

Garretón, Manuel Antonio. 1989. *The Chilean Political Process*. Boston: Hyman.

———. 1996. "Social Movements and the Process of Democratization. A General Framework." *International Review of Sociology* 6 (1): 39–49.

———. 1999. "Social and Economic Transformations in Latin America: The Emergence of a New Political Matrix?" In Oxhorn and Starr 1999, 61–78.

———. 2003. *Incomplete Democracy: Political Democratization in Chile and Latin America*. Translated by R. Kelly Washbourne, with Gregory Horvath. Chapel Hill: University of North Carolina.

———. 2007. *Del postpinochetismo a la sociedad democrática: Globalización y política en el Bicentenario*. Santiago: Random House Mondadori.

Garro, Alejandro M. 1999. "Access to Justice for the Poor in Latin America." In Méndez, O'Donnell, and Pinheiro 1999, 251–66.

Gay, Robert. 1990. "Popular Incorporation and Prospects for Democracy: Some Implications of the Brazilian Case." *Theory and Society* 19:447–63.

Gellner, Ernest. 1991. "Civil Society in Historical Context." *International Social Science Journal* 129 (August): 495–510.

Gil, Federico. 1966. *The Political System of Chile*. Boston: Houghton Mifflin.

Gil Olmos, José. 2004a. "En el filo . . ." *Revista Proceso*, July 4, 12–17.

———. 2004b. "Última llamada." *Revista Proceso*, June 27, 8–14.

Gisselquist, Rachel. 2005. "Bolivia's 2004 Municipal Elections." *Focal Point: Spotlight on the Americas* 4 (1): 1–2.

Goldfrank, Benjamin. 2003. "Making Participation Work in Porto Alegre." In *Radicals in Power: The Workers' Party (PT) and Experiments in Urban Democracy in Brazil*, edited by Gianpaolo Baiocchi, 27–52. London: Zed Books.

Goldthorpe, John, ed. 1984. *Order and Conflict in Contemporary Capitalism*. Oxford: Clarendon Press.

Gray-Molina, George. 1998. "Exclusion, Participation and Democratic State-Building." Paper presented at the Democratic Viability in Bolivia seminar, St. Antony's College, University of Oxford, February 25.

———. 2003. "The Offspring of 1952: Poverty, Exclusion and the Promise of Popular Participation." In *Proclaiming Revolution: Bolivia in Comparative Perspective*, edited by Merilee S. Grindle and Pilar Domingo, 345–63. Boston: David Rockefeller Center for Latin American Studies, Harvard University; London: Institute of Latin American Studies, University of London.

Greaves, Edward F. 2004. "Municipality and Community in Chile: Building Imagined Civic Communities and Its Impact on the Political." *Politics and Society* 32 (2): 203–30.

Grebe López, Horst. 1997. "La Ley de Participación Popular." In Secretaría Nacional 1997, 171–84.

Griffin, Keith, and Amy Ickowitz. 2003. "Confronting Human Development in Mexico." In Middlebrook and Zepeda 2003a, 577–95.

Grindle, Merilee S. 2000. *Audacious Reforms: Institutional Invention and Democracy in Latin America*. Baltimore: Johns Hopkins University Press.

Grupo de Trabajo del Diálogo Nacional. 1998. *Propuesta contra la pobreza*. La Paz: Vicepresidencia de la República.

Guerrero, Isabel, Luis Felipe López-Calva, and Michael Walton. 2009. "The Inequality Trap and Its Links to Low Growth in Mexico." In Levy and Walton 2009b, 111–56.

Gugliano, Alfredo Alejandro. n.d. *A Caixa de Pandora da participação cidadã: O orçamento participativo e a governança solidária local em Porto Alegre*. Porto Alegre, Brazil: Universidade Federal do Rio Grande Sul.

Guidry, John A., and Mark Q. Sawyer. 2003. "Contentious Pluralism: The Public Sphere and Democracy." *Perspectives on Politics* 1 (2): 273–89.

Gurrieri, Adolfo, and Pedro Sáinz. 2003. "Empleo y movilidad estructural: Trayectoria de un tema prebischiano." *Revista de la CEPAL* 80:141–64.

Guzmán Boutier, Omar. 1998. "Denuncias del comité de vilancia o cuándo efectivo es el control social." In Unidad de Investigación y Análisis 1998b, 132–53.

Habermas, Jürgen. 1992. "Further Reflections on the Public Sphere." In *Habermas and the Public Sphere*, edited by Craig Calhoun, 421–61. Cambridge: Cambridge University Press.

Hamilton, Nora. 1985. *The Limits of State Autonomy: Post-Revolutionary Mexico*. Princeton: Princeton University Press.

Hann, Chris. 1996. "Introduction: Political Society and Civil Anthropology." In Hann and Dunn 1996, 1–24. London: Routledge.

Hann, Chris, and Elizabeth Dunn, eds. 1996. *Civil Society: Challenging Western Models*. London: Routledge.

Heller, Patrick. 2001. "Moving the State: The Politics of Democratic Decentralization in Kerala, South Africa, and Porto Alegre." *Politics and Society* 29 (1): 131–63.

Helwege, Ann. 1995. "Poverty in Latin America: Back to the Abyss?" *Journal of Interamerican Studies and World Affairs* 37 (Fall): 99–123.

Henríquez, Helia, and Verónica Uribe-Echevarría. 2004. *Trayectorias laborales: La certeza de la incertidumbre*. Santiago: Dirección del Trabajor, Gobierno de Chile.

Heredia, Blanca. 1992. "Profits, Politics, and Size: The Political Transformation of Mexican Business." In *The Right and Democracy in Latin America*, edited by Douglas A. Chalmers, Maria do Carmo Campello de Souza, and Atilio Borón, 277–301. New York: Praeger.

Herrera, David. 1997. "Voices on the Left." *NACLA Report on the Americas* 31 (July/August): 10–12.

Hilgers, Tina. 2008. "Causes and Consequences of Political Clientelism: Mexico's PRD in Comparative Perspective." *Latin American Politics and Society* 50 (4): 123–53.

Hirschman, Albert. 1979. "The Turn to Authoritarianism in Latin America and the Search for Its Economic Determinants." In Collier 1979, 61–98.

Hobson, Barbara, and Marika Lindholm. 1997. "Collective Identities: Women's Power Resources and the Making of Welfare States." *Theory and Society* 26 (August): 475–508.

Holzner, Claudio A. 2007. "The Poverty of Democracy: Neoliberal Reforms and Political Participation of the Poor in Mexico." *Latin American Politics and Scoeity* 49 (2): 87–122.

Huber, Evelyne. 2002a. "Conclusion: Actors, Institutions, and Policies." In Huber 2002b, 439–80.

———, ed. 2002b. *Models of Capitalism: Lessons for Latin America*. University Park: Pennsylvania State University Press.

Huber, Evelyne, Dietrich Rueschemeyer, and John D. Stephens. 1997. "The Paradoxes of Contemporary Democracy: Formal, Participatory, and Social Dimensions." *Comparative Politics* 29 (3): 323–42.

Huneeus, Carlos. 2007. *The Pinochet Regime*. Translated by Lake Sagaris. Boulder: Lynne Rienner.

Hunter, Wendy. 2003. "Education Policy Reform in Latin America: New Opportunities, Old Constraints." In *Latin American Democracies in the New Global Economy*, edited by Ana Margheritis, 173–95. Miami: North-South Center Press.

Huntington, Samuel. 1996. *The Clash of Civilizations and the Remaking of World Order*. New York: Simon and Schuster.

IDB (Inter-American Development Bank). 1998. *Facing Up to Inequality in Latin America: Economic and Social Progress in Latin America, 1998–1999 Report*. Washington, D.C.: Inter-American Development Bank.

———. 2003. *Good Jobs Wanted: Labor Markets in Latin America; 2004 Economic and Social Progress Report*. Washington, D.C.: Inter-American Development Bank.

Iglesias, Enrique V. 1990. "From Policy Consensus to Renewed Economic Growth." In *Latin American Adjustment: How Much Has Happened?*, edited by John Williamson, 345–50. Washington, D.C.: Institute for International Economics.

ILDIS (Instituto Latinoamericano de Investigaciones Sociales). 2004. *Municipalización: Diagnóstico de una década; Treinta investigaciones sobre participación popular y descentralización*. 2 vols. La Paz: Plural / United States Agency for Development / Friedrich Ebert Stiftung / ILDIS.

Jaquette, Jane, and Sharon L. Wolchik. 1998. *Women and Democracy: Latin America and Central and Eastern Europe*. Baltimore: John Hopkins University Press.

Jusidman, Clara. 2009. "Desigualdad y política social en México." *Nueva Sociedad* 220:190–206.

Karl, Terry Lynn. 1986. "Petroleum and Political Pacts: The Transition to Democracy in Venezuela." In O'Donnell, Schmitter, and Whitehead 1986, 196–219.

———. 1990. "Dilemmas of Democratization in Latin America." *Comparative Politics* 23 (October): 1–21.

———. 1997. *The Paradox of Plenty: Oil Booms and Petro States*. Berkeley and Los Angeles: University of California Press.

———. 2003. "The Vicious Cycle of Inequality in Latin America." In Eckstein and Wickham-Crowley 2003, 133–57.

Karl, Terry Lynn, and Philippe C. Schmitter. 1991. "What Democracy Is . . . and What It Is Not." In *The Global Resurgence of Democracy*, edited by Marc F. Plattner and Larry Diamond, 39–52. Baltimore: John Hopkins University Press.

Katznelson, Ira. 1986. "Working-Class Formation: Constructing Cases and Comparisons." In *Working-Class Formation: Nineteenth-Century Patterns in Western Europe and the United States*, edited by Ira Katznelson and Aristide Zolberg, 3–41. Princeton: Princeton University Press.

Keane, John. 1988a. *Civil Society and the State: New European Perspectives*. London: Verso.

———. 1988b. "Depotism and Democracy." In Keane 1988a, 33–71.

———. 1998. *Civil Society: Old Images, New Visions*. Stanford: Stanford University Press.

Keck, Margaret E., and Kathryn Sikkink. 1998. *Activists Beyond Borders: Advocacy Networks in International Politics*. Ithaca: Cornell University Press.

Kincaid, Douglas A., and Eduardo A. Gamarra. 1996. "Disorderly Democracy: Redefining Public Security in Latin America." In *Latin America in the World-Economy*, edited by Roberto Patricio Koreniewsicz and William C. Smith, 211–28. Westport, Conn.: Praeger.

Klein, Herbert. 1969. *Parties and Political Change in Bolivia, 1880–1952*. Cambridge: Cambridge University Press.

Kliksberg, Bernardo. 2000. "Diez falacias sobre los problemas sociales de América Latina." Unpublished manuscript. Washington, D.C.

Knight, Alan. 1986. *The Mexican Revolution*. Cambridge: Cambridge University Press.

Korzeniewsicz, Roberto Patricio, and William C. Smith. 2000. "Poverty, Inequality, and Growth in Latin America: Searching for the High Road to Globalization." *Latin American Research Review* 35 (3): 7–54.

Kudelka, Ana María. 2004. "Análisis de las políticas de género desde un enfoque gerencial y su impacto a nivel municipal." In ILDIS 2004, 2:503–58.

Kurth, James. 1979. "Industrial Change and Political Change: A European Perspective." In Collier 1979, 363–97.

Kurtz, Marcus J. 2004. *Free Market Democracy and the Chilean and Mexican Countryside*. Cambridge: Cambridge University Press.

Labastida Martín del Campo, Julio, and Miguel Armando López Leyva. 2004. "México: Una transición prolongada (1988–1996/97)." *Revista Mexicana de Sociología* 66 (4): 749–806.

Lagos, Marta. 1997. "Latin America's Smiling Mask." *Journal of Democracy* 8 (July): 125–38.

———. 2003a. "Latin America's Lost Illusions: A Road with No Return?" *Journal of Democracy* 14 (2): 163–73.

———. 2003b. "Public Opinion." In Domínguez and Schifter 2003, 136–61.

Laraña, Osvaldo. 2001. "Distribución de ingresos: 1958–2001." In *Reformas, crecimiento, y políticas sociales en Chile desde 1973,* edited by Ricardo Ffrench-Davis and Barbara Stallings, 295–328. Santiago: Comisión Económica para América Latina y el Caribe.

Laserna, Roberto. 2000. "Cochabamba: La guerra contra el agua." *Observatorio Social de América Latina* 1 (2): 15–20.

———. 2003. "Bolivia: Entre populismo y democracia." *Nueva Sociedad* 188:4–14.

———. 2004. *Bolivia: La crisis de octubre y el fracaso del ch'enko; Una visión desde la economía política.* Fundación Milenio. http://www.fundacion-milenio.org/documentos/doc_details/ 149-bolivia-la-crisis-de-octubre-y-el-fracaso-del-chaenko.html.

Lastra Vía, Noemí M. 2004. "Cobro de impuestos." In ILDIS 2004, 1:101–47.

Latinobarómetro. 2003. *Summary Report: Democracy and Economy.* Santiago: Latinobarómetro.

———. 2008. *Informe 2008.* Santiago: Latinobarómetro.

———. 2009a. "Banco de datos." Latinobarómetro Corporation. Accessed February 7, 2011. http://www.latinobarometro.org/.

———. 2009b. *Informe 2009.* Santiago: Latinobarómetro.

Laurell, Asa Cristina. 2003. "The Transformation of Social Policy in Mexico." In Middlebrook and Zepeda 2003a, 320–49.

León, Arturo, and Javier Martínez. 2007. "La estratificación social en Chile hacia fines del siglo XX." In *Estratificación y movilidad social en América Latina: Transformaciones estructurales de un cuarto de siglo,* edited by Rolando Franco, Arturo León, and Raúl Atria, 303–37. Santiago: LOM.

Levy, Santiago. 2006. *Progress Against Poverty: Sustaining Mexico's Progresa-Oportunidades Program.* Washington, D.C.: Brookings Institution.

———. 2008. *Good Intentions, Bad Outcomes: Social Policy, Informality, and Economic Growth in Mexico.* Washington, D.C.: Brookings Institution.

———. 2009. "Social Security Reform in Mexico: For Whom?" In Levy and Walton 2009b, 203–44.

Levy, Santiago, and Michael Walton. 2009a. "Equity, Competition, and Growth in Mexico: An Overview." In Levy and Walton 2009b, 1–42.

———, eds. 2009b. *No Growth Without Equity? Inequality, Interests, and Competition in Mexico,* Washington, D.C.: Basingstoke; New York: World Bank / Palgrave Macmillan.

"Ley de emergencia contra la delincuencia: ¿Un estado de sitio?" 1996. *Proceso* 16 (March 20): 8.

Lipset, Seymour Martin, and Stein Rokkan. 1967. "Cleavage Structures, Party Systems, and Voter Alignments: An Introduction." In *Party Systems and Voter Alignments: Cross-National Perspectives,* edited by Seymour Martin Lipset and Stein Rokkan, 1–64. New York: Free Press.

Londoño, Juan Luis. 1996. *Poverty, Inequality, and Human Capital Development in Latin America, 1950–2025.* Washington, D.C.: World Bank.

López, Ramón, and Sebastian J. Miller. 2008. "Chile: The Unbearable Burden of Inequality." *World Development* 36 (12): 2669–95.

López Leyva, Miguel Armando. 2009. "La influencia de los movimientos sociales en la definición de políticas públicas: La(s) marcha(s) contra la inseguridad pública." Paper presented at the Vigésimo Séptimo Congreso de la Asociación Latinoamericana de Sociología, Buenos Aires.

Loveman, Brian. 1979. *Chile.* New York: Oxford University Press.

Luizaga, Jorge Miranda. 2004. "El desarrollo social y económico de los municipios frente a la problemática territorial y limítrofe en Bolivia." In ILDIS 2004, 1:403–36.

Luján Veneros, María del Rosario. 2004. "Governabilidad municipal: Análisis de la aplicación del voto constructivo de censura." In ILDIS 2004, 2:145–85.

Lynch, John. 1984. "The Origins of Spanish American Independence." In *From Independence to c. 1870*. Vol. 3 of *The Cambridge History of Latin America*, edited by Leslie Bethell, 3–50. Cambridge: Cambridge University Press.

———. 1992. *Caudillos in Spanish America, 1800–1850*. Oxford: Clarendon Press.

Mahoney, James. 2001. "Path-Dependent Explanations of Regime Change: Central America in Comparative Perspective." *Studies in Comparative International Development* 36 (1): 111–41.

Maier, Charles S., ed. 1987. *Changing Boundaries of the Political: Essays on the Evolving Balance Between the State and Society, Public and Private in Europe*. Cambridge: Cambridge University Press.

Mainwaring, Scott, and Timothy Skully, eds. 1995. *Building Democratic Institutions: Party Systems in Latin America*. Stanford: Stanford University Press.

Malloy, James. 1968. "Revolution and Development in Bolivia." In *Constructive Change in Latin America*, edited by Cole Balsier, 177–232. Pittsburgh: University of Pittsburgh Press.

Maloney, William F. 2009. "Mexican Labor Markets: Protection, Productivity and Power." In Levy and Walton 2009b, 245–81.

Mann, Michael. 1996. "Ruling Class Strategies and Citizenship." In *Citizenship Today: The Contemporary Relevance of T. H. Marshall*, edited by Martin Bulmer and Anthony M. Rees, 125–44. London: UCL Press.

Marshall, T. H. 1950. *Citizenship and Social Class and Other Essays*. Cambridge: Cambridge University Press.

Martínez, Javier, and Alvaro Díaz. 1996. *Chile: The Great Transformation*. Washington, D.C.: Brookings Institution / Research Institute for Social Development, United Nations.

Martínez Sánchez, Tomás 2009. "Movimientos sociales y seguridad nacional." In *Atlas de la seguridad y la defensa de México, 2009*, edited by Raúl Benítez Manaut, Abelardo Rodríguez Sumano, and Armando Rodríguez Luna, 150–53. Mexico City: Colectivo de Análisis de la Seguridad con Democracia.

Maydana, Raúl. 2004. "El comité de vigilancia y la participación y control social en el modelo municipalista de descentralización del estado boliviano." In ILDIS 2004, 2:186–246.

Mayer-Serra, Carlos Elizondo. 2009. "Perverse Equilibria: Unsuitable but Durable Institutions." In Levy and Walton 2009b, 157–99.

Mayorga, René Antonio. 1997. "Bolivia's Silent Revolution." *Journal of Democracy* 8 (January): 142–56.

McSherry, Patrice J. 1998. "The Emergence of Guardian Democracy." *NACLA Report on the Americas* 32 (November/December): 16–24.

Mejía, Fabrizio. 2004. "La marcha del día después." *Revista Proceso*, July 4, 24–27.

Melucci, Alberto. 1985. "The Symbolic Challenge of Contemporary Movements." *Social Research* 52 (4): 789–816.

———. 1989. *Nomads of the Present: Social Movements and Individual Needs in Contemporary Society*. Edited by John Keane and Paul Mier. Philadelphia: Temple University Press.

Méndez, Juan E. 1999a. "Institutional Reform Including Access to Justice: Introduction." In Méndez, O'Donnell, and Pinheiro 1999, 221–26.

———. 1999b. "The Problems of Lawless Violence: Introduction." In Méndez, O'Donnell, and Pinheiro 1999, 19–24. Notre Dame: University of Notre Dame.

Méndez, Juan E., Guillermo O'Donnell, and Paulo Sérgio Pinheiro, eds. 1999. *The (Un)Rule of Law and the Underprivileged in Latin America*. Notre Dame: University of Notre Dame.

Méndez de Hoyas, Irma. 2006. *Transición a la democracia en México: Competencia partidista y reformas electorales, 1977–2003*. Mexico City: Facultad Latinoamericana de Ciencias Sociales, Sede Académica de México.

Mendoza, Nelson. 2004. "El ordenamiento territorial: Política para profundizar la descentralización departamental y municipal." In ILDIS 2004, 1:367–401.

Mesa-Lago, Carmelo. 1978. *Social Security in Latin America: Pressure Groups, Stratification, and Inequality*. Pittsburgh: University of Pittsburgh Press.

Middlebrook, Kevin J. 1995. *The Paradox of Revolution: Labor, the State, and Authoritarianism in Mexico*. Baltimore: John Hopkins University Press.

Middlebrook, Kevin J., and Eduardo Zepeda, eds. 2003a. *Confronting Development: Assessing Mexico's Economic and Social Policy*. Stanford: Standford University Press.

———. 2003b. "The Political Economy of Mexican Development Policy." In Middlebrook and Zepeda 2003a, 3–52.

Migdal, Joel S. 1994. "The State in Society: An Approach to Struggles for Domination." In Migdal, Kohli, and Shue 1994, 7–35.

Migdal, Joel S., Atul Kholi, and Vivienne Shue, eds. 1994. *State Power and Social Forces: Domination and Transformation in the Third World*. Cambridge: Cambridge University Press.

Molina Saucedo, Carlos Hugo. 1997. "Justificación de motivos." In Secretaría Nacional 1997, 33–36.

———. 1999. "Relatorio: Entrevista con Carlos Hugo Molina, Taller de Expertos: Municipios y cultura institucional democrática." Unpublished paper. La Paz: Programa de las Naciones Unidas para el Desarrollo.

Montambeault, Françoise. 2009. "Models of (Un)changing State-Society Relationships: Urban Participatory Governance and the Deepening of Democracy in Mexico and Brazil." Ph.D. diss., McGill University, Montreal.

Moore, Barrington. 1966. *The Social Origins of Dictatorship and Democracy*. Boston: Beacon Press.

Moreno-Brid, Juan Carlos. 2009. "La economía mexicana frente a la crisis internacional." *Nueva Sociedad* 220:60–83.

Morley, Samuel A. 2000. "The Effects of Growth and Economic Reform on Income Distribution in Latin America." *CEPAL Review* 71:23–40.

———. 2003. "Distribution and Growth in Latin America in an Era of Structural Reform: The Impact of Globalisation." In *Globalisation, Poverty, and Inequality*, edited by Richard Kohl, 63–69. Paris: Development Centre of the Organisation for Economic Co-operation and Development.

Morley, Samuel A., Roberto Machado, and Stefano Pettinato. 1999. *Indexes of Structural Reform in Latin America*. Serie reformas económicas 12. Santiago: Economic Development Division, Economic Commission for Latin America and the Caribbean, United Nations.

Morrison, Andrew, Mayra Buvinic, and Michael Shifter. 2003. "The Violent Americas: Risk Factors, Consequences, and Policy Implications of Social and Domestic Violence." In Frühling, Tulchin, and Golding 2003, 93–122.

Mostajo, Rossana. 2000. *Gasto social y distribución del ingreso: Caracterización e impacto redistributivo en países seleccionados de América Latina y el Caribe*. Serie reformas económicas 69. Santiago: Comisión Económica para América Latina y el Caribe, Naciones Unidas.

MUCD (México Unido Contra la Delincuencia). 2010. Incidencia delictiva nacional (1997–2009). http://mucd.org.mx/assets/files/NACIONAL%20%20040310.pdf. Accessed January 19, 2011.

Muñoz Armenta, Aldo. 2006. "Control sindical y gobernabilidad: Paradojas de la democracia mexicana." In *Democratización y tensiones de gobernabilidad en América Latina*, edited by Darío Salinas Figueredo, 325–39. Mexico City: Friedrich Ebert Stiftung / Gernika.

Muñoz Goma, Oscar. 2007. *El modelo económico de la Concertación 1990–2005: ¿Reformas o cambio?* Santiago: Facultad Latinoamericana de Ciencias Sociales–Chile.

Murillo, Maria Victoria. 1997. "Union Politics, Market-Oriented Reforms, and the Reshaping of Argentine Corporatism." In *The New Politics of Inequality in Latin America: Rethinking Participation and Representation*, edited by Douglas A. Chalmers, Carlos M. Vilas, Katherine Hite, Scott B. Martin, Kerianne Piester, and Monique Segarra, 72–94. Oxford: Oxford University Press.

———. 2003. "Latin American Labor." In Domínguez and Schifter 2003, 100–17.

Nandy, Ashis. 1997. " A Critique of Modernist Secularism." In *Politics in India*, edited by Sudipta Kaviraj, 329–41. Delhi: Oxford University Press.

Navarro, Marysa. 1989. "The Personal Is Political: Las Madres de la Plaza de Mayo." In Eckstein 1989, 241–58.

Navia, Patricio. 2010. "Living in Actually Existing Democracies: Chile; Democracy to the Extent Possible." Special Issue, *Latin American Research Review* 45:298–328.

Neild, Rachel. 1999. *From National Security to Citizen Security: Civil Society and the Evolution of Public Order Debates.* Montreal: International Centre for Human Rights and Democratic Development.

Nelson, Joan M. 2004. "The Politics of Education Reform: Cross-National Comparisons." In *Crucial Needs, Weak Incentives: Social Sector Reform, Democratization, and Globalization in Latin America,* edited by Robert R. Kaufman and Joan M. Nelson, 23–64. Washington, D.C.: Woodrow Wilson Center Press.

Nuñez, Javier, and Cristina Risco. 2004. "Movilidad intergeneracional del ingreso en un país en desarrollo: El caso de Chile." Working paper, Departamento de Economía, Universidad de Chile, Santiago.

O'Donnell, Guillermo. 1979a. *Modernization and Bureaucratic Authoritarianism.* Berkeley and Los Angeles: University of California Press.

———. 1979b. "Tensions in the Bureaucratic Authoritarian State and the Question of Democracy." In Collier 1979, 285–318.

———. 1988. "State and Alliances in Argentina, 1956–1976." In *Toward a Political Economy of Development: A Rational Choice Perspective,* edited by Robert H. Bates, 176–205. Berkeley and Los Angeles: University of California Press.

———. 1994. "Delegative Democracy." *Journal of Democracy* 5 (1): 56–69.

———. 1998. "Poverty and Inequality in Latin America: Some Political Reflections." In *Poverty and Inequality in Latin America: Issues and New Challenges,* edited by Victor E. Tokman and Guillermo O'Donnell, 49–71. Notre Dame: University of Notre Dame Press.

O'Donnell, Guillermo, and Philippe C. Schmitter. 1986. *Transitions from Authoritarian Rule: Tentative Conclusions About Uncertain Democracies.* Baltimore: Johns Hopkins University Press.

OECD (Organisation for Economic Co-operation and Development). 2009. *OECD Reviews of Labour Market and Social Policies: Chile.* Paris: Organisation for Economic Co-operation and Development.

Offe, Claus. 1984. *Contradictions of the Welfare State.* Cambridge: MIT Press.

———. 1987. "Challenging the Boundaries of Institutional Politics: Social Movements Since the 1960s." In Maier 1987, 63–106.

Olivera, Mercedes. 2006. "Violence Against Women and Mexico's Structural Crisis." *Latin American Perspectives* 33 (2): 104–14.

Olvera, Alberto J. 2003a. Introducción. In Olvera 2003b, 13–41.

———. 2003b. "Movimientos sociales prodemocráticos, democratización, y esfera pública en México: El caso de Alianza Cívica." In Olvera 2003b, 351–409.

———, ed. 2003c. *Sociedad civil, esfera, y pública democratización en América Latina: México.* Veracruz: Universidad Veracruzana; Mexico City: Fondo de Cultura Económica.

———. 2003d. "Las tendencias generales de desarrollo de la sociedad civil en México." In Olvera 2003b, 42–70.

———. 2010. "The Elusive Democracy: Political Parties, Democratic Institutions, and Civil Society in Mexico." Special Issue, *Latin American Research Review* 45:79–107.

Oportunidades. 2008. *Oportunidades: A Program of Results.* Edited by Oportunidades. Mexico City: Oportundades Press and Media Office.

Organización Internacional del Trabajo. 1993. *El trabajo en el mundo.* Geneva: Organización Internacional del Trabajo.

———. 1996. *La situación sociolaboral en las zonas francas y empresas maquiladoras del istmo centroamericano y República Dominicana.* San José, Costa Rica: Organización Internacional del Trabajo.

Ortega, Eugenio. 2006. "Chile: La brecha entre sociedad y representación politica; Algunas hipótesis." *Boletín de la Revista Latinoamericana de Desarrollo Humano* 24:1–9.

Oszlak, Oscar. 1981. "The Historical Formation of the State in Latin America: Some Theoretical and Methodological Guidelines for Its Study." *Latin American Research Review* 16 (2): 3–32.

Oxhorn, Philip. 1995a. "From Controlled Inclusion to Coerced Marginalization: The Struggle for Civil Society in Latin America." In *Civil Society: Theory, History, and Comparison,* edited by John Hall, 250–77. Cambridge: Polity Press.

———. 1995b. *Organizing Civil Society: The Popular Sectors and the Struggle for Democracy in Chile.* University Park: Pennsylvania State University Press.

———. 1998a. "Is the Century of Corporatism Over? Neoliberalism and the Rise of Neopluralism." In Oxhorn and Ducatenzeiler 1998, 195–217.

———. 1998b. "The Social Foundations of Latin America's Recurrent Populism: Problems of Class Formation and Collective Action." *Journal of Historical Sociology* 11 (June): 212–46.

———. 1999. "The Ambiguous Link: Social Movements and Democracy in Latin America." *Journal of Interamerican Studies and World Affairs* 41 (Fall): 129–46.

———. 2006. "Conceptualizing Civil Society from the Bottom Up: A Political Economy Perspective." In Feinberg, Waisman, and Zamosc, 59–84.

———. 2003. "Social Inequality, Civil Society, and the Limits of Citizenship in Latin America." In Eckstein and Wickham-Crowley 2003, 35–63.

Oxhorn, Philip, and Graciela Ducatenzeiler, eds. 1998. *What Kind of Democracy? What Kind of Market? Latin America in the Age of Neoliberalism.* University Park: Pennsylvania State University Press.

———. 1999. "The Problematic Relationship Between Economic and Political Liberalization: Some Theoretical Considerations." In Oxhorn and Starr 1999, 13–41.

Oxhorn, Philip, and Pamela K. Starr, eds. 1999. *Markets and Democracy in Latin America: Conflict or Convergence?* Boulder: Lynne Rienner.

Paige, Jeffrey M. 1997. *Coffee and Power: Revolution and the Rise of Democracy in Central America.* Cambridge: Harvard University Press.

Paley, Julia. 2001. *Marketing Democracy: Power and Social Movements in Post-dictatorship Chile.* Berkeley and Los Angeles: University of California Press.

Panfichi, Aldo, ed. 2002. *Sociedad civil, gobernabilidad, y democratización en América Latina: Andes y Cono Sur.* Mexico City: Fondo de Cultura Económica.

Peeler, John A. 2003. "Social Justice and the New Indigenous Politics: An Analysis of Guatemala, the Central Andes and Chiapas." In Eckstein and Wickham-Crowley 2003, 257–84.

Piester, Kerianne. 1997. "Targeting the Poor: The Politics of Social Policy Reform in Mexico." In *The New Politics of Inequality in Latin America: Rethinking Participation and Representation,* edited by Douglas A. Chalmers, Carlos M. Vilas, Katherine Hite, Scott B. Martin, Kerianne Piester, and Monique Segarra, 469–88. Oxford: Oxford University Press.

Pinheiro, Paulo Sérgio. 1999. "The Rule of Law and the Underprivileged in Latin America: Introduction." In Méndez, O'Donnell, and Pinheiro 1999, 1–15.

Pinto, Aníbal. 1970. "Desarrollo económico y relaciones sociales." In *Chile, hoy,* edited by Aníbal Pinto, 5–52. Mexico City: Siglo Veintiuno.

PNUD (Programa de las Naciones Unidas para el Desarrollo). 1998. *Desarrollo humano en Bolivia, 1998.* La Paz: Programa de las Naciones Unidas para el Desarrollo.

———. 1999. "Relatorio: Taller de Expertos; Municipios y cultura institucional democrática." Unpublished paper. La Paz: Programa de las Naciones Unidas para el Desarrollo.

———. 2004. *Democracia en América Latina: Hace una democracia de ciudadanas y ciudadanos.* New York: Programa de las Naciones Unidas para el Desarrollo.

PNUD-Chile (Programa de las Naciones Unidas para el Desarrollo–Chile). 1998. *Desarrollo humano en Chile: Las pardojas de la modernización.* Santiago: Programa de las Naciones Unidas para el Desarrollo–Chile.

Polanyi, Karl. 1944. *The Great Transformation: The Political and Economic Origins of Our Time.* New York: Farrar and Rinehart.

"Política y politiquería." 1996. *Proceso* 15 (March 27): 6–7.

Porcel, Abdón, and Laurent Thévoz. 1998. "Asignación, ejecución, y rendición de cuentas del POA municipal." In Unidad de Investigación y Análisis 1998b, 92–131.

Portes, Alejandro. 1985. "Latin American Class Structures: Their Composition and Change During the Last Decades." *Latin American Research Review* 20 (3): 7–39.

———. 1994. "By-passing the Rules: The Dialectics of Labour Standards and Informalization in Less Developed Countries." In *International Labour Standards and Economic Interdependence,* edited by Werner Sengenberger and Duncan C. Campbell, 159–76. Geneva: International Institute for Labour Studies.

Portes, Alejandro, and Kelly Hoffman. 2003. "Latin American Class Structures: Their Composition and Change During the Neoliberal Era." *Latin American Research Review* 38 (1): 41–82.

Posner, Paul. 1999. "Popular Representation and Political Dissatisfaction in Chile's New Democracy." *Journal of Interamerican Studies and World Affairs* 41 (Spring): 59–85.

———. 2004. "Local Democracy and the Transformation of Popular Participation in Chile." *Latin American Politics and Society* 46 (3): 55–81.

Power, Timothy. 2010. "Brazilian Democracy as a Late Bloomer: Reevaluating the Regime in the Cardoso-Lula Era." Special Issue, *Latin American Research Review* 45:218–27.

Przeworski, Adam. 1985. *Capitalism and Social Democracy.* Cambridge: Cambridge University Press / Editions de la Maison des Sciences de l'Homme.

———. 1986. "Some Problems in the Study of the Transition to Democracy." In O'Donnell, Schmitter, and Whitehead 1986, 47–63.

Psacharopoulos, George, Samuel A. Morley, Ariel Fiszbein, Haeduck Lee, and Bill Wood. 1997. "Poverty and Income Distribution in Latin America: The Story of the 1980s." *World Bank Technical Paper.* Washington, D.C.: World Bank.

Putnam, Robert. 1993. *Making Democracy Work: Civic Traditions in Modern Italy.* Princeton: Princeton University Press.

Ramírez Sáiz, Juan-Manuel. 1997. "Contribuciones democráticas de la 'Alianza Cívica.'" In *El debate nacional, IV: Nuevos actores sociales,* edited by Juan-Manuel Ramírez Sáiz and Jorge Regalado Santillán, 341–64. Mexico City: Centro Universitario de Ciencias Sociales y Humanidades, Universidad de Guadalajara/Diana.

———. 2002. "Contribuciones de las organizaciones cívicas al cambio político." In *La sociedad civil ante la transición democrática,* edited by Lucía Álvarez, 105–24. Mexico City: Plaza y Valdés.

Rayelo, Ricardo 2004. "Ya había un diagnóstico criminal . . . y Fox lo guardó." *Revista Proceso,* July 4, 18–23.

Rea Rodríguez, Carlos R. 2001. "¿Historicidad sin movimientos sociales? Reflexión introductoria a partir de las experiencias Alianza Cívica y el Baronismo." *Espiral* 21:161–200.

Reinecke, Gerhard, and Jacobo Velasco. 2006. *Chile: Informe de empleo para el año 2005.* Santiago: Oficina Internacional del Trabajo.

Rendón, Armando 2008. "El poder popular y la Asamblea Popular de los Pueblos de Oaxaca." *Polis* 4 (1): 39–70.

Roberts, Bryan R. 1981. *Cities of Peasants: The Political Economy of Urbanization in the Third World.* London: Arnold.

———. 2005. "Citizenship, Rights, and Social Policy." In Wood and Roberts 2005b, 137–58.

Roberts, Bryan R., and Alejandro Portes. 2006. "Coping with the Free Market City: Collective Action in Six Latin American Cities at the End of the Twentieth Century." *Latin American Research Review* 41 (2): 57–83.

Roberts, Bryan R., and Charles H. Wood. 2005a. "Introduction: Rethinking Development in Latin America." In Wood and Roberts 2005b, 1–23.

———, eds. 2005b. *Rethinking Development in Latin America*. University Park: Pennsylvania State University Press.

Roberts, Kenneth M. 1994. "Neoliberalism and the Transformation of Populism in Latin America: The Peruvian Case." Paper presented at the Annual Meeting of the American Political Science Association, New York, September.

———. 1995. "Neoliberalism and the Transformation of Populism in Latin America: The Peruvian Case." *World Politics* 48 (October): 82–116.

———. 1998. *Deepening Democracy? The Modern Left and Social Movements in Chile and Peru*. Stanford: Stanford University Press.

———. 2002. "Social Inequalities Without Class Cleavages in Latin America's Neoliberal Era." *Studies in Comparative International Development* 36 (4): 3–33.

Robinson, James A. 2003. "Where Does Inequality Come From? Ideas and Implications for Latin America." In *Globalisation, Poverty, and Inequality*, edited by Richard Kohl, 69–75. Paris: Development Centre of the Organisation for Economic Co-operation and Development.

Roca, Mónica. 2004. "Manejo económico municipal y relaciones de daño económico entre municipios." In ILDIS 2004, 1:149–78.

Rojas Ortuste, Gonzalo. 1998. *Censura constructiva, inestabilidad, y democracia municipal*. La Paz: Instituto Latinoamericano de Investigaciones Sociales de la Fundación Friedrich Ebert Stiftung.

Rojas Ortuste, Gonzalo, and Laurent Thévoz. 1998. "Presentación general." In Unidad de Investigación y Análisis 1998b, 11–23.

Roman, Richard, and Edur Velasco Arregui. 2006. "The State, the Bourgeoisie, and the Unions: The Recycling of Mexico's System of Labor Control." *Latin American Perspectives* 33 (2): 95–103.

Rubin, Jeffrey W. 1997. *Decentering the Regime: Ethnicity, Radicalism, and Democracy in Juchitàn, Mexico*. Durham: Duke University Press.

Rueschemeyer, Dietrich, Evelyne Stephens, and John D. Stephens. 1992. *Capitalist Development and Democracy*. Chicago: University of Chicago Press.

Ruiz Tagle, Jaime. 1985. *El sindicalismo chileno después del Plan Laboral*. Santiago: Programa de Economía del Trabajo.

Rustow, Dankwart A. 1970. "Transitions to Democracy: Toward a Dynamic Model." *Comparative Politics* 2 (April): 337–63.

Safford, Frank. 1987. "Politics, Ideology, and Society." In *Spanish America After Independence, c. 1820–1870*, edited by Leslie Bethell, 347–422. Cambridge: Cambridge University Press.

Salas, Carlos, and Eduardo Zepeda. 2003. "Employment and Wages: Enduring the Costs of Liberalization and Economic Reform." In Middlebrook and Zepeda 2003a, 522–58.

Salinero B., Jorge. 2006. *Veinte años de afiliación sindical y negociación colectiva en Chile: Problemas y Desafíos*. In Cuaderno de investigación 29. Santiago: Departamento de Estudios Dirección del Trabajo, Gobierno de Chile.

Sánchez de Lozada, Gonzalo. 1997. "Bolivia debe cambiar." In Secretaría Nacional 1997, 19–20.

Schedler, Andreas. 2000. "Mexico's Victory: The Democratic Revelation." *Journal of Democracy* 11 (4): 5–19.

Schmitter, Philippe. 1974. "Still the Century of Corporatism?" *Review of Politics* 36 (January): 85–131.

———. 1986. "An Introduction to Southern European Transitions from Authoritarian Rule: Italy, Greece, Portugal, Spain, and Turkey." In *Transitions from Authoritarian Rule: Southern Europe*, edited by Guillermo O'Donnell, Philippe Schmitter, and Laurence Whitehead, 3–10. Baltimore: Johns Hopkins University Press.

Schöpflin, George. 1990. "The Political Traditions of Eastern Europe." *Daedalus* 119 (Winter): 55–90.

Schteingart, Martha. 2000. "Las políticas sociales para los pobres: El caso de Progresa." In *Los dilemas de la política social: ¿Cómo combatir la pobreza?*, edited by Enrique Valencia

Lomelí, Mónica Gendreau, and Ana María Tepichín, 187–203. Mexico City: Universidad de Guadalajara/Instituto Tecnológico y de Estudios Superiores de Occidente/Universidad Iberoamericano.

Scully, Timothy. 1992. *Rethinking the Center: Party Politics in Nineteenth- and Twentieth-Century Chile.* Stanford: Stanford University Press.

Secretaría Nacional de Participación Popular. 1997. *El pulso de la democracia: Participación ciudadana y descentralización en Bolivia.* La Paz: Ministerio de Desarrollo Humano / Secretaría Nacional de Participación Popular/Nueva Sociedad.

Segovia, Carolina. 2009. "¿Crisis de la política en Chile? Percepciones y valoraciones sobre los partidos." In *La sociedad de la opinión: Reflexiones sobre encuestas y cambio político en democracia,* edited by Rodrigo Cordero, 197–224. Santiago: Portales.

Seligman, Adam. 1992. *The Idea of Civil Society.* New York: Free Press.

Seligson, Mitchell A. 1998. *The Political Culture of Democracy in Bolivia: 1998.* Mimeo draft. La Paz: U.S. Agency for International Development.

Sheahan, John. 2002. "Alternative Models of Capitalism in Latin America." In Huber 2002b, 25–52.

Shefner, Jon. 2008. *The Illusion of Civil Society: Democratization and Community Mobilization in Low-Income Mexico.* University Park: Pennsylvania State University Press.

Shils, Edward. 1991. "The Virtue of Civil Society." *Government and Opposition* 26 (Winter): 3–20.

Shirk, David A., and Alejandra Ríos Cázares. 2007. "Introduction: Reforming the Administration of Justice in Mexico." In *Reforming the Administration of Justice in Mexico,* edited by Wayne A. Cornelius and David A. Shirk, 1–47. Notre Dame: University of Notre Dame Press.

Siavelis, Peter. 2000. *The President and Congress in Postauthoritarian Chile.* University Park: Pennsylvania State University Press.

Skidmore, Thomas, and Peter Smith. 2005. *Modern Latin America.* 6th ed. New York: Oxford University Press.

Skocpol, Theda. 1973. "A Critical Review of Barrington Moore's Social Origins." *Politics and Society* 4 (Fall): 1–34.

———. 1985. "Bringing the State Back In: Strategies of Analysis in Current Research." In *Bringing the State Back In,* edited by Peter Evans, Dietrich Rueschemeyer and Theda Skocpol, 3–37. Cambridge: Cambridge University Press.

———. 1996. "Unravelling from Above." *American Prospect* 25:20–25.

Smith, William C., and Roberto Patricio Korzeniewsicz. 1997. "Latin America and the Second Great Transformation." In *Politics, Social Change, and Economic Restructuring in Latin America,* edited by William C. Smith and Roberto Patricio Korzeniewsicz, 1–20. Coral Gables: North-South Center Press, University of Miami.

Smulovitz, Catalina, and Enrique Peruzotti. 2000. "Societal Accountability in Latin America." *Journal of Democracy* 11 (4): 147–58.

Somers, Margret. 1993. "Citizenship and the Place of the Public Sphere: Law, Community, and Political Culture in the Transition to Democracy." *American Sociological Review* 58 (October): 587–620.

Sorroza, Carlos. 2008. "La crisis política de Oaxaca: Componentes, alcances, y propuesta de salida." *Cotidiano* 23 (148): 21–36.

Spalding, Hobart. 1977. *Organized Labor in Latin America: Historical Case Studies of Workers in Dependent Societies.* New York: New York University Press.

Stallings, Barbara. 1978. *Class Conflict and Economic Development in Chile, 1958–1973.* Stanford: Stanford University Press.

Stallings, Barbara, and Wilson Peres. 2000. *Growth, Employment, and Equity: The Impact of the Economic Reforms in Latin American and the Caribbean.* Washington, D.C.: Economic Commission for Latin America and the Caribbean, United Nations / Brookings Institution Press.

Task Force on Education, Equity, and Economic Competitiveness in the Americas. 2001. *Lagging Behind: A Report Card on Education in Latin America*. Washington, D.C.: Partnership for Educational Revitalization in the Americas.

Taylor, Charles. 1990. "Invoking Civil Society." Working Paper 31, Center for Psychosocial Studies, Chicago.

———. 1998. "The Dynamics of Democratic Exclusion." *Journal of Democracy* 9 (October): 143–56.

Taylor, Marcus. 2006. *From Pinochet to the "Third Way": Neoliberalism and Social Transformation in Chile*. London: Pluto Press.

Teichman, Judith. 2008. "Redistributive Conflict and Social Policy in Latin America." *World Development* 36 (3): 446–60.

Tello Peón, Jorge. 2009. "La seguridad pública en México: Síntesis social." In *Atlas de la seguridad y la defensa de México, 2009*, edited by Raúl Benítez Manaut, Abelardo Rodríguez Sumano, and Armando Rodríguez Luna, 21–24. Mexico City: Colectivo de Análisis de la Seguridad con Democracia.

Thévoz, Laurent, and Ernesto Velasco. 1998. "La dinámica de los procesos municipales de implementación de la LPP." In Unidad de Investigación y Análisis 1998b, 203–22.

Thorp, Rosemary. 1998. *Progress, Poverty, and Exclusion: An Economic History of Latin America in the Twentieth Century*. Washington, D.C.: Inter-American Development Bank.

Tilly, Charles. 1981. *As Sociology Meets History*. New York: Academic Press.

———. 1996. "Citizenship, Identity and Social History." In *Citizenship, Identity, and Social History*, edited by Charles Tilly, 1–18. Cambridge: University of Cambridge.

———. 1998. *Durable Inequality*. Berkeley and Los Angeles: University of California Press.

Tocqueville, Alexis de. 1969. *Democracy in America*. Edited by J. P. Mayer. Garden City, N.Y.: Anchor Books.

Tokman, Víctor. 2002. "Jobs and Solidarity: Challenges for Labor Market Policy in Latin America." In Huber 2002b, 159–94.

Toranzo Gutiérrez, Julia Gabriela. 2004. "Los recursos de la iniciativa HIPC para la reducción de la pobreza." In ILDIS 2004, 2:347–62.

Transparency International. 2010. Corruption Perceptions Index. Accessed December 10. http://www.transparency.org/policy_research/surveys_indices/cpi/2010/results.

Tulchin, Joseph S., and Graig Fagan. 2003. "Introducción: Perfil actual de la seguridad ciudadana e impacto en la gobernabilidad democrática; Aportes desde Latinoamérica." In *Entre el crimen y el castigo: Seguridad ciudadana y control democrático en América Latina y el Caribe*, edited by Lilian Bobea, 13–29. Caracas: Facultad Latinoamericana de Ciencias Sociales–República Dominicana/Woodrow Wilson Internacional Center for Scholars / Nueva Sociedad.

Turner, Bryan. 1992. "Outline of a Theory of Citizenship." In *Dimensions of Radical Democracy: Pluralism, Citizenship, Community*, edited by Chantal Mouffe, 33–63. London: Verso.

UIA (Unidad de Investigación y Análisis). 1998a. *Participación popular: Una evaluación-aprendizaje de la ley, 1994–1997*. La Paz: Viceministerio de Participación Popular y Fortalecimiento Municipal, Ministerio de Desarrollo Sostenible y Planificación.

———. 1998b. "El proceso social de introducción de demandas." In Unidad de Investigación y Análisis 1998b, 69–91.

———. 1999. *Lectura de los datos del voto constructivo de censura*. La Paz: Viceministerio de Participación Popular y Fortalecimiento Municipal, Ministerio de Desarrollo Sostenible y Planificación.

UNDP (United Nations Development Program). 1999. *Human Development Report*. New York: Cambridge University Press.

———. 2004. *Human Development Report 2004: Cultural Liberty in Today's Diverse World*. New York: United Nations Development Program.

———. 2010. *Human Development Report 2010: The Real Wealth of Nations; Pathways to Human Development*. New York: United Nations Development Program.

Valdés, Teresa. 2010. "El Chile de Michelle Bachelet ¿Género en el poder?" Special Issue, *Latin American Research Review* 45:248–73.

Valenzuela, Arturo. 1977. *Political Brokers in Chile: Local Government in a Centralized Polity*. Durham: Duke University Press.

———. 1978. *The Breakdown of Democratic Regimes: Chile*. Baltimore: Johns Hopkins University Press.

———. 1999. "Chile: Origins and Consolidation of Latin American Democracy." In *Democracy in Developing Countries: Latin America*, edited by Larry Diamond, Jonathan Hartlyn, Juan José Linz, and Seymour Martin Lipset, 191–247. Boulder: Lynne Rienner.

Van Cott, Donna. 2000. *The Friendly Liquidation of the Past: The Politics of Diversity in Latin America*. Pittsburgh: University of Pittsburgh Press.

Vargas, Humberto. 1998. *Los municipios en Bolivia: Son evidentes los avances con participación popular*. Cochabamba, Bolivia: Centro de Estudios de la Realidad Económica y Social.

Velasco, José Luis. n.d. "Carencias sociales y fragilidad política: Las movilizaciones populares." In *Documentos de Trabajo*. Mexico City: Facultad Latinoamericana de Ciencias Sociales.

Véliz, Claudio. 1980. *The Centralist Tradition of Latin America*. Princeton: Princeton University Press.

Veras Soares, Fábio, Rafael Perez Ribas, and Rafael Guerreiro Osório. 2010. "Evaluating the Impact of Brazil's Bolsa Família: Cash Transfer Programmes in Comparative Perspective." *Latin American Research Review* 45 (2): 173–90.

Verdesoto, Luis. 2004. "¿Hacia dónde va Bolivia?" *Nueva Sociedad* 291:38–49.

Vilas, Carlos, and Steve Ellner. 1999. "The Decline of the Steady Job in Latin America." *NACLA Report on the Americas* 32 (January/February): 15–20.

Walby, Sylvia. 1994. "Is Citizenship Gendered?" *Sociology* 28 (May): 379–95.

Waltzer, Michael. 1992. "The Civil Society Argument." In *Dimensions of Radical Democracy: Pluralism, Citizenship, Community*, edited by Chantal Mouffe, 89–107. London: Verso.

———. 1999. "Rescuing Civil Society." *Dissent* (Winter): 62–67.

Wampler, Brian, and Leonardo Avritzer. 2004. "Participatory Publics: Civil Society and New Institutions in Democratic Brazil." *Comparative Politics* 36 (3): 291–312.

Waylen, Georgina. 1994. "Women and Democratization: Conceptualizing Gender Relations in Transition Politics." *World Politics* 46 (April): 327–54.

Weeks, John. 1999. "Wages, Employment and Workers' Rights in Latin America, 1970–98." *International Labour Review* 138 (2): 151–69.

Weyland, Kurt. 1997. "'Growth with Equity' in Chile's New Democracy?" *Latin American Research Review* 32 (1): 37–68.

———. 1999. "Neoliberal Populism in Latin America and Eastern Europe." *Comparative Politics* 31 (July): 379–401.

———. 2001. "Clarifying a Contested Concept: Populism and the Study of Latin American Politics." *Comparative Politics* 34 (1): 1–22.

Whitehead, Laurence. 2001. "Bolivia and the Viability of Democracy." *Journal of Democracy* 12 (2): 6–16.

Winn, Peter. 2000. "Lagos Defeats the Right by a Thread." *Nacla Report on the Americas* 33 (5): 6–10.

Woldenberg, José. 2009. "México de cara a las elecciones." *Nueva Sociedad* 220:97–111.

Womack, John, Jr. 1968. *Zapata and the Mexican Revolution*. New York: Knopf.

World Bank. 2006. *Decentralized Service Delivery for the Poor: Mexico*. Washington, D.C.: World Bank.

Wuhs, Steven T. 2008. *Savage Democracy: Institutional Change and Party Development in Mexico*. University Park: Pennsylvania State University Press.

Yashar, Deborah J. 1998. "Contesting Citizenship: Indigenous Movements and Democracy in Latin America." *Comparative Politics* 31 (October): 23–42.

———. 2005. *Contesting Citizenship in Latin America: The Rise of Indigenous Movements and the Postliberal Challenge*. New York: Cambridge University Press.

Zapata, Francisco. 1998. "Trade Unions and the Corporatist System in Mexico." In Oxhorn and
    Ducatenzeiler 1998, 151–67.
Zepeda Lecuona, Guillermo. 2007. "Criminal Investigation and the Subversion of the Principles
    of the Justice System in Mexico." In *Reforming the Administration of Justice in Mexico*,
    edited by Wayne A. Cornelius and David A. Shirk, 133–74. Notre Dame: University of
    Notre Dame Press.

index

Acción Democrática y Nacionalista, 147
Acuerdo Nacional para una Transición a la
    Democracia Plena, 106
Administrative Decentralization Law, 169,
    247n14
agency, 19, 21, 30
agency, citizenship as
    Bolivian mobilizations and, 184–85
    in Chile, 91
    controlled inclusion and, 49
    introduction to, 29–31
    in Mexico, 228–29
    and participatory budgeting in Porto
        Alegre, 234–36
    political democracy and, 230
    social construction of citizenship and, 45,
        48
    state and quest for, 236–38
Agenda Pro Participación Ciudadana, 124
agriculture
    commercialization of, 25–27
    decreased participation in, 35–36
Aguilar, Gloria, 168, 169–70
Alessandri, Arturo, 95–96, 98
Alessandri, Jorge, 96, 99, 100
Alianza Cívica, 213–15, 218–19, 249n24
Alianza Democrática, 105–6
Allard, Cristian Pizarro, 113–14
Allende, Salvador, 38, 96, 97, 99, 100–101
Altimir, Oscar, 60, 112
Ameller Terrazas, Vladimir, 180
Archondo, Rafael, 163, 166
Argentina
    controlled inclusion in, 46
    mobilization in, 2, 45
    poverty in, 66
Arica, Chile, 126–28
Asamblea para la Soberanía de los Pueblos,
    175–77

Asamblea Popular de los Pueblos de Oaxaca,
    225–28
Assale, Héctor, 86
Assembly for the Sovereignty of Indigenous
    Peoples, 175–77
authoritarian government, 26–27, 52–56, 75, 87,
    102–9, 119
Aylwin, Patricio, 108, 134
Ayo, Diego, 177, 180–81

Bachelet, Michelle, 109, 124
Bánzer, Hugo, 180, 246n10
Barbery, Roberto, 154
Base-Level Territorial Organizations (OTB),
    140–41, 150, 153–56, 162–66, 174
Bendix, Reinhard, 5
Bitar, Sergio, 122, 127, 128
Bizberg, Ilán, 196
Bocal, Ramiro, 162–63
Bolivia
    characteristics of, 89 (table)
    Comités de Vigilancia in, 170–73
    conclusions on LPP and, 178–85
    indigenous groups and, 174–78
    LPP limits and, 165–70
    LPP success in, 156–59
    mobilizations in, 1–2
    municipal governments in, 159–62
    1952 revolution in, 142–49, 158
    overview of, 88–90, 138–41, 150–56
    role of OTBs in, 162–65
Bolivian Workers Central (COB), 144–45, 149
Bolsa Família program, 65
Bonaparte, Napoleon, 32
boundaries, between private and public
    spheres, 19–20
bourgeoisie, informal petty, 38–39
Brachet-Márquez, Viviane, 200–201
Brazil, 234–37

Britain
    citizenship rights and, 23–27
    democratic transitions and, 55
Brockmann, Erika, 152
bureaucratic authoritarian regimes, 248n5
business participation, 126–28
Bustillo, Inés, 66

Calles, Plutarco Elías, 193
Cantador, Carlos, 125–26
capitalism, 23–27, 239n8
Cárdenas, Cuauhtémoc, 211–12, 214
Cárdenas, Lázaro, 191–92, 193
Cárdenas, Víctor Hugo, 150–51, 155
Cardoso, Fernando Enrique, 5
cash transfer programs, 65, 79
Castells, Manuel, 95
Catholic Church, 105, 183–84, 188, 190, 232–33
caudillos, 32–33, 93, 188, 190, 193
centralization, controlled inclusion and, 36–38
Central Obrera Boliviana (COB), 144–45, 149
CESCO (Consejo Económico-Social Comunal), 124, 125
Chaco War (1932), 143
Chapare, Bolivia, 175–77
Chávez, Hugo
    controlled inclusion and, 47
    institutional legitimacy and, 243n14
    mass media opposition and, 20
    mobilization and, 3, 4, 242n15
    resurgence of populism and, 85–86
Chile
    characteristics of, 89 (table)
    conclusions on, 136–37
    consolidated democracy in, 230
    elections in, 129–36, 245n23
    historical context of, 92–101
    military dictatorship and democratic
        transition in, 102–9
    neopluralist democracy in, 109–29
    overview of, 88–92
Chilean Human Development Report (1998),
    117
Chile Solidario, 125
Chile Solidarity, 125
Christian Democratic Party, 96–101, 105,
    122–23, 130
citizen insecurity, 68–74, 116–18, 123, 219–25
citizen participation, 123–26, 128–29, 231, 233,
    235–36. *See also* Popular Participation
    Law
Citizen Participation Project, 124
citizenship. *See also* agency, citizenship as; consumption, citizenship as; co-optation,
    citizenship as

democratic, 59–74
    economy and quality of, 87
    struggles, 25, 29–30, 31–34
citizenship rights. *See* rights of citizenship
Civic Alliance, 213–15, 218–19, 249n24
civic committees, 148–49, 154, 246n14
civil rights, 23–27, 49, 55, 73, 240n16. *See also*
    rights of citizenship
civil society
    citizenship rights and, 23–28
    collectivist perspective of, 9–15
    intellectual and normative concepts of, 6–7
    liberal perspective of, 7–9
    public sphere and, 15–20
    public sphere and social constructions of
        citizenship rights and, 22 (figure)
    relevance of, 230–38
    social construction of citizenship and,
        20–23
    theories of, 5–6
civil society movement, 16–17, 210–15
civil society organizations
    challenges to, 16–17
    in Chile, 104–6, 107
    class and, 240n23
    in Mexico, 212–15, 218–19
class
    citizenship rights and, 24
    civil society organizations and, 240n23
    controlled inclusion and, 38–41
    and education in Chile, 115
    Mexican revolution and, 190–93
    neopluralism and, 80–81
    participation and, 11–12
    populism and, 43–44
clientelism, 94, 142, 146, 194
Coca, Oscar, 149, 158
cocaleros, 175–76, 247n17
Cochabamba, Bolivia, 182–84
Cochabamba Civic Committee, 182, 183
coerced marginalization, 46–48, 51, 242n13
co-financing, 169
collective action, 36–37
collectivist perspective of civil society, 7, 9–15
Colombia, 47
colonialism, 31–32
Comité Cívica de Cochabamba, 182, 183
Comité Popular de Solidaridad y Reconstrucción, 197–98
comités cívicos, 148–49, 154, 246n14
Comités de Vigilancia, 141, 170–73, 247n30
Command for the No, 108, 245n15
communism, women's rights under, 27–28
Communist Party, 93, 245nn14,15
communist revolution, 26

Community Economic and Social Councils, 124, 125
Compromise State, 95–101
Concertación de los Partidos por la Democracia, 108, 109, 134, 136
Concertación por el No, 108, 245n15
Confederación de Trabajadores Mexicanos, 192–94, 199, 201, 202, 204
Confederación Nacional Campesina, 192–94
Confederation of Mexican Workers, 192–94, 199, 201, 202, 204
Consejo Económico-Social Comunal (CESCO), 124, 125
Consejos Consultivos de los Comités de Vigilancia, 247n30
consensus, societal, 12–13, 24, 29, 231
consolidated democracy, 230
constructive censure vote, 160, 161
consumption, citizenship as
    Chile's democratic transition and, 91–92, 103–4, 109–10
    effects of, 230
    in Mexico, 206–7, 209
    neopluralism and, 58
controlled inclusion
    in Chile, 95–101
    demise of, 45–48, 51
    education and, 67
    neopluralism and, 56, 57–58
    overview of, 34–43
    and revolution in Mexico, 189–98
    social construction of citizenship and, 49–50
    United States and, 242n12
co-optation, citizenship as
    in Bolivia, 142, 155–56
    in Chile, 96–97
    controlled inclusion and, 34, 49
    effects of, 228
    in Mexico, 206–7
    overview of, 30
    populism and, 44
    racism and, 178
Coordinadora Departamental del Agua y la Vida, 182
Coordinadora Única de Damnificados, 197–98
coparticipación, 150, 151, 153, 165–66
Copper Workers' Union protests, 105
Cordero, Gonzalo, 132–33
corporatism, 153–54, 196, 198–210, 216
Corque, Bolivia, 175
Corriente Democrática, 211
corruption, government
    in Bolivia, 147–48, 179
    citizen insecurity and, 72–73

Corruption Perceptions Index rankings, 88
    crisis of representation and, 79
Corruption Perceptions Index rankings, 88
Costa Rica, 46–47, 242n14
crime, 68–74, 116–18, 219–25, 233–34
criollo elite, 32–33
Cristeros Rebellion, 190, 191

Dagnino, Evelina, 83
Dammert, Lucía, 117
da Silva, Luís Inácio ("Lula"), 20
decentralization, 83–84, 90
de la Huerta, Adolfo, 190
de la Madrid, Miguel, 198
de la Rúa, Fernando, 2
demobilization, 53–54, 104–9
democracia de los acuerdos, 108–9, 122–23
democracy
    citizenship as agency and, 30–31
    civil society's role in, 9
    in Latin America, 230–31
    neopluralism and, 56–58
    popular mobilizations and, 4–5
    relevance of, 86–88
    resurgence of, 51–52
    support for and satisfaction with, 74–79, 119, 120–21 (table), 217, 218 (table)
democracy by agreements, 108–9, 122–23
Democratic Alliance, 105–6
democratic citizenship, 59–74
Democratic Current, 211
Democratic Labor Party, 234–35
Democratic Party, 93
democratic transition(s)
    in Chile, 102–9
    in Mexico, 186–87, 210–15
    social construction of citizenship and, 52–56
Departmental Coordinating Committee for Water and Life, 182
development, municipal, 167–70
Díaz, José de la Cruz Porfirio, 188–89
dictatorship, 26–27, 52–56, 75, 87, 102–9, 119
Dresser, Denise, 207

earthquake, 196–98
Eckstein, Susan, 145, 198
economic crisis, 51, 199–201
economy
    Chile's democratic transition and, 102–3
    citizenship quality and, 87
    citizenship rights and, 23–25
    civil society's relationship to, 11–12
    commercialization of agriculture, 25–27
    controlled inclusion and, 35–36, 38–41

economy (*continued*)
corporatism and transition of Mexican, 198–210
economic inequality, 59–66
economic insecurity, 59–66, 110–14, 123
growth in, 65–66
Mexico and world, 188–89
neopluralism and, 57, 80–85
popular mobilizations and, 4–5
reforms, 51–52
state-controlled resources and, 239n8
Ecuador, 2–3
education
citizen participation and, 128–29, 233
democratic attitudes and, 75–76
employment and, 111
by income in Chile, 117 (table)
Mexican economic transition and, 202–3
neopluralism and, 66–68, 82
privatized, in Chile, 114–16
Education Law Reform (2002), 202–3
Ejército Zapatista de Liberación Nacional, 213, 215, 249n26
ejido, 192, 199
El Alto, Bolivia, 184–85
elections
Chilean, 93, 96, 99–100, 129–36, 245n23
electoral reform, 213–15
Mexican democratic transition and, 210–15
political parties and, 20
popular mobilizations and, 4
populism and, 43–44
voter apathy in, 78
Ellner, Steve, 83
El Salvador, 71–72
Emergency Law Against Crime (1996), 71–72
employment. *See also* organized labor
Chile's democratic transition and, 103, 110–12
citizen insecurity and, 70
economic inequality and insecurity and, 59, 60–62
in Mexican manufacturing positions, 199–200
Mexican social protection and, 205
Escalante Gonzalbo, Fernando, 192
Estado de Compromiso, 95–101
Europe
citizenship rights and, 23–28
colonialism and, 31–32
democratic transitions and, 55
resistance to state subordination in, 10–11

Evans, Peter, 240nn12–13
extreme poverty, 138, 165–66, 178, 208–9, 243n6

Faletto, Enzo, 5
fascism, 26–27
Fondo de Control Social, 173
Fox, Vicente, 186, 228
Frei, Eduardo, 38, 96–100, 123
Fujimori, Alberto, 4, 20, 78, 85–86

Garretón, Manuel Antonio
on business participation, 126
on Chile's democratic transition, 101, 123
on Latin American politics, 86, 92
on new political style, 136–37
on welfare systems, 65
General Education Law, 128
geographic centralization, 36–38
Gil, Frederico, 96
Gonzalez Macchi, Luis, 3
government
authoritarian, 26–27, 52–56, 75, 87, 102–9, 119
citizen exclusion from, 77–80
civil society's relationship with, 232–34, 237–38
corruption, 72–73, 88, 147–48, 160, 179
municipal, 159–62
support for democratic, 74–79, 119, 120–21 (table), 217, 218 (table)
trust in, 77, 243nn14–15
Great Britain
citizenship rights and, 23–27
democratic transitions and, 55
Great Depression, 34, 35
"Great Transformation," 34
Guatemala, 78
Gutiérrez, Lucio, 2, 3, 4

Habermas, Jürgen, 15–16
Hamilton, Nora, 191
Hann, Chris, 8
Hapsburg, Maximilian von, 188
health care, 104
Heavily Indebted Poor Countries initiative, 168, 180–81
Henríquez, Helia, 111
Herrera, Alejandro, 133–34
HIPC (Heavily Indebted Poor Countries) initiative, 168, 180–81
Hoffman, Kelly, 63, 70
Huber, Evelyne, 64
Huerta, Adolfo de la, 190
human rights, 130–31

Ibáñez, Carlos, 96, 244n6
identity, national, 13
import substitution industrialization (ISI)
    model, 5, 35, 40, 99
inclusion, 10–11, 13, 15, 17, 40. *See also* controlled inclusion
income inequality, 61–65, 67, 103, 112–14
independence, struggle for, 31–34
Independencia, Bolivia, 176
indigenous groups
    in Bolivia, 138–40, 142
    constructive censure vote and, 161
    jurisdictional boundaries for, 157
    marginalization of, 246n3
    in Mexico, 188
    mobilization of, 242n4
    Popular Participation Law and, 174–78, 182
    property rights of, 34
individualism, 8–9, 83
industrialization, 12, 25–27, 35–36, 40–41, 42
inequality
    in Chile, 96–97, 103, 112–16
    citizenship rights and, 24
    controlled inclusion and, 37–39, 194
    crime and, 70
    economic, 59–66, 67
    foundations of, 31, 33–34
    neopluralism and, 80
    organized labor and, 43
    popular mobilizations and, 4–5
informal petty bourgeoisie, 38–39
informal proletariat, 38–39
insecurity
    citizen, 68–74, 116–18, 123, 219–25
    economic, 59–66, 110–14, 123
institutional legitimacy, 243n14
Institutional Revolutionary Party, 193–94, 198, 206–7, 210–12, 226
intellectual concept of civil society, 6–7
investment, productive, 165–68, 177
ISI (import substitution industrialization) model, 5, 35, 40, 99

Jefferson, Thomas, 13
Jiménez, Manuel, 245n17
job creation, 60, 103, 110, 179–80
Juárez, Benito, 188
juntas de vecinos, 124–25
jurisdictional boundaries, 157

Keane, John, 13, 18

labor codes, 61
labor insurgency (1970), 196

labor movement. *See* organized labor
Labraño, Moises, 245n18
Lagos, Marta, 75
Lagos, Ricardo
    Chile Solidario and, 125
    citizen participation and, 123, 124
    election of, 109, 246n26
    on inequality and insecurity, 4
    1999–2000 presidential election and, 129–30, 134–35
    on organized labor, 112
land reform
    in Bolivia, 139, 144–45, 149
    controlled inclusion and, 38
    in Mexico, 192, 199
Laserna, Roberto, 149, 182
Lavín, Joaquin, 130, 131–34, 135
Law for Social Defense (1996), 71–72
laws
    enforcement of, 71, 72–73, 74, 223–24, 243n15
    public sphere and, 18–19
Le Blanc, Luis, 127, 128
Lema, Ana Maria, 178
Levy, Santiago, 204, 208, 209, 217
Ley de Descentralización Administrativa, 169, 247n14
Ley de Diálogo Nacional, 167
Ley de Participación Popular (LPP). *See* Popular Participation Law
Ley de Partidos Políticos, 159
Ley General de Educación, 128
Ley Orgánica Constitucional de Enseñanza, 114, 128–29
liberal perspective of civil society, 7–9
Lockean perspective of civil society, 7–9
López Obrador, Andrés Manuel, 227, 228
"lost decade," 51, 56, 62, 200

Madrid, Miguel de la, 198
Mahoney, James, 46
Malloy, James, 145
Mann, Michael, 27
manufacturing, 36, 199–200
Marin, Gladys, 135
Marshall, T. H., 5, 23–25, 49, 55, 66, 153
Martínez, Arturo, 245n17
Marx, Karl, 12
mass media, 20, 23, 71
Maydana, Raúl, 171
Mayer-Serra, Carlos Elizondo, 229
media, 20, 23, 71
Mejia, Victor, 85
Menem, Carlos, 2
Mesa, Carlos, 1

Mexico
  characteristics of, 89 (table)
  conclusions on, 228–29
  criminal violence in, 219–25
  democratic transition and civil society
      movement in, 210–15
  economic transition and corporatism in,
      198–210
  history of revolution in, 187–89
  introduction to, 186–87
  nature of neopluralist democracy in, 215–18
  overview of study on, 88–90
  revolution and controlled inclusion in,
      189–98
Middle Ages, 27
middle-sector inclusion, 40
migration, 36, 167
military
  as law enforcement, 71
  military governments, 248n5
minifundias, 149
minimum wage, Mexican, 200
mobility, neopluralism and social, 66–68, 80
mobilization(s)
  Alianza Cívica and, 214
  causes of, 4–5
  Chile's democratic transition and, 104–9,
      128
  controlled inclusion and, 43
  against criminal violence in Mexico,
      219–25
  democratic transitions and, 52, 54–55
  in El Alto, 184–85
  electoral, 212–13, 249n22
  in Europe, 25
  following water wars, 178–79, 182–84
  impact of, 45–46
  of indigenous groups, 242n4
  in Mexico, 186, 191–93, 195–98
  of middle sectors, 40
  organization and, 14
  overview of, 1–4
  political will and, 233
  Popular Assembly of the Peoples of Oaxaca
      and, 225–28
  populism and, 43–44
  public sphere and, 16–17
  social construction of citizenship and, 21
  societal consensus and, 13–14
  through Chilean political parties, 94–95,
      98–99
  through Chile's political elite, 100–101
  working-class, 240n23
modernity, 25–27
modernization, 35–36

Molina, Carlos Hugo, 151, 153
Moore, Barrington, 5, 25–27, 240n21
moral consensus, 13
Morales, Evo, 179, 185, 246nn4, 8
Mostajo, Rossana, 63
Movimiento Democrático Popular, 105–6
Movimiento Izquierda Revolucionaria, 93–94
Movimiento Nacionalista Revolucionario,
      143–46, 147
Moxa, Bolivia, 175
municipal development, 167–70
municipal governments, 159–62, 167–73
Muñoz Goma, Oscar, 110
Murat, José, 226

NAFTA (North American Free Trade Agree-
      ment), 198–99
National Accord for the Transition to Full
      Democracy, 106
National Action Party, 190, 216, 219, 227–28
National Dialogue Law (2001), 167, 180
National Dialogues, 180, 181
National Educational Workers Union, 202–3,
      226–27
national identity, 13
nationalism, 190
Nationalist Democratic Action, 147
Nationalist Revolutionary Movement, 143–46,
      147
National Peasant Confederation, 192–94
National Revolutionary Party, 193–94
National Solidarity Program, 207
National Union of Autonomous Peasant
      Regional Organizations, 196
Navia, Patricio, 129
neglect, 177–78
neighborhood councils, 124–25
neoliberalism, 5, 51
neopluralism
  Chile and, 91–92
  crisis of representation and, 74–86
  democratic citizenship limits and, 59–74
  democratic relevance and, 86–88
  effects of, 230
  electoral dimension of, 210–15
  and existing democracies, 56–58
  introduction to, 51–52
  Mexican economic transition and, 199
  nature of, in Mexico, 215–18
  overview of studies, 88–90
Nicaraguan Revolution (1979), 246n1
Noboa, Gustavo, 2–3
normative concept of civil society, 6–7, 12
North American Free Trade Agreement
      (NAFTA), 198–99

Nueva Política Económia, 147
Nuñez, Jose Luis, 155

Oaxaca, Mexico, 225–28
oligarchic rule, 31–34, 38
Olvera, Alberto, 196, 211, 212
opinion polls, 78–79
Oportunidades, 208–10
Organic Constitutional Law for Education,
    114, 128–29
Organizaciones Territoriales de Base (OTB),
    140–41, 150, 153–56, 162–66, 174
organization(s). *See also* civil society
    organizations
    democratic transitions and, 54
    in generating political power, 14
    public sphere and, 16, 17
organized labor
    Bolivian Revolution and, 143–45
    in Chile, 97–98, 103, 112, 245nn17,18
    controlled inclusion and, 41–43, 45
    democratic transitions and, 55
    Getúlio Vargas and, 241n8
    indigenous groups and, 176–77
    in Mexico, 192, 196, 201–3, 204, 216
    National Educational Workers Union,
        226–27
    neopluralism and, 81–83
    representation and, 231
Ortega, Eugenio, 126, 136
OTB (Organizaciones Territoriales de Base),
    140–41, 150, 153–56, 162–66, 174

Pact for Stability and Economic Growth, 201
Pacto para la Estabilidad y el Crecimiento
    Económico, 201
Pacto por la Democracia, 147
Paige, Jeffrey, 46, 47
participation. *See also* Popular Participation
    Law
    business, 126–28
    citizen, 123–26, 128–29, 231, 233
    in Porto Alegre, 235–36
    rights of citizenship and, 231
participatory budgeting, 165–67, 234–37
participatory planning, 165–70
Partido Acción Nacional, 190, 216, 219,
    227–28
Partido Communista, 93, 245nn14,15
Partido de la Revolución Democrática, 211–12,
    216, 219, 227
Partido Democrática Cristiana, 96, 97, 98,
    99–100, 101
Partido Democrático, 93
Partido Democrático Trabalhista, 234–35

Partido dos Trabalhadores, 234–35
Partido Nacional Revolucionario, 193–94
Partido Radical, 93, 99
Partido Revolucionario Institucional, 193–94,
    198, 206–7, 210–12, 226
Partido Revolucionario Mexicano, 193–94
Partido Socialista, 93
Party of the Democratic Revolution, 211–12,
    216, 219, 227
Party of the Mexican Revolution, 193–94
patronage. *See* clientelism
Paz Estenssoro, Victor, 144, 146, 147
peasantry, mobilization of, 191–93
Pinheiro, Paulo Sérgio, 71, 73
Pinochet, Augusto, 20, 102, 107–8, 119, 130,
    245n24
Pinto, Aníbal, 96
Pizarro Allard, Cristian, 113–14
Plan Arica, 126–28
plebiscite, in Chile, 107–8, 131
pluralism, 86–87
poblaciones, 105–6
police corruption, 71–74, 223–24, 243n15
political elite
    in Chile, 95, 100–101, 122
    controlled inclusion and, 41
    in public sphere, 78–79
political parties
    in Bolivia, 148–49, 159–61, 162
    Chile's democratic transition and, 91,
        93–95, 97–100, 105–8, 131–32
    controlled inclusion and, 41–42
    democracy by agreements and, 122–23
    democratic transitions and, 53–54
    in Mexico, 186, 212, 213
    as political class, 79
    public sphere and, 20, 23
    support for and satisfaction with, 217
    trust in, 77
Political Party Law, 159
political rights of citizenship, 27
politics
    class relations and, 80
    cynicism and disconnect in, 77–80
    welfare reform and, 83–84
polling, 78–79, 243n17
Popular Assembly of the Peoples of Oaxaca,
    225–28
Popular Committee for Solidarity and Recon-
    struction, 197–98
Popular Democratic Movement, 105–6
Popular Participation Law
    citizenship as agency and, 236
    Comités de Vigilancia and, 170–73
    conclusions on, 178–85

Popular Participation Law (*continued*)
  impact of, 151 (table)
  indigenous groups and, 174–78
  introduction to, 140–41
  limits of, 165–70
  municipal governments and, 159–62
  1952 revolution and, 142–49
  overview of, 90, 150–56
  role of OTBs in, 162–65
  success of, 156–59
Popular Unity coalition, 100
popular upsurges. *See* mobilization(s)
populism, 43–44, 85–86
Porcel, Abdón, 169
Porfiriato, 188–89
Portales, Diego, 93
Portes, Alejandro, 38–39, 63, 70
Porto Alegre, Brazil, 234–37
positive dimension, of state and civil society
      synergy, 19
poverty
  in Bolivia, 149, 180–81
  Chile's democratic transition and, 104,
      109, 113–14
  controlled inclusion and, 37–38, 42
  criminalization of, 70–73
  democratic transitions and, 54
  education and, 67
  extreme, 138, 243n6
  income inequality and, 62–66
  indigenous groups and, 177–78
  in Mexico, 200, 206, 207–10
  neopluralism and, 83–85
  productive investment and, 165–66
  reduction of, 59–60
  state relationship with, 79–80
power relations, 9–14
power resources, 22, 26–27, 240n21
prescriptive dimension, of state and civil
      society synergy, 18
private security firms, 74, 224
private sphere, 19–20, 240n14
privatization, 178–79, 182–84
Pro-Citizen Participation Agenda, 124
productive investment, 165–68, 177
Programa Nacional de Solidaridad, 207
Progresa, 208–10
proletariat, informal, 38–39
PRONASOL (Programa Nacional de
      Solidaridad), 207
property rights
  of indigenous communities, 34
  land reform and, 38
proscriptive dimension, of state and civil
      society synergy, 19

public opinion polls, 78–79, 243n17
public sphere
  civil society and social construction of
      citizenship rights and, 22 (figure)
  composition and effectiveness of, 16–20
  controlled inclusion and, 48
  overview and definition of, 15–16
  participation in, 231
  shrinking of, 85–86
  social construction of citizenship and,
      20–23
Puerto Villarroel, Bolivia, 176–77
Putnam, Robert, 7

racism, 177–78
Radical Party, 93, 99
redistribution
  in Bolivia, 165, 167
  in Chile, 100, 103–4
  controlled inclusion and, 37–38
  economic insecurity and, 63–65
Reforma de la Ley de Enseñanza (2002),
      202–3
Reilly, Thomas, 166
relevance of civil society, 230–38
rent seeking. *See* clientelism
representation, crisis of, 74–86, 118–29
Revolución en Libertad, 97, 98, 100
revolution
  from above and below, 26–27
  in Mexico, 187–98
Revolutionary Left Movement, 93–94
Revolution in Liberty, 97, 98, 100
rights of citizenship
  Chilean political parties and, 94
  coerced marginalization and, 46
  controlled inclusion and, 34, 42, 49
  for disadvantaged groups, 8
  in Europe, 23–28
  neopluralism and, 59–74
  participation and, 231
  popular mobilizations and, 4–5
  public sphere and, 18–19
  social construction of citizenship and,
      21–23
  struggle for, 29–30
Roberts, Bryan, 84
Rojas Ortuste, Gonzalo, 158
Roman, Richard, 216
Rúa, Fernando de la, 2
Rueschemeyer, Dietrich, 240n23
Ruiz, Ulises, 226, 227–28
rule of law, marketization of, 68–74, 117,
      223–24
Rustow, Dankwart, 13

Salinas, Carlos, 207, 211, 214
Sánchez de Lozada, Gonazalo, 1, 2, 151, 155, 178–79, 182
Schmitter, Philippe, 41
security firms, private, 74, 224
Sendero Luminoso, 14
sexenio, 193
Siles, Hernán, 146
Sindicato Nacional de Trabajadores de la Educación, 202–3, 226–27
social class. *See* class
social construction of citizenship
  controlled inclusion and, 49–50
  defined, 5
  democratic transitions and, 52–56
  public sphere and, 20–23
  public sphere and civil society and, 22 (figure)
Social Control Fund, 173
Socialist Party, 93
social mobility, neopluralism and, 66–68, 80
social protection funding, 204–6
social rights of citizenship, 27
social security system, Mexican, 204–5
social services, Chilean, 96–97
societal consensus, 12–13, 24, 29, 231
societal corporatism, 41
Soriano, Walter, 148, 152
Soviet Union, 27–28
Spain, 31–32
state
  citizenship as agency and, 236–38
  civil society and public sphere and, 22
  civil society's relationship to, 14–15, 17, 48, 232–34, 237–38
  labor movement and, 41–42
  public sphere and, 15, 17–20
Stephens, Evelyne, 240n23
Stephens, John D., 240n23
Stroessner, Alfredo, 48
struggles, citizenship, 25, 29–30, 31–34
subordination
  controlled inclusion and, 48
  public sphere and, 17
  resistance to, 10–11
suffrage, in Chile, 96
synergy, 18–19, 240nn12–13

targeted assistance, 63, 64–65, 79, 83
taxation system, Chilean, 113
Taylor, Charles, 16
Tello Peón, Jorge, 222
theories of civil society, 5–16
Thévoz, Laurent, 158, 169
Thorp, Rosemary, 37

Tilly, Charles, 21
Tlatelolco Massacre, 195–96
Tocqueville, Alexis de, 7, 19
Tokman, Victor, 60
Toranzo, Carlos, 148
Toranzo, Julia, 181
Torres, Osvaldo, 128
Transparency International, 88
trust
  in Chilean institutions, 119, 122 (table)
  in governing institutions, 77, 243nn14–15
  interpersonal, 84–85

unemployment, 59, 60, 61, 70
Unión Nacional de Organizaciones Regionales Campesinas Autónomas, 196
unions. *See* organized labor
Unitary Committee of Earthquake Victims, 197–98
United Nations Development Program, 110
United States, 10, 242n12
United Workers Central, 245nn17,18
Universal Access with Explicit Guarantees in Health, 104
urbanization, 36–38, 84, 167, 206
Uribe-Echevarría, Verónica, 111
Urzúa, Raúl, 83

Valenzuela, Juan Pablo, 115
Vargas, Daniel, 87
Vargas, Getúlio, 241n8
Vargas, Humberto, 163–64
Vega, Miguel, 122–23
Velasco, Andrés, 135
Velasco Arregui, Edur, 216
Venezuela
  controlled inclusion in, 47
  institutional legitimacy in, 243n14
  mobilizations in, 3
  voter apathy in, 78
Verdesoto, Luis, 179
victimization rates, 69
Vigilance Committee Consultative Councils, 247n30
Vigilance Committees, 141, 170–73, 247n30
Vilas, Carlos, 83
violence, 68–74, 116–18, 219–25, 233–34
voting. *See* elections

wage structures, 62–63, 67, 110–11
Walton, Michael, 217
War of the Pacific (1879-1883), 93
water wars, 178–79, 182–84
welfare systems
  Chilean, 96–97

welfare systems (*continued*)
  crime and, 70
  Mexican, 204, 207–10
  mobilization and, 45
  neopluralism and, 63–65
  targeted, 79, 83–85
Winn, Peter, 135
Woldenberg, José, 216, 217
women
  employment of, in Chile, 110–11
  local participation of, 164–65
  as victims of violence, 69, 179
  women's rights, 27–28, 231
Wood, Charles, 84

Workers' Party, 234–35
working class
  mobilization of, 24–25, 26, 55, 101, 240n23
  organized labor and, 41, 143–44, 191, 195
World War II, 34, 35

youth employment, in Chile, 110

Zaldívar, Andres, 130
Zapata, Francisco, 201
Zapatista Army of National Liberation, 213,
  215, 249n26
Zedillo, Ernesto, 208, 214
Zelaya, Manuel, 239n1